HELP!

The Beatles, Duke Ellington,
and the
Magic of Collaboration

Also by Thomas Brothers

Louis Armstrong's New Orleans (2006)
Louis Armstrong, Master of Modernism (2014)

HELP!

The Beatles, Duke Ellington,
and the
Magic of Collaboration

Thomas Brothers

W. W. NORTON & COMPANY
INDEPENDENT PUBLISHERS SINCE 1923
NEW YORK • LONDON

For information about permission to reproduce selections from this book, write to
Permissions, W. W. Norton & Company, Inc., 500 Fifth Avenue, New York, NY 10110

For information about special discounts for bulk purchases, please contact
W. W. Norton Special Sales at specialsales@wwnorton.com or 800-233-4830

Manufacturing by LSC Communications, Harrisonburg
Book design by Lisa Buckley
Production manager: Anna Oler

Library of Congress Cataloging-in-Publication Data

Names: Brothers, Thomas David, author.
Title: Help! : the Beatles, Duke Ellington, and the magic of collaboration / Thomas Brothers.
Description: First edition. | New York : W. W. Norton & Company, [2018] | Includes
    bibliographical references and index.
Identifiers: LCCN 2018010059 | ISBN 9780393246230 (hardcover)
Subjects: LCSH: Popular music—History and criticism. | Jazz—History and criticism. |
    Composition (Music)—Collaboration. | Beatles—Criticism and interpretation. | Ellington,
    Duke, 1899–1974—Criticism and interpretation.
Classification: LCC ML3470 .B76 2018 | DDC 781.65092—dc23
LC record available at https://lccn.loc.gov/2018010059

W. W. Norton & Company, Inc., 500 Fifth Avenue, New York, N.Y. 10110
www.wwnorton.com

W. W. Norton & Company Ltd., 15 Carlisle Street, London W1D 3BS

1 2 3 4 5 6 7 8 9 0

There is such a thing as magic,

and the Beatles were magic.

—PAUL McCARTNEY

The Beatles, like Duke Ellington,

are unclassifiable musicians.

—LILLIAN ROSS, *THE NEW YORKER* (JUNE 24, 1967)

For Tekla

CONTENTS

PRELUDE

IN THE SPRING OF 1863, journalist Charles Carleton Coffin traveled from Boston to South Carolina. His intention was to file a report on the imminent recapture of Fort Sumter by the Union Army. Though that event took longer to unfold than he and his fellow Yankees had expected, he took the opportunity of his extended stay to observe religious services of recently freed slaves. After the war he wrote an account of what he saw.

At the African Baptist Church in Port Royal, near Beaufort, Coffin was pleased to hear the hymn *St. Martin's*, composed by William Tans'ur. The singers took considerable liberty with the melody, adding, as Coffin described it, "crooks, turns, slurs, and appoggiaturas not to be found in any printed copy." At the end of the formal service they transitioned into an even stranger phase, with benches pushed to the walls and everyone moving around in a display of spiritual rapture. They shuffled in jerking motions, clapping their hands and stamping their feet, with impressive precision and vigorous syncopation. As they rotated in a circle, their voices louder and louder, they seemed to repeat the same song again and again. Unlike the hymn from Tans'ur, Coffin did not recognize this song. The leader of the group fixed his eyes in a trancelike stare, prompting swelling tides of emotion. When the shouters eventually tired they simply stopped for a few minutes before starting another tune. Coffin was amazed by the fluid and independent motion of legs, arms, head, body, and hands, as if "every joint hung on wires."

This report of a musical vision radically different from anything the author had known in New England is matched and extended by others, scattered in time and place throughout the South. The most common name the participants gave their circle ritual was "ring shout." In the postwar years Daniel Alexander Payne, an African American preacher and one of the founders of Wilberforce University, admonished former slaves to forget all about the ring shout and adopt more dignified, Eurocentric forms of worship. But there was tremendous momentum in the opposite direction. Ring shout observers described strained vocal production indicating heightened emotions, precise synchrony between body and music, bending pitch, blue notes, hard initial attack, and the fixed and variable format for organizing rhythm. Today, the entire package is familiar through the recorded history of jazz, rock, gospel, blues, soul, and funk.

The ring shout combined emotional release with spiritual fulfillment, and it included another dimension that was just as important: the ritual was deeply communal. One of the great, central truths of music's role in the African diaspora was its power to bring people together. Which sister supplied the slurs, which brother the hooks, which the bends, which the growls? The practice was designed to make it easy for each person to find his or her place in a collective whole. Ethnomusicologist John Chernoff, working in the 1970s with the Ewe people of Ghana, observed that "music's explicit purpose, in the various ways it might be defined by Africans, is, essentially, socialization." That purpose and the techniques for achieving it were fully transmitted to the New World, where people from different parts of Africa came together and discovered what they had in common. In spite of vicious annihilation of social networks—or *because* of that—the community-building role of music only grew stronger.

Interaction among those present mattered more than a precise rendition of Tans'ur's hymn or any hymn. The ring shout was open-ended and accommodating. Tunes could be reduced to simple fragments—"riffs," as they are called in jazz. Participants standing outside the inner circle formed the "base." The predictability of the base made it easy to add claps, stamps, crooks, portamentos, "delicate variations," syncopations, accents, and ecstatic outbursts without losing a sense of continuity and togetherness. It made it easy to sonically and visually connect with one another.

There was plenty of room for creativity. Basers could change harmonies if they felt like it, while shouters added effects of "marvelous complication and variety." Robert Anderson, who had been enslaved in Kentucky, remembered how "all of them could sing and keep time to music, improvise extra little parts to a melody already known, or make up melodies of their own." The singers jumped through different vocal registers and they shifted from words to vocalization, hushed murmurs, soft croons, assertive urgings, and forceful confessions.

Leaders had a knack for inventing. There was some allegiance to tunes that had been carried over from Africa and some borrowing from white hymnody, but it was more fun to get in touch with the Holy Spirit and watch a new "spiritual" unfold on the spot. The base alternated with the leader to give him or her time to think of what was coming next. "They'd all take it up and keep at it, and keep a-adding to it, and then it would be a spiritual," as another former slave remembered. Musicians in Duke Ellington's Orchestra and the Beatles used similar words to describe how they generated material.

It was all done without musical notation, of course, a key for producing results so dramatically different from scripted music. One observer quipped that ring-shout music was "as impossible to place on score as the singing of birds." Nonliteracy, perceived as a lack by outsiders, was the starting point for the open-ended harvest of communal synergy. What appeared to be a disadvantage produced a distinctive field of musical creativity.

It may seem odd to join together Duke Ellington's Orchestra and the Beatles in a single study, and odder still to begin the account in Port Royal, South Carolina, in 1863. Ellington's upwardly mobile childhood in Washington, D.C., did not expose him to the ring shout or anything close to it. His parents would have been more sympathetic to the assimilative agenda of Daniel Alexander Payne. The Beatles were even more remote, across the Atlantic Ocean and across the boundary of race, almost a century later.

Nevertheless, the African American communal tradition was the foundation for what these musicians accomplished, both in musical style and creative process, which was highly collaborative. Jazz emerged directly from the African American vernacular and so did rock; both idioms carried a feeling for the communal vision with them. In New Orleans around 1900, Buddy Bolden played his cornet in a way that reminded people of preaching. Joe Oliver, the son of a Baptist minister, made his reputation playing his version of a hymn on his cornet. Louis Armstrong learned to sing in a Baptist church and was then tutored in jazz by Oliver. As for rock, consider this historical assessment from Armstrong himself, speaking in 1966: "All these different kinds of fantastic music you hear today—course it's all guitars now—used to hear that way back in the old Sanctified churches where the sisters used to shout till their petticoats fell down." And a couple of years later: "All that music that's got a beat, it comes from the same place, the old Sanctified churches. It's the same old soup warmed over." Early jazz and early rock each started as "Everyman music," easy to relate to and easy to join in with, the legacy of the ring shout still delivering the goods. Stylistic norms invited amateur participation and interaction.

A tradition of communal music-making was ripped out of Africa and survived through sheer force of will. It shaped the African American musical vernacular, which in turn shaped the American scene. The African American vernacular became an always-available source of renewal, functioning for white America something like Greek and Roman antiquity did in the high-art traditions of Europe, where it is impossible to speak of a single "renaissance" since so many generations of artists and intellectuals dipped into this inexhaustible well for inspiration. One difference is that the African American source never went away. The music was best learned by observing, which was relatively easy to do since black communities continued to train virtuosos by the dozens, generation after generation: Louis Armstrong, Little Richard, Aretha Franklin, James Brown, and countless others.

The communal tradition reached Ellington and the Beatles, and each group did something special with it. One could say that they each brought a composer's vision to the dynamics of collaboration. The ring shout was the indispensable background. It could not have happened any other way.

INTRODUCTION

WHAT DO THE BEATLES and Duke Ellington's Orchestra have in common? Besides high musical quality, both groups relied on collaboration to an extraordinary degree. Their collective methods were the primary reason for the high quality, which just seems to loom larger and larger as the decades pass. One could even say that they were the two greatest collaborations in music history.

Ellington misled the public by exaggerating his own role, keeping collaborators out of sight and off the credits on record labels. Today the situation is much clearer than it used to be, thanks to research on Billy Strayhorn and increasingly honest assessment of the entire phenomenon. To emphasize collaboration runs counter to Ellington's elite status. His exceptional standing has been strong for a long time, but at what cost? Today more value is placed on collaborative creativity than used to be the case, so the time may be right for recognizing Ellington as a genius collaborator.

The Beatles, on the other hand, embraced a communal image. Lennon and McCartney grew so close that they decided to sign their compositions jointly, no matter who wrote what. The movie *A Hard Day's Night* cemented the image of a tightly knit ensemble, "the boys" bantering around like a family of brothers—like the Marx Brothers, to whom they were compared—with the same haircuts and suits, the same weird accents, the dry humor, and the tight rock-and-roll fun. Deliberate obfuscation about collaboration did not come until after the group broke up, the source being Lennon, who aggressively puffed up his own role. Though he later acknowledged the distortions ("I was lying"), his revisionist account was massively influential. More than a few found it agreeable to identify the politically aware innovator as the Beatle worth glorifying the most. Some of the finest writers on the Beatles' music were misled into thinking that the two principals collaborated as composers only during the early years.

The first step toward understanding how these two bands worked is to locate their methods within the African American musical vernacular. Jazz had its origins in music-making by former slaves and their descendants. The funky wind bands of uptown New Orleans emerged as a stylized and professionalized transformation of interactive music-making. By the 1950s those connections seemed remote, as musicians explored how far and in how many directions they could take improvisational virtuosity. As if on cue, rock emerged to reset a participatory paradigm. The debt of rock and roll to music-making in the African American church was obvious to insiders. Rock and roll differed from early jazz in featuring the electric guitar instead of the wind instruments of New Orleans, and in being a song idiom, blended with dance music. Yet its origins in communal music-making were similar.

Ellington and the Beatles worked at the nexus of vernacular practice, where creativity from all participants was welcomed, and commercial pop, which required a single-minded focus on compositions that can be filed for copyright. You could say that these groups shared an ability to impose compositional vision on collaborative music-making. Or to put that in a slightly different way, they each found ways to tap into creative fields opened up by collaboration and to use that resource in the service of compositional definition.

In his landmark study *Art Worlds*, sociologist Howard Becker demonstrates how it takes a village to create a work of art—any artwork, not just the collectively generated compositions of Ellington and the Beatles. Becker begins with a story about novelist Anthony Trollope, who depended on a butler to wake him up, bring him coffee, and get him to his desk by 5:30 a.m.

every day, so he could knock off a handsome chunk of prose before breakfast. Trollope would not have been able to do what he did without his butler. The story is a small demonstration of a universal truth—what Buddhists call interdependence—as it plays out between internal creativity and external conditions. The dynamics between the two are infinite. Becker argues that all art is collaborative in some sense, that it is virtually impossible to say where creative roles end and where the roles of passive "supporters" begin. Still, there are distinctions. We could even imagine quantifying them. If Trollope's butler tips him off to a character or a theme, then the meter goes up a notch. Ellington and the Beatles light up the far end of the spectrum. Their results simply could not have been achieved by a solitary composer, no matter how much coffee he drinks or how early he gets out of bed.

What I am addressing is *relationships designed to promote collective creativity*. The different arts follow different trends, and they change according to context. Painting workshops, for example, were well established in Renaissance Italy. A team of artists led by Domenico Ghirlandaio, including his young apprentice Michelangelo, set to work on elaborate frescoes for the church Santa Maria Novella, in Florence. Ghirlandaio's participation would have been spelled out in a contract: the patrons did not want him turning over key features of design and execution to anyone else. If a helper got too good, he had little choice but to break off on his own. The system was conceived in terms of design (articulated through a drawing) and execution (the painted realization of the drawing), and the master painter was expected to make the design and render the primary figures. This resembled a composer handing carefully crafted products of creative genius to performers, whose job it is to follow directions.

Becker highlights the serialized market for novels in nineteenth-century London, where books unfolded chapter by chapter, month after month. The product was heavily monitored by the businessman's close readings of sales, something like a record company tracking the Top 40, except that in this case the feedback determined a product that had already begun but was not yet finished. Editorial intervention in literature varies a great deal. Literary works positioned on the artistic side of the social spectrum may benefit from creative collaboration, though that often remains hidden. The large investments required for mass production mean that corporate control is taken for granted. In music this kind of intervention entered surprisingly late. A strong role for editors did not emerge until around the mid-twentieth century, as recording studios started to manage their products with an iron grip.

What we find with Ellington and the Beatles is an unusually strong ebb and flow of ideas. The collaboration is face to face (rather than sequential) and it is music-music (rather than music-dance, music-literature, and so on). As a rule, this is rare in classical music. The differences are structurally determined: classical music relies on notation instead of the unnotated "head arrangements" that make it easy to constantly exchange and adjust; classical music highlights a division of labor between specialized composers and specialized performers, in contrast with performer-centered creativity in the African American vernacular; and in classical music, emphasis on weight of authority accrues to a specialized work of art while the popular marketplace is much looser.

"Boy, you're gonna carry that weight," wrote McCartney as a sort of sad farewell to his fellow Beatles, in the grand medley on side two of *Abbey Road*, his way of saying that the four individuals would never be able to achieve apart what they had accomplished together. Less poetically he might have said, "Boy, you're never gonna be able to match, by yourself, this harvest we have reaped from vigorously creative interdependence." Ellington understood this fully. His response was to rarely fire anyone and to subsidize salaries out of his own pocket, doing whatever it took to sustain the most stable swing band in history.

*   *   *

To the point of view being argued here, that Ellington and the Beatles were unrivaled composer collectives, there are two immediate obstacles. One, already alluded to, involves evidence: the historical record was deliberately obscured, with some principals exaggerating their own importance. There will always be controversies since the details were never documented fully. Still, over time, clarity emerges.

The other obstacle involves a conceptual problem: in popular music, what, precisely, does it mean to identify the "composition"? In a general sense this question applies to all kinds of music, but it is acute in popular music. At the center of the problem stands copyright. The legal definition of what the composition is and what it isn't saturates the entire system of popular music so thoroughly that everyone, not just the businessman, has been conditioned to think in the terms it defines.

To illustrate the problem, consider the Beatles' *Strawberry Fields Forever,* one of their most celebrated recordings.

In the fall of 1966, Lennon traveled to Spain for six weeks to try his hand at acting in the film *How I Won the War.* During the downtime in filmmaking he composed a song that he called *Strawberry Fields Forever.* The reference was to a place in Liverpool, a woodsy garden where he liked to hang out as a child. He had been experimenting with LSD for many months. Earlier, in the spring of 1966, he had led the fab four in a search for musical manifestations of those experiments with startlingly fresh songs like *Tomorrow Never Knows, Rain,* and *She Said She Said. Strawberry Fields Forever* was the next step.

Lennon brought his acoustic guitar to Spain, and with it he composed a contemplative song, with simple melody and chords that support interesting lyrics, a casual atmosphere that is slightly disorienting. The singer invites the listener to join him as he goes "down" to Strawberry Fields. We might resist. The implications are uncertain, especially because of the way he delivers the word "down," with slight and mysterious hesitation and heavy, varispeed (manipulation of a tape recorder) distortion. He says that Strawberry Fields is a place where nothing is real, and he assures us that there is no reason to worry. As the lyric wanders through a reticent stream of consciousness, the singer tries to articulate an inner search, an "awareness," as Lennon put it, carried by the drifty melody. Gentle harmonies support the tune without claiming too much attention. One can appreciate this dreamy song without any thought of psychoactive drugs, as Beatles producer George Martin did, as an invocation of the slippery allure of childhood memory. Back in London, Lennon picked up a guitar and sang the song for his bandmates and Martin. A demo tape issued on *Anthology 2* (1996) must carry the spirit of this first hearing.

On one level, the compositional identity of *Strawberry Fields Forever* is defined by this demo. This was how Lennon worked out the song in his head, feeling his way forward with guitar and voice. The demo is very close to the composition as it would eventually be defined for copyright. Had the commercial recording released in February 1967 remained faithful to this simple conception, I doubt that *Strawberry Fields Forever* would have reached the status it enjoys today. What can definitely be said is that as the band worked and reworked the song over many sessions, it became something Lennon never could have imagined in Spain and, indeed, no single member of this creative alliance could have imagined by himself.

Inside the studio the Beatles and Martin (with help from engineer Geoff Emerick) expanded the song into a breathtakingly original recording. Not only do words, melody, and chords work together in beautiful synthesis, so does what we could call, for lack of a better word, the "arrangement," which dramatically extends the expressive core. The recording released in 1967 is the product of diverse creative forces working together in the service of a single compositional vision, which is never an easy trick and nowhere realized more spectacularly than here.

The four Beatles first developed a backing track that reflects years of playing together by ear in the ensemble tradition of rock and roll, with areas of responsibility predetermined by tradition while still granting a range of choices. Starr's role, easily missed in the heady Beatles mix, is notable. McCartney created a haunting introduction that in a simple stroke gave the mood more musical richness. His flutelike line is hard to identify because it was created on a Mellotron, a primitive synthesizer new to the group. George Harrison introduced the swarmandal, a zither-like instrument from India. He was deepening his interest in Indian music in the fall of 1966 thanks to tutorials with sitar master Ravi Shankar. The touch of India directs the disorienting lyric away from hedonistic drug entertainment and toward a genuine spiritual tradition. It did not take much in late 1966 to do that, since the connection between Indian spirituality and psychoactive drugs had been dramatically advanced by Timothy Leary and colleagues in *The Psychedelic Experience*, which explicitly took an ancient Buddhist text as a resource for how to use LSD. Lennon quoted Leary in *Tomorrow Never Knows*, where Harrison made aural connections to India with sitar and tamboura.

McCartney's ears were impressively open in 1966. It is hard to imagine the range of his curiosity being matched by any other composer of the moment, no matter what idiom they were working in. He was keeping up with current pop and rock, of course, and he was listening to classical music by Vivaldi (which shaped *Eleanor Rigby*) and J. S. Bach (which shaped *Penny Lane*). It was McCartney who brought in high-modern techniques from composers like Karlheinz Stockhausen and Luciano Berio. While Lennon holed up at his suburban estate, dazzled by LSD, McCartney hopped around central London like a king, dipping at will into avant-garde circles of electronic music, movies, and paintings. Starr summed up the comparison: "Paul was mixing with an unconventional crowd, but he was very conventional, while John was being unconventional at home." McCartney had introduced electronic composition with backward tape loops in *Tomorrow Never Knows*, and *Strawberry Fields Forever* was the perfect opportunity to go further.

At one point during the fifty-five hours of studio time, Lennon and the others listened to what George Martin and his staff thought was a finished product. Lennon stumbled to articulate his sense that the piece could become greater. McCartney suggested orchestral instruments and a sonic collage started to form, with a wide range of musical signifiers drifting in and out of the dreamworld—Stockhausenian fragments of slide guitar, swarmandal, the rock band, the hard-to-identify Mellotron, prepared piano, backward cymbals, trumpets, and cellos. In the normal world these instruments do not belong together, and some of them don't even exist. They communicate different kinds of expression, different states of mind, different parts of the globe. Lennon's simple song began to float, with all the little touches occupying discrete moments of consciousness. Varispeed tape manipulation bent the sounds even further. As McCartney said in December, he was keen to discover how "to take a note and wreck it and see in that note what else there is in it, that a simple act like distorting it has caused." The arrangement is conceived dynamically rather than statically: each time the chorus returns there is more momentum and greater urgency, putting the formal parts in constant motion.

The dynamic arrangement includes a serendipitous moment about one minute in. Lennon liked part of one take and part of another, so he asked Martin to fuse the two. Since they were in different keys and different tempos this seemed unlikely, but with speed adjustments in the tape recorders the engineers matched them up fairly well. You can hear a slight dislocation, an oozy slither into a slightly brisker tempo and brighter sound compared with the opening section, which is slower, slightly slurred, and darker. The transition is felt rather than measured. The fade-in at the end infuses everything with added doses of electronic weirdness, and the song melts from solid to liquid to vapor.

Martin compared *Strawberry Fields Forever* to a tone poem by Debussy, and fifty years later the comparison holds up. Debussy, with a lot of theoretical training, commitment to musical notation, and the sustained focus of a single composer, reached a certain kind of musical achievement. The Beatles reached comparable value without notation and through extraordinary synergy between multiple creative forces. Lennon's song moved from one to two to four to five to six, a collaborative hierarchy where everyone understood his place.

In his fitful, post-Beatle years Lennon distanced himself from the complexities of the end product, which he blamed on McCartney and Martin. If he had those concerns in the fall of 1966, he wisely kept them to himself. It had long been clear to him—he probably had some sense of it from their very first meeting, back in 1957—that McCartney's musical skill far exceeded his own, and that they could be of great benefit to each other. By late 1966 the creative process of making Beatles music included, by default, a huge opening for McCartney's interventions.

To return to the question: if we think of Ellington and the Beatles as composers working collectively, how, precisely, do we define their compositions? This can be answered only by ignoring the narrow definition of copyright and splitting the stages of composition. Lennon composed a good song; based on that, the creative team composed a tremendous recording. The recording preserves a finished product that is a composition in every meaningful way. The phonograph was essential for shaping, documenting, and transmitting the collaborative practices that concern us in this book.

Lennon's song functioned something like a script in a movie. The script is the movie's foundation, though it is not necessarily the most important ingredient in the movie's success. The director, not the scriptwriter, is usually the one who receives the most creative credit. The director may rewrite the script, reject it, or ask for revisions. It is easy to distinguish the script from the movie and to understand its role without diminishing it or inflating it. With *Strawberry Fields Forever,* the analogy clarifies the role of the original song, which forms one but not the only basis for success of the recorded composition. Lennon composed the script but he shared the role of director and yielded many decisions, large and small, to his colleagues.

A division of creative labor became standardized in popular music in much the same way that it did in movies, though it took longer to settle into place. By the 1950s, composers, performers, arrangers, singers, and producers all had roles in making records, with varying creative expectations. To take a small example: George Harrison added a riff at the beginning of McCartney's song *And I Love Her.* In a legal sense Harrison is not co-composer and the riff is not part of the song, but it is very much part of the song's identity, as McCartney himself acknowledged. There are countless examples of this in jazz and rock.

Art music traditionally excludes this kind of flexibility. I am not saying that it has never happened, just that it is not traditional. The concept of the artist is simply too grand. A "script" produced by an artist is supposed to be loaded with genius and it is supposed to be complete, not dependent on anyone else's intervention or subordinated to someone else's vision. Collaboration is accepted across disciplines, with a librettist supplying words to an opera composer, for example, the two of them staying out of each other's way as much as possible. This is why it is still challenging for many to accept how heavily Ellington's accomplishments were dependent on creative collaboration. If Ellington was the greatest composer in the history of jazz, perhaps even the greatest composer in the history of the United States—many think that he was—then he has to call the important shots. Ellington was practical and accepted good results however they came. Yet it was also useful for him to be thought of as a great composer, so he was not always forthright about routine reliance on communal creativity.

The point is not to advocate one method over another, but to understand the differences. Nothing like the Beatles and Ellington collaborations has ever existed in classical music, nothing even remotely close. Musicologist Richard Taruskin argues that the central role of musical literacy is what makes classical music cohere as a tradition. What are the consequences of so much emphasis on notation? What are the social implications, and how does it shape the range of expression? We could form parallel questions for the collaborative and unnotated traditions of the African American vernacular. Ellington knew how to notate music, but that was a small part of a multidimensional approach that privileged unnotated music; the Beatles never bothered. The expressive markers of the African American vernacular, as impossible to notate as the singing of birds, were central for both groups, and so was the creative back and forth that the ring shout was designed to promote. What Ellington and the Beatles achieved would simply not have been possible if most of the creative process had to be written down. The easy flow of ideas would have become cumbersome. Each method carries its own set of advantages.

Of course many jazz and rock musicians foreground the African American vernacular, not just blue notes and rhythms but also creative interaction. Jazz musicians, especially, cultivate responsive ears. Ellington and the Beatles aimed not for improvisational spontaneity but crafted compositions. More typically the two realms are kept apart, with specialists staking out their respective territories. What can be achieved by bringing them together?

The phonograph was their indispensable aid. Classical composers adapt to the limitations and benefits of notation, while the phonograph made it possible to capture a much fuller range of the African American vernacular. This meant that a recording could define a composition, including details that could not be notated. Without the phonograph, the Beatles and Ellington would have come up with wonderful material, but they would not have participated in music history as they did, with massive distribution bringing financial reward, fame, portfolios that could be studied and imitated, and legacy. With the phonograph, they made their marks on the twentieth century. The African American vernacular provided the lifeblood of commercial genres like jazz and rock. That commercial entry, in turn, linked the music to recording technology, which made compositional histories like these possible. This is similar to movies, where the technology of film documents collaborative creativity in a way that writing cannot.

Ellington and the Beatles were hothouse collaborations that grew under particular conditions, but the starting point for what each accomplished was the cultural-economic nexus where the African American vernacular, orally based and communally purposeful, met the commercial expectations of popular music. It was an epoch-making collision, contradictory and fitful, with collateral damage everywhere you looked. Tension was unavoidable. In order to have compositional definition, you have to have someone making decisions, and in order to succeed commercially, you have to have someone pushing for high standards. The process more or less guaranteed conflict between balanced group dynamics and individual vision. That problem did not emerge in the ring shout, and solo composers never have to worry about it. But for the two greatest collaborations in music history, it was inevitable.

PART I

The Duke Ellington Orchestra

CHAPTER 1

ELLINGTON *and*
EARLY JAZZ

New Orleans

IN JANUARY 1923, Duke Ellington first heard Sidney Bechet, already well on his way to becoming a legend. Bechet started out playing clarinet, but by this time his preferred instrument was the soprano saxophone. His performance at the Howard Theatre, in Washington, D.C., was Ellington's first exposure to African American jazz from New Orleans, and it came as a complete shock: "I had never heard anything like it," he remembered. "It was a completely new sound and conception to me."

Recordings of Bechet from 1923 and 1924 make it easy to understand Ellington's enthusiasm. The first impression one gets from *Wildcat Blues*, *Texas Moaner Blues*, and *Cake Walking Babies from Home* (all with Clarence Williams' Blue Five) is of immense confidence. The playing is forceful and precise, with no false steps. With blistering attack, intense vibrato, blues saturation from start to finish, and nuances of conversational rhythm and phrasing, there is no doubt about the cultural origins of this music: this is ear-based, performer-centered music from the African American vernacular, as it was professionalized in New Orleans. Bechet has a good sense of melodic contour, nicely varied and interesting. There is a surplus of ornamentation, yet nothing feels out of place.

1.1 James P. Johnson, Sidney Bechet, and Pops Foster

Ellington was hardly alone in being so impressed, and not just by Bechet but by so many of the great players from New Orleans who were conquering jazz on nearly every instrument. Bass players Bill Johnson and George "Pops" Foster, drummers Warren "Baby" Dodds and Arthur "Zutty" Singleton, trombonist Edward "Kid" Ory, clarinetists Johnny Dodds and Jimmie Noone, pianists Tony Jackson and "Jelly Roll" Morton (born Ferdinand Joseph LaMothe), cornetists Fred Keppard and Tommy Ladnier—these and many others were admired and imitated as the musicians traveled and recorded.

Cornetist Joseph "King" Oliver may have topped them all. Oliver arrived in Chicago in 1918 to lead a band of homeboys who lit up the Lincoln Gardens dance hall. On his first night there, the master of ceremonies placed a paper crown on his head, men threw hats in the air in celebration, and the crowd proclaimed him "King." The key to Oliver's success was "freak" playing, the name musicians from New Orleans gave to the manipulation of hats, bottles, and toilet plungers on wind instruments to create bluesy, talking effects.

Trumpeter James "Bubber" Miley heard Oliver in 1921 as he was passing through Chicago. Just like Ellington when he heard Bechet, Miley was overwhelmed. "Bubber and I sat there with our mouths open," remembered clarinetist Garvin Bushell. "That's where Bubber got his growling, from Joe Oliver." Miley perfected the technique and made it his own. We could say that he was Oliver's greatest follower in freak playing. Toward the end of the decade he became the one who, more than anyone, helped Ellington's band achieve a distinct identity.

Following Oliver even more directly was his protégé Louis Armstrong. In New Orleans, Armstrong constantly followed his mentor in parades and memorized his solos. Armstrong preferred straight cornet playing over freak music. Like Miley, he became one of a kind, unmistakable and compelling, and by 1927 he was the most influential soloist in all of jazz. Trumpeter Charles "Cootie" Williams patterned his style after Armstrong and joined Ellington in 1929. Like Miley, Williams became one of Ellington's key collaborators.

Clarinetist Albany "Barney" Bigard was raised in the Seventh Ward of New Orleans, a hotbed of luscious clarinet playing in the Creole tradition. He joined Ellington in 1928. Together, he and Ellington produced the band's first megahit, *Mood Indigo* (1930), and he contributed to many pieces after that. Alto saxophonist

Johnny Hodges was yet another 1928 addition to the Ellington band. Hodges grew up in Boston, and the experience that shaped his playing most was hearing Sidney Bechet. Ellington said that Bechet took Hodges "under his arm and taught him everything." Of Ellington's many collaborators, Hodges may have been the most prolific.

It wasn't just solo playing that made New Orleans so distinctive and important. African American musicians there perfected the funky and vigorous practice known as "collective improvisation," which transferred the interactive style of the ring shout to wind instruments. The transfer is not surprising since the formative musical experiences for most musicians took place in church. Early jazz from New Orleans was created by the same people who defiantly turned their backs on cultural assimilation and cultivated the participatory model. One observer explained that marching bands and their second-line followers basically brought the ring shout into the neighborhood streets.

Collective improvisation is organized around a known tune, usually carried by the cornet, around which the others improvise, embellish, extend, and invent figures that must have resembled the crooks, turns, slurs, and appoggiaturas of the Port Royal ring shouters. Drums, tuba (or trombone or bass viol), and guitar (or banjo) "base" the ensemble with a steady beat. Clarinet, second cornet, and trombone weave lines against the lead to produce a stylized version of church heterophony. The entire package is there—rough and ready emotional intensity, movement of the body joined to music, flagrant bending of pitch, percussive attack, strained timbre, the universal invitation to join in. The splendid series of recordings made by King Oliver's Creole Jazz Band in 1923 is the earliest and best documentation of this ear-based practice.

Collective improvisation stands as one of New Orleans' greatest cultural gifts to the world. As the 1920s began to roar, the practice found a cultural niche it has never let go of. Establishment figures condemned the music as primitive, degenerate, uncivilized, racially contaminated, and licentious. It was blamed for rising rates of illegitimacy. Born out of a vision of social unity, a way to achieve balance between the assertion of the individual and the cohesion of the group, collective improvisation was read by opponents in the opposite way, as social anarchy, an "impulse for wildness . . . traceable to the Negro influence." The same kind of hysterical outrage would be repeated in the 1950s in opposition to rock and roll. This was no accident, since rock and roll renewed the same set of basic principles—easy to follow, easy to learn, funky, participatory, rhythmically exciting, full of blue notes, associated with African Americans.

Jazz from New Orleans carried tremendous artistic power, and it also carried a firm definition of black authenticity. In New Orleans, African Americans had been the main audience for the music, but even there, by the mid-1910s, a few white musicians were admiring the music from a distance. The (white) Original Dixieland Jazz Band made a nationwide splash in 1917 with a simplified version of collective improvisation. Their recording of *Livery Stable Blues* sold over a million copies. The ODJB was received as part novelty, part fun, part rebellion, and part subliminally racial fantasy, a white conveyer of African American energy. When Oliver and his colleagues arrived in Chicago, a group of young white musicians stumbled on the "real thing" and fell in love with it. The New Orleanians nicknamed them "alligators."

"I was not only hearing a new form of music but was experiencing a whole new way of life," gushed saxophonist Bud Freeman. Clarinetist Mezz Mezzrow went further than most. In 1928 he moved to Harlem and, in his words, "became a Negro." Similar behavior and sentiments surface among white rock and rollers decades later.

The sounds of New Orleans offered the surest way for Ellington to establish black authenticity in his compositions. All of jazz was indebted to the New Orleanian achievement, but Ellington discovered a way to use it with special purpose. That soloists like Miley, Bigard, Hodges, and Williams also turned out to be superb collaborators was an unexpected benefit that he was uniquely prepared to exploit.

Edward Kennedy Ellington

Edward Kennedy "Duke" Ellington was born in Washington, D.C., on April 29, 1899, not exactly with a silver spoon in his mouth but with advantages that set him on a path toward musical leadership. His was the largest African American community in the nation (eighty-seven thousand people). The familiar categories of low, middle, and upper classes don't go very far in explaining his family's position. "I don't know how many castes of Negroes there were in the city at that time, but I do know that if you decided to mix carelessly with another you would be told that one just did not do that sort of thing," he remembered. His parents understood who was above and who below, and like everyone else they found ways to culturally articulate their social aspirations.

His father, James Edward Ellington, known as "J.E.," was described by daughter Ruth as a "Chesterfieldian gentleman who wore gloves and spats, very intellectual and self educated." J.E. sometimes worked as a butler and caterer, and he had enough social polish and connections to land occasional jobs in the White House. He mastered the terms of service—proper table settings, politeness, and how to interact with empowered whites. "The way the table was set was just like those at which my grandfather had butlered," remembered Mercer Ellington, Duke's son. "This you might say is where the dukedom began." Ellington acknowledged copying his father's sharp dress and "vocabulary," by which he meant strategies of charm and persuasion. His father had an "unsurpassed aura of conviviality" and also entrepreneurial skills, landing contracts and hiring servants for one-time events—precisely the model his son used to break into the music business.

Ellington's mother, Daisy, came from a social position a notch or two above J.E. Her father was one of only forty African American policemen in the entire District, while his parents had both been slaves; she completed high school, while his formal education ended in grade school. Daisy gave her son the confidence to believe he could take all the good that was provided for him—anything personal, social, or cultural—and develop it to the highest degree.

1.2 Edward Kennedy "Duke" Ellington, age four

She was a deeply religious person for whom nose glasses and lipstick were sinful. She convinced her son that he was blessed. Like countless African American parents she was determined to overcome the limitations of the past and move forward with conviction, faith, and hope.

Throughout his illustrious career, Ellington was described as someone who connected with people very easily. This was perhaps the most important gift of all that he got from his parents, his greatest asset, the one that made him a collaborator without peer. Ellington's confidence was further nurtured by the neighborhood. "My strongest influences, my inspirations, were all Negro," he reported, but this environment had little in common with the vernacular arena that shaped early jazz in New Orleans. It is impossible to imagine traces of the ring shout at the churches of Ellington's youth. That kind of cultural expression was viewed as regressive, something to turn away from without looking back. The atmosphere was very different from the Sanctified full immersion that surrounded Oliver and Armstrong in New

Orleans. Ellington watched churches and school groups perform pageants on the history and progress of the Negro race, elaborate productions with props, costumes, sets, actors, and musicians, themes that would later surface in his extended pieces like *Black, Brown and Beige*, which he subtitled a "tone parallel of the history of the American Negro."

Social life for the Ellington family included regular mixing with whites. "In our house," explained sister Ruth, "while I was growing up, people of all colors were there. More whites than coloreds. My father was like that." This kind of social confidence was useful throughout his career.

At home Daisy read through uplifting parlor songs on the piano, and J.E. played "old standard operatic things" by ear. Young Edward took a few piano lessons with a teacher improbably named Mrs. Clinkscales, but he lacked patience, didn't practice, and skipped the lessons whenever he could. Years later Ruth remembered hearing her brother's band broadcasting live from the Cotton Club in New York City, she and her mother "sitting in this very respectable Victorian living room" and not knowing quite what to make of the "jungle music" coming through the radio.

"All through grade school, I had a genuine interest in drawing and painting, and I realized I had a sort of talent for them," Ellington recalled. His skill in visual arts earned him a scholarship from the NAACP to attend Pratt Institute in Brooklyn, but he turned it down. Here is a biographical parallel with John Lennon, who attended art school in Liverpool for several years. Both composers were clever in surrounding their music with visual imagery, Ellington through titles and publicity material, Lennon through lyrics. An ability to bring strong conceptual definition to their music may have had something to do with talent in the visual arts. Though Ellington declined the art scholarship, he put his visual talent to practical use and set up a shop for painting signs. Yet music pulled him. A piano piece by Harvey Oliver Brooks called *Junk Man Rag* caused a musical epiphany at age fourteen.

"I cannot tell you what that music did to me," he remembered. He sought out Brooks and persuaded him to pass on some tips at the piano. He had enough basic ability to move ahead while he gathered stray tips from ragtime pianist Oliver "Doc" Perry and music teacher Henry Grant.

Ragtime was the music that set Ellington on fire during his teenage years. Most piano rags follow a formal approach known as "strain form," which conditioned the way Ellington thought about music for decades to come. Strain form goes like this: the piece begins with a substantial phrase or section—a "strain"—that is repeated literally to form a couplet. A contrasting idea follows, and it too is repeated. After that there might be a return to the first idea, followed by yet another new idea or two, again with literal repetition. The process just described could be represented as AABBACCDD, the plan of many piano rags, including the most famous one ever written, Scott Joplin's *Maple Leaf Rag*.

Strain form made it easy to combine material from different sources—floating bits of hymns, marches, popular songs, blues, arias, rags, and folk tunes—and for Ellington it opened up a natural way to collaborate. Even Joplin, who had high, artistically minded goals for himself, was not above adding a new strain to one already composed by Louis Chauvin: the two of them produced the elegant *Heliotrope Bouquet* (1907) in that way. Patching together material like this became standard practice in 1920s jazz. For example, Louis Armstrong composed a theme that became the foundation for *Dippermouth Blues* ("Dippermouth" was one of his nicknames). Joe Oliver then added a solo, and Johnny Dodds contributed two more strains. On the record label Oliver and Armstrong were identified as co-composers, but the lead sheet sent to the U.S. Copyright Office credited only Oliver. Oliver's solo was the standout moment in the piece, and the recording helped spread his reputation. This was how a piece begun by Armstrong (and named after him) became identified with Oliver. We shall see similar stories with Ellington.

There are countless examples like this, most with gestations that are less clearly documented. Strain form made it easy to pull a piece together from various sources and slap your name on it. Bandleaders routinely took more credit than they were entitled to. This naturally became Ellington's preferred approach for organizing material from different people.

His ragtime passion drove him to hang around pianists, ask questions, and gradually pick up repertory by ear. He learned how to play the different dance tempos—the one-step, two-step, waltz, tango, and fox trot. Someone showed him how to slow down a piano roll recorded by the great James P. Johnson so that he could track Johnson's notes and get them under his fingers. When the master himself came to town, Ellington's friends urged him onto the stage to play Johnson's *Carolina Shout* (the reference is to the ring shout). Johnson warmly acknowledged him and the two became friends after Ellington moved to New York City.

In the summer of 1918, with his girlfriend Edna pregnant, it was time to think more seriously about increasing his income. On one job, a musician who had contracted the gig and hired Ellington to play piano explained that he himself couldn't be there, so could Ellington please collect the one-hundred-dollar fee, keep ten dollars, and hand the rest over? This little eye-opener inspired Ellington to set up his own business. He had in front of him his father's example of contracting and hiring, and he had picked up some of his interpersonal savvy. Saxophonist Otto Hardwick, who started playing with Ellington around this time and stayed with him for decades, described how Ellington started to pull in a lot of "dicty" (that is, high-class) jobs at embassies and private mansions. "Sometimes he had two or three jobs going at the same time and would rush around to make an appearance with each group he'd sent out." Nothing original was expected at these gigs. The music was light and polite, in the background and "under conversation," service with a smile. Ellington attributed his success to one-inch ads in the telephone book.

It was not exactly what his parents had raised him for, yet they were proud. "Well he picked up the piano by ear and now he's making more money than I am," his father bragged. He took a few lessons in music theory and notation with a teacher from Dunbar High School, but this kind of knowledge remained very sketchy. His greatest assets were on the management side. "Duke drew people to him like flies to sugar," said Sonny Greer, a drummer who also began a long association in the early 1920s. In spite of his success, no one was overestimating his musical future. On the legitimate side of the spectrum he lacked solid musicianship, and on the bluesy vernacular side he didn't have much exposure or obvious talent.

Indeed, the case could be made that it was Ellington's *distance* from vernacular practices, not any close familiarity with them, that made it possible for him to later make them the basis for something new and original. The same argument can be made about the Beatles, whose contact with American rock and roll during their formative years was largely limited to 45 "singles." "There was an awareness of what was happening in America, but an enormous ignorance about it," observed one British contemporary. "We took on the PR of it, rather than the reality of it, so it wasn't absolutely imitative, and that was what was so important and that's why it was interesting and that's why it was creative."

In February 1923 a musician named Wilber Sweatman invited Greer, the drummer, to join his band in New York City, to which Greer replied that he would make the trip only if Sweatman hired Ellington and Hardwick as well. Sweatman conceded. In Harlem, Ellington got to know more stride pianists, including Willie "The Lion" Smith. "If anybody taught Ellington theory it was Willie," claimed son Mercer. "He taught him things pianistically and he taught him things instrumentally."

After a few transitions, Ellington, Greer, and Hardwick ended up in a six-piece band called the Washingtonians, which was led by Elmer Snowden. When they discovered that the leader was

1.3 The Washingtonians, 1924

cheating them they decided to fire him, with Greer leading the way. Greer declined to assume leadership himself, however, and nominated Ellington: "He didn't want it, but his disposition was better balanced than ours. He could keep us in line without doing much."

New York City has long been the capital of the jazz world, but this was hardly the case in 1923. The New Orleanians made Chicago the cutting edge of jazz, and New York City caught up gradually. Yet Harlem was exploding with other kinds of intellectual and cultural energy, and it was increasingly well organized as an entertainment center supplying cultural labor for wealthy whites. Black musicians playing for white pleasure is a very old phenomenon in the United States, and now it was taking new form in the "black and tans." The most famous and expensive black and tans meant (at least in New York City) exclusively black performances for exclusively white patrons. These clubs framed African American culture in a devious synthesis of stereotypical degradation and show-biz sophistication. They reassured wealthy whites of black inferiority and servitude at the same time that they paid top wages. They became a powerful cultural force. The Washingtonians landed a black-and-tan job at the Hollywood Café, a basement club on Forty-Ninth Street near Broadway, in the autumn of 1923. For the next decade or so, Ellington's career would be largely based at black and tans, which heavily shaped his creative output.

This was where Bubber Miley entered Ellington's band. Miley's freak technique quickly gained notice in the *New York Clipper*: "This colored band is plenty torrid and includes a trumpet player ... who exacts the eeriest sort of modulations and 'singing' notes heard." Miley's allure, Ellington remembered, caused him and the band to "forget all about the sweet music."

Miley's freak playing was soon supplemented with the hire of Charlie Irvis, a friend who played trombone. Their vocalized effects, regarded as deeply emotional inside African American communities, nicely fit the primitivist interests of whites at the black and tans, where they were heard as exotic and primitive. By autumn of 1926, Ellington and Miley would figure out a powerful recipe for extending the impact of this kind of music.

In the meantime Ellington tried his hand at composing and publishing. New York City may not have been the capital of jazz, but it was indeed the capital of the music industry, which included the publication of sheet music. Before he left Washington, Ellington had composed a couple of pieces. In New York he wrote some songs with Joe Trent, an established lyricist. When they sold one for fifty dollars Ellington was hooked. The Washingtonians recorded three tunes with at least partial compositional credit to Ellington in November of 1924. In the spring of 1925, Trent landed a contract to supply songs for an "all-colored" Broadway show called *Chocolate Kiddies*, and he invited Ellington to work with him.

Musicals with African American casts had exploded in popularity after the 1921 smash hit *Shuffle Along*, with songs by Eubie Blake and Noble Sissle, including *I'm Just Wild About Harry*. A Broadway show could launch a career like nothing else. James P. Johnson wrote *The Charleston* (1923) and *If I Could Be with You (One Hour Tonight)* (1926) for all-colored Broadway productions, and Fats Waller wrote *Honeysuckle Rose* and *Ain't Misbehavin'* (1929). It was a huge break for Ellington to enter this commercial world. But *Chocolate Kiddies* was a disappointment. While the backers tried it in Europe, the show never made it to Broadway. The songs composed by Trent and Ellington are undistinguished.

Ellington's failed dip into Broadway show music naturally gives rise to a question: since the big money was here, why didn't he develop further in this direction? Broadway hits fanned out across the country and just went on and on, as the famous tunes from Gershwin, Waller, and Blake still do. Ellington's most recent biographer has suggested a provocative answer to the question that will not be to everyone's liking: Ellington was simply not very good at writing tunes.

But what about *Mood Indigo* (1930) and *Sophisticated Lady* (1933)? Or *In a Sentimental Mood* (1935), *Caravan* (1936), *I Let a Song Go Out of My Heart* (1938), *Do Nothin' Till You Hear from Me* (1943), and *I'm Beginning to See the Light* (1944)? By anybody's standards, there are a lot of great tunes in this list, hummable melodies that people still identify with Ellington. The problem is that he didn't write those tunes. Barney Bigard, Otto Hardwick, Johnny Hodges, Juan Tizol, and Cootie Williams wrote them, and Ellington then made songs out of them, sometimes with co-credit and sometimes with sole credit, falsely claimed.

When the critic Alec Wilder got around to Ellington in his book *American Popular Song: The Great Innovators, 1900–1950*, he first explained that Ellington was primarily a composer of instrumental pieces, not songs. Some of his most popular pieces were adapted to become songs, and Wilder reviewed a few. He noted a big drop in quality at the bridge for *Don't Get around Much*

Anymore (1942). "It simply hasn't the verve of the main strain," he wrote. Indeed—the verve part was composed by Johnny Hodges. When Ellington took one of his sidemen's catchy tunes and made a piece out of it, as happened here, the bridge was typically where he inserted his own ideas to fill out the chorus. Hodges's name does not appear on record labels as co-composer, and it does not appear in Wilder's discussion, just Ellington and, with this song, a complete misunderstanding of what the leader accomplished.

As a composer of melody, Ellington was no Waller, no Blake, no Gershwin, no McCartney. Inevitably there will be arguments about this or that tune, but it seems wise to simply hold in a suspended state of curiosity the idea that he didn't become a composer of Broadway hits because he lacked the talent to do so. This could also be framed more positively: he didn't devote himself to Broadway hits because he turned out to be much better at something else. He figured out how to compose collaboratively, according to a quirky set of exchanges and relations that made him one of a kind. His principal partners would not be lyricists, in the Broadway model, but the musicians who worked in his band. Collaborative composition turned out to be a perfect way to compensate for his weaknesses and maximize his strengths.

In the spring of 1925 the Hollywood Café reopened as the Kentucky Club, and Duke Ellington's Washingtonians, as the band was soon called, continued to build their reputation. White musicians stopped by to hear them. The famous bandleader Paul Whiteman gave him a fifty-dollar tip one evening. Work like this was good for professional development if you could hack the grueling hours. "Once you put your horn to your mouth, you didn't take it out until you quit," remembered Freddy Guy. The band expanded to seven players and then eight, sometimes reaching ten and increasing its expressive range.

Meanwhile, there were more opportunities to record. "Race records," as they were known during this period, were made by African American musicians and marketed to African American audiences. Without race records, music history would be very different: we would lack recordings of the King Oliver Creole Jazz Band, Bessie Smith and dozens of blues singers, Louis Armstrong's Hot Five, Jelly Roll Morton's Red Hot Peppers, and much, much else. In 1920, Okeh Records took a chance and recorded Mamie Smith singing *Crazy Blues*. The company was handsomely rewarded for its risk. Competitors followed, each with their own label, color coded to keep everything separate from the main (white) part of the business. The business model for race records was low budget, with little rehearsal, low pay, and little oversight.

The production of race records was monitored slightly, if at all. The recordings were so cheap to make that flops were not a big deal, which allowed musicians to experiment, as Armstrong did, for example, with his scat hit *Heebie Jeebies* (1926). The situation was very different from the 1950s, where studio producers, representing the company, intervened at many levels. A by-product of this business model was that performers were expected to record their own compositions so that the company didn't have to pay royalties; instead they could simply pay the composer-performer a modest fee. This inspired those performers to compose more, and it is one of the reasons why we have a lot of recorded compositions during this period from Joe Oliver, Louis Armstrong, and Duke Ellington.

The performers didn't get paid much for race recordings but they got good publicity, as Oliver found out with *Dippermouth Blues*. If their compositions got recorded by others, then the copyright holder of the tune could reap a windfall. Following the success of the blues singers, dance bands found their way onto race records with ensembles like King Oliver's Creole Jazz Band in 1923, the Clarence Williams' Blue Five in 1924, and Louis Armstrong's Hot Five in 1925. In November 1924, Ellington's band recorded seven sides, followed by two sides in the fall of 1925 and four in the spring of 1926. But Bubber Miley, the star trumpeter who had put the band on the map and made Ellington forget all about the sweet stuff, irresponsibly missed every one of them. These recordings offer nothing noteworthy, certainly nothing that would predict the recordings that would soon make him famous.

Modern Black Music

Jazz acquired so much momentum that it became one of the defining cultural features of the 1920s, maybe even the most defining of all. That was partly thanks to the protean nature of the word itself, which soon came to mean many different kinds of music. Jazz became a sprawling field of almost infinite blends, a heady play between black music and white music, blues and ragtime, popular and classical, soloists and groups, ear-based playing and notation, collective improvisation and fixed arrangements, song and dance, and rough-and-ready tone production and conservatory-based sound. New Orleans got it started, but that was not necessarily everyone's first thought when they heard the word "jazz." The idea of making music modern, a huge theme for this period, helped drive innovation. As Ellington settled into his career he had to contemplate where in this large arena of possibility his place would be.

He was doing well at the Kentucky Club, but he was still small potatoes compared with big-name white bandleaders like Paul Whiteman, Isham Jones, and Paul Ash. More within reach was Fletcher Henderson's Orchestra, probably the most successful African American dance band in the country by 1926. Henderson had a regular gig at the Roseland Ballroom, on Broadway between Fifty-First and Fifty-Second Streets, not far from the Kentucky Club. "My biggest ambition was to sound like Fletcher," Ellington remembered. His eventual breakthrough depended on being different from Henderson, but he got there through mastering the model Henderson established. This meant figuring out how to satisfy white audiences.

Henderson (1897–1952) arrived in New York City in the summer of 1920 fresh from Atlanta University, where he majored in chemistry and served as university organist. His intention was to attend Columbia University, but he soon hooked up with the Pace and Handy Music Company and put his academic plans aside. Most of the advantages enjoyed by Ellington when he was growing up were cleanly trumped by Henderson. W. E. B. Du Bois's concept of a "talented tenth," the African American elite who were, in Du Bois's view, destined to lead "The Race" forward, could have been framed with Henderson in mind. Henderson's father, Fletcher Sr., taught Latin and served as school principal in Cuthbert, Georgia. Fletcher Jr. practiced classical piano daily beginning at age six, locked in the family parlor. Even after his son became famous, Fletcher Sr. refused to allow jazz recordings to be played in his house.

The Pace and Handy Music Company was loaded with prestige, first because of partner W. C. Handy's accomplishments in composing and publishing, with huge hits like *St. Louis Blues*, and second because of Black Swan Records, formed by Harry Pace. The company's goal was to put forward the best The Race had to offer, and they did not mean jazz, at least not initially. Black Swan's cultural vision of high-brow classical music was sanctioned by the NAACP, which bought shares in the company. Pace, too, was a graduate of Atlanta University (1903 valedictorian) and he welcomed young Henderson as "musical director and recording manager." Henderson stepped into the expanding scene with promise and optimism. But before he knew it he was leading a dance band of his own. His was not a jazz band but a step above, which was precisely what the Roseland Ballroom was looking for when they hired him. This whites-only ballroom was slightly upscale. Every night it featured two bands that took turns and provided continuous music without a break. Henderson went head-to-head with first-rate white bands led by Vincent Lopez and Sam Lanin. The interracial competition must have given the scene a touch of daring.

Henderson was inventing a new talented-tenth script by competing with white dance bands on their own turf. The African American press loved to write about his success. He made records with major labels like Vocalion and Columbia, both marketing to whites. Henderson's was not a jazz band when he entered the Roseland, but it was just around this time that jazz was starting to infiltrate the repertory of the fancy white bands. Henderson naturally followed suit. He enjoyed one advantage over his white rivals: he could hire African American soloists, many of whom were better at playing the "hot" solo style. In the fall of 1924 he brought in trumpeter Louis Armstrong and clarinetist Buster Bailey.

Since Henderson was recording not on the cheaper race labels but on high-end white labels, the companies set him up with recent hits, for which they paid royalties to composers. This meant that he could record all the tunes he was performing at the Roseland rather than slapping together ad hoc pieces and arrangements made for recording sessions, as Oliver, Armstrong, Ellington, and most other African American bands were forced to do. Bands like Henderson's had well-rehearsed sections of instruments—a trumpet section and a saxophone section, maybe even a couple of trombones—the opposite in some ways to the spontaneous and participatory sound of collective improvisation. When a song became popular it was turned into a dance-band arrangement. The same published arrangements were purchased and played by virtually everyone. Or you could skip the sheet music and wander over to a bar with a "fistful of nickels," as Mercer Ellington described his father doing, play a recording over and over again on the jukebox and gradually crib the details. This continued to be standard practice into the 1950s, when the Beatles learned how to do it. It was also common to "doctor the stocks," which meant personalizing the arrangement in some way to distinguish your version from everyone else's.

But by the mid-1920s, more and more elite bands were hiring arrangers as a way to distinguish themselves even further.

The arranger played a creative role every bit as important as an improvising soloist or a composer of tunes. Henderson hired arranger Don Redman in 1923, and it was Redman's work, more than anyone else's, that defined the band's sound until he departed in 1927.

Redman's primary focus was to pack as much variety into the three-minute arrangement as could be managed. There always needed to be a catchy intro and ending, as well as space for one or more hot soloists. Instrumentation might change as often as every measure. Tunes and melodic fragments tossed through the orchestra in a dizzying back and forth. Redman could direct a soloist to play the lead melody or an entire section to do it, accompanied by subdued chords or with exciting call and response, all of it moving with soft demure or toward vigorous climax. Emphasis was on novelty and surprise, high values for the Jazz Age.

In 1925, Redman took the Oliver-Armstrong *Dippermouth Blues* from 1923 and made a fresh arrangement of it. He renamed it *Sugar Foot Stomp*, and asked Armstrong himself to contribute a version of his mentor's famous solo. *Sugar Foot Stomp* is a clever reconceptualization of the original. In the 1923 recording from the Oliver band, bass player Bill Johnson yells out, at a climactic moment, "Oh play that thing!" as if Oliver and his musicians were all in church, urging one another to spiritual ecstasy. In the Henderson version Redman delivers the outburst, but more subdued and understated. "Play" now means playful. Jazz Age cool replaces the feverish intensity of the ring shout. Redman's achievement was to capture that lighthearted playfulness throughout the arrangement, through bouncy new melodies, through Armstrong's confident but understated solo, and with some slick harmonic turns.

Redman and other arrangers were also experimenting with ways to integrate soloists into their arrangements. *T.N.T.*, recorded in October 1925, is a good example. *T.N.T.* has the usual respect for variety, with the main theme tweaked differently almost every

time it returns. In several strains
Armstrong is set in dialogue
with the orchestra, with nice
movement between his hot solo
style and the more orderly lines
of the arranged theme. In *Carolina Stomp*, recorded in the same
month, Redman scripts vigorous
responses to Armstrong in a crisp
dialogue. Redman and Henderson were not just framing their
featured hot soloist but learning
from him. Armstrong inspired
a melodic style in their arrange-

1.4 Fletcher Henderson

ments that was more expansive and more driving. He "changed our
whole idea about the band musically," Redman insisted.

When Ellington said that he wanted to be like Henderson, he
had all of this in mind—the ability to compete with the best white
dance bands, high-end white patronage, personalized arrangements, a nice array of hot soloists, and polished ensemble playing.

Henderson's success automatically established him as an
emblem of black modernity. The search for a modern African
American identity during the 1920s was fueled from three different directions—the Great Migration and the historic aspirations attached to it; Du Bois's talented-tenth vision for the future
of The Race; and the nationwide fervor for a seemingly endless
stream of cultural, social, economic, and technological inventions.
African American journalists viewed Henderson's band as the
direction African American jazz should take. "Modernism will
always rule," wrote music columnist Dave Peyton in the *Chicago
Defender*, and what he had in mind was exactly the kind of music
Henderson specialized in.

With the 1920s showering financial rewards on those who
were good at coming up with new inventions, there was no

shortage of musical talent stepping forward. From a direction quite different than Henderson's came Jelly Roll Morton. Less engaged with established paths into commercial success, Morton found his own way. Ellington paid attention and picked up something very different from the nearby examples in midtown Manhattan.

Morton was a pianist, composer, arranger, entertainer, and tall-tale huckster who, like many of his fellow New Orleanians, filed a lot of tunes for copyright. A number of them carried far beyond the U.S. Copyright Office: Morton's *King Porter Stomp*, for example, became Benny Goodman's theme during the Swing Era. In 1926, Morton organized a band of clarinet, cornet, trombone, banjo, drums, and bass, with himself on piano. Everyone was from New Orleans. He named the band "Jelly Roll Morton's Red Hot Peppers." The intention was to work out fresh arrangements of Morton's own compositions, but only for the recording studio. The band never performed in public.

The results stand as one of the greatest series of recordings in jazz history. In tune after tune Morton frames solos, changes textures and combinations of instruments, uses contrasts of loud and soft, and micromanages the production of elegant little gems. The series is an early example of a composer who regards the phonograph as a chance to make a compositional statement he could not have otherwise made. The musicians got paid to rehearse, a rare thing at the time, which allowed Morton to develop his ideas in direct contact with the band.

Morton launched the series with *Black Bottom Stomp*, a reworking of an earlier piano rag. This is one of many pieces (for example, *Charleston Rag, Heebie Jeebies, Georgia Grind, Mess Around, East St. Louis Toodle-O*) from the period that links to a dance. It is one of the best. Like countless dances throughout American history, the Black Bottom emerged from the African American community and made its way into white society as a cut-loose bit of fun. By the time Morton recorded on September 15, 1926, the dance had

1.5 Jelly Roll Morton, 1926

just made a big splash on Broadway, and the Dancing Masters of America had declared it the Charleston's successor. The Prince and Princess of Romania announced their intention to learn the steps on their upcoming visit to the United States, in October. "You clap your hands on your rear end," went one description. "Then you bend your legs and go down, down to the floor, twisting and turning, close to your partner. Then you come back up and move away from your partner and give him the come-on with your fingers down here." The Juvenile Protection Agency of Chicago complained that the Black Bottom "has ceased to be a dance at all and is merely an immoral exhibition," but that was not enough to derail its momentum and may have had the opposite effect. Black and tans were hopping with the Black Bottom in 1926.

Morton captured the pizzazz of the whole phenomenon

and gave it lasting musical definition in this recording. Gunther Schuller has described the musical form:

Intro A1 A2 A3 Interlude B1 B2 B3 B4 B5 B6 B7 Coda

Many race recordings from this period are organized in this way. What usually happens is that a theme is stated completely, then followed by a string of improvised solos that are based on the chords supporting the theme. Morton's strategy is to bring in tricks from the arranger's table. He blends elements of variety with touches of continuity while taking full advantage of his musicians' New Orleanian skill set.

His A theme is nothing fancy but it is crisp and attractive, the kind of thing Ellington would have swapped his cummerbund to be able to compose in 1926. According to Barney Bigard, who played with both men, Morton "wrote more damn tunes than Duke Ellington ever thought about writing." It is played by full orchestra, but the way it is constructed implies a sort of call and response. A2 makes that explicit: the trumpet improvises (or is it scripted?) over the chords, and it is answered by the second part of the theme, played by the orchestra. A3 brings another improvisation, now by the clarinet, but without the call and response. The plan produces a gradual metamorphosis from highly organized to seemingly spontaneous.

As if to ratchet up formal strength once again, the interlude, a quick call and response between trumpet and orchestra, modulates with strong focus to set up the new theme. There was a tradition in New Orleans of bringing performances to a rousing finish in the final chorus with collective improvisation and a vigorous thump on every beat, especially on bass. Morton puts this texture here, at the first statement of the B theme. The effect is to electrify the entire second half of the piece. The B statements that follow are neatly varied with changing details of instrumentation, rhythmic accompaniment, texture, countermelodies, range, melodic variation, dynamics, and improvisation. Each is energized by a two-bar "break," dashes of solo vigor of which Morton was especially fond.

With the Red Hot Peppers Morton found a splendid way to mix writing with improvisation, arrangement with spontaneity, micromanagement from the central controller with intuitive ear playing from the vernacular tradition. The musicians were happy to yield to his preference or assert themselves, whatever he wanted. It can be hard to tell where the break is between Morton's writing and improvised solos, which seems to have been part of his conception. It is a splendid response to the available resources, sui generis. Morton picks and chooses with unrivaled ease between the unnotated approach favored by Oliver and the notated approach preferred by Henderson. The composer-arranger's control is loose enough to bring in the musicians' performer-centered creativity, yet firm enough to work with principles of variety, contrast, and formal patterns of design.

In this strategy he anticipated Ellington. Morton never ran a band for very long, but if he had done that, with a working orchestra continuously at his fingertips, he might have gone even further in the direction Ellington ultimately followed. Temperamentally he was a lone cowboy who never could have sustained the complex musical-business relationships that Ellington was born and raised to finesse.

From yet another direction still came James P. Johnson, whom we have already met when Ellington learned his rag *Carolina Shout* from a piano roll. Like Henderson, Johnson had solid training on classical piano. He was also a good composer. His hit *If I Could Be with You (One Hour Tonight)* became one of the decade's enduring standards (1926; lyrics by Henry Creamer). Johnson's reach for musical innovation included classically inspired compositions built around "folk" material. His *Yamekraw: A Negro Rhapsody* (1927) was a model for Ellington's extended compositions a few years later. Johnson described *Yamekraw* as "a genuine Negro treatise on spiritual, syncopated and 'blue' melodies." There are scattered examples throughout music history of one composer orchestrating another's composition, a collaborative relationship though not necessarily one that involves active exchange. Ferde Grofé brilliantly orchestrated Gershwin's *Rhapsody in Blue*, for example, which was the model for Johnson's *Yamekraw*. The composer William Grant Still, who made a specialty out of the art of orchestration, built on Grofé's achievement and orchestrated *Yamekraw*, lifting it to a higher level.

In 1926, Ellington and his band were doing well, especially when the recreant Miley showed up. But when he mulled over ways to advance further, Ellington must have seen the obstacles. He had neither the ear-playing skills of Morton nor the technical skills of Henderson. He lacked Johnson's command of harmony and melodic craft. The dozen or so pieces he had recorded through the fall of 1926 put him nowhere near any of these musicians. He studied the arrangements of Redman, Morton, Oliver, and anyone else who caught his fancy, though he lacked their training and abilities. Yet in this vigorously expanding marketplace, there was plenty of opportunity for African American bandleaders who could combine, in some fresh package, the skills of manager, leader, entrepreneur, arranger, composer, performer, and cultural visionary. When the talented tenth thought of how to move The Race forward, they did not have in mind the commercial wheeling and dealing of popular culture. Jazz musicians surprised them. Fertile synergy between creative exploration and popular culture turned out to be a potent mix that could explode with powerful results.

In Harlem, Ellington stumbled upon a connection that made a difference, not in career opportunities or musical models but on a deeper level. Will Marion Cook was an old-school professional on Broadway, a member of the talented tenth before the phrase was coined. Cook was born in 1869 in Washington, D.C., where his father was the dean of Howard University School of Law. At age 15 he attended Oberlin College, from which both of his parents had graduated, to study violin. From there he made his way to the Berlin Hochschule für Musik and took violin lessons with the legendary Joseph Joachim, a close associate of Brahms. Back in the United States he studied composition with the equally legendary Antonín Dvořák at the National Conservatory of Music of America, in Manhattan. By the time Ellington met him he had a career as a composer, arranger, and conductor, especially for all-colored Broadway shows.

Cook had a good sense of tunes, arrangements, and what it meant to be a professional African American musician, though he lacked the interpersonal skills to make the most of his abilities. Ellington started to hang around with him in the mid-1920s. "I can see him now with that beautiful mane of white hair flowing in the breeze as he and I rode uptown through Central Park in the summertime in a taxi with an open top," he wrote in his autobiography. "I would ask questions and get my education."

A few choice words stuck. "First you find the logical way," Cook told him, "and when you find it, avoid it, and let your inner self break through and guide you." At least once this general guideline was illustrated in specific detail. "I'd sing a melody in its simplest form," Ellington recalled, "and he'd stop me and say, 'Reverse your figures.'" Cook's authority gave Ellington confidence. Jazz originality was bursting out all over during the mid- and late 1920s, and though it took him some time, Ellington was figuring out how he could participate.

The solution was to collaborate. In itself this was not surprising, since virtually all of the musical greatness we have covered so far involved some kind of gathering of creative forces into a single musical statement, from Oliver's collective improvisation to Redman's distribution of hot soloists and arranged parts to Morton's savvy blend of compositional control and improvisational freedom to Johnson's reliance on William Grant Still. Ellington discovered a collaborative model different from all others. It involved a fresh blend of performance, arrangement, and composition. We could say that he took the logical way of organizing these three activities and flipped it.

Until the last few months of 1926, arrangements in the Ellington band do not seem to have been a very high priority. Like most bands, Ellington doctored the stocks. The band typically worked out a "head arrangement," which meant finding its way as a group, trying out various ideas, and memorizing without recourse to writing. Bechet described going to Ellington's apartment (we don't know exactly when this happened), where the musicians talked through the possibilities, experimented on the piano, and got "the feeling for the band, playing together . . . The arrangements, they came out of that," he explained. It was easy to make suggestions and include the best from each musician. Hot solos, the head arrangement, and the preexistent tune and its harmonies all stood in a fairly conventional relationship with one another.

Ellington's flip of the conventional way depended on one voice emerging from the band and standing above all others. In the summer of 1926, Bubber Miley, the flamboyant trumpet player who had put the band on the black-and-tan map of Manhattan, came up with a stunning solo that got Ellington thinking differently. Ellington's creative stroke followed Miley's, and it involved an ingenious way to blur the boundaries between the largely separate categories of composition, performance, and arrangement. This unconventional move would become Ellington's recipe for making the biggest mark of all in the burgeoning world of jazz.

CHAPTER 2

THE MILEY METHOD *and the* ELLINGTON PROBLEM

JAMES "BUBBER" MILEY (1903–1932) and Duke Ellington jointly created a musical modernism that still sounds very fresh. Neither could have done it without the other, yet history has not fully acknowledged this, with Miley's role routinely diminished or relegated to the shadows.

We might compare their relationship with that of Pablo Picasso, the most famous painter of the twentieth century, and his lesser-known colleague Georges Braque. The two young painters met in Montmartre, France, in March 1907. By 1909 they were visiting each other's studios at the end of every day, critiquing each other's work and sharing ideas. Their paintings were so similar that few could distinguish one from the other. Urging each other to become bolder and more experimental, they overturned pictorial conventions to an unprecedented degree by emphasizing a geometric play of abstract form with fragmented representation, thus engaging the viewer's intuition.

Their closeness made them reluctant to sign their canvases. "We were trying to set up a new order and it had to express itself through different individuals. Nobody needed to know that it was so-and-so who had done this or that painting," said Picasso. "We were prepared to efface our personalities in order to find originality," explained Braque. Later they gave up and signed them, but usually on the back. The marketplace they were aiming for did not accommodate collaboration. Nevertheless, one of the foundational moments of high modernism depended on it. Braque said that they were like "two mountaineers roped together." Less charitably, Picasso used a different metaphor and described Braque as his wife.

Unlike the painters, Miley and Ellington worked in a tradition where collaboration was normal. Two traditions actually—on one side the ring shout, with its firm social purpose and easy exchange, on the other composers who cosigned popular tunes and songs. Some of the reasons Miley has not received the recognition he is due were personal, including alcoholism, professional irresponsibility, and early death. The bigger impediment was Ellington's tendency to gather all of the credit around himself, using their mutual efforts to establish his image as a composer-genius.

2.1 Bubber Miley, December 1928

Little is known about Miley's life. He was born in 1903 in Aiken, South Carolina, and moved to New York City with his family at age six. By 1920 he was good enough to play professionally, and he soon joined a backup band for Mamie Smith, the successful blues diva. The key development of his style came after exposure to Joe Oliver's freak playing on a visit to Chicago in 1921 (see Chapter 1).

Whatever bluesyness Miley had internalized by 1921 prepared him well enough to absorb Oliver's style and personalize
it. Miley played with Bechet in Ellington's band during the summer of 1926. They had a blast taking turns in improvisational
cutting sessions, trading choruses back and forth, "growling at
each other something awful," as Ellington described it, musicians dropping by to witness the torrential flow of creativity.
Miley became a brilliant innovator, one of a kind, unmistakable
and compelling. If Ellington's distance from the African American musical vernacular helped him think of fresh ways to use
those styles and techniques, then Miley was the connection who
made that possible.

East St. Louis Toodle-O, Black and Tan Fantasy, *and* Creole Love Call

The story of *East St. Louis Toodle-O* begins in the summer of 1926,
on a tour with the Ellington band in Massachusetts, where Miley
noticed a dry cleaning shop named "Lewandos." He thought the
word sounded musical and started singing it, "Oh Lee-wan-dos!"
This was the seed for *East St. Louis Toodle-O*. Miley turned the
little call into a substantial melody full of pungent blue notes and
rapid, speech-like chatter. There is no recorded precedent. Still
today, people are stunned when they hear this solo, which was
recorded for the first time on November 29, 1926. What makes
the solo so compelling is the entire conception, not simply the
mastery of freak technique. Miley does not merely add ornaments
to a preconceived tune. The strength comes from the inseparability of freak expressivity with the design of his melody.

This solo dominates the recordings of *East St. Louis Toodle-O*.
By March 1928, Ellington had recorded the piece seven times,
with this solo pretty much intact. (My favorite is the December 19,
1927, Victor recording, with its slower, more atmospheric tempo
and with Miley in elegant refinement.) Miley plays throughout

the opening section, lasting well over a minute, and he returns at the end to take up almost half of the recording. Like most great jazz solos from the 1920s, this one was composed rather than improvised. When Oliver rerecorded *Dippermouth Blues*, for example, his solo stayed the same, and that was standard practice. Hot soloists *could* improvise, and many race records hastily pulled together to fill out a recording date demonstrate the results. But it was better to carefully shape a solo to perfection if you had the time to do so, much like a short vaudeville act that gave a performer his or her brief moment in the spotlight.

In November 1926, in Chicago, Armstrong was recording with his Hot Five unit. Their performance of *Big Butter and Egg Man* includes a solo that was his featured number at the Sunset Cafe. Beautifully sculpted, it is now recognized as his first great solo on record, one that took him to a higher level of accomplishment and prestige. It is a marvelous coincidence to observe Oliver's two greatest followers recording their first great solos around exactly the same time.

Even though these solos by Oliver, Armstrong, and Miley were carefully composed they could still *seem* to be improvised. That was because they incorporated so much of the African American musical vernacular. Many listeners did not make a distinction between improvised music that was mostly spontaneous and ear-playing music that was mostly prearranged. They conflated all "hot solos"; since they were all distinctly African American, it seemed like they must have been spontaneously created. In 1926 the novelist Mary Austin wrote, in the *Nation*, how Bill "Bojangles" Robinson's splendid dance moves could be chalked up to the "sincere unconsciousness of his genius." They came to him in dreams, Austin believed, "as inspiration has always come to tribal man." Austin was simply summing up in a vivid way the period's standard view, relevant as much for music as it was for dance. The primitivist mind-set granted African American artists creativity but not calculation, intuition but not analysis, emotion but not reason. These projections went hand in hand with social and legal justifications for second-class citizenship.

By the late 1920s hot solos were a big part of jazz. Arrangers left room for the soloist to work his primitive magic, but they were less concerned about integrating the material with the rest of the performance. The soloist might paraphrase a popular tune that the arrangement was based on, but could just as easily not. The main purpose was a dash of spice and contrast. All of Armstrong's great solos from the 1920s were like this. An arrangement was put together and Armstrong created a solo for it. If he came up with a good one, it defined the record and even the piece itself.

"The band became the accompaniment to this music," was how trombonist Lawrence Brown explained Miley's importance during this period. What happened next to *East St. Louis Toodle-O* is not documented. Joe "Tricky Sam" Nanton said that Miley was the "backbone of the band . . . His ideas and tunes he wrote set the band's style," and he gave the example of *East St. Louis Toodle-O*. Nothing is known about who created what beyond Miley's solo, but Ellington's subsequent history suggests that it was he who decided to build a piece around it. He probably came up with the effective accompaniment to Miley's main theme. The recording begins with just the accompaniment, all by itself, as an introduction, a moody sequence of minor chords, rising mysteriously from a very low range and then falling back down. Then these chords splendidly frame Miley's fiercely chattering, majestic trumpet.

Miley's solo is so brilliant, and it is extended so effectively by the moody accompaniment, that it really doesn't matter how mediocre the rest of the piece is. Once Miley drops out, the material barely qualifies as adequate for contrast, a foil to set up Miley's return at the end. With the moody chords fused so powerfully to the main melody, the results stand as a strong compositional statement. It is an arrangement masquerading as a composition. Will Marion Cook's advice to flip the logical way has taken an unexpected turn. The logical way was to start with a composition (a popular song), make an arrangement of it, and drop in an unprescribed hot solo for contrast. *East St. Louis Toodle-O* started with a well-defined hot solo by Miley, Ellington arranged it, and the two musicians ended up with a composition.

In 1926, Ellington was not a leader in any of the primary categories of musical creativity—composing a popular song, arranging a popular song for jazz band, or creating a hot solo. Why not blur the categories and see what happens? Miley's soulfulness now stood at the center of a piece in ways that had not been tried before. At age twenty-seven, Ellington figured out a way to make his mark. This was late in the game for the trajectory usually associated with great composers; when Paul McCartney was twenty-seven, for example, the Beatles were finished. But, as it turned out, it was not too late at all to launch a career based on creative collaboration.

East St. Louis Toodle-O put Ellington on the map. "People heard it and said, 'Here they come!'" enthused drummer Sonny Greer. It was followed by another Miley gem, *Black and Tan Fantasy*, first recorded on April 7, 1927.

Miley's inspiration this time was the religious anthem *The Holy City*, by Stephen Adams (1892, lyrics by Frederic Weatherly). In African American neighborhoods of New Orleans and elsewhere there was an easy back and forth between church, dance hall, and parades that included featured numbers for trumpet. When cabaret singer Ollie Powers died in 1928, for example, Armstrong played unaccompanied the anthem *Going Home* at his funeral. The gesture came straight out of the famous "funeral with music" that Armstrong had grown up with in New Orleans. Miley is known to have played that melody as well. Also in Chicago, Oliver and Armstrong worked out a duet version of the theme from *Holy City*, just the two of them, again with no accompaniment. Blues singer Alberta Hunter said that their performance at Lincoln Gardens was so powerful that it made "the hair on your head rise." It didn't take much to tweak the melody from *Holy City* to make it fit blues form. Oliver and Armstrong inserted it into their compositions *Canal Street Blues* and *Chimes Blues*, both recorded in April 1923 with King Oliver's Creole Jazz Band.

The version of *Holy City* that Miley plays to open *Black and Tan Fantasy* has a different character from the Creole Jazz Band recordings from 1923. The tempo is slowed down and the melody has been shifted to a plaintive minor key. Like *East St. Louis Toodle-O*, the popularity of *Black and Tan Fantasy* is indicated by how frequently Ellington recorded it—five times between April 1927 and June 1930. Again, Miley's solos and the arrangement stay pretty much the same, with Jabbo Smith substituting for him on the November 1927 Okeh recording and sticking to Miley's conception.

In the opening section, Miley is harmonized by trombonist Nanton, both instruments muted and soft, with the trombone slightly strained in its higher range. The accompaniment is stark, just a sparse marking of the beat. The effect is dark and mysterious, an imaginative counterpart to the opening of *East St. Louis Toodle-O*. But instead of dominating the entire first section as he does in the earlier piece, Miley gives way to a contrasting theme, whimsical and mellow, played on alto saxophone. The contrasting sections in *East St. Louis Toodle-O* are trite and drag the piece down, but this material in *Black and Tan Fantasy* is better. It effectively functions as a call-and-response extension of Miley's monumental presence. Saxophonist Otto Hardwick claimed that he composed this theme (contrary to the assumption of most writers that it was Ellington's), and frankly there is no reason to doubt him.

Next come two blues choruses for Miley. They open with the trumpeter holding a single high note over sixteen beats (in the Victor recording from October 1927), muted and soft and strained, like an alarm sounding from a distant place. Again the accompaniment is bare. He then tumbles down with a rush of virtuoso, chatter-like freak music, full of dramatic tension. Next Ellington takes a lackluster chorus on piano, followed by Nanton. Then

Miley returns for one more chorus at the end, his more assertive plunges now punctuated with bracing blasts from the band. He quantitatively dominates this performance even more than he does *East St. Louis Toodle-O*, and since his playing stands several notches above everything else, this is a recipe for success. The piece finishes with one more arranging trick, a rallentando dash of Chopin's *Funeral March* (the same passage was used previously by Morton and others in a similar way). The bluesy vernacular has been framed by two musical signifiers of somber weight, *Holy City* at the beginning and Chopin at the end, yet it is Miley who commands attention. "'Bub' is responsible for all that slow, weird music," explained an article in the *New York Tribune*. Ellington was smart enough to stay out of his way.

It was probably Ellington who came up with the strong title, which gathers the diverse elements into a mysterious whole and invites the listener to decide what it means. The strategy for his title may have been as simple as aiming for a job at the Cotton Club, the premiere black-and-tan cabaret in Harlem. Another possibility would be an allusion to how the soulful interior of the piece (Miley's trumpet) is framed with white music (Stephen Adams and Chopin). The title was designed to engage the listener's imagination. The title *East St. Louis Toodle-O* sounds more evocative today than it did in 1926: it was primarily a marketing ploy to sell the record in that majority African American city, where the *Toodle-O* (or *todalo*) dance was popular; it was like Morton's *Black Bottom Stomp* in this regard. The title *Black and Tan Fantasy* invites interpretation, which is a matter of entering the realm of *art*. A "fantasy" was something like a "rhapsody," for which Gershwin had already demonstrated the possibilities.

Ellington has again made an arrangement and sold it as a composition, with the added twist of a title that aims to place the piece higher on the scale of cultural production. His main contribution was to *conceptualize* the spectacular playing of his featured soloist. It is a conceptual stroke that puts him on com-

mon ground with Lennon and
the art school sensibility of late
1950s and early 1960s Britain.
Miley's inspired rendition of *The
Holy City*, the bookend of Chopin's *Funeral March*, and having
everything in the same key to
suggest a sustained mood—the
title put the whole thing in imaginative motion.

2.2 Adelaide Hall, 1934

The third important Miley-
Ellington collaboration was *Creole Love Call*, first recorded on
October 26, 1927. Here the collaborative range extends beyond
the band to include an outsider, the singer Adelaide Hall. This
piece began as an adaptation of *Camp Meeting Blues*, yet another
Oliver recording from 1923. The first theme of *Creole Love Call*,
played by a clarinet trio, is a harmonization of a riff-based melody that Oliver composed for that earlier piece. Hall was touring
alongside the Ellington band in the fall of 1927, and when she
heard the arrangement she started scatting a lovely countermelody to go with the riff. Her vocal style is vigorous and imaginative.
It is similar to Louis Armstrong's singing, and this is no coincidence since she had been performing with him on a regular basis
at the Sunset Cafe in Chicago during the summer. Ellington liked
what Hall was doing so much that he asked her to join the recording session. Hall uses her voice like an instrument and provides a
counterpart not just to Oliver's riff tune but also to Miley's freak
trumpet—blues on blues on blues.

Creole Love Call was filled out with an additional melody lifted
from *Camp Meeting Blues*, plus there is a delightful surprise. After
the third statement of the riff, with call and response between
brasses and winds, low and mellow, like most of the performance,

comes the surprise in statement four, where the winds suddenly propel the riff up an octave and belt it out, with vigorous punctuation from the brasses. The quick change of mood makes a beautiful point of contrast before the fifth and final statement, which retreats down in range, volume, and mood, laced once more with Hall's effective scatting. It was an inspired arranging detail that helps bring out the intensity of the more subdued material that dominates the piece.

For *East St. Louis Toodle-O,* Ellington composed several weak themes and one terrific sequence of mysterious chords for the background. The combination of Miley with the mysterious chords carried the whole piece. Ellington composed less for *Black and Tan Fantasy,* and virtually nothing for *Creole Love Call,* where bluesy inspirations from Oliver, Miley, and Hall dominate from beginning to end. Morton's model of cannily mixing vernacular elements with new compositional material did not work for Ellington, basically because he did not yet have Morton's compositional ability. Instead, he was learning how to work as an innovative arranger. This was the strategy for generating the three most outstanding pieces (by far) in the Ellington canon through 1927 (and beyond).

Miley's impact was probably greater than we can ever know. Nanton insisted that Miley "was an idea man . . . For instance we'd have a printed orchestration and Bubber would always have some stuff of his own and soon we'd have a trio or quartet on the part and if one of us didn't know the chorus the others would tell us what to play." Ellington's son Mercer concurred: "As I remember the story from Pop," he explained, "Bubber was considered the most prolific musician in the band up until he left, early in 1929 . . . He was responsible for many licks and the development of arrangements." In other words, the commonly held assumption that Miley's contribution is limited to his own playing, and that everything else gets credited to Ellington, is unsupported. Dancer Roger Pryor Dodge, who performed with Miley after he left Ellington and knew the trumpeter well, said that Miley overflowed with strong musical ideas, but he needed Ellington to "see to it that any good idea was completed." But when most writers talk about *East St. Louis Toodle-O*, *Black and Tan Fantasy*, and *Creole Love Call*, the hierarchy is inverted, with Miley put in secondary position. Given that Miley died in 1931 at age twenty-eight, an impoverished alcoholic, while Ellington died in 1974 as one of the most heralded musicians in the history of American music, this is not surprising.

Gunther Schuller, one of the great writers on jazz and on Ellington, did not subscribe to the consensus view. "It is possible to theorize that without Miley, Duke Ellington might never have become a composer of any significance," Schuller wrote. "In the mid-1920s, the main creative thrust of Ellington's work came not from Ellington himself but from [Miley] . . . In many of these pieces, the best, the most original, and the most striking material comes from Miley, while the more ordinary sections, hailing more from a kind of Broadway show-tune world, come from Ellington." Dodge was right that Miley needed Ellington, and Schuller was right that Ellington needed Miley. We would not have the splendor of these three magnificent pieces without this collaborative entanglement, which must be put in the foreground if we are to understand most of Ellington's greatest achievements.

The Miley-Ellington collaboration achieved a unique statement of black modernity. What made the 1920s so exciting—and still makes it so—were the nearly constant explosions of original music. People recently arrived from the Deep South regarded Joe Oliver's band at Lincoln Gardens as an updated version of what they knew from the plantations. Fletcher Henderson hired hot soloists and an arranger to beat white bands at their own game, the kind of modernism that was always going to win, in talented-tenth critic Dave Peyton's view. Jelly Roll Morton merged his compositional ideas with the vernacular expertise of his musicians to record three-minute gems that had no precedent. Louis Armstrong crafted a solo style that was bluesy and vernacular yet more complicated, more controlled, more virtuosic, with bigger tone and better melodic ideas than anyone else could match. James P. Johnson drew on his command of the keyboard and of composition to create an extended piece, following Gershwin's lead but with strong connections to the African American vernacular. Miley was capable of achieving an original style all by himself, with solo strength that rivaled Armstrong, but together, he and Ellington were untouchable.

Ellington flipped normal practice by making the hot solo the starting point for a composition, rather than a dash of spice inserted into an arrangement. No one *extended* Oliver's solo on *Dippermouth Blues* or Armstrong's solos with Henderson in the way that Ellington extended Miley's solos. The relationship between hot solo and polished arrangement was reconceived, the energy of the black vernacular framed in a unique way. *East St. Louis Toodle-O*, *Black and Tan Fantasy*, and *Creole Love Call* unveiled a new synthesis between the vernacular and the cultivated, between the seemingly improvised and the composed, between the talented tenth and what Langston Hughes called "the low-down folks, the so-called common element" of African American society.

The key was not to condescend to the vernacular, not to drop it in for decoration or as a strained reach for authenticity, but to make it the dominant feature. These Miley-Ellington pieces glorify the vernacular. Armstrong was doing the same thing, though in a completely different way. Their respective approaches opened up fields of creativity that yielded rich harvests for decades. It's not that jazz musicians *had* to proceed in this way in order to reach greatness. It's more that proceeding in this way opened a path of intertwined musical and social possibilities. That is part of the recipe that made Armstrong and Ellington the two central figures in jazz history.

If we think about the approaches of Armstrong and Ellington on a more metaphorical level we can detect another important difference. "If music is a language, then who is speaking?" is a useful question to ask as we reflect on Ellington's achievement. When Armstrong played it was obvious whose voice was coming through. With Ellington, the answer is multidimensional, and this becomes a source of the music's power.

On the literal level, Bubber Miley was speaking through his vocalizing trumpet. There are reports that Miley's superb playing was matched with a strong sense of physical presence. This was a key to the performer-centered tradition the New Orleanians had gathered up and professionalized: the music seems to emanate from a position of personal power. Since Miley's physical presence was absent on phonograph records, and since his voice stood alongside arranging details (like the accompanying chords in *East St. Louis Toodle-O*) and conceptual details (like the title *Black and Tan Fantasy*), the records begged the question "Who is speaking?" and suggested a more complicated set of answers.

Phonograph records, and, in parallel, radio, extended Ellington's reputation dramatically in the early 1930s. As his name became more familiar, these disembodied forms of transmission led to the conviction that it was actually Ellington who was speaking through *East St. Louis Toodle-O*, *Black and Tan Fantasy*, and *Creole Love Call*. In this way, the phonograph promoted his status as a great composer. This is partly why the reception history of Ellington's bands overwhelmingly leans toward the view that he is the author of these path-breaking compositions. One writer even referred to Miley as Ellington's "muse," thus reducing the trumpeter to passive inspiration for the great master rather than the backbone and idea man of the orchestra.

Another way to respond would be to regard Miley's freak trumpet as the voice of the low-down folks, the so-called common element, which had been professionalized in the tradition of Oliver and Armstrong. But what is different from Oliver and Armstrong is the particular way in which the black vernacular is framed through contrasting and complementary gestures, details of musical form, evocative titling, the demand for interpretation—the various materials of art. All of this points in the direction of classical music and cultural values that were dear to the talented-tenth cream of African American society (see Chapter 1).

It often seemed like the values of the talented tenth and those of the low-down majority were irreconcilable, with rigid conflict across political, religious, aesthetic, and social fields. This played out in South Side Chicago churches, for example, with a long list of contested practices—"folk styles" of preaching versus "message" preaching; moving and clapping versus quiet reflection; repertory; heterophony versus precise part singing; bending pitch versus diatonic discipline; rhythmic embellishment versus prescribed rhythms. In 1932, a few years after Mahalia Jackson arrived in Chicago and started singing in public, a friend urged her to take voice lessons. The two of them visited a teacher named DuBois, an African American tenor who had a career singing classical music. "You've got to learn to stop hollering," DuBois scolded Jackson. "It will take time to build up your voice. The way you sing is not a credit to the Negro race." One had to choose. You could acquiesce, compromise, or dig in your heels. Arguments in favor of cultural assimilation carried some force, since the talented tenth was not, after all, occupying a neutral position but one of relative privilege. Many must have felt a real inner struggle.

In that context we may hear *East St. Louis Toodle-O*, *Black and Tan Fantasy*, and *Creole Love Call* as catalyzing a *complete* African American identity. These three pieces, introduced on records over a period of eleven months, resolved tension between the black vernacular and the black elite. They solved the problem with music so strong that you never got tired of spinning the disc for one more play. They are not overtly ideological. The titles are evocative rather than didactic. They are loaded with artistic persuasion rather than rhetorical persuasion, the emotional-dramatic power of music taking over.

Great art is often plugged into the most highly charged social currents of its time, and the honor of "greatest" often goes to art that is emblematic in this way. Consider how novelist and critic Ralph Ellison heard this music as a teenager in Oklahoma, in the early 1930s:

> Whenever his theme song *East St. Louis Toodle-O* came on the air, our morale was lifted by something inescapably hopeful in the sound. Its style was so triumphant and the moody melody so successful in capturing the times, yet so expressive of the faith which would see us through them. And when the *Black and Tan Fantasy* was played we were reminded not only of how fleeting all human life must be, but in its blues-based tension between content and manner, it warned us not only to look at the darker side of life, but also to remember the necessity for humor, technical mastery and creative excellence . . . it was not until the discovery of Ellington that we had any hint that jazz possessed possibilities of a range of expressiveness comparable to that of classical European music.

With such powerful analogies close to hand, it is no wonder that Ellington has been revered as a genius composer rather than as a genius collaborator.

With un-notatable soul standing at the center of compositional sophistication, *East St. Louis Toodle-O*, *Black and Tan Fantasy*, and *Creole Love Call* carried an ethical dimension that was hard to match. This black modernity gave equal weight to the full range of black experience, the talented tenth defined not in opposition to the base but in full communal embrace. Miley needed Ellington and Ellington needed Miley: collaboration promoted diversity of expression, contributed to the music being regarded as *art*, and established Ellington as a cultural leader.

Ellington's collective method separated him from composer-collaborators like the Gershwins on the one hand and from performer-collaborators like the King Oliver Creole Jazz Band on the other. The compositions emerged from performance, not from the songwriter's pen. Most of the work took place independently of notation, putting vernacular details in the foreground. The phonograph was the technological miracle that preserved and distributed the results for study and imitation, an opportunity to enter into historical dialogue no less powerfully than a written score.

Morton, the flamboyant and itinerant pianist-composer, worked out his collaborative gems in the recording studio and then hustled down the road for more solo work, his primary focus. Ellington, more domesticated and with stronger managerial instincts, used his band to create and refine compositions for the next forty years. The usual sequence of the music moving from composer to arranger to performer no longer held priority. There was no precedent for doing all three in one collaborative cauldron, and we can probably assume that the credit for recognizing this fresh possibility goes to Ellington. His discovery carried him to the top of the musical world.

The Cotton Club

Robert Donaldson Darrell was a journalist who covered jazz recordings for magazines like the *Phonograph Monthly Review*, *Music Lovers' Guide*, *Saturday Review*, and *High Fidelity*. In 1936 he published a discography dedicated to classical music, and he loved Ellington so much that he slipped in some coverage. Darrell claimed that, since Ellington had done more than anyone to "invest American jazz with the imagination and craftsmanship vital to aesthetic worth," he was worthy of inclusion alongside the classical greats. Earlier, in 1932, he described a sequence of laughing at the "gargling and gobbling" of the freak effects in *Black and Tan Fantasy* when he first heard the record, but after repeated hearings he was haunted by the effects in a profound way. The same sequence must have been familiar to more than a few of the privileged whites who taxied to the black and tan cabarets of Harlem.

The Miley-Ellington vision of black modernity, just like all the others that we have looked at, was automatically available to serve the interests of white primitivism. Henderson aimed to match the standards of elite white dance bands and beat them at their own game. Ellington followed his example, and through the immense talent of his solo trumpeter discovered a distinct niche. On December 4, 1927, his band began work at the Cotton Club. Over the next few years they turned it into one of the most famous venues in jazz history.

Primitivist thinking in the 1920s was a major component of white supremacy, a complement to Jim Crow regulation and vigilante terrorism, and the black and tans brought this mind-set to life. The basic assumption of all-around black inferiority recognized a few special areas where the subordinate race actually held advantages. It was taken as an obvious fact that nonwhites lacked reason and the capacity for advanced civilization, but at the same time these absences carved out a space for creativity, spontaneity, emotional intensity, and sexual energy to break through. The entire set of assets was vividly framed at the black and tans through dance, song, comedy, and music. Everything was managed through meticulously controlled social-cultural rituals. The whole package offered whites an "emotional holiday," as one writer put it. The institution became an icon for the Jazz Age.

In 1927 the black and tans of Harlem were in the ascent, led by Connie's Inn, Small's Paradise, and the Cotton Club. Rudolph Fisher, a Harlem resident, left his hometown in the early 1920s, and when he returned in 1927 he was stunned by the slumming scene. He strolled around to his favorite places and usually got turned away at the door. When he was allowed to enter he found himself isolated. He sat and watched whites

2.3 Ellington's Cotton Club Band, 1933

"playing Negro games" as they tried out the Charleston and its many variants. He described the scene as something like "Virginians on the veranda of a plantation's big house—sitting genuinely spellbound as they hear the lugubrious strains floating up from the Negro quarters."

The Cotton Club was the most elite black and tan of all, the "Aristocrat of Harlem" as Lady Edwina Mountbatten quipped, with admission a vertiginous two and a half dollars and illicit alcohol similarly dear. Elite, in this case, meant exclusively white patronage. The black press in Harlem hated the Cotton Club because they were forbidden to enter. Police protection, paid off through gangster ownership, was strong.

The Cotton Club offered racist pageantry of unrivaled potency and glamour. The name promised to take customers back in their imaginations to the white comforts of slavery, but the decoration of the interior leaped back even further with "jungle" décor. The black house staff serviced up to seven hundred guests. The stage jutted into the seating area and was barely elevated, providing intimate, almost-touching proximity to the performers. The women of the chorus line were invariably "café au lait" complexion, five feet six inches or taller, twenty-one years old or less, looking good in minimal clothing. "The big attraction are the gals," wrote *Variety*, "10 of 'em, the majority of whom in white company would pass for Caucasians. Possessed of the native jazz heritage, their hotsy totsy performance of working sans wraps could never be parred by a white gal."

Ellington's titles for the three big hits were practically calling cards for the Cotton Club. Most patrons would have been willing to step onto the dance floor and try out a few steps of *East St. Louis Toodle-O*. Some would have been titillated by the erotic implications of *Creole Love Call*. *Black and Tan Fantasy* could have been the nickname of the entire outfit. Any black music could be sold as primitivist fodder, but this innovative Miley-Ellington mix was special, since it was so distinctly black and so accessibly sophisticated. British jazz musician Spike Hughes described the Cotton Club as "run by a white man for white patrons who sincerely believed that when they visited the place they were seeing Harlem at its most authentic." Miley's freak virtuosity was irresistible.

The Cotton Club polished black and tan trappings to a high gloss. The centerpiece was the "revue," a sequence of fast-paced acts, loosely thematicized with a professional producer, stage manager, costume designer, and in-house composer backing up the comedians, dance teams, singers, and musicians, all of it framed by stage sets and lighting. The goal of Cotton Club revues was to make it to Broadway as all-colored shows. It turned out to be a lucrative business model aided by a steady flow of ambitious talent, including Edith Wilson, Bojangles Robinson, Earl "Snakehips" Tucker, Ethel Waters, and many others.

This was the environment Ellington stepped into in December 1927. The first thing to do was expand the orchestra from six to ten players, an easy task thanks to the excellent salaries. His impressive hires in 1928 and 1929 include Barney Bigard, Johnny Hodges, Cootie Williams, and Juan Tizol. Each would soon become an integral part of the creative collective.

Bigard (1906–1980) joined in January 1928 and before long launched one of Ellington's greatest hits, *Mood Indigo* (1930). Hodges (1907–1970) joined a few months later, in May. Benny Goodman identified Hodges as the greatest alto saxophone player in all of jazz, while Charlie Parker quipped that he was the Lily Pons (a famous operatic soprano) of the saxophone. Like his idol Sidney Bechet, Hodges had a huge vibrato, but the creamy quality of his tone, described by Ellington as "so beautiful it sometimes brought tears to the eyes," was all his own. Hodges stayed with Ellington until 1951, when he formed his own band. Then he returned in 1955 and kept going until his sudden and untimely death in 1970, bringing to a close an association of thirty-eight years.

Hodges's greatest contribution to Ellington's collective may have been his gift for melodic invention. Like Miley he was "full of ideas," testified Mercer Ellington. A melody crafted and played by Hodges is usually full of florid richness and blues expressivity. As with Miley, it is difficult to separate ornament from structure, both cut from a single cloth, whether the idiom is blues, ballad, or up-tempo. Hodges could uplift virtually any performance with an improvised solo, and he could turn someone else's melodic banality into gold. He contributed a lot of tuneful gems for Ellington to build pieces around. Publicist Helen Oakley Dance, who was close to the band, described Hodges as "an absolute song factory." Ellington's frequent failure to give Hodges legal or public recognition as co-composer was a cause of resentment and considerable bitterness during the years they worked together.

In January 1929, Ellington finally gave up on Miley after a damaging string of missed gigs and recording dates. Cootie Williams (1911–1985) was hired in March to replace him, even though Miley's freak style was completely foreign to him. Williams soon figured out that he was expected to take Miley's solos, and Nanton, who had learned from Miley, showed him how to do it. Williams rose to the challenge to become a great soloist with an individual style. One of his early featured numbers was *Ring Dem Bells* (1930), where he scatted a vocal chorus in call and response with Hodges's saxophone and improvised two trumpet choruses. The excellent *Echoes of the Jungle* (1931) is co-credited compositionally to Williams and Ellington.

Valve trombonist Juan Tizol (1900–1984) joined in the summer of 1929. Tizol grew up in Puerto Rico, with strong training in classical technique. His flawless reading skills—far better than Ellington's—made him an obvious choice for the band's copyist. Ellington did not usually look to Tizol for improvised solos, but he loved his suave and "legitimate" sound, melodies played straight and pretty, with the valves giving him more agility than a regular slide trombone would have. And he also liked Tizol's compositions, of which there were dozens. Tizol said that he spent a lot of time composing immediately after joining Ellington, music pouring through him like an "open faucet." His first composer credit on a disc dates from 1935, while earlier accomplishments remained anonymous.

Later, Tizol composed three pieces that helped define the Ellington sound at midcareer—*Caravan* (1936), *Perdido* (1941), and *Conga Brava* (1940). Ellington recorded *Caravan* more than one hundred times, and there were vast numbers of covers by other bands. Lyrics were added and it became one of the most covered pieces associated with Ellington. A radio station in Los Angeles played the piece continuously for twenty-four hours with the intention of never playing the same recording twice. The very first recording of *Caravan* gave credit solely to Tizol as composer, but subsequent discs gave credit to Irving Mills (Ellington's manager), Ellington, and Tizol. Tizol was a loyal employee, a company man who respected his boss. In one interview, however, he admitted, "Yeah, he did some bad things to me, but he was a nice fellow, too." His wife Rose was more candid: "Juan was disgusted with being cheated." In his autobiography Ellington described Tizol as "a very big man, a very unselfish man and one of the finest musicians I've ever known."

Ellington's first revue at the Cotton Club, in December 1927, included several featured numbers for the band, including *Creole Love Call*. Special arrangements were made to bring in Adelaide Hall to sing her part. *East St. Louis Toodle-O* and *Black and Tan Fantasy* must have also been featured. But most of the music for the revue was created by the in-house composer Jimmy McHugh. McHugh joined up with lyricist Dorothy Fields to form one of history's great song-writing partnerships. The Ellington band recorded a handful of their songs written for the Cotton Club stage, including *Harlem River Quiver* (December 1927), *Diga Diga Doo* (July 1928), *I Can't Give You Anything but Love* (October 1928), and *Doin' the New Lowdown* (September 1929), the last with Bill Bojangles Robinson featured on vocal and tap dance.

The leader's job description was to work with the various performers, with McHugh and the rest of the (white) staff behind the scenes, and with his musicians. His skill set was just right—a feeling for elegance, a knack for originality, and confidence in dealing with whites. The New Orleanians had the bluesy vernacular in their pockets, but musicians like Morton, Oliver, Bechet, and Armstrong did not have much experience dealing with the white business world, at least not at the level of Henderson and Ellington. Oliver was offered the Cotton Club job in late 1927 and he turned it down. Ellington, with the help of his manager, used the opportunity to elevate his career above all others.

The highlight of 1928 was *The Mooche*. Although the disc for this tune did not credit Miley as co-composer (he was probably gone from the band by the time the disc was released), his presence is very strong. *The Mooche* was put together for a Cotton Club revue as an evocation of the barbaric underworld. Sprung loose from its original trappings, it is a powerful piece of music. The opening strain, a relaxed and expansive stretch of forty-five seconds, splendidly joins Miley's chattering trumpet with an arranged theme. If it was Ellington who came up with the arranged theme, then he has gone far beyond the trite contrasting ideas of *East St. Louis Toodle-O* and caught up with his featured soloist. This minor mode section of the piece nicely yields to contrasting major mode sections, which are followed by a series of minor blues choruses, with effective obbligato and a strong scat chorus from singer Baby Cox (who is also used well on *Hot and Bothered*).

Radio was a surprise benefit of the Cotton Club gig. The band was first heard on station WHN, which broadcasted "on location" from a number of Manhattan spots. In February 1929 the Cotton Club advanced a step and hooked up with WABC, the main station in the CBS radio network. This meant distribution through some forty stations across the country, mostly in the northeast and around the Great Lakes. The *Chicago Defender* started to reference "Duke Ellington and his famous broadcasting orchestra." Louis Armstrong remembered gathering around the radio with his bandmates from the Savoy Ballroom in Chicago, late at night in an apartment, to cherish Ellington broadcasts during the spring of 1929. *East St. Louis Toodle-O* became their radio theme song.

Ellington had been tracking Fletcher Henderson, but he was now ahead of his role model. In October 1929 the band landed another claim to fame playing for a Florenz Ziegfeld Jr. production called *Show Girl*, starring Jimmy Durante and Ruby Keeler with songs by Gershwin. The Ellington Orchestra performed from the stage in a nightclub scene, then they all rushed back to the Cotton Club by 11 p.m. for the nightly gig there. There were many ways to break the color line, and this one was noticed far and wide. It caused the *Defender* to dub Ellington the "Black Paul Whiteman" in a November column. We should note the careful analogy: Whiteman was the most prestigious bandleader of the day, but he was not a composer. Ellington's image as a great composer had not yet been established, and in 1929, his path toward celebrity was still the Henderson model of playing at prestigious white venues.

Mood Indigo: *The Ellington Effect, the Miley Method, and the Ellington Problem*

A clarinet and a flute have different tonal qualities, which are often described as "colors." An orchestrator who takes a composition and assigns the parts to various instruments, as Ferde Grofé did for George Gershwin and as William Grant Still did for James P. Johnson, has to be an expert in combining different colors to make new, more complex ones. Ellington developed a strong sense of how to do this, and *Mood Indigo* is one of his finest achievements.

The synesthetic metaphor, with "color" describing qualities of sound, alerts us again to his interest in visual arts. His son Mercer described the talent on his grandmother's side of the family, with several accomplished painters. The orchestrator does more, of course, than simply combine instruments in unusual ways. It is a matter of experimenting with how instrumental color can enhance melody, harmony, or form. That is how orchestrating becomes an area for creativity and distinction.

Ellington liked to stack his band with different colors and styles of playing—Juan Tizol's smooth trombone, Tricky Sam Nanton's raucous one, the bell-like trumpet of Arthur Whetsol, the silky alto saxophone of Otto Hardwick, the brusque baritone sax of Harry Carney, and so on. (All of them played in the Cotton

Club band.) The story of *Mood Indigo* began with the lush clarinet of Barney Bigard.

Bigard was raised in the Seventh Ward of downtown New Orleans, where "Creole" meant something a little different from elsewhere in the United States. For the people Bigard grew up with it meant a sense of belonging to this city, a family connection back through history and all the way to France, an identity that invoked social distinction, especially in matters of competition with the Americans on the other side of Canal Street. Bigard was a Creole of color, though this was not a social category he and his family used. They just thought of themselves as Creoles. Music was the most reliable marker of cultural distinction within reach of the Seventh Ward Creoles. They passionately valued their Eurocentric musical traditions, sustained by tight social networks and maintained with a rigorous pedagogy that set them up for good-paying employment. Music was always there for pleasure and sociability, Creole front parlors turning into little concert halls on Sunday afternoons, with violin, piano, and clarinet performing gestures of cultural distinction.

Bigard took lessons as a young teenager with a Creole of color clarinetist named Lorenzo Tio Jr. A single lesson easily lasted two hours. Every fundamental of musical technique was drilled thoroughly before going to the next one. The clarinet has the advantage of being able to move quickly through a big musical range, from high to low. The low end is known as the "*chalumeau* range," and Creole clarinetists were known for their ability to play it with a rich, woody sound. When listeners heard them play like this they immediately understood (if so inclined) their cultural superiority to the untutored, blues-based clarinetists uptown.

And that is how Bigard developed the big, round sound that Ellington was instantly drawn to. After sustained training Bigard stepped out and started playing jazz. He learned how to improvise, to play the blues, and to spin the obbligato parts that were so important for collective improvisation. What he didn't master before he left New Orleans he had plenty of time to soak up during an extended stay with King Oliver's band from 1925 to 1927.

In the summer of 1930, Bigard had a tune he wanted Ellington to hear. The story got told a little differently on various occasions, but what seems likely is that the melody originated with his teacher in New Orleans, Lorenzo Tio Jr. Bigard tinkered with it and added a bridge to make something that was "mostly my own but partly Tio's." Ellington added the introductory strain— "I gave him some ideas for it too," insisted Bigard—with harmonizing turns worked out on the piano. The different sections of *Mood Indigo* were kept in the same key to maintain continuity of mood rather than sharp contrast, building on the precedent of *Black and Tan Fantasy*.

Ellington described the origins of *Mood Indigo* very differently: "We had a little six-piece date in 1930 at OKeh. So we went down, and that night when I was waiting for my mother to cook dinner, why, I said, 'Yeah, I need another number, I better scratch out something while I wait.'"

"I had to laugh when I read that article," remembered Bigard. Ellington also claimed that *Mood Indigo* was the "first tune I wrote specially for microphone transmission."

One thing everyone agrees on is that Ellington orchestrated the introductory strain. Instead of having trumpet in the middle, clarinet above, and trombone below, as would be typical, the trombone is pushed high in its range, just below the trumpet, with clarinet on the bottom. This was similar to the opening of *Black and Tan Fantasy*, with Miley and Nanton, now with the addition of Bigard's lush and low chalumeau-range clarinet. Everything is muted and soft. The sound is mysterious, saturated color from a distance, subtly glowing yet dark. Putting the clarinet far below the muted trombone is a classic example of finding the logical way and flipping it, the mid-1920s advice from Will Marion Cook. "The Ellington Effect" is a phrase coined by Billy Strayhorn to describe his approach to arranging. "Each member of his band is to him a distinctive tone color and set of emotions, which he mixes with others equally distinctive to produce a third thing, which I like to call the Ellington Effect," Strayhorn explained in 1952.

Mood Indigo is further distinguished by unusual harmonies, chromatic and slightly unpredictable, in the introductory section. *Black Beauty* (1928) was one Ellington precedent for thinking outside the typical harmonic box of jazz. Its introduction is based on the whole-tone scale, which gives it an edgy, otherworldly feeling. The brief introduction nicely frames the rest of the piece. (*Black Beauty* is also another egregious example of Miley's role being diminished in literature on Ellington: contrary to most discussions, which solely credit Ellington, Miley probably composed the main tune, which critic Gary Giddins has described as "the most enchantingly beautiful melody ever conceived in the stride idiom.")

Even more direct preparation for *Mood Indigo* was the impressive first strain of *The Mystery Song* (first recorded August 1930), likewise built around several attractive harmonic turns. Lyricist Don George described Ellington's "strange way of composing. Most tune writers wrote the melody first, then worked out the chord structure behind it, but Duke wrote the chords and that was that . . . " This explains why some of Ellington's most striking material revolves around moody progressions. It also explains why his own melodies rarely rank among the best. The first strain of *The Mystery Song* is a splendid example of what the harmonically oriented Ellington could come up with, sitting at his piano, experimenting with chords. The introduction to *Mood Indigo* benefits from Bigard's addition of melodic definition to Ellington's chords.

Ellington, the failed tunesmith, found his niche first in arranging and second in fresh harmonies. It's hard to create an entire piece out of interesting chords, but as a framing device it works beautifully. After the introduction, the clarinet melody takes over the main section of *Mood Indigo*, wistful and beautifully delivered by Bigard, the best of Creole New Orleans. Microphones helped transmit the intimacy through recordings and radio. Mills promoted Ellington as the "Rudy Vallée of the Colored Race." Vallée was the premiere crooner of the day, soft and mellow and heavily dependent on the new technology. It was a strange analogy, but the intention was to place pieces like *Mood Indigo* in that crooning context, beaming into bedrooms over the radio and conjuring romance with the aid of the microphone.

Marrying fresh tone colors to quirky harmonies produced stunningly atmospheric results, and both became favored devices for Ellington. "For instance if we played an old hat number like *Who's Sorry Now*, out would come those 'funny' chords even for a number like that," remembered Bigard. "I understand that he got a lot of his chord ideas from an old guy named Will Vodery that used to arrange for shows." Trumpeter Freddie Jenkins described how Ellington would rehearse the band, "pay us union scale, maybe for four or five hours, just to help him formulate chords. He'd assign different notes to every instrument and say 'Play that, B-a-a-m!' and it might produce a big C13th, what we call a Christmas chord. Then he'd take those same notes and switch them to different instruments and while you'd still have a big C13th, it would sure sound a lot different. Sometimes he'd do that three or four times until he found the combination he wanted." Ellington's sense of how to use an orchestra came from constant, on-site experience.

It was Vodery who helped Ellington land the prestigious job with Ziegfeld in the fall of 1929. "[Vodery's] chromatic tendencies penetrated my ear, and are largely responsible for the way I think music, even today," remembered Ellington. Perhaps the opening strain of *Mood Indigo* is a demonstration of Vodery's lessons to his open-eared colleague. "You see, Ellington is a Doctor of music, I'll call him," said bass player Wellman Braud, "because he can make a tune a little better, sound a little better than what it is." In this case the doctoring produced a megahit that spread across the nation. Radio's ability to sell sheet music was unrivaled, and *Mood Indigo* made a lot of money for the copyright holder.

Bigard sold his composition to Ellington for twenty-five dollars. For twenty-eight years the song accrued royalties to Ellington and his manager but not to Bigard. Bigard eventually sued and won, receiving royalties beginning in 1958. *Mood Indigo* is another example of what we might call the "Miley method." The piece started as a solo from a member of the band, then Ellington made an arrangement that extends the solo. Since the method originated with Miley's great solos, it seems fitting to honor his role.

Mood Indigo represents a moment of compositional maturity for Ellington, at age thirty-two. Atmospheric "mood" pieces were part of the Cotton Club scene, right alongside the exotic jungle pieces, and Ellington's unusual harmonies served both types. Dance pieces were played everywhere, but Ellington was the right person to explore these more imaginative directions. He slowed *East St. Louis Toodle-O* down from the original fox trot tempo and transformed it into a mood piece. He assembled *Mood Indigo* by combining Bigard's tunefulness, his own interest in chromatic harmonies, and the unusual scoring of *Black and Tan Fantasy*, enhanced by Bigard's chalumeau range. But "assembled" is not quite the right word. The whole is greater than the sum of the parts. What makes the piece so successful is the synthesis of these components into a coherent musical vision.

His compositional identity was fully formed. The ingredients are easy to itemize: first, the multidimensional voice that emerged naturally from the Miley method, which became thoroughly identified with Ellington; second, inventive and chromatic harmonies; third, unusual scoring; fourth, evocative titling. This piece synthesized all of that, matched with musical excellence. From now on, any composition with Ellington's name on it could invoke his public identity simply by touching on any of these parts, regardless of whether or not he had the primary role in composing it. This is still the case today: Ellington fans hear *him*, a consistent voice, from 1926 through the very end. Year after year, devotees multiplied as he extended the range of this approach.

2.4 *Mood Indigo* trio: Sam Nanton, Arthur Whetsol, Barney Bigard, ca. 1935

You could enjoy these compositions at the Cotton Club, and you could listen to them on the radio, but with a record you could play them over and over. Records gave the performances a documented status and allowed them to play a sustained role in cultural history. Tin Pan Alley songwriting turned out not to be Ellington's thing, but through collaboration and recordings he discovered a powerful alternative. Like Ellington, Louis Armstrong composed tunes, notated them, and sent them to the U.S. Copyright Office for copyright. But over the course of the 1920s Armstrong realized a more rewarding way to channel his creativity: he could create brilliant hot solos, full of melodic invention and thoroughly located in the African American musical vernacular. The payoff came not through sheet music but through recordings that enhanced his reputation. With Mills's guidance, Ellington merged this new model with the old one. The recording of *Mood Indigo* supported sheet music sales of the basic tune, which is where royalties accrued.

Bigard claimed authorship of thirteen tunes from the Ellington playbook, including *Rockin' in Rhythm*, a longtime favorite credited to Mills, Ellington, and Harry Carney, Ellington's close confidant ("He put Harry's name on there," Bigard scoffed. "Harry couldn't compose nothing if he tried"). "[Ellington's] pretty smart and he's shrewd," Bigard acknowledged. "You might make what we call a riff . . . He gets that riff and he makes a tune out of it, and that's the way he does. A lot of tunes that he gets credit for is from the boys in the band . . . I mean, like if anybody stood up and took a solo, you know, and he heard something that he made playing that he liked, he'd tell them, 'Play the solo, play it again,' until he got it. When he got it, then that's it. Then the next thing you know there's a tune coming out of it. He'd put his name onto anything." It's easy to imagine the happy melody for *Rockin' in Rhythm* having been generated in this way.

Bigard was hardly the only disgruntled sideman. *Sophisticated Lady* (1932) was the biggest hit to follow *Mood Indigo*. Ellington recorded it dozens of times, the last barely two months before his death in 1974. Phonograph discs and sheet music usually credit Ellington as the composer, plus Mitchell Parish, who eventually supplied lyrics, plus the unstoppable Mills. Usually missing, after the initial release, is the name of trombonist Lawrence Brown, who composed the main theme, and saxophonist Otto Hardwick, who composed the bridge to complete the entire thematic content. "Me and Lawrence Brown," joked Hardwick, "we used to call ourselves 'the co-writers.'" Ellington made up another origin story that omitted the co-writers and instead had him writing at a piano, trying to "capture a real sophisticated lady, you know, one who is traveled and learned."

"I don't consider you a composer," was Brown's scornful dismissal of Ellington in a fit of pique. "You are a compiler."

Trumpeter Clark Terry concurred, describing Ellington as a "compiler of deeds and ideas." We have already talked about the dissatisfaction of Hodges and Tizol. The musician who probably suffered most of all from this system was Billy Strayhorn, whose compositional and arranging skills saturate the band's repertory during the 1940s and '50s.

"It wouldn't cost him nothing to credit them—he was a genius," reflected Bigard. To the contrary, it would have cost him plenty. Noncrediting was part of Ellington's ecosystem for sustained big-band success. First, it would have cost him massive streams of revenue, and second, it would have undermined his carefully managed image as a composer-genius, unique in the sprawling field of jazz.

"My loot comes from publishing," Ellington once acknowledged. Manager Mills understood this side of the business thoroughly. The logic of adding Mills as a copyright holder was that he would have a bigger incentive to promote the pieces. Since he was managing other performers, too, opportunities were expanding. A sideman-composer might get credit on the very first disc label, but the copyright was usually held by Ellington.

How did Ellington manage to pull off this kind of dissemblance, so many times over so many years, and still hold together his splendid band? His legendary powers of persuasion and managerial savvy were helpful. "You'll be talking to Duke and you'll want to say, 'no,' and he'll make you say 'yes,'" explained drummer and bandleader Chico Hamilton. Many stories document his interpersonal effectiveness.

He also offered loyalty and longevity, huge benefits in the volatile world of entertainment. His was the most stable jazz band in history. At least some of his publishing loot helped subsidize salaries during slack times. Musicians can put up with a lot in exchange for that kind of job security. This was partly how he "inspired a togetherness that was, and still is, unique in the history of jazz," as Don George described the band in later decades.

There were also special agreements. The clearest case is Hodges, who did not become the band's highest paid musician simply because he was the Lily Pons of the alto saxophone.

He and Ellington had an unspoken system of communication whereby Hodges, the song factory, would recognize one of his own melodies in a new Ellington composition, make a silent little gesture to the leader, and know that his salary was about to jump up a notch. There must have been similar agreements with other soloists, who found themselves getting a bigger spotlight after an Ellington appropriation.

The musicians understood that their own hit-making creativity would be rewarded beyond the twenty-five dollars Ellington paid them to sell away their rights. There was a loose system at work, with indirect benefits. Not only was he not going to fire them, he might make them famous. Ellington climbed on the back of creative collaboration and used it to achieve nationwide fame. From there he constructed a virtuous loop with a business model that returned at least some of the rewards to the creative sidemen, thus promoting more collaboration. The Beatles discovered a different business model: Lennon and McCartney cosigned everything, which invited endless back and forth between the two creative principles. Compared with that, Ellington's model was covert, harder to manage, but totally in step with an era in which management routinely took creative credit for music that management did not create. Detailed discussion of Ellington's appropriations is often taken as an attack on his morals. Writers sometimes transfer the blame to others, Mills or Ellington's sister Ruth, who was involved with management. The intention here is not to arrive at moral judgment but rather to bring to light the quotidian realities of how the Ellington collective accomplished what it did.

The second reason it was difficult for Ellington to acknowledge creative collaboration is no less loaded and may actually be more highly charged today than ever before. Writers aiming to glorify Ellington—and that has been the standard approach—usually describe him as a genius composer, and this kind of praise does not naturally lead to thorough discussion of collective creativity.

The beginnings of the image trace back to these years, with Mills again in charge.

The creative breakthrough of *East St. Louis Toodle-O*, *Black and Tan Fantasy*, and *Creole Love Call* distinguished this band from all others, which in turn led Mills to promote Ellington as a great composer. There were plenty of precedents for jazz groups recording their own compositions, but usually as an economizing move: the companies insisted on it as a way to avoid paying royalties while offering the composer-performer a small flat fee. Now Mills presented the composer-performer as a mark of distinction. "I made his importance as an artist the primary consideration," he explained.

Ellington's son Mercer watched Mills layer "increasing veneers of sophistication on the music." Mills established a discourse of prestige that took visual form very quickly in the movie *Black and Tan* (1929, aka *Black and Tan Fantasy*), written and directed by Dudley Murphy. The movie opens with Ellington seated at a piano, pounding out "a new number I'm writing," that he teaches to trumpeter Arthur Whetsol. The number is, of course, *Black and Tan Fantasy*. Needless to say, Miley goes unmentioned.

Publicity releases put all the focus on the leader. "[Mills] wanted Duke to be the star, not the band," remembered guitarist Freddy Guy. "The men were just the rank and file. But I could see through him, man, and [Mills] hated me for it." Critic Abbe Niles wrote in 1929 that "there is more and better melody in one of the dances of this astounding Negro [Ellington] than in ten of the pallid tunes of the average operetta." Niles acknowledged that this might be hard for the first-time listener to appreciate because of the "hair-raising arabesques" from the musicians who were performing Ellington's great melodies. He identified Ellington's melodic gift as the reason for the success of *East St. Louis Toodle-O* and *Black and Tan Fantasy*.

This became the standard view of the Miley-Ellington pieces. In 1932, R. D. Darrell described how *Black and Tan Fantasy* "bore the indelible stamp of one mind, resourcefully inventive . . . tapping the inner world of feeling and experience . . . " For Darrell, that mind was, of course, Ellington's, not Miley's. It astonished Darrell how Ellington seemed to be "gifted with a seemingly inexhaustible well of melodic invention." The key to Ellington's success was not collaboration but solitary genius, everything "composed, scored, and played under one sure hand." Niles's and Darrell's mistakes have been repeated countless times.

In the summer of 1930, Mills placed Ellington's orchestra in another film, *Check and Double Check*, headlined by Amos 'n' Andy. *Check and Double Check* paid the Ellington unit a jaw-dropping $27,500 for four weeks of work and placed another plume in Ellington's hat. The movie featured an extended ballroom scene with the band playing *Old Man Blues*, one of the most stunning up-tempo numbers in the entire Ellington canon. Nanton, Carney, Hodges, and Jenkins deliver splendid solos, perfectly integrated into the arrangement, while Bigard's riveting obbligato drives below and then soars above the ensemble. The soloists are framed by a smart introduction, smart modulations, smart variety in the accompaniment, and smart contrasting themes. In the movie, the band is featured for the entire performance, with no cutaways for dialogue. The ballroom audience stops dancing and simply stands to attentively listen. It is an important moment in the formation of Ellington's elite status.

The *Defender's* high compliment from the fall of 1929, that Ellington was the "Paul Whiteman of the Race," had nothing to do with composition and everything to do with prestige as a performer. Mills spelled out in a publicity manual how to add the image of Ellington as a great composer to the mix: "Sell Ellington as a great artist, a musical genius whose unique style and individual theories of harmony have created a new music." He placed an article by Ellington in the British magazine *Rhythm* in March 1931, with the leader explaining how "the involved nature of my numbers prevents them being great popular successes." Having climbed to the top of the African American dance-band ladder, Ellington could present himself as a lofty artist shunning the lowest common denominators of the marketplace.

There were many ways to proclaim a composer's identity. The label of a record disc could say one thing, a copyright deposit another, sheet music something else, and a movie accomplished more than words. Origin stories about how Ellington created the pieces entirely by himself increased as time went on. Publicity mentioned Ellington and no one else. The multiple layers of information and disinformation are a source of confusion still with us today, often leading to the resigned conclusion that we'll never know all of the details so we might as well give the credit to Ellington. Alternatively, one could argue that whenever we see the smoke of creative collaboration, it is reasonable to assume there was fire.

We are still under the spell of Mills's promotional strategies. Ellington is often regarded as a composer even where his contribution was nothing more than a straightforward arrangement. The reason is that composing is higher on the hierarchy of creative work than arranging is. His status as a great composer is routinely taken as a starting point, generating layers upon layers of compromised commentary.

The Ellington problem, then, is simply this: we cannot assume that Ellington composed the material that he claimed. The default assumption of giving him credit is not sustainable. It makes more sense to assume collaboration than not. That is not to suggest that Ellington never composed anything of value, but rather that the default assumption cannot hold. Dissemblance was the norm.

With the Beatles we have a model of collaboration that was based on the central pair and then expanded to include others. With Ellington we have a leader working a highly flexible set of relationships and calling the shots. He had the skill set to pull it off. He was drawn to strain form because it made it easy to bring together material from different places in additive fashion. He made the most out of limited training by staying open-eared and taking lessons from old-school musicians like Cook and Vodery. He had a keen ear for quality. He was daring, willing to think outside the box. He saw possibilities others didn't see.

And he had strong powers of conceptualization. For many this makes his contributions more important than the "simply musical" contributions of the creative sidemen. Ellington conceptualized Miley's brilliant solos and that seems to make him the composer even if he didn't compose any of the strongest material. To counter that, one need only think about music that is interesting conceptually but not worth listening to. Conceptual sophistication went a long way in the twentieth century, though perhaps less far in music than other arts. In a museum it is easy to glance at work that offers an interesting concept but modest artistic skill, to chuckle a bit or nod in admiration at the cleverness, and then move on to the next item, all in a few seconds. Since music can only be experienced in real time, conceptual sophistication does not compensate so easily for modest musical talent. With Miley, Ellington didn't have to worry about a thing. After Miley's departure he identified a splendid array of creative talent to carry the band forward.

Ellington's status as a great composer is formidable, but what would it be like to fully factor in the essential contributions from Miley, Bigard, Hodges, Williams, Tizol, Stewart, Webster, Strayhorn, and all the rest? Ellington would become a different kind of cultural hero. It is frequently pointed out that when these musicians left the band they did not shine as they had with Ellington. The obvious response to that is that they needed him just as much as he needed them. The times are right to regard Ellington's primary gift as a genius collaborator. The only way to develop that view is by putting the Ellington problem in the foreground instead of keeping in the background, where he and his publicists worked hard to keep it.

The band entered the Cotton Club with one of jazz's top

soloists, who was bursting with musical ideas, and the generous payroll made it easy to uplift the ensemble and extend the range of collaboration. Cotton Club expectations for original material in a range of moods and styles encouraged Ellington's skills to grow. By 1931 he was without peer as a jazz arranger. We can trace his progress through the Miley jewels, then through out-standing numbers like *Hot and Bothered, Old Man Blues, Rockin' in Rhythm, Mystery Song,* and *Mood Indigo.* In the fresh version of an old standard like *Limehouse Blues* (1931), his arranging talent stands out clearly.

Mills wrapped the whole package with a silk bow. Nineteen hundred thirty-one was a year to harvest the band's radio repu-tation, with a lengthy tour of the nation topped off by a sold-out, six-week stay at the Oriental Theatre in Chicago. "Managers and promoters all agree that he is the biggest hit of all time," claimed the *Pittsburgh Courier,* "regardless of race or color."

"The chief number is *Black and Tan Fantasy,*" reported the *Cleve-land News.* The contribution to Ellington's glory made by the two greatest Miley-Ellington collaborations, *East St. Louis Toodle-O* and *Black and Tan Fantasy,* was sustained and incalculable.

More calculable is money. It has been estimated that in 1931, while the Great Depression ransacked the music industry with tanking record sales, folding black and tans (the Cotton Club was an exception), and fading vaudeville, Ellington's pay reached the highest level of his entire career, adjusted for inflation. "We worked clean through the Depression without even knowing there was one," quipped Bigard. The band's talent, Ellington's savvy, the Miley method, and Mills's veneers of sophistication combined to achieve one of the most stunning successes jazz has ever known.

THE 1930S:

An "ACCUMULATION *of* PERSONALITIES"

Decentralized Collaboration

ELLINGTON'S WORK AS A COMPOSER has been compared with auteur directors of movies—figures like Ingmar Bergman, Federico Fellini, and Alfred Hitchcock—who enlist the help of secondary collaborators to fulfill their vision. Sometimes Ellington did indeed work like that, but he never felt bound to any single approach. Indeed, one of the stunning developments during the 1930s was his ability to work in so many different ways. I will argue that his most fruitful method actually resembles a movie-making model that is much less centralized. The differences between that and the model of the auteur director highlight a lot about what has been falsely claimed and misunderstood about Ellington, and they also point to what was extraordinary.

There is no better demonstration of the decentralized model than the 1939 version of *The Wizard of Oz*. Louis B. Mayer, cofounder of MGM, hired ten screenwriters working more or less sequentially to turn the original book by L. Frank Baum into a movie script. Song lyricist Yip Harburg took a turn working over the script, too. He rewrote dialogues in rhyme as a clever way to lead into songs and integrate them into the story. He and composer Harold Arlen agreed that a ballad for Dorothy should be the central musical event. By any standard, they succeeded with *Over the Rainbow*. They delivered their songs to a team of musicians who arranged them and composed the rest of the music for the film. All of these musical layers contributed as much continuity and expression as the script did.

It was the job of four different directors, working one after the other, to take the script, songs, set designs, and actors who were handed to them and make a movie. The role of the director was limited. "I don't remember him ever saying, 'Don't do that,' or 'Don't do this,' or 'Try to do this,'" explained Margaret Hamilton, the wicked witch of the west, about Victor Fleming, the director who received screen credit. The film's producer, Mervyn LeRoy, and his assistant were in charge of everything that the ten screenwriters, four directors, two songwriters, and cast of actors created. Yet Louis B. Mayer could step in and override anything, as he tried to do when he ordered *Over the Rainbow* cut from the picture (intense persuasion won him over). The system was designed for robust distribution of creative control through a vast list of credited and uncredited participants. The producer hired the best professionals he could and let them go about their work. It was a sprawling mess of creative action, reaction, rejection, revision, and extension.

With Ellington things were often similar. There are many indications of a decentralized process with a producer-like figure having the final say, rather than a top-down process where everyone follows Ellington's vision. We've talked about the Miley method, Ellington's reliance on composed solos from his sidemen as the basis for new pieces. Other pieces were built more simply around solos that were improvised. Gunther Schuller felicitously described, in some of Ellington's arrangements from the early 1930s, the "generous parade of uniquely individual voices." Smart foregrounding of superb talent surfaces in pieces like *Drop Me Off in Harlem* and *Bundle of Blues*, both from 1933.

More hidden were the recipes for shaping arrangements, where, according to many reports, collaboration was normal. Ellington was in charge, but an egalitarian spirit was in place. In the early years, remembered alto saxophonist Otto Hardwick, "We would have an arrangement, but if there was something you felt you wanted to put in it, you were free to do it, privileged to make suggestions, just spontaneously burst out with it . . ."

That same atmosphere continued into the 1930s. "Everyone made suggestions," explained Cootie Williams. "It was a family thing."

And it remained strong even under the pressures of making a record. "For instance when you go into a recording studio, you might have an arrangement all made, yet it'll probably be changed," said Harry Carney. "Guys come up with ideas of injecting something. That still goes on."

"Everybody pitches in—all the time," interjected Johnny Hodges in the same interview. "Somebody might have ideas to make it a little better."

Wellman Braud described how Hodges and Bigard were good at "filling the holes," the classic responsibility of a clarinetist from New Orleans. "All bands at that time [early 1930s] were most ear bands," explained Lawrence Brown. "Whatever you heard you'd pick up a place to fit in, a part to fit in. Whatever you heard was missing that's where you were." The musicians rarely claimed ownership of their contributions to an arrangement. Unlike the fast-moving small print at the end of a movie, there was no room on a phonograph disc to acknowledge all of this.

Sheik of Araby (May 1932) was a surprisingly effective recording of an old standard, with trombonist Lawrence Brown making his first mark with Ellington. Brown had spent many months in Los Angeles playing behind Louis Armstrong, and this solo proves that he was paying attention. Hodges, who offers a stunning solo on soprano sax on the same record, said that Sidney Bechet "taught" the Ellington band this arrangement for *Sheik of*

Araby. "He played that for us, and Tizol put it down," which is to say that Bechet demonstrated his ideas, the band learned them, and Juan Tizol notated the results.

A 1933 article in *Metronome* magazine described a back and forth process for making an arrangement: first through the sections of the band; then into notation; then back to Ellington's apartment for tinkering; and finally a return to the musicians the next day for further commentary, adjustments, and improvements. At the end the arrangement was memorized. The process typically began without notation and ended there, but included notation along the way. A 1944 *New Yorker* article reported something similar and credited the role of Tizol once again.

3.1 Lawrence Brown, 1933

Tizol, the classically trained trombonist from Puerto Rico, was known as the "extractor." The term carried several meanings. It could mean notating ideas worked out collectively in performance, or it could mean notating individual parts. How much Tizol edited and arranged while he did this will never be answered. Tizol was modest and self-deprecating, and he downplayed his ability to create arrangements. Nevertheless, he composed some of the band's greatest hits, had facility with musical notation far superior to anyone else, and was a marvelous trombone player. His strong musicality and high standards must have quietly shaped the whole process.

"Extended" Compositions

Ellington was more like an auteur director of a movie in what he called his "extended" compositions. These pieces lean toward art music for the concert hall—their connections to jazz, dance, and popular music are often thin or nonexistent. The first one was *Creole Rhapsody* (1931). Later came *Reminiscing in Tempo* (1935), *Diminuendo and Crescendo in Blue* (1937), *Black, Brown and Beige* (1943), and many more. For the extended pieces Ellington tends to script a more or less complete vision, conceived for specific musicians who have the ability to bring out his ideas, much like a movie director imagines his concept being brought to life by specific actors.

The extended pieces have been frequently written about, even though they rarely rank in the top tier of Ellington's recorded legacy. It is a lot easier to write about all the biographical and cultural issues surrounding them than it is to write about what makes Bubber Miley's trumpet playing so magnificent. We will see precisely the same phenomenon with the Beatles: Lennon's conceptually provocative but musically simple songs are much easier to talk about than McCartney's musically rich songs.

The idea of composing an extended piece came from Irving Mills. It is easy to get Mills's logic: Ellington, the great composer, should write longer pieces, just like other great composers. This would be an excellent way to enhance his status. *Creole Rhapsody* was a modest step in that direction. The first recording, from January 1931, lasts a little more than six minutes; a revised version from June lasts around eight minutes. After you played the first part on side one, you flipped the disc over and played the second part. A sign of the success of Mills's strategy was an invitation from composer Percy Grainger for Ellington to visit a composition seminar at New York University; the Ellington Orchestra played *Creole Rhapsody* there in the fall of 1932. Paul Whiteman's orchestra performed the piece at Carnegie Hall three months

3.2 Basil Cameron, Percy Grainger, and Ellington, 1933

later. This was the kind of thing Mercer Ellington was thinking of when he described Mills adding increasing veneers of sophistication to Ellington's music.

The connection to Whiteman followed indirectly from connections to Gershwin's *Rhapsody in Blue,* which Whiteman had famously premiered in 1924. But *Creole Rhapsody* is no *Rhapsody in Blue.* There are two main problems. First, the melodic themes are not of the highest quality, and second, the handling of longer form leaves much to be desired. Both problems turn up regularly in Ellington's extended pieces.

The first problem, to put it bluntly, has to do with the fact that the themes of *Creole Rhapsody* came exclusively from Ellington himself, not from the hit makers in his band. The second comes from trying to do something for which he had no preparation. Mastery of short forms does not automatically convert to mastery of longer ones. Classical composers invest considerable time learning how to craft longer pieces. Working with teachers, they study the masterpieces and learn how to hold interest, how to transition from one section to another, and how to make the material hang together. "It would be a pity if Ellington started to produce rambling, pseudo-highbrow fantasies," wrote the British composer Constant Lambert in response to *Creole Rhapsody*. Similar sentiments have been articulated by others. Lambert was a huge admirer of Ellington's shorter recordings. He called him the "first jazz composer of distinction," and he cited the standard-length *Hot and Bothered* and *Mood Indigo* as examples of Ellington's best.

Reminiscing in Tempo (1935) is stronger than *Creole Rhapsody*, though it, too, is hardly a composition upon which to build a legacy. Ellington wrote the piece after his mother's untimely death "in a soliloquizing mood," as he later reflected. The piece exists in different versions. The original recording followed the double-sided plan times two: now there are two discs, four sides, four parts to a single piece. These discs were twelve inch, the typical size for classical music, rather than ten inch, the size usually reserved for popular music. (This distinction was still current in 1963, when Ringo Starr quipped to George Martin that the classically trained producer was "very twelve inch.") The thirteen-minute *Reminiscing* is organized around a moody set of chromatically shifting chords, just the kind of thing Ellington liked to experiment with at his piano. Sometimes the chords are heard in slithering arpeggiations and sometimes they shift in blocks, coolly in the background, behind the main theme. Various thematic episodes enter and then return to the interesting harmonies. The lack of tight musical direction paints a meandering atmosphere that can be felt as pensive.

Schuller was impressed by how Ellington, in *Reminiscing in Tempo*, targeted specific players and how this orientation is integrated with his larger vision for the piece. He doesn't just write for trombone, trumpet, and alto sax, he writes for Lawrence Brown,

Arthur Whetsol, and Johnny Hodges. Ellington loved to talk about writing "to the musician."

"Aren't there marked similarities between you and Bach?" an admirer asked him in 1944.

"Well, Bach and myself both write with individual performers in mind," was his response.

The elite image Ellington and Mills were striving for could not be summed up better than in statements like this. Ellington wrote for his musicians just like Bach did. That formula took what was so special about the band's collaboration and turned it into prestige for Ellington. This is the view R. D. Darrell articulated in 1932, when he credited Ellington as the composer of the great melodies that were actually created by Bubber Miley. But it was not true in that case and it was not true in countless other cases, where Bigard or Williams or Tizol or some other musician created the compelling melodies that outsiders heard as Ellington's. *Reminiscing in Tempo*, on the other hand, appears to have come from Ellington alone. There is no doubt that the players bring a lot to sustain interest and help the piece along.

Perhaps the most successful of the 1930s extended pieces was *Diminuendo and Crescendo in Blue*, another double-sider, about seven minutes long. This piece works so well because it circumvents both of the problems that tend to mar the extended pieces. The title signals the unusual formal plan. Part one, *Diminuendo*, gradually declines in volume, and part two, *Crescendo*, gradually increases. This was a clever response to the artifice of distributing a single piece over two sides of a record with a complete break in the middle: part one gets softer and softer until it fades into nothing and side one comes to an end; then part two starts softly and grows in volume. The listener's flip of the record and the resulting moment of silence becomes part of the performance. The other formal solution is to organize most of the piece through repeated blues choruses, one after the other. The risk here is redundancy, but that is taken care of partly by the diminuendo and the crescendo, partly by effective modulations, and partly by movement from complexity to simplicity (in *Diminuendo*), then simplicity to complexity (in *Crescendo*). The problem of how to organize a seven-minute piece is deftly solved, though this sui generis solution could not be repeated.

Stylistically, the piece has much more jazz than either *Creole Rhapsody* or *Reminiscing in Tempo*, and this also works to its benefit. Vigorous riffs keep driving ahead, with rapid call and response, both staples of the Swing Era though spiked here with an edgy, dissonant ferocity. It is easy to imagine this piece evolving within the band—indeed, it is hard to imagine any other way. *Diminuendo and Crescendo in Blue* is thus a blend of Ellington as auteur director and Ellington as a less controlling collaborator. In a candid moment he described the process:

> We had a recording date scheduled for the next morning and in our usual custom we intended to work up an original composition . . . After two hours of musical battling at the studios the next morning we knew we really had something. Another hour at this sort of thing and we finally had our "blues in rhythm." One disc side we named "Blues Crescendo" and the other, "Blues Diminuendo" . . . Each member of the band feels and knows that it is his orchestra and regards the achievements of the band as his achievements and his success. This communal spirit is typified in our method of composition . . . the name "Duke Ellington" is synonymous with "The Duke Ellington Orchestra."

The alignment with blues invited the musicians to do what they did best. Two decades later that invitation gave rise to one of the most celebrated performances in jazz history. In the 1950s, Ellington reached back to revive the piece as a vehicle for tenor sax soloist Paul Gonsalves, who was alloted an expansive stretch to improvise during the interlude between *Diminuendo* and *Crescendo*; this became known as the "wailing interval." At the 1956 Newport Jazz Festival the piece turned into something like a giant ring shout for the seven thousand mostly white, middle-class, youthful audience. Ellington urged on his tenor sax soloist, "sic-ing that stuff on just as if it's all happening somewhere in a tobacco shed or a corn likker joint," as Albert Murray put it. Gonsalves produced twenty-seven wailing choruses. No one moved in a circle, though a "platinum-blonde girl in a black dress began dancing in one of the boxes," fervently synchronized with the enraptured saxophone. The crowd took to its feet and roared. All of this was the rousing lead-in to *Crescendo*. It is not too much to say that this moment revived Ellington's career. A cover story in *Time* magazine appeared in August and an LP called *Ellington at Newport*—which remains Ellington's best-selling LP—was issued in the fall.

What distinguished Ellington, then, was his *flexibility* in collaborative relationships. Sometimes he built arrangements around his musicians' solos; sometimes he used the voicings and instrumental colors that his sidemen came up with and sometimes he used those musicians to test out his own ideas; sometimes he watched a group arrangement get tossed around until it gelled; sometimes he was simply the doctor, as Wellman Braud put it, who edited and improved. Sometimes he was like a movie producer, sometimes like an auteur director. Always he was an eager collaborator, smart about finding the best way for himself to get involved. It was not a question of ego, since he got all of the credit no matter what. Since he was also good at coming up with titles after the fact, it can seem like he had the guiding conception all along, but this was rarely how things worked.

It all took an immense amount of work and superb discipline on the level of reading people and their music, as well as staying power, to see through an evolving piece in every detail to its finish. The idea that Ellington was lazy, as some authors have asserted, is simply ridiculous.

Collaboration was everywhere, yet his public image as a genius who did it all by himself just got firmer and firmer. From the nineteenth century there was a strong tradition of classical composers using folklike melodies to invoke national identities (or "races," in casual parlance) in their compositions. This legacy became a way to strengthen Ellington's status as a great composer. Ordinary folk songs were the key to expressing a nation's soul. Franz Liszt, for example, wrote a set of piano pieces he called *Hungarian Rhapsodies* that included folk songs from western Hungary, where he was born. Tchaikovsky in Russia, Grieg in Norway, Sibelius in Finland, Vaughan Williams in England, the list goes on and on. Composers might use actual folk songs but it was even better if they composed folklike material themselves. Virtually all of the Western nations had the opportunity to hear their collective souls articulated in this way.

It seemed natural to think of Ellington as doing the same thing for the African American race. His goal, as he explained to the *Christian Science Monitor* in 1935, was to "make new, unadulterated music expressing the character and moods of the Negro." This was part of the recipe that made him, in the words of Constant Lambert (1934), "the first jazz composer of distinction, and the first Negro composer of distinction." Lambert also made explicit his assumptions about the racial dynamics entwined in that assessment. Jazz recordings, he explained, typically represented the work of many people, with more than one composer, more than one soloist, and so on. "Usually the Negro element is confined to the actual arabesques of the execution," he bluntly insisted. In other words, African Americans were good at performing but not creating, at least not usually. This was not a peculiar idea of Lambert's but a widespread racial stereotype.

Lambert even put a creative powerhouse like Louis Armstrong under this umbrella. It is "the greatest mistake to class Louis Armstrong and Duke Ellington together as similar exponents of Negro music," he wrote. "The one is a trumpet player, the other a genuine composer." In other words, Armstrong was a typical African American musician, just like the ones who performed Ellington's compositions, their creative contributions limited to ornamenting someone else's ideas. I have argued elsewhere that we should think of Armstrong as one of the greatest composers of melody in the history of American music. Lambert's purpose was to elevate Ellington above all others, composing great music all himself.

Lambert is frequently cited for his early recognition of Ellington's achievement, but this layer of prejudice is always omitted, even though it is essential to his analysis. A potent and fatal dose of racism was deeply embedded in the foundational discourse on Ellington as a composer. Miley, Bigard, Williams, Tizol, Hodges, and all the other collaborators didn't stand a chance. Meaningful collaboration wasn't even a possibility since Ellington was one of a kind. He was not just exceptional as a jazz composer, *he was exceptional among his race.*

This false and unjust analysis is infused with considerable irony. The entire performer-centered tradition of musical creativity that flowed from the ring shout arose as a way of compensating for the fact that the rewards of copyright were simply not available to slave musicians. Instead those musicians could "rag the tune," which meant adding their own creativity to received melodies. This paradigm continued into the Jim Crow era, when early jazz in New Orleans ran with the possibilities and largely accepted the limitations, the rewards of copyright not becoming easily available until the migration North. In New Orleans and before it was better to *embody* the creativity, to make it part of how you performed, as a group or individually, to win cutting contests in dance halls and street parades and become a celebrated local hero.

The phonograph allowed Ellington to document an arrangement that was built around not just a folklike melody but all of the performer-centered creativity that went with it, a powerful move unavailable to Sibelius, Vaughan Williams, and all the others, who were limited to what could be captured in writing. Not only that, he could co-opt the whole thing under his own name. The irony is that performer-centered creativity had flourished as a way to deal with limitations imposed on African American musicians from a racist society. Now it was being subsumed into the ideology of a great composer who used it to express the "character and moods" of the entire race. This required reducing the performer-creators to mere executors of the genius's great ideas. Ellington and Mills could never have pulled off this hoax all by themselves. They needed a powerful ideology and a long lineage of willing writers to assist them, and they got it.

The Swing Era

The Swing Era, as it is known, is one of the most glorious periods in the history of American music. As a social phenomenon it began around 1935, when white dance bands such as Benny Goodman's reached nationwide fame playing up-tempo jazz. But there was never any doubt about where Goodman got his inspiration: it was from African American jazz musicians; New Orleanians like Johnny Dodds, Jimmie Noone, and Louis Armstrong whom he heard growing up in Chicago; and arrangers like Fletcher Henderson, Don Redman, and Duke Ellington. Swing emerged from these lineages as the music was adapted by white jazz bands and appreciated by young white audiences.

The causal relationship between swing and the Great Depression was only partly a matter of happy music as an antidote to desperate times. Musicians were willing to work for low wages, which fostered an elaborate hierarchy of employment and commerce, something like baseball with its multiple levels of minor leagues feeding into the majors. Leaders worked their way up, and so did sidemen, soloists, and arrangers. Intense competition raised quality all around. The successful bands traveled, and good ideas quickly spread around. In 1935, when Goodman broke

3.3 Jitterbug

through, swing popularity was more a response to the growing hopefulness of the New Deal than to the despair of the Depression. Young people exploded with the energy of dance and music, and the phenomenon kept going for more than a decade. As in the 1920s before and the 1950s after, black dance moves swept the nation. High school and college students were the largest group of fans, and "hot clubs" formed on campuses. "Every aspect of my life and that of my friends revolved around big bands, jazz, dancing, jitterbugging, in my formative teens," remembered a white working-class fan from Massachusetts. Jazz had never before and would never again reach these levels of popularity.

Ellington secured some location gigs, but nothing as long as his stay at the Cotton Club (1927–1931). His band racked up thousands of miles on the road, an exhausting way of life. Someone came up with the idea of renting two Pullman cars and a baggage car that the band could hook up to trains. That made it easier to avoid the irritations and threats of racism by circumventing the need to find places to sleep and eat. Ellington had his own roomette. He loved the plush accommodations, the easy mix between privacy and hanging out with the others, the food, and the relaxing flow of scenery.

In February 1932 the band recorded a prescient anthem for the entire swing phenomenon, *It Don't Mean a Thing (If It Ain't Got That Swing)*. Hodges is again superb on alto sax, and this was the first Ellington recording for singer Ivie Anderson, who would continue with the band through 1942. Ellington explained that the catchy title was something Bubber Miley used to walk around saying. We have seen from the genesis of *East St. Louis Toodle-O* how Miley related to language musically. In the case of *It Don't Mean a Thing (If It Ain't Got That Swing)*, the words match the musical setting so perfectly that we might imagine Miley *singing* this phrase—he didn't just *speak* it—which would make this another Miley-Ellington collaboration. Also effective is the doo-wha riff in the brasses, set up in dialogue with Anderson's vocal, the literal answer to her insistence that life is meaningless without musical verve. Anderson's growling scat is a salute to Louis Armstrong.

A few days later they recorded another vocal tribute to Armstrong with the old standard, *Dinah*. Here Sonny Greer lamely imitates Armstrong's elegant way of moving between words and scat, from tune to improvised invention, now in sync with the foundational rhythms and now radically out of phase. The best way to hear the Ellington *Dinah* is simply as comedic parody—and there were many such parodies of Armstrong's distinctive voice during these years. Armstrong's own recording of *Dinah* (1930) helped establish his breathtakingly fresh modernity, based on the bluesy vernacular he had learned when he was growing up, then developed in the decade after he left New Orleans. Not only was his new style stunningly modern, it was also feverishly popular: it has been claimed that he sold more records in 1931 than anyone, regardless of genre.

Ellington was aiming for that same rare blend. This was one of the challenges facing him as the Swing Era unfolded: how to continue to be both modern and popular, two ideals that do not automatically fit together. Modern meant original, sophisticated, and advanced, while popularity depended on being instantly like-able to a broad slice of the population. The key for Armstrong was his voice. He was still the leading trumpet soloist in jazz, but then as now, vocals were the primary path to commercial success.

In most bands singers like Anderson were marginal, brought out only for a few numbers during a dance or concert. They were usually women, and instrumentalists condescendingly called them "canaries." Some of them—Billie Holiday and Ella Fitzger-ald, to take the two most famous examples—transcended these limitations. Anderson was a strong asset, but, as we have already seen, the main problem for Ellington in creating hit songs was his limited ability as a composer of melody. One possibility was to mix modern touches into a song, as he does effectively in *It Don't Mean a Thing*. Anderson's conventional and accessible singing contrasts with an imposing interlude of jarring and effec-tive chord progressions. Armstrong had created a one-of-a-kind synthesis of modern and popular; most others found it easier to blend the two sequentially.

Ellington naturally gravitated toward instrumental music, where he had first made his mark. The years 1932–1936 wit-nessed a series of stunning achievements, mostly sitting on the modern side of the equation rather than the popular. *Lazy Rhap-sody, Blue Harlem, Blue Ramble*, and *Slippery Horn* (all 1932) are full of sparkling details and imaginative ideas. Jimmie Lunce-ford's band, a main rival to Ellington during this period, was also producing thrilling arrangements packed with one splendid invention after another. For the Lunceford recording *Flaming Reeds and Screaming Brass* (1933), the arranger writes to match the virtuosity of the musicians but without lapsing into flashiness for its own sake. Lunceford's *Jazznocracy* and *White Heat* (1934) are equally compelling in ensemble brilliance and arranging ingenuity. All of these performances sound like the players have invited the arranger to have fun with what they might be able to do; then the players respond to the arrangement with more inspiration of their own.

Ellington's greatest achievement along these lines was *Daybreak Express* (1933). His love of trains, the sense of moving forward without a care in the world, everything under control, shines through in this piece. Part of the magic comes from how he uses strain form to keep boosting the energy of the train. The sections move ahead with a sense of destinational purpose. In this regard *Daybreak Express* is like *Diminuendo and Crescendo in Blue*: each piece demonstrates a unique approach to form that could not be repeated. In the introduction the train accelerates gradually as the chords rise one slight half step after another. Then come the fabulous whistles (CD 0:22). In the next section the train sounds like it is still accelerating as Bigard's clarinet wails high (0:47); the impression is not due to an increase in tempo but rather to continuing harmonic tension. Finally things even out as the train reaches a plateau that launches an energetic theme in four-part harmony from the saxophone section (1:18). The theme is full of standard ragtime syncopations, smoothly performed, an elegant Pullman car cruising through the beautiful countryside on frictionless wheels that are moving very fast. A sudden modulation then pops out (1:45) to give the impression of yet another acceleration. The velvet saxophones yield to an elaborate mosaic of call and response that seems to involve the entire orchestra. All the time the rhythm section keeps chugging along without missing a note. Inside the dazzling layers you can hear the doo-wha riff from *It Don't Mean a Thing*, some references to *Tiger Rag* (which provided background chords), high-note trumpet playing in the style of Armstrong, and vigorous doses of call and response. The final slowdown into the station is brief but imaginatively equal to the initial pullout.

Though it ranks very high in the Ellington portfolio, *Daybreak Express* may not be the greatest Ellington train piece. It would be tough to put it either ahead or behind Billy Strayhorn's *Take the "A" Train*, Ellington's theme song for many years. But in terms of a match between compositional vision and targeted virtuosity of the musicians, *Daybreak Express* has a place in the top echelon of jazz, on a par with pieces like Charles Mingus's *Haitian Fight Song* and John Coltrane's *Love Supreme*. Here is Ellington the auteur director at his very finest.

Yet in the Swing Era songs claimed the biggest financial rewards, just as they always have and always will in popular music. Dance bands had to offer at least a few current hits. You could make an instrumental arrangement of a popular tune, or you could have a vocalist step out and sing. If you had too much—too much of a mediocre tune in a single arrangement or too many mediocre tunes in your repertoire—you risked being thought too "commercial," a simplistic but deadly word that echoes through the decades and into modern-day criticism. If you had too little, your bottom line was jeopardized. It was easy for purists to forget that there were two sides to commercialism. It was not just a matter of pandering to the lowest common denominator but also one of positive artistic inspiration. After all, a good popular song has its own qualities of beauty that come through any arrangement. Those qualities inevitably had impact, even on jazz that positioned itself on the noncommercial end of the spectrum.

Ellington arranged and recorded plenty of popular tunes, and he also tried to produce originals. From the early 1930s his four biggest hits were *Mood Indigo* (1930), *Sophisticated Lady* (1933), *(In My) Solitude* (1934), and *In a Sentimental Mood* (1935). All of them were conceived as instrumental numbers and then adapted with lyrics to make songs. Musically, none of them feels too popish or commercial (though the lyrics, added by hired professionals, are a different matter), and Ellington's elite reputation remained intact.

We have already looked at the collective generation of *Mood Indigo* and *Sophisticated Lady*. Notably, Cootie Williams said that Ellington composed *Solitude* by himself. The piece is harmonically driven, like *The Mystery Song* from a few years earlier, which makes this claim easy to believe. The melody is very simple but effectively moves through nonchord tones with a firm shape, supported by a rich flow of harmonies. The song version of *Solitude* has been recorded countless times, making it the most successful of any composition that can securely be credited to Ellington alone.

Trumpeter Rex Stewart called *In a Sentimental Mood* a "communal effort." Otto Hardwick, who plays lead at the beginning of the original 1934 recording, composed the well-defined and engaging main section of the melody. (Rarely acknowledged is the likelihood that Hardwick also contributed the main idea for *Prelude to a Kiss*, a huge hit in 1938.) We have already seen Ellington's fondness for inventing stories about how he created pieces, and *In a Sentimental Mood* was one of his more colorful efforts. These stories had three purposes. First, they advanced the image of Ellington's deep well of intuitive inspiration, implying no need for help from anybody else. Second, they gave the public something to imagine about an instrumental piece, making it easier to relate to. And third, they were an offering to journalists and musicologists to repeat and thus guarantee that the two main points stayed in circulation.

The stories are so entertaining that writers have been happy to oblige. They know better, and they usually hedge a bit, but still they repeat the stories as if they might be true. For *In a Sentimental Mood*, Ellington claimed that he offered the piece spontaneously at a late-night social event in the North Carolina Mutual Building in Durham, North Carolina, after a dance. Two women were arguing with each other, so Ellington invented the lovely melody as a way to pacify them. Ellington's actual contribution to the song was probably limited to the harmonies of the main section, chromatic and effective, and the conventional bridge as a routine point of contrast.

One of Ellington's main rivals as an arranger in the mid-1930s was Sy Oliver, who worked for Lunceford. Many of Oliver's arrangements inspire superb performances from Lunceford's musicians to produce some of the greatest mid-decade swing. Oliver's playful arrangement of *Mood Indigo*, for example, is a sterling transformation of Ellington's more weighty arrangement of the material Bigard brought from New Orleans. Oliver's harmonic daring and the high standards of musicianship in the Lunceford band allowed them to match Ellington in modernity and sophistication.

Oliver liked to do one thing that Ellington usually did not do: he was fond of blending novelty, modernity, and swing. Sometimes the results are a little too cute, but at its best this approach reaches a winsome and cosmopolitan humor that is not easy to attain in instrumental music. *Organ Grinder's Swing* (1936) is the most famous example and one of the great treasures of the period. The humor comes from the manipulation of the simple street song through swing sophistication, strong blues, imaginative instrumental colors, modulation, and a good sense of drama achieved through dynamics.

When Ellington did aim for novelty the results were, inevitably, classier. We could think about the series of "concerto" pieces recorded beginning in 1936 in this way. A concerto is a type of piece from the classical world written for soloist and group. In 1936, Ellington recorded four pieces with the word "concerto" in the title, each for a different musician in his band: *Echoes of Harlem (Cootie's Concerto)*, *Clarinet Lament (Barney's Concerto)*, *Yearning for Love (Lawrence's Concerto)*, and *Trumpet in Spades (Rex's Concerto)*. Here was a new three-minute way to catch high-brow credentials.

3.4 Ellington calling out trumpeter Rex Stewart, 1939

Trumpet in Spades (Rex's Concerto) is designed for Rex Stewart, who had been with the band since 1934. The cadenza-like displays of rapid playing instantly recall virtuoso figures typical of classical concertos, but the quality here is very weak. In 1937, Stewart developed a technique known as "half valve." This was yet another way to get quirky vocal effects from the instrument, a fresh alternative to the full-throated freak playing of Oliver, Miley, Nanton, and Williams. Like those players, Stewart's technical control helped him establish his own creative voice, which Ellington then incorporated into the band. *Boy Meets Horn* (1938) puts the half-valve technique front and center. It was followed by the lovely *Morning Glory* in 1940. Discs for both give co-composing credit to Ellington and Stewart.

Clarinet Lament (Barney's Concerto), co-credited to Ellington and Bigard, shows off the Creole clarinetist with classical-like flourishes blended with an abundance of blues. As with *Trumpet in Spades*, the classical touches are the weakest parts of the piece. The harmonic foundation for the main part of the piece is borrowed from *Basin Street Blues*, and at times *Clarinet Lament* almost sounds like an arrangement of that famous tune. Discs for *Echoes of Harlem (Cootie's Concerto)* show co-credit to Ellington and Williams in early pressings but not later ("Duke got his name on the label," explained Williams. "I didn't mind"). *Echoes of Harlem* may be the best of the four concertos from 1936, with superb melodic invention from Williams. As with so many Ellington recordings, subtle details in the accompaniment enrich everything.

Meanwhile Johnny Hodges continued to produce. Ellington did not craft a concerto for him, but *Jeep's Blues* (Jeep was one of Hodges's nicknames) was a jukebox hit in 1938. The disc co-credits Ellington and Hodges; the latter was undoubtedly responsible for the splendid tune. Like *Diminuendo and Crescendo in Blue, Jeep's Blues* found powerful renewal at the Newport Jazz Festival in 1956. The later performance moves at a more majestic tempo than the original, and it is more firmly framed as a vehicle for Hodges. Today it is better known than the version from 1938.

Left uncredited were Hodges's vital contributions to the songs *I Let a Song Go Out of My Heart* (1938), *Never No Lament* (1940), and *Don't Get Around Much Anymore* (1942). *I Let a Song Go Out of My Heart* was another big seller that quickly generated an attractive revenue stream for its copyright holders—Mills, Ellington, and lyricist Henry Nemo—through many cover versions. *Don't Get Around Much Anymore*, based on another melodic hook from Hodges, also enjoyed great success. Among its many covers is one by Paul McCartney (1987), who cleverly arranged it as a retrospective rocker. All of these songs were initially conceived as instrumental numbers, and in their initial recordings the band is so good performing them that they should take first place in any assessment.

Hodges brought exquisite passion to any melody he was assigned to play, improvised first-rate blues and hot solos, and crafted melodic hooks that became hits. He was central to the Swing Era success of the Ellington collective. "Corner after corner there were jukeboxes, and you could go forty blocks up Harlem and never stop hearing Johnny Hodges," recalled publicist Helen Oakley.

Ellington's small-group spinoffs from the late 1930s—Rex Stewart and His Fifty-Second Street Stompers, Barney Bigard and His Jazzopaters, Cootie Williams and His Rug Cutters, Johnny Hodges and His Orchestra, and Ivie Anderson and Her Boys from Dixie—are very much part of the period. Other bands were following this model, too. Recordings like these were cheap to make and they satisfied the hungry market. The performances tend to be less fancy in arrangement with plenty of great solos, showing a more informal side of the Ellington band. Writers sometimes frame them as a chance for the leader to make trial runs on new material, but they were also a strategic, late 1930s extension of the Ellington ecosystem: they gave his collaborators a chance to put their creativity on a record with their names prominently displayed. Some of them rank among the finest jewels in the Ellington discography.

Swing was also fruitful for Juan Tizol, the composer, extractor, and trombone virtuoso from Puerto Rico. Tizol developed a specialty in so-called Latin jazz. Ellington has received high praise for this side of the band's portfolio, but there is no doubt that Tizol was the central figure.

Tizol himself did not use the term "Latin jazz" but instead talked about his "Spanish melodies." The first recorded by Ellington was *Porto Rican Chaos* (1935); the title was soon changed to *Moonlight Fiesta*. The traditional clave rhythm prominent throughout the Caribbean and Sub-Saharan Africa is immediately recognizable. Next came the celebrated *Caravan* (1936). The first recording of *Caravan*, made by Barney Bigard's Jazzopators, does not use the clave rhythm as a foundation but instead features a vigorous riff accompaniment. The entire basis for the success of *Caravan* is there in this 1936 recording—the effective combination of the haunting melody, its skillful harmonization, and the driving riff. The disc names only Tizol as composer, so we may assume that it represents something close to his original vision for the piece. Ellington apparently composed the place-holding bridge and he probably came up with the title.

When Ellington changed the title of *Porto Rican Chaos* to *Moonlight Fiesta*, he was aiming to stimulate the listener's imagination. The title *Porto Rican Chaos* belongs to the same tradition of 1920s dance pieces as *Black Bottom Stomp* and *East St. Louis Toodle-O*. The title *Moonlight Fiesta* is less dance oriented and more evocative, along the lines of *Mood Indigo*. The title *Caravan* points toward the Middle East. It frames Tizol's most successful piece—by measure of number of covers it may be the most successful piece ever associated with Ellington—with a tease of exoticism.

Tizol biographer Basilio Serrano notes how easy it was for Tizol's Spanish melodies to include a Middle Eastern flavor, and he suggests that the medieval history of the Iberian Peninsula, with cultural connections to northern Africa and the Middle East, is audible here. After the initial 1936 recording, subsequent recordings from the Ellington Orchestra pile on big wet splashes of exoticism, with more emphasis on the harmonic minor scale, odd dissonance from the piano, a gong from Burma, clave, and unusual scoring. When a piece becomes this successful, follow-ups will be expected, and Tizol delivered. In the next few years he moved between compositions that were partly Latin and partly exotic in this Middle Eastern way. These include the important piece *Bakiff* (1941), which paved the way for *The Far East Suite* album (1963–1964) by Ellington and Strayhorn, just as *Caravan* paved the way for Dizzy Gillespie's *A Night in Tunisia*.

The unassuming Tizol was quietly extraordinary. He may have been the only musician in the world who had this global set of sensibilities—Latin jazz with African-derived grooves, European classical technique at a high level, Spanish-Middle Eastern flavor, and jazz phrasing. He brought to that breadth of musical experience an exceptional skill set of performance, arrangement, and composition. His contributions were singular, but he largely remained in the shadows.

Perdido (also known as *Tizol's Stomp*) is another quasi-Latin standby, second in popularity to *Caravan* among Tizol's compositions. Tizol composed it on a train on the way to New Orleans. He said it was his response to the sound of the word itself, which is the name of a street in the neighborhood Louis Armstrong grew up in. *Perdido* is a riff-based tune very much in the New Orleans tradition (*Canal Street Blues, Muskrat Ramble*). Ellington's orchestra recorded it in 1941, and it did not take long before "every orchestra began to play my number," as Tizol proudly reflected. As with *Caravan*, lyrics were later added to turn it into a song, causing not just Ellington's name but also a lyricist's name to be added to the credits. "[Duke] took credit for everything I did," Tizol said.

Tizol's compositional talent blossomed further in 1938, which turned out to be a rich year for him in slow-tempo ballads. *Have a Heart*, with lyrics added later to turn it into *Lost in Meditation*, is a lovely ballad that ranks with the very best. *Pyramid* is another first-rate composition, and so is *Gypsy Without a Song*, which became one of Tizol's personal favorites from his own portfolio. The late 1930s were challenging for Ellington, but Tizol was coming up with fantastic material. Ellington's name got attached to all of these tunes as co-composer, though it is not clear what, if anything, he had to do with them. Together with Tizol and others in the orchestra he probably worked on details of the arrangements. But one might assume that Tizol's compositions were typically more complete than those from other sidemen.

Renewal

To have a career in popular music means learning how to deal with contradiction and compromise, and for African American musicians especially, this challenge has long been daunting. The possibility of reaching large white audiences, with tastes and expectations that are not necessarily the same as those of black audiences, perpetually beckons. Choices must be made. During the Swing Era, with its unprecedented audience base for jazz, climbing this ladder meant segregated white venues. "Our type of music wasn't really for black people," was how Cootie Williams saw things. "While we were on tour we were playing for white audiences. The rich, upper class of blacks would come but mostly we would be playing for whites." Writers like Ralph Ellison and Albert Murray, the cream of the talented tenth, adored Ellington and wrote about his music with great eloquence, but they were hardly representative of African American society as a whole. There were sold out, "colored-only" dances on his tours, but these were a small part of the business plan. Ellington was hardly unusual in facing this dilemma, but since his artistic identity was centered on "authentic Negro music," the tension must have been keenly felt.

The money was in chasing white audiences, yet more and more white bands were mastering up-tempo jazz so the competition was strong. Goodman was leading the way, and right behind were Jimmy Dorsey, Tommy Dorsey (who picked up Sy Oliver as arranger in 1939), Artie Shaw, Glenn Miller, and Woody Herman. They all became household names. So did Armstrong, Ellington, Calloway, Lunceford, Webb, and Basie, but not at the same level. More than a few of Ellington's song hits sold much better when recorded by white bands than by his band.

One had to have a niche in such a large field of competition, especially given the structural disadvantages for African Americans. For Ellington this meant sophistication, modernity, and art. This inevitably gave rise to a second set of contradictions and compromises that he aimed to solve with an elusive blend of accessibility and sophistication, popularity and modernity, commercialism and art. A 1936 article from *Variety* surveyed the musical preferences of college students, with a correspondent from Dartmouth complaining how Ellington's "weird chords have grown stale." The student noted that Ellington's was one of several African American bands "who fail to impress noticeably."

Along with these challenges, Ellington was no longer receiving the same level of preferential treatment from Mills he had enjoyed during the early 1930s. Benny Goodman's band performed a celebrated and lucrative swing concert at Carnegie Hall in January 1938, and it was prominently featured in the movie *Hollywood Hotel*. Ellington expected Mills to make similar things happen. When they didn't, he decided, in early 1939, to hire new management. Ellington could measure success through sustained gigs at the new Cotton Club in midtown Manhattan, through Pullman cars and high-level touring, through a second whirlwind trip to Europe, and through a number of successful recordings. But at the height of the Swing Era there was still a sense that African American bands were second tier. A 1940 article in the trade magazine *DownBeat* summed up the imbalance with a less than subtle subtitle: "Negro Leaders Could Make More Money Running a Rib Joint."

It is in this context that we should understand Ellington's opinion, headlined in *DownBeat*, that "Swing Is Stagnant." In four articles (February, April, May, and July, 1939), he made his case. "Nothing of importance, nothing new, nothing either original or creative has occurred in the swing field during the last few years," he blasted. He blamed the problem on adolescent audiences, unqualified and uninformed critics, and commercialism (not necessarily in that order). Swing relied too much on formulaic arrangements with the same ideas repeated again and again. Exciting rhythm cannot stand on its own for very long but thrives when accompanied by imagination and expressive range, he explained.

He had high praise for William "Count" Basie, though. "Basie's outstanding musical quality has been unpretentiousness . . . Undoubtedly the greatest rhythm section in the business, they are the greatest exponents of that emotional element of bouncing buoyancy, otherwise known as swing." The Count Basie Orchestra was a primary force in the late 1930s, and Ellington, like every other bandleader, had to pay attention. Basie grew up in New Jersey but made a name for himself in Kansas City, Missouri, where by 1929 he had taken a position as pianist and arranger for Bennie Moten. In the early 1930s, while most of the country was in severe retraction, Kansas City thrived as a center for the cattle industry with a busy entertainment district. It magnetized musical talent from neighboring states to the south and west. By 1935, Basie was leading a band that included some of the best musicians from the entire region, including tenor saxophonist Lester Young. He took his all-star unit to New York City and in 1937 scored a hit record with *One O'Clock Jump*.

In 1938, with the help of on-location radio broadcasts from the Famous Door on Fifty-Second Street, Basie swept through the Swing Era like a prairie fire, a tremendous infusion of regional energy into the national scene. As Ellington implied, the music was rich but not complicated in a conceptual way. Basie was not aiming to inspire the listener to interpret his music and think about it as art. As Albert Murray put it, "Refining the basics that make blues music swing is the Basie trademark."

The rhythm section in Basie's band was based on a new approach to how the bass player (Walter Page), the piano player (Basie), the guitarist (Freddie Green), and the drummer (Jo Jones) all worked together to lay down the foundational groove for the band and dancers. These musicians took Kansas City's regional practice to the highest level. The rhythm section was bluesy and driving, but it was also light and airy. On top of this came vigorous riffs, subtle and imaginative. On top of the riffs came soloists such as Young and Buck Clayton, each bluesy, driving, light, and airy in his own way. Young, Basie, and their colleagues infused their music with blues understatement. The Basie band flourished in 1938 as the newest, most modern thing around, and anyone interested in "authentic Negro music" could hardly ignore them.

The jam session, the jazz institution that most directly carried forward the communal focus of the ring shout, played a huge role in Kansas City. The scene reminded bass player Gene Ramey of church revival meetings, "where the preacher and the people are singing, and there's happenings all around." A regional, ear-playing tradition shaped the Basie band and invigorated jazz; it was similar to what the New Orleanians had done when they moved to Chicago in the early 1920s. Ellington channeled jam session ideas into meticulously managed compositions and arrangements; the Basie band did something similar, though with less intervention.

Riff-based arrangements were not new. There are many recordings from the 1930s that prominently feature riffs, including, most famously, the Fletcher Henderson band's arrangements (1928, 1932, and 1933) of Jelly Roll Morton's *King Porter Stomp*, which Goodman purchased and turned into his theme music (1935). Basie's band did more riff arrangements and did them more imaginatively. Sidemen competed with one another good naturedly to toss off new riffs for trial runs. "We always had somebody in those sections who was a leader, who could start something and get those ensembles going," explained Basie. "I mean while somebody would be soloing in the reed section, the brasses would have something going in the background, and the reed section would have something to go with that . . . And the thing about it that was so fantastic was this: Once those guys played something, they could damn near play it exactly the same the next night."

In some of the greatest Basie recordings, riffs combine to form complex, interlocking structures, a sort of riff mosaic. The final few choruses of *One O'Clock Jump*, indebted to earlier achievements from Kansas City, put this kind of energy on the national map. *Every Tub* (1938), arranged by trombonist Eddie Durham, finds the rhythm section and soloists (and certainly the dancers) bouncing off the riff mosaics one after the other, each chorus freshly made. In *Volcano* (1939), one riff stays steady while others are added in successive blues choruses to create a layered and

3.5 Johnny Hodges and Jimmie Blanton, 1940

building effect. Five months later Ellington did something similar in his celebrated *Ko-Ko*.

How could Ellington be the most modern thing in jazz in 1927 and still keep that position a dozen years later? He succeeded during the Cotton Club era because he and Miley invented a fresh black modernity, delivered with compelling beauty. His solution in 1939 and early 1940 was to find a new compromise with swing. It was based on three important hires who immediately reinvigorated the band: Billy Strayhorn, Jimmie Blanton, and Ben Webster. The results were so spectacular that for many Ellington fans the 1940–1941 band produced the greatest music of Ellington's entire career. Strayhorn stayed the longest and his impact was pervasive until his death in 1967 (see Chapter 4). Both Blanton and Webster were from the region that was responsible for the special qualities of the Basie band. They helped to instantly integrate Ellington with the current stylistic field.

Ellington once described his band as "an accumulation of personalities, tonal devices." As we have seen, the idea that the band's diverse personalities were mere "tonal devices" that inspired the leader to write in idiosyncratic ways is more misleading than it is informing. In this case, as in many others, the three new tonal devices in 1940 were tremendous musicians whose creative labors account for some of the greatest accomplishments of the year.

Blanton (1918–1942) was born in Chattanooga, Tennessee. He died young, before he was interviewed extensively, so little is known of his life. During his few years with Ellington he was known to practice the string bass incessantly, a habit that must have begun as a child, inspired by his mother who was a professional musician. He studied violin, string bass, and music theory at Tennessee State University. In October 1939 several of Ellington's musicians heard him playing at an after-hours place in St. Louis. They quickly fetched Ellington from his hotel room and he hired the twenty-year-old on the spot. He was featured in front of the band, dressed in a new white suit, the very next night. His teacher provided a list of symphonic bass players with whom Blanton could take refresher lessons while he toured with Ellington.

Blanton instantly strengthened the rhythm section. He had a rich and focused tone, a flawless ear, and, as Ellington put it, "those precision notes in the right places, so that we could float out on the great and adventurous sea of expectancy with his pulse and foundation behind us." By the time the band got to Indianapolis Blanton was taking a solo in *Sophisticated Lady*. He could improvise as if one of the horn soloists at fast tempos. Ellington featured him in a series of recorded duets for piano bass (for example, *Pitter Panther Patter*, 1940) that established a new model for how to play a jazz solo on bass.

Jack the Bear (March 1940) was a delightful if modest feature for him. A favorite of Albert Murray's, the recording begins with a playful mosaic of riffs, light and not too busy, to make a nice call and response between the band and Blanton. At the end, Blanton stretches out with a full sixteen-bar solo, increasingly highlighted as the others drop out. Improvised choruses and a section of call-and-response riffs from the horns fill out the performance. But even when he was not featured like this Blanton's presence was huge. "His amazing talent sparked the entire band," insisted Rex Stewart.

Blanton's tragically short life ended on July 30, 1942, in California at a sanatorium for victims of tuberculosis. In his room, the only decoration was a photograph of his close friend and bandmate, Ben Webster.

Webster's entry into Ellington's band on January 22, 1940, was not the same sort of rescue from anonymity that Blanton's was. He had already played with Ellington during 1935 and 1936, and after that he established himself as a soloist in bands led by Moten, Henderson, Calloway, Andy Kirk, and Benny Carter. This hire was a plum for Ellington. With Webster, Bigard (when he swapped out his clarinet for alto sax), Hodges, Hardwick, and Carney, Ellington could make claim to having the world's greatest saxophone section.

Webster (1909–1973) was born and grew up in Kansas City where he soaked up the style. As a child he learned violin and piano, facilitated by the natural gift of perfect pitch. At age sixteen he was befriended by the great pianist and arranger Mary Lou Williams, then a precocious fifteen-year-old who worked with him on his piano skills. He attended Wilberforce University in Ohio, where he was a classmate of Horace Henderson, soon to be an arranger for his brother Fletcher. Back in Kansas City he got to know Basie, who coached him on piano some more. In Amarillo, Texas, he took sax lessons from Lester Young's father. He was the same age as Lester Young and the two of them frequently practiced together in the summer of 1929. He was five years younger than Coleman Hawkins, whom he greatly admired. By 1930 he was playing with a touring band that moved through Oklahoma City, Tulsa, Kansas City, and the entire region.

Young and Hawkins were the leading tenor saxophonists of the late 1930s. At his best, Webster was in their league, and he was at his best with Ellington. Suddenly, Ellington had a tenor who could match the swing and drive of Blanton yet also had considerable flexibility. Perhaps Ellington also knew that Webster liked to compose. "Ben Webster is not only one of the greatest exponents of the tenor saxophone," explained Rex Stewart, "but he is also a talented arranger, composer . . ." Webster's stature as a soulful performer has overshadowed these abilities, but given his distinguished upbringing they are hardly surprising. His compositional ability contributed to two of the greatest Ellington pieces from the glorious year of 1940.

"A lot of guys didn't know that *In a Mellotone* is Ben's tune," explained bass player and friend Milt Hinton, an impeccable source. He's right: there is no disc credit for Webster, and his name is rarely mentioned in connection with this much-loved piece. It was one of the hits of 1940, and it has been covered many times. *In a Mellotone* is based on the chords for *Rose Room* (composed in 1917 by Art Hickman), which was the piece that the legendary guitarist Charlie Christian, from Oklahoma, improvised on for forty-five minutes when he auditioned for Benny Goodman in 1939 (the Goodman Sextet's recording from October must provide a glimpse of what Christian played on that occasion). *Rose Room* was undoubtedly one of the pieces that were routinely used for jam sessions. That made it easy for Webster to compose a tune to go along with the chords, a common way of creating new pieces. Superb solos by Williams and Hodges add to the stunning success of the original recording of *In a Mellotone* from September 1940. As usual, there is no information about where the arranging details came from; they may have come from Webster, from Ellington, from the group, or from some informal combination. It has been assumed that Ellington arranged the call and response between the theme and the trombones, followed by the riveting dialogue between Williams and the saxophones.

As successful as *In a Mellotone* was, the first and most important tune that Webster gave to Ellington was something he had named "Shuckin' and Stiffin'." He offered this piece soon after joining in January. "I just wrote this tune and Duke is gonna record it," he excitedly told Hinton. Ellington substituted *Cotton Tail* for Webster's risqué title. *Cotton Tail* has been highly praised—Gunther Schuller gushed that it "changed the face of jazz"—but most of the credit has indefensibly gone to Ellington. It now seems clear that Webster contributed the main theme, two choruses of terrific improvisation, and an arranged chorus for the sax section. What is left are superb musicianship from the band and splendid arranging touches (either from Ellington or Strayhorn or both) that lifted Webster's great material to the highest level.

Four months earlier, in September 1939, the Basie band had recorded *Lester Leaps In*, a display piece for Lester Young, Webster's teenage friend and now a well-known soloist. A month after that Coleman Hawkins recorded his legendary version of *Body and Soul*, a stunning, three-minute, tour de force entirely dominated by Hawkins. It must have seemed natural to introduce Ellington's new tenor saxophonist with a display piece of his own. And all the better that Webster had written the theme himself: Ellington could claim composer credit, and in exchange Webster would get his moment in the spotlight, the Ellington ecosystem holding strong. Just as *In a Mellotone* is based on the chords for *Rose Room*, *Cotton Tail* is based on a modified version of the chords for Gershwin's *I Got Rhythm*, another standard of the jam sessions.

There is no introductory material for *Cotton Tail*, just an eruption of high energy from Blanton and Greer in support of Webster's splendid theme, which emphasizes nonharmonic tones on the ninth, fourth, flatted fifth, and sixth degrees above the changing chords. This theme is very hip, a strut down Fifty-Second Street, the center of jazz modernism in 1940. It has been related to proto-bebop with prescient credit to Ellington, but it is much more likely that the connection to bebop here came from Webster, who had been making a study of Coleman Hawkins. Hawkins (and also Young, to a lesser extent) was experimenting with precisely this set of intervals to invent a new melodic idiom in solos like *Body and Soul*. Webster picked up the modern vocabulary and turned out a sharp melody. It is possible that Ellington (or more likely Strayhorn, who was also studying nascent bebop closely) edited and improved Webster's theme. We will probably never know. All we know is that Ellington took credit for the whole thing.

After the theme Webster begins his famous solo, two choruses lasting over a minute and occupying a third of the piece. The solo packs the power of Webster's Kansas City tutorial. It is a worthy answer to *Lester Leaps In* and *Body and Soul*. Just as Ellington said about Basie, there is nothing pretentious here, just robust melody that builds nicely and is full of wonderful effects. Webster offers an impressive range of sax vocalizations, from breathy and suggestive near the beginning to shrieking at the high point. As critic Stanley Crouch put it, Webster was good at making "a chord as much an assemblage of colors as pitches." The logic of the solo is enhanced by the transitional section between the two choruses, where Ellington and Blanton provide harmonic tension. The lively chorus for the saxophone section that follows was also composed by Webster.

Another Webster highlight from 1940 is the ballad *All Too Soon*. Here his contribution is a wonderful solo. Lawrence Brown's muted solo is beautiful, too, and when Webster follows him with less reserve and more effusion the combined effect is marvelous. Someone (either Ellington or Strayhorn) had the cogent idea of distinguishing the two solos by modulating up a half step with a fresh riff in the accompaniment. The flexible Webster was studying not just Hawkins and Young (and Hilton Jefferson, another tenor as well) but also his sectionmate Johnny Hodges, a connection that is evident in his ballad solos.

The reliable Juan Tizol also made a vital contribution in 1940. *Conga Brava* started as his elegant melody. The rhythmic-harmonic groove that supports the theme is moody and instantly engaging, a strong part of the piece's identity. Tizol's melody is stylistically similar to *Caravan*, except that it has a length of ten bars. A ten-bar phrase is irregular, in terms of the stylistic norms of popular music and dance music, which rely on the predictability of four-bar subphrases that form eight-bar phrases that are then combined into thirty-two-bar choruses. The contrasting section following the main phrase (repeated) is seven bars. Ellington had experimented with irregular phrases before, in pieces like *Creole Rhapsody*. Here the technique is used in a more effortless way.

Webster has a long solo in *Conga Brava* that works well, though he seems a little uncertain about how to handle the ten-bar phrases. Building a piece in pastiche style out of contrasting strains—one theme after another, often with a single repetition, the procedure that dominated the ragtime era—was still Ellington's preferred strategy in 1940. It made it easy to combine material from different people, in this case Tizol, Webster, and the work of the arrangers. The shifts of mood in *Conga Brava* can seem jarring, as we go from the lovely and mysterious atmosphere of the main theme to the mocking, brassy contrast of the seven-bar theme, then to Webster's earthy saxophone. It helps that each section is so strong on its own. If any of the various parts of the piece were weaker, the quirky combination would not be quite so palatable.

Concerto for Cootie is one of the classics from the 1940 "miracle year," as one biographer has described it. No piece captures Ellington's public image of elegance and innovation better than this one. Though it is firmly associated with the leader, *Concerto for Cootie* was the product of a collaborative method, like most of the 1940 highlights.

R. D. Darrell wrote about the great Miley pieces around 1930 with the false assumption that Ellington was the sole creative force, reducing Miley to mere executer of the great composer's melodic genius. *Concerto for Cootie* inspired equally influential commentary, and it has been equally one-sided. In 1954, André Hodeir, a composer and critic trained at the Conservatoire de Paris, devoted an entire book chapter to it. Never before had there been such close attention to details of an Ellington piece. Hodeir's book was highly influential through the English translation, *Jazz: Its Evolution and Essence* (1956), which shaped the thinking of Gunther Schuller and Martin Williams, for example, two writers whose work still looms large in jazz criticism.

The title of Hodeir's chapter—"A Masterpiece: Concerto for Cootie"—is revealing: masterpieces are written by isolated geniuses, not by collectives. Hodeir argues that the greatest thing about the piece is its unity, such as never could have come from improvising musicians, even an Armstrong or a Charlie Parker. It could come only from someone dedicated to composition "in the real sense of the word." This sense of distinguishing "real" composition from "less real" composition does a lot of earnest but ham-fisted work in the discourse of prestige that surrounds Ellington.

Hodeir observed how well the piece had aged during the fourteen years since it was first recorded, and that impression still holds today. It sounds fresh and vital, not at all a dated piece of Swing Era ephemerality. What stands above all is the brilliant performance from Cootie Williams. Just as people today who first hear *East St. Louis Toodle-O* and *Black and Tan Fantasy* are stunned by the freshness and integrity of Bubber Miley's playing, so does Cootie Williams's playing here immediately capture the listener.

Here is another piece generated by the Miley method, with Williams creating a melody that was the starting point. As with Miley, what is critical is Williams's conception of how to perform the melody. With virtuoso brilliance, each section features a different skill set. First he uses a mute, and he plays the theme with a saucy vibrato. In the next section he uses a tighter mute with less vibrato. Then comes the kind of freak music he first learned to play when he took over for Miley in 1929. To round off this first part of the piece (which we could describe as AABA), he returns to the tight mute of section one, now with only slight vibrato.

There follows an expansive middle section, with a new theme and a new key, and to deliver it Williams breaks into the fully open sound of his golden trumpet. It is a glowing, radiant moment. This section is also marked by pronounced bending of pitch. The new theme nicely contrasts with the more confined theme of the first section: one turns in on itself, the other expands, and the differences are beautifully complemented by the varied performing techniques. It is a bravura demonstration of jazz trumpet playing, variety of technique splendidly harnessed to expressive melodic invention. *Concerto for Cootie and No One Else*, might have been the title.

Like *Cotton Tail* and *Conga Brava*, some of the phrases in *Concerto for Cootie* fall in ten-bar lengths. We may assume that Ellington added this detail. The phrasing is irregular, with sprightly details of extension and retraction, and this becomes part of the dynamic texture. The unfolding dialogue between soloist and group is loaded with a snappy variety of crisp and engaging exchange, the orchestra following Williams's lead like a deft jitterbugger. The responses harmonically turn the phrase in different directions, always hip and always tight. In classical music, dialogue between soloist and group is a fundamental feature of concerto form, and it is something for which Ellington, with expertise in the African American tradition of call and response, was well suited. Too much emphasis on the soloist in a concerto can make the group seem superfluous while the soloist strays into empty display. If the group is too rich, then the soloist feels hampered and diminished.

What remains to discuss from *Concerto for Cootie* is the first thing the listener hears—the stunning introduction. This passage gracefully puts the main theme in a slightly different emotional context—a *classier* context, we could say. That is due to its greater harmonic and contrapuntal complexity, all of it flowing by more rapidly and with greater richness relative to the main body of the piece. In the 1936 concertos *Clarinet Lament (Barney's Concerto)* and *Trumpet in Spades (Rex's Concerto)*, Ellington scrambled to compose pseudo cadenzas as allusions to the classical tradition of concertos. The results were ineffective. For the introduction to *Concerto for Cootie* he didn't have to scramble.

In the meantime, Ellington had hired someone who knew a lot about that world and could deliver it on demand. It now seems that the introduction was composed by Billy Strayhorn. It is a moment of grandeur, an instant atmosphere of expansive elegance, almost like a fanfare to the virtuoso display that will follow. This single stroke of majesty, understated in some ways, is completely appropriate to the occasion. It is very different from the simpler—and often unfocused—introductions Ellington himself routinely added to many pieces.

Strayhorn's authorship of this phrase was not publicly suggested until 2002, thanks to intensive study of his music by musicologist Walter van de Leur. The question immediately arises: how else might Strayhorn have contributed to the miracle year of

1940, in ways that are not quite so obvious? The more one studies Strayhorn and the marvelous accomplishments of this period, the clearer the answer seems to be: Strayhorn's contribution was as important as anyone's. It may even be that he was the musician most responsible for the brilliant surge in quality that happily defines the swing renewal of the Ellington collective.

CHAPTER 4

BILLY STRAYHORN

IN THE NOVEL *East of Eden*, John Steinbeck's narrator articulates, with special emphasis, a conventional view of solitary creativity:

> Our species is the only creative species, and it has only one creative instrument, the individual mind and spirit of man. Nothing was ever created by two men. There are no good collaborations, whether in music, in art, in poetry, in mathematics, in philosophy. Once the miracle of creation has taken place, the group can build and extend it, but the group never invents anything. The preciousness lies in the lonely mind of man.

That this view is held so widely explains how the image of Ellington as a self-sufficient, great composer has acquired such relentless traction—which, in turn, is why any honest assessment requires considerable effort to identify and draw out the collaborative practices that Ellington thoroughly depended on. Ellington and Billy Strayhorn, along with Lennon and McCartney, are the pre-eminent musical cases contradicting the *East of Eden* view.

A huge step forward in understanding Strayhorn's role was made in two books published around the year 2000: *Lush Life: A Biography of Billy Strayhorn* (1996) by David Hajdu, was followed by *Something to Live For: The Music of Billy Strayhorn* (2002) by Walter van de Leur. Strayhorn's contributions were so strong that

Ellington's career inevitably divides into two parts—before Strayhorn and after. People often wonder how Ellington was able to keep his creative engines going through the 1940s and all the way into the 1960s. There is only one answer: Billy Strayhorn. Literature on Ellington divides along similar lines—books written before Strayhorn's role was so carefully documented and books written after (and among the after, authors who have been paying attention and those who haven't).

The story of how Lennon and McCartney first met circulated soon after the Beatles became famous, but the first encounter between Ellington and Strayhorn was not revealed to the public until almost thirty years after Strayhorn's death. Ellington was thirty-nine, a famous figure, Strayhorn a twenty-three-year-old unknown outside of his hometown, when they were introduced on December 2, 1938, backstage, after a concert in Pittsburgh. Ellington was playing a weeklong gig at the Stanley Theater, and a friend of Strayhorn's arranged for the pianist to play a couple of his compositions for the leader between shows. "Mr. Ellington, this is the way you played this number in the show," Strayhorn confidently announced as he sat down and played *Sophisticated Lady*. It did indeed sound just like what Ellington had played on stage. "Now this is the way *I* would play it," he continued, and he produced an interpretation that his friend described as "pretty hip-sounding and further and further 'out there' as he went on." Ellington was impressed. He asked Strayhorn if he could do that again, so the pianist repeated his comparative exercise, this time with *Solitude*. Before Strayhorn left the theater Ellington asked him to arrange a song for Ivie Anderson, which the band performed a few days later, without a rehearsal but with glowing success.

Our central collaborative pairs, Ellington-Strayhorn and Lennon-McCartney, share a similar biographical moment: in each case, the leader was introduced to a younger musician, eager to join, who was clearly the leader's musical superior. On the level of musical chops, McCartney was unequivocally beyond Lennon, and one can make that same case for Strayhorn and Ellington. That will sound outrageous to anyone who is used to hearing how equal Lennon and McCartney were, and to anyone who is accustomed to thinking of Strayhorn as Ellington's helpful assistant. Each leader had enough confidence to bring in the younger and superior talent, which turned out to be a very smart move.

Ellington had built his career around hiring excellent musicians and using them in ways that did not occur to others. In Pittsburgh he must have sensed the possibilities right away. Occasionally he described Strayhorn as his lyricist and orchestrator, which would be something like the Yankees saying they acquired Babe Ruth for his pitching skills. But after Strayhorn's death he gave a heartfelt account of how closely the two had worked together: "Billy Strayhorn was my right arm, my left arm, all the eyes in the back of my head, my brain waves in his head, and his in mine." That was the level of creative intimacy that made it possible for Strayhorn to modernize the Ellington collective at the height of the Swing Era more powerfully than anyone else possibly could have.

William Thomas Strayhorn (1915–1967) was born in Dayton, Ohio, to parents who had both grown up in North Carolina. Each parent enjoyed modest advantages. His mother Lillian graduated from a two-year program at Shaw University in Raleigh, and his father James's family had once owned a whiskey distillery. His father's parents lived in a handsome home in Hillsborough (at the corner of Hillsborough Avenue and West Margaret Lane), where Billy spent summers when he was young. Even though he grew up in slum houses, in marginal neighborhoods, and with debilitating family tension, he also was in touch with a sense of greater possibilities; these he embraced in his vivid imagination. The family moved several times before landing in Pittsburgh in 1920.

His mother was a loving, caring woman, devoted to her son. Reading about their relationship makes one think of the Daisy-Edward relationship back in Washington, D.C. Strayhorn's father, however, was no J. E. Ellington. His daughter described

4.1 Strayhorn and Ellington

him as "bright" with "lots of personality," but "back then, who needed a bright black man with personality?" He grew bitter and frustrated as he drifted through jobs of unskilled labor. Heavy drinking led to physical abuse and cruelty. Billy, quiet and small, got used to taking his father's worst. His mother sent him to Hillsborough during the summers, where his grandparents doted on him. His grandmother, a church pianist, happily watched the child pick out hymns he heard on Sundays on her piano. A record player was part of the fun in Hillsborough.

As a young teenager Billy worked odd jobs and saved enough money to buy a piano for himself. He took lessons at a music store. His childhood was marked by a degree of racial integration that included schools. Smart and somewhat shy, he spent a lot of time at the music store, buying whatever sheet music he could afford, and also at the town library, reading constantly. "He would ask me if I had heard of César Franck," said a childhood friend. He was finding ways to nurture his intelligence and artistic sensitivity through music and literature, creating an alternative world for himself that did not depend on traveling to North Carolina, hiding from his father, or analyzing why he was so different from other children. "I think my brother really dove with full force into everything my mother always wanted for him—music, books, art, the whole world of culture," explained his sister.

The public high school he attended offered a distinguished education in music that produced Strayhorn and then jazz pianist Ahmad Jamal. The music teacher, Carl McVicker, welcomed all talent, black or white, rich or poor, and he valued not only classical music but jazz as well. Strayhorn "learned everything we could teach him," remembered McVicker. Strayhorn's main interest was classical music, and he passionately embraced theory, piano, and repertory. He brilliantly performed Grieg's *Piano Concerto in A Minor* in 1934, his senior year, with the school orchestra. "He kept to himself, since there weren't too many black fellows in classical music back then," recalled a classmate. He read *The New Yorker*. His nickname was "Dictionary," and he liked to speak French.

By the time Ellington met him in late 1938, Strayhorn had assembled an impressive portfolio, including student pieces inspired by Chopin. He composed a concerto of his own that was stylistically indebted to Gershwin's *Rhapsody in Blue*; it was performed at the commencement for his high school class. For a revue called *Fantastic Rhythm* he wrote ten songs, dance music, and incidental music. The production enjoyed some local success, and two Pittsburgh legends, singer Billy Eckstine and pianist Erroll Garner, performed in it for stretches. He enrolled at the Pittsburgh Musical Institute and returned his focus to classical music. Someone gave him an Art Tatum record and he wore it out, fascinated with the audacious harmonies and pianistic virtuosity. He was attracted to the elegant playing of pianist Teddy Wilson. "What he realized, we talked about, was that everything he loved about classical music was there, in one form or another, in jazz—and here was a place he could apply himself," remembered a musician friend.

Compared with Ellington, Strayhorn's musical education was more systematic, more notation based, theoretical, with much stronger cultivation of performance and much stronger awareness of classical repertory. His training came through in his early compositions from Pittsburgh, several of which were good enough to achieve world-class standing.

By 1936 he had finished *Lush Life*, one of his most admired songs. He began composing it in 1933 at age eighteen and then tinkered with it for three years. It took a long time for the song to break out of his private world. Singer Kay Davis premiered it at Carnegie Hall in 1948, with Strayhorn accompanying her from the piano. Recordings by Nat "King" Cole, Sarah Vaughan, Ella Fitzgerald, Johnny Hartman, John Coltrane, Linda Ronstadt, and many others followed. The long gestation and the very long delay to professional performance reflect *Lush Life*'s complexity, which pushes it closer to classical music than popular music. The intricate chords resolve irregularly, and the melody is also irregular, with very little repetition. Sparkling rhymes and chromatic details flicker by. The lyrics are clever ("relaxes" is quickly rhymed with "axis," for example) but they feel too world weary for such a young composer. Everything is integrated at a sophisticated level, the result of three years of polishing. "Every now and then I'd go back to it, and add a little more to it," Strayhorn remembered. It is easy to imagine how Ellington, attacked in the press for being too artistically ambitious and aiming above the heads of his audiences, might have been reluctant to challenge them with *Lush Life*. His band never issued a recording of it.

By 1937 he had completed another song, *Something to Live For*, which became the first of his pieces recorded by Ellington (March 1939). This tender ballad has a very different feeling from the delicate flamboyance of *Lush Life*. It was one of the compositions he sang and played during his Pittsburgh audition. The recording sold well in the spring of 1939, with Ellington's name slapped on the disc as co-composer. *Your Love Has Faded* was another Pittsburgh composition recorded by the Ellington Orchestra in 1939, with Ellington's name again added as co-composer. This became the first Strayhorn vehicle for Johnny Hodges, a long and fruitful pairing.

Before departing Pittsburgh to begin his new job, in January 1939, Strayhorn reportedly composed *Take the "A" Train*. At their first meeting Ellington had given the job applicant a couple of arranging tests, which he passed with honors. As he got ready to assume his new position he was nervous, so he thought to impress his boss once again by taking the directions Ellington had written out on how to get to his apartment in Harlem (don't take the new D train, you'll end up in the Bronx) and give them musical shape. *Take the "A" Train* is very modern, very hip, and instantly likeable, an effortless mix of relaxed swing, angular bebop, and experimental Bartók, all of it coming out as excellent Strayhorn. The recording from January 1941 became a best seller, and Ellington started using the piece as his theme number. Over the decades it became the number most associated with Ellington, though he never claimed credit for it. To the contrary, he explained many times to surprised admirers that it was in fact Strayhorn who had composed the most famous of all Ellington pieces. As we shall see, Ellington's choice of making this song his emblem naturally followed Strayhorn's success in changing the band's sound.

Take the "A" Train is as much a part of early 1940s New York City optimism and modernity as Piet Mondrian's *Broadway Boogie Woogie* (1943). Dynamic, fresh, and colorful—this was how the city felt to two outsiders grateful to be there. Mondrian arrived in Manhattan in 1940, in flight from the Nazis, already with an appreciation of jazz. This painting and this piece of music each find a sweet spot of modernist integrity that is also instantly accessible. They convey the energy of democratized cosmopolitanism, powerful and inviting.

This was Strayhorn when Ellington first met him and practically hired him on the spot: super talented, intellectual, articulate, ambitious, well trained, and slightly diffident. When he arrived in Manhattan he was nobody's baby, even though he sort of looked like one. His soft facial features reminded people of the cartoon character Swee'Pea, in the Popeye comic strip series, so that became his nickname. It is not clear how much his sexual identity was evident, even to himself, but it did not take long for Manhattan to inspire confidence in his homosexuality. "There wasn't a lot of guys [besides Strayhorn] who was homosexual and acted like that, like there it was and you have to accept it," explained clarinetist Jimmy Hamilton. "And if you don't—that's your problem."

His first Manhattan residence was the Harlem YMCA, but within a few days he moved into Ellington's apartment, where he remained for almost a year, sharing the spacious accommodations with Ellington's girlfriend Mildred Dixon, his sister Ruth, his son Mercer, and of course Ellington himself when he wasn't touring. Strayhorn, Dixon, Ruth, and Mercer were all fairly close in age, and Strayhorn felt like part of the family. Ellington sent him songs and asked for quick arrangements for a recording session. In late March the band toured Europe, leaving Strayhorn behind, footloose and fancy-free in Manhattan. He took the opportunity to compose the lovely, aching *Day Dream* (recorded by the Ellington Orchestra in 1940 with Ellington given co-credit) and *Passion Flower* (recorded in 1941 with credit solely to Strayhorn).

Both became specialties for Hodges. The harmonic language of *Passion Flower* recalls Debussy, quite distinct from the quirky harmonies Ellington liked to experiment with at his piano. "At that time people weren't writing with that extensive level of theory," said composer-arranger Locksley "Slide" Hampton. "His compositions were very involved. But the thing that stood out was that, with all that theory that was there, you still had a very human spiritual side to his music."

"You'll do whatever you feel like doing," Ellington promised his new assistant when the two of them agreed to work together. Here he was in a luxury apartment in Manhattan, figuring out how to bring the sensitivity of contemporary classical music to jazz pieces with popular aspirations. He was indeed doing exactly what he felt like doing.

As we look at the dramas of their relationship over the next decades, Ellington often seems like an exploiter of his assistant's talent. But imagine these initial years from Strayhorn's point of view. You are young, unconnected, slightly introverted, nerdy, African American, and homosexual, with musical talent bursting out all over the place. What are your options? You would perhaps like to be associated with one of the great classical institutions of the United States, one of its symphony orchestras, conservatories, or opera houses. In 1939 they are not exactly begging you to join them. Or even better, to have a career as a concert pianist or a renowned composer. The point has often been made that during the Jim Crow era jazz benefited in a perverse way from discrimination. More than a few gifted African American musicians who were blocked from careers in classical music were delighted to find in jazz an idiom that valued sophistication and refinement. For no one is that truer than for Strayhorn. And within the vast, increasingly diverse world of jazz, there was no better place for him to be than with Ellington, who had been rubbing up against the prestige of classical music for a decade. Ellington offered a secure existence with one of the best

dance bands in the country, on retainer with few steady obliga-
tions, a gig that was tough to top.

Strayhorn and the Ellington Miracle, 1940–1941

Can it really be coincidence that Ellington's miraculous, midlife
renewal at age forty-one dates from just after Strayhorn joined?
In most accounts of this period Strayhorn's role is underplayed.
Webster, Blanton, and Strayhorn are always mentioned, but there
is a tendency to emphasize Blanton and Webster. This follows
from the view of Ellington "writing for his musicians," just as Bach
did. Blanton and Webster are understood as unique performers who inspired the master to compositional renewal. We have
already seen how they were more than that, with Webster making
significant contributions in composing, including most of the celebrated *Cotton Tail*. Strayhorn seems to have been as important
as any member of the creative collective during this special period.

There were three main areas for Strayhorn to work in. The
first was composing by himself. In the winter of 1940–1941 he
wrote *Chelsea Bridge* and *Rain Check*, both with disc credit given
solely to him. These two pieces demonstrate how well the young
composer had settled into his position.

Chelsea Bridge, elegant and ambitious, is one of Strayhorn's
triumphs. He said later that the original title was *Battersea
Bridge*, after James Whistler's painting *Nocturne: Blue and
Gold—Old Battersea Bridge* (ca. 1875). Whistler alluded to
music in the titles for many of his paintings, for example, *Symphony in White*, *Arrangement in Gray*, and *Harmony in Gold*.
Nocturne is an unmistakable reference to a set of atmospheric
piano pieces by Chopin. Strayhorn returns the compliment and
implies a connection between his own *Chelsea Bridge* and Whistler's misty sensibility.

Nocturne: Blue and Gold—Old Battersea Bridge was the kind of
painting the famous art critic John Ruskin couldn't stand. Ruskin

objected to Whistler's emphasis on the subjective arrangements and nonrepresentational harmonies at the expense of realistic naturalism and moral clarity. Whistler was "flinging a pot of paint in the public's face," he sneered. Many decades later, the inspiration of Whistler's painting turned Strayhorn's mind toward two composers whose music he knew very well—the great French impressionists Debussy and Ravel.

The main theme of *Chelsea Bridge* is close to a theme from Ravel's *Valses Nobles et Sentimentales*. The resemblance lasts for only a few bars, and it is mainly a matter of a distinctive harmonic progression. Debussy and Ravel both liked to take highly charged chords and spring them loose from their directional tendencies, making the harmonic progressions seem to float, like images in the mist. *Chelsea Bridge* brings this language to jazz. When Ben Webster enters with a solo the segue feels completely natural.

Yet, not all jazz critics were convinced. Critic Stanley Dance (who later helped Ellington write his autobiography) reacted in a way that recalls Ruskin's response to Whistler, accusing Strayhorn of "originality at the expense of beauty . . . an obsession for tone color and voicing which excludes everything else that matters." But *Chelsea Bridge* was widely appreciated by jazz musicians, not only instrumentalists and singers (lyrics were added in 1958) but composers and arrangers. Arranger Gil Evans, for example, remembered how "From the moment I first heard *Chelsea Bridge*, I set out to try to do that." Webster loved the piece so much that he kept performing it into the 1950s and '60s.

Rain Check is another up-tempo jump number swinging with vibrant themes and bright musical wit. Harmonic adventurousness is less in the forefront and more a nuance around the edges. Strayhorn's intricate themes and arrangement take over and we are far from the collective world of the Miley method. *Chelsea Bridge* and *Rain Check* are among the first of many strong associations between Strayhorn and Webster. A sax chorus presents a new theme that just keeps climbing in intensity. Aside from brief

4.2 Juan Tizol and Strayhorn (seated), with Ben Webster and Barney Bigard

improvised solos, it is Strayhorn from start to finish, the young composer at the top of his game.

Strayhorn himself played piano on the first recording of *Rain Check*. Webster, Blanton, and Strayhorn, the three newcomers, were close friends, and they occasionally performed in public as a stunning jazz trio. This opportunity must have been satisfying to Strayhorn since he never performed with the full band and received sparse acknowledgment. It must have been a touching scene to see and hear these superb musicians, so different from one another in background and personality, yet so close through their dedication to music.

The second area where Strayhorn set to work with Ellington was taking charge of arrangements for the small-group sessions and the vocal sessions. Soon after he arrived in 1939, Ellington put him in charge of the spinoff combos that had been going since 1936. When the band departed for its seven-week tour of Europe in the spring of 1939, Strayhorn hunkered down in Ellington's apartment and pored over his boss's portfolio of scores. He already had a passion for collecting and studying classical scores; he owned a copy of Stravinsky's *Rite of Spring*, for example. This sustained access to the band's library was his chance to master the Ellington effect and all other details of the leader's style, while the small-group arrangements were a perfect opportunity to try things out. By the end of 1939 he was in charge of arrangements for singers.

His first impact through a vocal arrangement came with the song *Flamingo* (composed by Ted Grouya and Edmund Anderson, recorded by Ellington in December 1940). In Chapter 3 we saw how Armstrong blended modernity and popularity in a unique singing style that could not be imitated, while Ellington mixed in modern touches between straightforward renditions of the melody for *It Don't Mean a Thing*. For *Flamingo*, singer Herb Jeffries puts on his smoothest crooning voice, which Strayhorn surrounds with an intricate formal play of motives, dramatic punctuations, surprising modulations, bold dissonance, and lavish musical commentary. "It sounded as if Stravinsky were a jazz musician," insisted pianist, composer, and arranger John Lewis. The daring experiment was rewarded with terrific sales. Jeffries, the singer, identified with the song so much that he named his nightclub after it in Florida, years later. Ellington described *Flamingo* as a "renaissance in elaborate ornamentation for the accompaniment of singers."

The third area of work for Strayhorn was direct collaboration with Ellington. When Strayhorn's name stands alone on the composer credit, there is no question about his authorship. In other cases it seems fairly obvious that Ellington's name was added to a piece composed by Strayhorn. When the two created together things are inevitably less clear. Sometimes there is anecdotal evidence for a specific contribution from Strayhorn, and sometimes there is stylistic evidence. Since the overwhelming tendency has been to credit Ellington at Strayhorn's expense, it is worth pushing the matter in the other direction.

Debussy, Ravel, Bartók, Stravinsky—Strayhorn had a grasp of their modern sounds, for their lean and sleek themes, and he brought that to the Ellington Orchestra. His best pieces feel rich yet crisp and economical, sophisticated yet accessible. By 1940 he had matured as a composer whose mastery of craft allowed his personality to shine through. After his study of Ellington's portfolio he was in a position to add to Ellington's own efforts in a way that was fresh yet blended, a perfect meeting ground for collaboration. This was perhaps the most important ingredient that made the miracle year of 1940 what it was. Recognizing it relegates claims for an unexplainable Ellington miracle to the publicity manuals, which is where they belong.

We have seen the likelihood, based on stylistic evidence, that Strayhorn composed the introduction for *Concerto for Cootie*. The introduction is so unlike those composed by Ellington and so like Strayhorn's identifiable style, that the conclusion seems inescapable. It is hardly surprising that Ellington welcomed his assistant's improvements. *Jack the Bear*, already considered in Chapter 3 as a vehicle for bass player Jimmie Blanton, is another example. Ellington had been composing a piece he called *Take It Away*.

"It didn't work out, and the piece was dropped," explained Strayhorn. "Then Jimmie Blanton came into the band, and Duke wanted to feature him as a solo man. We needed some material quickly, so I reworked *Take It Away* as a showpiece for Blanton's bass." They called the new piece *Jack the Bear*.

A different collaborative sequence produced *Sepia Panorama*. Here is another illustration of Ellington's method of building a composition by stringing ideas together, which goes back to strain form from the ragtime era. We saw with *Conga Brava* how this process can lead to abrupt contrasts, and the same thing happens in *Sepia Panorama*. Music is capable of accommodating what we might call the beautiful non sequitur, a juxtaposition of ideas that do not logically follow but still hold together. *Sepia Panorama* has been criticized as "fragmented," with "conflicting juxtapositions," but Ellington liked it enough to make it his theme music during the second half of 1940.

Sepia Panorama apparently started out as a composition by Ellington. Around the same time he asked Strayhorn to make an arrangement of *Tuxedo Junction*, a recent hit for Glenn Miller. From Strayhorn's arrangement he especially liked a phrase that he decided to use in *Sepia Panorama*. Following this came another of Ellington's clever experiments with schematic form. He created an extended palindrome, an unusual approach in music, several steps down the path of finding the normal way and doing the opposite.

The resulting pattern of themes looks like this: A (composed by Ellington), B (composed by Ellington), C (composed by Strayhorn), D (improvised blues chorus), D (improvised blues chorus), C, B (reduced), A. The piece starts with an assertive theme, a riff-based blues chorus. This yields to a more mellow yet harmonically adventurous second theme. Moving from the first to the second feels like a natural progression of lowering the energy a notch. Ellington then pasted in Strayhorn's passage from *Tuxedo Junction* to cause a bracing leap up in range and volume, as well as a sudden jump over to another key. Strayhorn's material is crisp, bright, clear and strong. The idea of the unprepared outburst probably came directly from the Glenn Miller recording of *Tuxedo Junction*, where something similar happens several times.

Two improvised blues choruses follow, both very mellow, one featuring Ellington and Blanton and the other Webster. Filling out the middle of a piece with blues choruses was a standard device, but Ellington had a trick up his sleeve. If, after the two blues choruses, he had simply repeated the order of themes A, B, and C, *Sepia Panorama* might have felt a bit routine. Instead, Strayhorn's passage leaps out ahead of time, freshly unexpected with its bright and forceful energy. The shaken-up order seems to legitimize the non sequitur of Strayhorn's material: we are encouraged to listen not for logical continuity but for some higher-level emotional synthesis. *Sepia Panorama* replaced *East St. Louis Toodle-O* as Ellington's theme music until it was bumped by *Take the "A" Train*.

Concerto for Cootie and Jack the Bear were both recorded in March 1940. Also recorded in that month was *Ko-Ko*, one of the greatest pieces in the entire Ellington canon. There is no direct documentation of Strayhorn's role in this celebrated landmark, but much of the evidence for collaboration has not come to light until relatively recently. Since we have nothing close to a full picture of how things worked, the question inevitably arises: is it likely that Ellington did not involve his brilliant assistant, who was turning out terrific material left and right, in one of his most famous pieces?

While Basie's *Volcano* was a precedent for *Ko-Ko*, the comparison also reveals an emphatic difference. *Ko-Ko* is built around seven blues choruses, plus introduction and conclusion (with an added tag), all in a minor key, which automatically distances the piece from typical Swing Era buoyancy. The vitality is in step with Basie, but *Ko-Ko* is much darker and dramatic. Blanton's bass is picked up well by the microphone, and he pulses through the piece like a throbbing heart.

The taut riffs come in call and response and they come in layers, like Basie except laced with dissonant punctuations. Nanton's talking trombone dominates choruses two and three. For chorus four Ellington's fragmented piano dialogues with dissonant shards from the horns. In chorus six, the band swells to heightened volume and dissonance only to break off surprisingly, with

Blanton dramatically popping out all by himself for three unaccompanied breaks. The explosive climax and stark contrast are potent. It's hard to imagine what the light-footed jitterbuggers thought of *Ko-Ko*. It could easily have been one of the pieces that "sailed over all but a few heads," as *DownBeat* described an Ellington concert in May 1940.

We might speculate about Strayhorn's contribution. Ellington asked him to rework *Jack the Bear* by incorporating bass player Jimmie Blanton after he joined the band in October 1939. *Ko-Ko* dates from around the same time, and it also appears to have been a piece that Ellington drafted before the bass virtuoso's arrival. It would have seemed natural to have Strayhorn rework *Ko-Ko* to include Blanton. *Jack the Bear* and *Ko-Ko* were both ready to go for a recording session on March 6, 1940.

If Strayhorn added a chorus for Blanton, that would have been chorus six, with his three solo breaks. This is the climax of the entire piece. It involves part writing that is not particularly characteristic of Ellington: a little motive is imitated, bounced from saxophones to trombones to trumpets in quick succession; it then rises to a crisp rhythmic kick (half note followed by two eighth notes ending on beat three) at the top. Most of the piece, in contrast, is based on call and response. The idea of tossing a motive back and forth like this would come easily to anyone who has studied a lot of classical music.

Moreover, the third punctuation, which moves to the "V" chord of the blues form, is a massive but controlled scream, with flat seven and flat nine in tension with the root of the chord, flat thirteen in tension with the fifth, and eleven in tension with the third (a flat ten is thrown in for good measure). Previous arrivals at this spot in the blues form are not nearly so loaded with dissonance, and the dissonances are not so prominent, either. Here they are placed on the top end of the range in high relief, which is something Strayhorn liked to do. The effect resembles the famous and equally climactic horn blast in *Take the "A" Train*, where we also find the same rhythmic kick (half note followed by two eighth notes on beat three). If Strayhorn was responsible for this chorus, he probably also added the little tag at the end of the piece, which uses the same imitative figures, again for climactic effect.

Gunther Schuller admired how the small group of winds sounded so massive in *Ko-Ko*, and he compared the fullness of the arrangement to pieces like Stravinsky's *Symphony for Wind Instruments*, his *Symphony of Psalms*, and Bartók's *Concerto for Orchestra*. Any connection to Stravinsky and Bartók would have come from Strayhorn. In early 1941, Strayhorn made some arrangements for a seven-piece band led by Lee Young in California. "Billy got a great, full sound out of those seven pieces," the grateful leader remembered. "He made us sound like fourteen." Strayhorn had reached an uncommon fluency. "It was so natural, so easy to him, like writing a letter," said another arranger to whom Strayhorn had given some tips. "I don't think he had any realization that what he could do was incredible. It just doesn't come like that to other people."

Frankly, it is easier to assume that Strayhorn was involved with *Ko-Ko* than it is to assume that he was not. "I'd see Billy walk into Duke's dressing room, and Duke would say, 'Oh, Billy, I want you to finish this thing for me,'" recalled Ellington's sister Ruth. "Just like that: 'I want you to finish this thing for me.' And Billy would sit and stare into his eyes for about ten minutes, and Duke would stare back, and then Billy would say, 'Okay.' They wouldn't exchange a word. They'd just look into each other's eyes, and Billy would go out and write what Duke wanted."

From later years there are reports of the two of them composing together on the telephone, bouncing around ideas. "In music as you develop a theme or a musical idea, there are many points at which direction must be decided," remembered Ellington, "and any time I was in the throes of debate with myself, harmonically or melodically, I would turn to Billy Strayhorn. We would talk and then the whole world would come into focus."

"I don't think your strain is melodic enough," Strayhorn once told Ellington on a train. It is unlikely that the surviving evidence captures the full richness of their quirky back and forth. After the arrival of Strayhorn the default assumption that Ellington gets primary credit becomes more suspicious than ever. He had long been in the habit of hiring first-rate talent, giving them autonomy, and absorbing their best work. In 1940, Strayhorn extended the entire project.

The two found their collective stride, and sparks flew so fast that the record companies could barely keep up. Strayhorn's 1939 year of apprenticeship paid off, and by 1940 he was ready to assume a position as Ellington's right arm, his left arm, the eyes in the back of his head, his brain waves, whatever the situation called for. Rather than "the summit of [Ellington's] compositional achievement," as one writer has put it, 1940 looks more like the summit of his new collaboration with Strayhorn.

What distinguishes the miracle year of 1940 is not just the high quality of the music but also its persuasive modernity. Strayhorn helped Ellington reach a cutting-edge position in the world of big band jazz analogous to what he had achieved with Miley in 1926. It was easy for Ellington to make Take the "A" Train his new theme music in early 1941 because Strayhorn's modern touches had become so much a part of the Ellington sound. His talent came through in editing, arranging, orchestration, coaching (of the vocalists), composition, upgrades in elegance and classiness, and strategic doses of innovation.

The pattern continued. Take the "A" Train jump-started 1941. Also in 1941, Strayhorn reworked and improved I Got It Bad (and That Ain't Good), Rocks in My Bed, and C Jam Blues, with Ellington solely credited for all three.

C Jam Blues has very slight definition as a "piece" of music, though it has been a very happy success, recorded many times by many groups, from Bob Wills and his Texas Playboys to Charles Mingus. Compositions based on blues form and style, both vocal and instrumental, numbered in the thousands during the 1920s. Riff-based blues were especially popular following the success of Basie, as we have seen, with the riffs usually generated by session men. There is no reason to doubt the rumors that Bigard was responsible for this one.

The charm of *C Jam Blues* is the riff, which is simple but interesting enough to bear repetition. There are only two different pitches, one of them repeated seven times in a row, eight notes altogether, blues understatement brought to a point of logical conclusion. The riff carries through the harmonies of the blues chorus without a note being changed. Chorus two brings a snappy little countermelody into partnership. After that the various soloists improvise, one per chorus, just like a jam session, with violinist Ray Nance leading off. The very first recording (September 1941) of this casual piece carried the name *C Blues*. It was made, appropriately enough, by Barney Bigard and His Orchestra, one of the small-group spin-offs. For the recording by the full Ellington band in January 1942, Strayhorn reworked the arrangement. His new material gave the final chorus a crisp, dramatic finish, enriching the piece's identity and lifting it a notch up from the feeling of a casual jam session. His new material became as much a part of the piece's identity as Bigard's riff.

Rocks in My Bed and *I Got it Bad (and That Ain't Good)* were two of the standouts from the 1941 musical *Jump for Joy: A Sun-Tanned Revu-sical*. This project arose during the band's extended stay at Casa Mañana, a large nightclub near Los Angeles. The cast for the musical was entirely African American, and the themes were related to civil rights. A group of Left-leaning Hollywood writers and actors invited Ellington to compose the music. As many as fifteen writers worked on the show, supported by seven meddling backers.

Ellington had wanted to write a musical for a long time, including one with Langston Hughes in 1936 that never happened. This project resonated with two themes he cherished: racial pride and racial progress. The show's purpose, Ellington explained, was to "take Uncle Tom out of the theatre, eliminate the stereotyped image that had been exploited by Hollywood and Broadway, and say things that would make the audience think." In February 1941, he delivered a talk at an African American church in Los Angeles, in celebration of Annual Lincoln Day Services, and he argued there that the "Negro is the creative voice of America." The new musical would be an opportunity to put that view on full display.

Ellington's Left-leaning collaborators—all of them white— were motivated by a sharper political agenda. One of the songs was called "I've Got a Passport from Georgia," a satire about racism dominating that state so thoroughly that it was no longer recognizably part of the United States. Threats from the Ku Klux Klan caused the song to be cut from the show. The writers aimed to balance the seriousness of their political message with comedy and entertaining brilliance, which can be glimpsed today through a Soundie called *Bli-Blip*, where the charming Marie Bryant and Paul White perform a dance skit with jive talk and inventive jitterbug, accompanied by the Ellington band. The stage version of *Jump for Joy* in Los Angeles featured Dorothy Dandridge, Ivie Anderson, comedians, dancers, a choir, a dancing chorus, a cast of sixty, and Ellington's orchestra playing from the pit. The musical ran for only twelve weeks and never made it to the Big Apple. "That killed me," Ellington said to a friend about the show's mixed reception.

Ellington and Strayhorn wrote the music together, but composer credit was given only to Ellington, with Strayhorn barely mentioned in the program as having made some of the arrangements. "We should have listed Billy, too: 'By Duke Ellington and Billy Strayhorn,'" confessed Henry Blankfort, the producer and director.

"Billy really did write a whole lot of the show," added Sid Kuller, one of the writers and a catalyst for the entire project. "It was a big enough shock to the world to have Duke Ellington's name up there. Listen, the world wasn't ready to accept a show by Duke Ellington. It certainly wasn't ready to accept Duke Ellington *and* some other guy nobody ever heard of." Despite Kuller's argument to the contrary, the world probably would have accepted this without blinking. What really mattered to Kuller and his friends was the marketing advantage of Ellington's name.

I Got It Bad (and That Ain't Good) was good enough to survive the abbreviated run. Strayhorn made the arrangement; it is not clear how much he was involved with the composition. Ivie Anderson's recorded performance with the Ellington Orchestra became a hit. Strayhorn continued making new arrangements of the song for years, often with a featured role for Hodges.

An attempt was made to reenergize the show after a few weeks by bringing in blues singer Big Joe Turner (whose recording of *Shake Rattle and Roll* thirteen years later had considerable influence on rock and roll). Ellington and Strayhorn created a new number for Turner called *Rocks in My Bed*. Strayhorn's essential contribution to the success of this song is now clear. In the first recording of the song, performed by Turner, the harmonies are straight-ahead blues. But when it was time to record with the full band and Ivie Anderson, Strayhorn embellished the harmonies and transformed the melody as well. He enriched the piece and made it much more sustainable.

January 23, 1943, brought the debut of the Ellington piece about which more has been written than any other, the extended work *Black, Brown and Beige: A Tone Parallel to the History of the American Negro*. Since 1930, Ellington had been talking about composing on the theme of African American history, something longer than just a couple of disc sides, maybe even an opera. "It's time a big piece of music was written from the inside by a Negro," he told a journalist in 1941. *Black, Brown and Beige* was his strongest fulfillment of this vision.

The extended pieces had been key to establishing his reputation as a composer, and with Strayhorn now taking over so many responsibilities he could devote more time to this project. The first performance of *Black, Brown and Beige* at Carnegie Hall clocked in at forty-five minutes, far exceeding anything he had written. Ellington had been irritated at Irving Mills for not getting him a gig at Carnegie Hall in the 1930s, and now he had it. The performance was part of a publicity blitz that his new management called "National Ellington Week," described by one writer of the time as the "greatest pre-performance press ever accorded a jazz man." Eleanor Roosevelt, Glenn Miller, and Leopold Stokowski were among the luminaries in the audience for the Carnegie Hall premiere. A commemorative plaque presented to Ellington bore signatures of Marian Anderson, Aaron Copland, Benny Goodman, Earl Hines, and others.

Mercer Ellington explained the title as an allusion to color prejudice within the African American community, discrimination based on shades of skin tone, while Ellington himself suggested that it had to do with changing states of mind that were closer to or further from a white state of mind, black being further and beige being closer. Neither of these provocative interpretations was offered publicly, at least not for a long time. But at the premiere performance Ellington did speak before each of the three long movements, describing their content. There was also a printed program with extensive notes. The basic idea was a chronological representation of African American history, moving from 1620 through the Revolutionary War ("Black"), then from that war through the First World War ("Brown"), and finishing with the modern scene ("Beige").

"Black," Ellington explained, starts with work songs and then moves to spirituals, the aim being to show the close relationship between the two idioms. Highlights of "Black" include a muscular theme that returns several times. And then there is *Come Sunday*, the jewel of the entire piece, with a long, stand-alone afterlife. "Brown" has three divisions, first a salute to the West Indies, second, the Emancipation, and third, the blues. "Beige" gives a panorama of contemporary life in Harlem, from church to a penthouse in Sugar Hill.

The problems with *Black, Brown and Beige* are the same problems that plague the other extended pieces: the themes are of uneven quality and longer stretches of time are not organized convincingly. Critics complained, for example, how "the first movement . . . all but falls apart into so many separate pieces." Composer Paul Bowles opened his review by praising Ellington highly. "He is the composer of many of the finest popular melodies of the last 15 years," Bowles assured his readers, a false claim that no one in 1943 (and far beyond) would have even thought to question. Then he dismissed *Black, Brown and Beige* as "formless and meaningless . . . nothing emerged but a gaudy potpourri of tutti dance passages and solo virtuoso work. (The dance parts used some pretty corny riffs, too.) There were countless unprovoked modulations, a passage in 5/4, paraphrases on well-known tunes that were as trite as the tunes themselves, and recurrent climaxes that impeded the piece's progress."

Yet it is easy to admire this piece even with its defects. There is enough integrity to sustain appreciation for the innovation of composing *A Tone Parallel to the History of the Negro.* "The Negro was put ahead twenty years culturally as a result of this affair," commented one white observer, and the nobility of Ellington's vision is audible. It has been suggested that a more prominent role for the programmatic storytelling that lay behind the shifting musical events might enhance the audience's experience. Maurice Peress's arrangement for string orchestra shows that there is no need to halt the Ellington tradition of adaptation and collaboration.

Ellington relied on two of his strongest collaborators for key moments. For the spiritual-like *Come Sunday* he looked to Johnny Hodges. The tempo is extremely slow. It takes Hodges two full minutes to play through the thirty-two-bar theme. The pace invites the great alto saxophonist to do what he did best: he treats the theme in the manner that African Americans sometimes used to call "long meter," meaning the performance of a spiritual or hymn at a very slow tempo with overwhelming ornamentation. It is a breathtaking performance. Moody harmonies and voicings shimmer behind Hodges and animate the piece further. Hodges, a master at sustaining interest at such a slow tempo, was later matched by Mahalia Jackson, who also knew something about ornamenting power and who made her contribution after lyrics were added in the late 1950s.

It comes as no surprise to learn that Ellington brought in Strayhorn for *Beige*, since that is where the tone parallel arrives at the modern moment in African American history. It has been estimated that Strayhorn wrote about a third of this thirteen-minute section. Especially effective is his jazz waltz depicting the sophisticated fun of the Harlem elite in a penthouse on Sugar Hill. It hardly needs to be said that the entirety of *Black, Brown and Beige* was credited solely to Ellington. This was, after all, "National Ellington Week," and his moment in the spotlight at the most famous monument to great composers in the United States. When asked about his involvement Strayhorn characteristically ducked the issue. For the same Carnegie Hall concert, Ellington asked Strayhorn to rework, without credit, a composition from 1938 called *Blue Belles of Harlem*, where one reviewer heard "overtones suggestive of Ravel" without knowing that it was Strayhorn rather than Ellington who accounted for that connection.

Hodges was making $190 per week in December 1943, the highest salary in the band, and he was responding with first-rate material that continued to feed Ellington's revenue stream. This included Ellington's big hit of 1944, *I'm Beginning to See the Light. Don't Get Around Much Anymore* had been a success for the Ink Spots in early 1943, with the creative product from Hodges leading to copyright and credit for Ellington. *I'm Beginning to See the Light* also started as a catchy tune from Hodges, to which Don George added some sharp lyrics, among the best of any Ellington song.

George pitched the piece to some big-name white bands, though Ellington was skeptical and advised him not to waste time on it. Selling a song like this was standard practice, based on the reality of much stronger market potential for white bands. *In a Sentimental Mood*, for example, had been a far bigger hit for Benny Goodman than it was for Ellington. Harry James said yes to George's pitch, and Johnny Thompson made a nice arrangement of *I'm Beginning to See the Light* for the James Orchestra. The James recording sold well and made the tune known. The disc showed composer credit for James, Ellington, Hodges, and George, proving that there was enough room for multiple credits when the politics required it. In 1945 the Ink Spots once again (now with Ella Fitzgerald joining them) stepped into the picture. Their recording made *I'm Beginning to See the Light* an even bigger hit, and George felt vindicated. In the summer of 1944 the song was heard as a patriotic statement; according to George, the record "played on every loudspeaker on every PT boat that carried our boys to the attack on the beaches of Normandy."

Ellington's *Black, Brown and Beige* may not have been the success he was hoping for, but his appearance (and subsequent appearances) at Carnegie Hall worked well for him. He won awards from *DownBeat* magazine in 1944 and *Esquire* in 1945. Feature stories in the *Saturday Evening Post* and *The New Yorker* followed, also in 1945, with a weekly radio show on the ABC network, broadcasting across the country and to armed forces abroad. Yet the war years were stressful for all swing bands. Transportation was challenging, shellac for making phonograph records was in short supply, and musicians were being drafted, thus creating shortages of qualified players. Ellington suffered a string of departures: Williams left in 1941, Bigard in 1942, Blanton died in 1942, Webster went out to lead his own combo in 1943, Tizol joined Harry James in 1944 (and later returned), and Ray Nance and Rex Stewart left in 1945 (Nance later returned).

How much of Strayhorn's contributions were known during

these years? Very little, and what was known could easily be down-played or ignored, a situation that carries into the present day. The band's radio audience did not know that Strayhorn, rather than Ellington, had created most of the new arrangements they were listening to. Crediting on discs continued according to the quirky patterns we have seen: some of their collaborations were cosigned (*Out of This World*), sometimes Ellington had Strayhorn rewrite an earlier piece without credit (*Blutopia*), some of Stray-horn's creations lacked any credit to him (*Air-Conditioned Jungle*), some showed sole credit for him (*Mid-Riff*), and some were simply shelved. Critic Alec Wilder wrote in 1948 that Ellington's "dis-ciple and associate Billy Strayhorn has contributed material of worth, but numerically its quantity is still small." The quantity was far greater than any outsider could have known.

There are many different kinds of evidence for composer credit, and all of them come with problems. Sometimes an orig-inal manuscript exists and the handwriting indicates authorship, yet the survival of this kind of evidence is so precarious that it can-not come anywhere close to telling the whole story. An original copyright deposit, a revised copyright deposit, an original record label, and a later record label—often these sources disagree with one another. Liner notes, program notes, and publicity releases further complicate the story. Isolated remarks from interviews are perhaps the most reliable evidence of all, but they are sparse. Strayhorn's and Ellington's names weave in and out of view, the former mostly out and the latter mostly in. Ellington, his family that worked for him (his sister, her husband, his son), his man-agers, and his close friends in the business all routinely pushed credit in his direction, under the premise that what was good for Ellington was good for the Ellington collective.

For Strayhorn the issue was only partly financial, since he was well taken care of. In 1941, Ellington gave him stock in his sheet-music publishing company. Strayhorn's reward, according to the Ellington ecosystem, would not be full artistic credit but

job security, generous pay, and a sense of belonging to an artistic
achievement that was highly regarded. As Cootie Williams put it,
"It was a pleasure, you know, to have the band to play your song."
Undoubtedly Strayhorn felt that way, too, at least for a while.

It has been claimed that Strayhorn preferred to remain hidden, that he didn't want publicity and was happy to serve his
boss. "Billy could have pursued a career on his own," insisted a
friend. "He had the talent to become rich and famous—but he'd
have had to be less than honest about his sexual orientation. Or
he could work behind the scenes for Duke and be open about
being gay. It really was truth or consequences, and Billy went with
truth." In the late 1940s the frustrations of this compromise were
beginning to show.

A theatrical production called *Beggar's Holiday* (1946) was
a turning point. "Ellington wanted the recognition of writing a
Broadway show," said his friend and collaborator Luther Henderson. "In fact, he wanted the recognition of writing a Broadway show
more than he wanted to write a Broadway show." It made perfect
sense to hand the assignment over to his assistant, with Ellington to be consulted by telephone. As with *Jump for Joy*, Ellington
received composer credit, with Strayhorn cited for "supervising"
the orchestration. "Mr. Ellington's score is a generous outpouring
of his individual talent, filled with the spirit and the warmth of
his music, the pulsing beat of his rhythms, the strength and the
refreshing colors of his modern harmonies," wrote one reviewer.
At the opening-night party Ellington circulated in full glory while
a demoralized Strayhorn quickly exited.

In April 1947 a friend of Strayhorn's from the music business
was surprised to discover that he had no formal contract with
Ellington and no sense of the value of his contributions. He was
also pondering his own sense of artistic mission. "He encouraged
me not to compromise," said an artist friend. "He said he knew all
about compromise, and things hadn't always worked out the way
he expected." The reality was that all swing musicians, not just

Strayhorn and Ellington, were forced to evaluate what they wanted to do and how they could make a living doing it, for the Swing Era was in decline. Leading bands experimented with reducing to smaller sizes. Bebop was increasingly capturing connoisseurs dedicated to the cutting edge. Blends of jazz with rhythm and blues were popular. Louis Armstrong enjoyed a surprising late-career resurgence with a New Orleans revival band. Singers like Bing Crosby, Ella Fitzgerald, Nat King Cole, Peggy Lee, and Doris Day claimed more and more attention, transforming the great dance bands into backup units. In an article for *DownBeat* (November 1952), Leonard Feather wrote that the only sustainable big bands left were those led by Ellington, Woody Herman, Count Basie, and Stan Kenton.

Ellington's royalty stream helped keep the band going. He increasingly relied on revisions of his famous pieces, which formed the core of his very first LP, the 1950 *Masterpieces by Elling-*

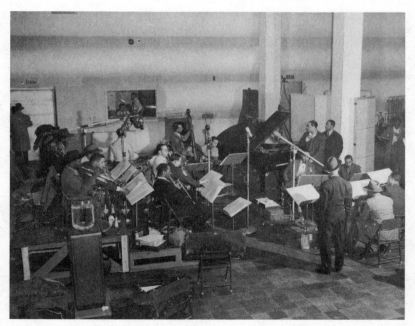

4.3 Ellington band in a recording studio, mid-1940s

ton. Strayhorn was again in charge. He reconceived and greatly extended *Mood Indigo* (fifteen and one-half minutes), *Sophisticated Lady* (eleven and one-half minutes), and *(In My) Solitude* (eight and one-half minutes). His contributions are so substantial, it has been observed, that a more appropriate title for the album would have been *Masterpieces by Ellington, Arranged by Strayhorn.* (Note the typical omission of the co-composers: a better emendation would be *Masterpieces by Bigard, Brown, Hardwick, and Ellington, Arranged by Strayhorn.*) Strayhorn's arrangement of *The Tattooed Bride* has been singled out as the finest version of that extended piece. Only Ellington was credited on the LP, further disgruntling his assistant.

Ellington offered him shares in a new record company he was launching, where Strayhorn would get full performing and composing credit, but the company folded quickly. *Satin Doll* was a bright spot in 1953. Strayhorn took an Ellington riff and ran it through a harmonic sequence with just the right touches, turning it into Ellington's last hit record and a jazz standard, with only Ellington's name listed as composer. In mid-1953 they drifted apart, each collaborating with others and working together only occasionally. "It was a situation where Duke still called him if he needed him, and Billy, he was there if he was needed," remembered clarinetist Jimmy Hamilton. "But their heads was somewhere else." As were the heads of the American record-buying public. In 1955, Bill Haley and the Comets reached the top of the pop charts with *Rock around the Clock*, while Fats Domino's *Ain't That a Shame* hit number one on the rhythm and blues charts.

A Jazz of Their Own

The Strayhorn-Ellington relationship was stunningly creative, thoroughly intimate, and highly unusual. They started out as master and assistant. There must have been a feeling of father and son, as well. It has also been claimed that they were lovers. Mercer Ellington said their sexual relationship was known among the band. "We had a relationship that nobody else in the world would understand," remarked Ellington.

"He had a very, very, very deep love for Strayhorn," said close friend Marian Logan, "and Strayhorn obviously loved Duke, too."

As David Hajdu puts it, they settled into "a jazz of their own." It is hardly surprising that this intertwining of personal closeness, artistic collaboration, and noncontractual business generated a set of deeply conflicted feelings for the junior partner.

The poignancy that automatically surfaces includes Strayhorn's descent into alcoholism. Performing musicians are routinely exposed to the dangers of substance abuse, with so many infamous examples in jazz and rock that the topic hardly needs to be mentioned. Musicians must be up when the late-night performance begins, and they need to come down when it is over. They live apart from family and social networks, with inverted hours, so they settle into an in-group culture where stimulants and alcohol are perceived as necessary and frequently regarded as creative aids.

Alcohol abuse was rampant in Ellington's band, and Strayhorn was part of the crowd. It contributed to his early death at age fifty-one, in 1967. His conflicting emotions about Ellington may have fueled his illness. Musicians who worked for Ellington reacted with a range of emotions when he claimed credit for their creative work, from bitterness to resignation to contentment. It was harder for Strayhorn since he was a composer and arranger, which meant that his identity was more thoroughly subsumed by the leader. Others could take a turn in the spotlight and play the solos they had created, while Strayhorn stayed behind the curtain.

His collaboration with Ellington, then, mixed personal and artistic tensions in a unique way—we could call it the Strayhorn problem. As he explored his options in the early 1950s, a question must have lurked in the back of his mind: what was his place in the world of professional musicians and how did that correlate with his artistic aspirations? His situation was unavoidably shaped by his formative work with Ellington.

Strayhorn drifted through several theatrical productions. A natural career choice would have been to work with vocalists. As different as Ellington and Strayhorn were, they shared a gift for musical empathy, each good at reading and responding to other musicians. This is hardly a skill that all great composers have, though it is one shared by all great collaborators. Strayhorn was frequently praised for his ability to work with singers. In 1955 he toured with Lena Horne and accompanied her on an LP. "He had a trick of hearing the breath," explained Horne. "He made a soft little bed right there to support the structure, so while you're taking your breath, nobody knows. It takes an awful lot of sensitivity."

"It was like he had a direct psychic link to Lena," remembered drummer Chico Hamilton. "When she was singing, he translated what she was feeling on the piano and sent back to her in his music at the same time. It went both ways."

He "could have done a million sessions, he was fast, he was good," said trumpeter Jimmy Maxwell. Temperament and self-identity got in the way. "Billy wasn't what you'd say a professional," was how Maxwell framed it. "He was an artistic man."

"The actual source of his frustration was artistic," insisted Leonard Feather, but one would have to immediately qualify that and say that the artistic frustration was completely bound up with his complicated history with Ellington, which turned out to be inescapable. His professional identity, from 1939 forward, had been completely formed around this relationship. The easiest way to solve the problem of how to proceed turned out, unsurprisingly, to be a return to Ellington.

As a creative collaborator, Ellington's formative moment came in 1926, at age twenty-seven, when he discovered a fresh way to combine vernacular performance with jazz arrangement, yielding new compositional possibilities. For Strayhorn, the parallel moment was his study of Ellington's portfolio in 1939, at age twenty-four, after which he went into action editing, adding, revising, and offering up his own work for the leader to process as he wished. The nature of creative synthesis in the two cases is very different. Ellington got a lot of mileage out of responding to someone else's first-rate material and coming up with fresh ways to frame it. His method was more open-ended than Strayhorn's bringing together of two different compositional sensibilities.

Just as the modern solution in 1926 would not do the trick in 1940, so did 1956 call for something fresh. The challenge may have been even greater this time around. In the mid-1950s heady innovations in jazz were spinning out in a dizzying array of directions. One of the leading lights, Charles Mingus, understood and admired Ellington's methods and his achievements. Compositions like *Pithecanthropus Erectus* (1956), *Haitian Fight Song* (1957), and *Wednesday Night Prayer Meeting* (1959) helped establish Mingus as one of the greatest jazz composers of all time, right alongside Ellington.

A first-rate bass player, Mingus actually joined the Ellington Orchestra briefly in the early 1950s. Mingus developed his own ways of bringing musicians into the creative process. One was to hum the themes he wanted them to play and then urge them to personalize their parts. He believed that writing everything out tended to fix the ideas too firmly. The group worked out the arrangement together by ear, with the leader tinkering as the process unfolded. Mingus was inspired not just by Ellington's collaborative method but also by his sense of a cutting-edge African American modernity based on the vernacular. He was the worthy follower who took the concept further. On the vernacular side were his dramatic uses of heterophony (two or more variations of a melody played simultaneously), evoking the "dark church where everyone was screaming" that he had experienced as a child. Collaboration with Mingus can have the aura of a militant statement of civil rights. Dissonances explode with rage that cannot possibly be controlled. Like Strayhorn, Mingus learned from classical composers, but since he was more collaboratively involved with his musicians than Strayhorn he achieved much greater vernacular intensity.

Haitian Fight Song, for example, has military-style drum cadences in the middle section, which is surrounded by blues choruses, one after the other, similar to examples from Ellington. What is unforgettable is the stunning ensemble performance from trombonist Jimmy Knepper, saxophonist Shafi Hadi, pianist Wade Legge, drummer Dannie Richmond, and Mingus himself in the great, tumultuous swells of collective improvisation that start and finish the piece. It sounds like a lot more than five people playing: it sounds like a congregation ablaze with the fire of the Holy Spirit and prepared to burn American racism to the ground. This is improvisation with a compositional purpose, led by Mingus with essential contributions from the others.

What Mingus lacked was Ellington's interpersonal skills. He liked to tell the story of how Ellington fired him. "The charming way he says it, you feel like he's paying you a compliment," he remembered. "Feeling honored, you shake hands and resign." Mingus's management style fell on the other, difficult end of the spectrum. The Ellington ecosystem of give-and-take, soft sell and high praise, you scratch my back and I'll scratch your back—that didn't come naturally to him. He routinely embarrassed musicians in the middle of performances and even attacked them physically, punching out a few front teeth on two occasions. Mingus said that his primary drummer, Dannie Richmond, who stayed with him longer than anyone, "gave me his complete open mind . . . to work with as clay." (Mingus here recalls Alfred Hitchcock: "All actors are cattle.") It is impossible to imagine Ellington ever regarding one of his musicians like that. Yet Mingus enjoyed a posthumous benefit that Ellington never got—a legacy orchestra dedicated solely to his music. Led by his widow Sue, and filled with dedicated Mingus collaborators mixed with younger players, the Mingus Big Band continues to keep alive the ear-based, collective method that Ellington pioneered and Mingus furthered.

4.4 Newport Jazz Festival, July 1956

There was no way for Ellington and Strayhorn to compete directly with someone like Mingus, but 1956 was the year of Ellington's surprise success at the Newport Jazz Festival, which suddenly thrust him into the spotlight. The centerpiece was Paul Gonsalves's solo in *Diminuendo and Crescendo in Blue*, and the performance included attractive arrangements of *Black and Tan Fantasy*, *Mood Indigo*, *Sophisticated Lady*, *Take the "A" Train*, and *Jeep's Blues*. But this was all in the basket of updated oldies, which could hardly satisfy high artistic ambitions. There was a solution in sight, represented in another type of piece performed at Newport. Columbia Records had approached Ellington, very near the performance date in July, with the idea of a "suite" celebrating this event. "Can you do it?" came the query. "Okay, I'll get Strays to work on it right away," was the reply. Given the rush, the *Newport Festival Suite* is unsurprisingly long on improvised solos.

But the genre of the suite turned out to be an attractive way to advance the Ellington-Strayhorn reconciliation. *Such Sweet Thunder* (1957), *The Nutcracker Suite* (1960), and *The Far East Suite* (1966) stand among their finest accomplishments. The suites also solved a set of four nagging problems, all in one stroke.

First, they relieved a point of tension related to artistic differences. Ellington, as we have seen, liked to fuse together diverse material, a typical 1920s approach to strain form. He shared this preference with John Lennon, who described composition as "doing little bits which you then join up." McCartney could unite with Lennon in this method, especially during the Beatles' early years, when one composer invented a verse and the other added a bridge, for example. But McCartney also mastered a more holistic approach to composing a single continuous statement, meticulously designed. *Yesterday* is a great example, as are many of McCartney's best songs. Strayhorn was like McCartney in this respect. Ellington routinely welcomed additions, extensions, edits, and substitutions to a score when he brought it to his musicians, while Strayhorn conceived a score as complete and final. He might leave space for improvisation, of course, but he didn't welcome revision. Ellington's abrupt transitions from one section to another expose his cut-and-paste method, while Strayhorn's more seamless transitions indicate a unified conception. Ellington's method taken to an extreme was described in a report from 1960:

> The final polishing of any Ellington arrangement is done as the band plays it, and Duke, to the bewilderment of people who have watched him record, writes and rehearses music in segments, usually of eight measures and almost always without a written conclusion . . . Duke's final instructions for a performance might go as follows: "Start at letter C. Then go to A and play it twice, only second time leave off

the last two bars. These bars are at the beginning of a sheet you have marked X. After X I'll play until I bring you in at C and you go out with letter D. Any questions?"

It is impossible to imagine Strayhorn ever embracing a strategy like this.

The problem was that Ellington did not hesitate to scramble Strayhorn's painstakingly crafted material when it suited him. When Ellington chopped up, abridged, pasted in, or simply rearranged his assistant's thoughtful designs, it must have been a source of irritation. But Ellington was in charge and could do what he liked. In the early days it would have been easy to take this as a gesture of inclusion, but as time went on Strayhorn must have found the practice frustrating. In the suites, however, Ellington could compose his small piece and Strayhorn could compose his. The two related as independent movements, each touching on a shared theme, and there was no need to force them together.

This is related to the second problem that the suites averted—the handling of extended form. Joining up phrases in a three-minute piece is one thing, but stretching that technique to the level of ten or fifteen minutes is another. With the suites there was no need. Only one of the twelve movements for *Such Sweet Thunder*, for example, exceeds four minutes. The idea of a suite accommodates diversity and doesn't require the tricks of the trade for organizing extended pieces. Yet a suite was automatically associated with the world of classical music, so it carried art credentials.

Plus, the concept was tailor-made for the newly invented LP. In this there is another parallel between the Ellington collective and the Beatles when the latter started to think in terms of albums rather than singles. Only two of the thirteen tracks on *Sgt. Pepper's Lonely Hearts Club Band* are longer than four minutes. The album is defined as a kind of psychedelic collage, the various components linked by the implied theme. Lennon and McCartney had no training in writing extended pieces, either, so this approach worked well for them. *Pepper* acquired the status of art like no rock album had ever done before.

By agreement, the suites solved a third problem: Ellington now assured his partner that he would be co-credited on all of them. He kept the promise even in cases where Strayhorn made no contribution at all. Here is an obvious comparison with Lennon and McCartney, who quickly recognized how cosigning all of their compositions, regardless of who wrote what, would be a boon to their collective enterprise.

And the fourth problem solved by the suite format was the central one for the final phase of Ellington's career: what would be the Ellington-Strayhorn niche amid the diversity of high-level 1950s jazz? The suites turned out to be a perfect way for Strayhorn to continue infusing the band's sound with modern sophistication. The concept played to his strengths, and that is the primary reason that they account for much of the best Ellington material from this period forward.

Such Sweet Thunder (1956, also known as *The Shakespeare Suite*) was conceived after the Stratford Shakespearean Festival requested Ellington to compose a new number to celebrate its annual gathering. An association with Shakespeare must have delighted Ellington, with the playwright's mix of classiness and popularity, plus the inevitable comparison of Shakespeare "writing to the actor" with Ellington "writing to the musician." The idea was to have music inspired by various characters in Shakespeare's plays, "thumbnail sketches," as Ellington described them. Included are four "sonnets" for subsets of the band that demonstrate, once again, Ellington's cleverness with musical form: each is built around fourteen phrases, with ten notes in each phrase, analogous to Shakespeare's poetry. In general, however, there are few direct connections to Shakespeare other than the imagery of the various titles, obliquely brought to life as musical moods.

The original recording of *Such Sweet Thunder* credited the entire suite to both Ellington and Strayhorn, with no indication that they had mostly worked separately on individual numbers. Their independence produced a satisfying range of expression analogous to the vivid characters. All of it is justified by the suite aesthetic, which had always, back to the earliest representations of the genre in classical music, leaned toward variety rather than unity. The plan for virtually every soloist to get a turn in the spotlight generated an attractive mix all by itself.

Ellington makes some imaginative contributions to *Such Sweet Thunder*, especially through titling. *Madness in Great Ones* uses the cut-and-paste method to evoke Hamlet's derangement in a string of non sequiturs. Virtuoso high-note trumpeter Cat Anderson is used to good effect. *Sonnet for Caesar* features plaintive writing for clarinet, which is effectively harmonized. But the three strongest numbers for the suite were composed by Strayhorn, who was devoted to Shakespeare and quoted him often.

Two of the three Strayhorn standouts were composed earlier. The static, moody harmony and the habanera ostinato in *Half the Fun* have led to apt comparisons with Debussy's piano prelude *La Puerta del Vino*. Superb playing from Hodges and percussionist Sam Woodyard bring Strayhorn's sure control of form to life. Strayhorn had earlier staked out his place in the tradition of Far Eastern musical exoticism with a fresh 1945 arrangement of Tizol's *Caravan*, and after *Half the Fun* he would have more to come with the stunning *Arabesque Cookie*, written for the 1960 adaptation of Tchaikovsky's *The Nutcracker Suite*.

Strayhorn's *The Star-Crossed Lovers* is the true highlight, with a strong and independent performing life. This exquisite ballad, also written earlier, is one of Strayhorn's greatest accomplishments, a superb example of meticulous craft and pithy inspiration from start to finish. Here is where the compatibility of the two close friends, Strayhorn and Hodges, reaches the musical sublime. With Bubber Miley's great masterpieces we observed how bending pitch and talking effects are inseparable from the construction of the melody. They do not feel added but rather part of the conception. That is not how *The Star-Crossed Lovers* came about, but still there is a comparison to make. Strayhorn's composition is an exquisite play between melodic and harmonic details that keep shifting, ever so slightly, as the piece unfolds. The richness of the harmonic motion works with melodic expectations, all of it subtly redirected and crafted according to the plan of the chorus. It is this melodic-harmonic *structure* that is the basis for the piece's success. But Hodges's magnificence (Gonsalves plays the first two phrases on tenor sax and Hodges follows) feels like it belongs to the piece. His performance is so powerfully imprinted that it cannot be escaped, and this followed directly from the long musical partnership between the two.

One writer has argued that the Strayhorn-Hodges ballads can sometimes feel like "overly scented confections," where Strayhorn pushes "his art to the very limits of sensualism and, at times, sentimentality." One can understand this reaction from listeners who prefer their musical emotions slightly dry. What makes *The Star-Crossed Lovers* exceptional is how Strayhorn's unexpected half steps are extended by Hodges with smaller, microtonal steps of bending, stretching, and sliding, a perfect match of composition and performer.

Equally dazzling is the piece Strayhorn wrote specifically for *Such Sweet Thunder*—*Up and Down, Up and Down (I Will Lead Them Up and Down)*. Here is where his passion for Shakespeare fueled his musical imagination. *Up and Down* is a musical illustration of Puck, the mischief maker in *A Midsummer Night's Dream*. It is a superb composition of wit and complexity. It paradoxically feels tightly managed and raucous at the same time. Trumpeter Clark Terry, one of Ellington's finest soloists of the 1950s, is cast as Puck, and he delivers his lines with just the right touch of bluesy subversion. Multiple strategies work their combined charms. Strayhorn's even-note runs of counterpoint recall Bach, and they are set off against Terry's very un-Bachian half-valving. The counterpoint flows in glittering streams of fairy dust, but it also pushes up against harmonic dissonance in a bracing, atonal way. And the basic strategy—basic to all of the Ellington-Strayhorn suites—of pitting classical against jazz emerges here in a fresh and skillful way as the composer strings out long, pedal-based washes of whimsical counterpoint followed by stocky, self-contained jazz phrases for the delicately sauntering Puck.

Up and Down is not exactly a *Take the "A" Train* crowd pleaser, and it might even fall under the category of pieces that "sailed over all but a few heads," as *DownBeat* complained in 1940. Perhaps someone even objected that it emphasizes "originality at the expense of beauty," as a critic said about *Chelsea Bridge*. If they did say that, they missed it. Strayhorn has carved out a beauty of his own, infused with concentrated originality.

Ellington was having fun trying to keep up with him. Nevertheless, one doesn't hear the same focus and richness of expression in Ellington's numbers for *Such Sweet Thunder* that one hears in Strayhorn's. The *Times* called this suite "the best work that Mr. Ellington has done in a decade." To take that claim seriously would be to rank Strayhorn's three standouts among the finest compositions to emerge from the Ellington collective during the 1950s. Rival nominations would include, on the weighty end of the spectrum, *A Tone Parallel to Harlem* (1951, also known as *Harlem* or *Harlem Suite*), one of the more successful of the old-style extended pieces. On the pop side would be *Satin Doll*. We have already seen Strayhorn's primary role in the latter; for the former he composed the final thirty seconds of the thirteen-minute piece, a crisp and bombastic conclusion to a piece that goes in a lot of different directions.

Ellington kept his word and co-credited his junior colleague, but since neither name was associated with individual numbers the superiority of Strayhorn's material was not apparent. Ellington started a cute tradition of having his assistant make a cameo appearance for *Half the Fun*. Jazz scholar Brian Priestley remembered seeing this in Leeds, England, in October 1958, the "closing rhythm-section vamp coinciding with the stage-lights fading to black as a spotlight picked out Strayhorn, who came on stage just to play a single low piano note." Meanwhile, publicist Joe Morgen was working in the opposite direction, doing everything he could to keep Strayhorn out of publicity materials so as not to distract attention away from the leader. Morgen hustled up praiseful articles in *Newsweek*, *Look*, and the *New York Times* during 1957, with Strayhorn's name nowhere in sight.

Strayhorn is the key to the success of the late suites because they play to his strengths—classy jazz, witty and refined. He was in his element. Ellington worked under deadlines, Strayhorn more when the muse moved him. Ellington had multiple responsibilities and always thought about the bottom line, which was less of a concern to Strayhorn. An observer watched them at work on the film score for *Paris Blues*, and he was surprised to see Ellington carrying most of the load. "Duke was a professional and a crowd pleaser, and the essence of his pieces was to please the crowd," he explained. "Strayhorn wasn't: the essence of his work was to satisfy himself. He didn't always have a lot of output. Duke kept Strayhorn around knowing the output might be small and getting smaller, but wanting it *all*."

Turner's painting inspired *Chelsea Bridge* in 1941, Shakespeare's play inspired *Up and Down* in 1957, and Tchaikovsky's charming ballet *The Nutcracker Suite* inspired some stunning music from Strayhorn in 1960. The ballet had risen in popularity thanks to George Balanchine's midcentury choreography and Christmastime entry into American living rooms through CBS television. *The Nutcracker Suite* was already a suite so it naturally fit the Ellington-Strayhorn model, and it automatically carried the magic formula of classy yet accessible, the best-loved piece by the quintessential middle-brow composer. Strayhorn convinced his boss, who was happy to come along for the imperial ride.

In an interview, Strayhorn explained the challenge. "It's always a struggle . . . to present [the music of] someone of the stature of Peter Ilyich Tchaikovsky and adapting it to our flavor without distorting him. . . . Actually, it sort of felt like we were talking to him, because we didn't want him turning over any more than he already was." Strayhorn's loyalty comes through in the final product. It was fine for Chuck Berry to riff on teenage rebellion and teasingly command Beethoven and Tchaikovsky to *Roll Over* (in their graves), but that was not Strayhorn's approach. He infuses his adaptation with respect at the same time that he feels no limitations. The project is a dialogue between creative adults, and the mature segment of the record-buying public is warmly invited to join the party.

The British critic Eddie Lambert wrote (around 1980) that "Ellington's aim in *The Nutcracker Suite* seems to have been to give full value to the three principal features of Tchaikovsky's score—its rich melodic content, its colorful textures, and its humor . . . Ellington ensures that the humor is wholly musical, giving an elegant glow to a set of performances of characteristic Ellington quality." This is spot-on if we replace "Ellington" with "Strayhorn." It is now clear that the *Nutcracker* is primarily Strayhorn's work. The surviving manuscripts establish that he wrote six of the nine movements and Ellington one (*Peanut Brittle Brigade*). Of the remaining two (for which manuscripts do not survive), one seems like Strayhorn (*Chinoiserie*) and the other seems like Ellington (*Volga Vouty*). The two contributions from Ellington are serviceable. Strayhorn's *The Nutcracker Suite* would have to be called an arrangement of Tchaikovsky, but he has so thoroughly reconceived everything that it is more like an independent composition.

At the initial meeting with Ellington, in Pittsburgh at the Stanley Theater, Strayhorn played *Sophisticated Lady* the way Ellington had played it and then showed him another way, "pretty hip-sounding" and pretty impressive. From the very first notes in the *Overture*, Tchaikovsky's material is easily recognizable but completely recast. The tempo, mood, form, and scoring are all different but the theme is clearly stated. Musical climax happens in Strayhorn's style rather than Tchaikovsky's style, and the same is true of the elegant transitions and the cool resolutions.

"Their scoring is among the most detailed and precise they ever wrote for the band," noted Lambert about *Nutcracker*, not knowing that it was Strayhorn whom he was praising. Tchaikovsky himself was a fine orchestrator, and Strayhorn was inspired. His magical use of instruments is evident in every movement. Inventive scorings include the introductions to *Toot Toot Tootie Toot* (*Dance of the Reed Pipes*) and *Chinoiserie*, which is so radically fractured with percussion and accompaniment that it sounds funny, yet the whole thing is done with so much integrity that it works. Strayhorn's humor is everywhere, delivered by musicians who know what to do with it. Jazzed-up Tchaikovsky could have sounded trite, but the intelligence of the arranger and his musicians avoids that hazard completely.

Another advantage to *The Nutcracker Suite* was that the original was music for dancing. This automatically provided a connection to jazz and suggested an approach: Strayhorn could transform the styles of movement, adding a playful dimension. The ballerina of Tchaikovsky's *Sugar Plum Fairy*, twinkling across the stage to the sounds of celesta and violin, yields to Harry Carney's lumbering baritone sax, the classic Ellington sound, spurred by Sam Woodyard's Latin-jazz groove. The movement is retitled *Sugar Rum Cherry*. This is not quite straight-ahead jazz and the texture is sparse and atmospheric. Tchaikovsky's theme is clipped and fragmented, modernist style, at several turns, including the clever conclusion where it whittles down abruptly to a little riff, repeated and fading away as Carney's character struts around the corner.

As a nod to the LP structure Strayhorn composed an *Entr'acte* to finish side one. It is built out of phrases from the *Overture* tossed around imaginatively through various soloists, now with paraphrase, now with counterpoint, now with riffs. *Chinoiserie* begins with a stunning mosaic of percussion, piano, and glissando bass (the mosaic reminds me of the groove McCartney invented for the Beatles' *Come Together*, I guess because each is so strikingly original). This becomes the basis for an increasingly layered texture. Quirky Monk-like (or Webern-like, or both) dots of dissonance accommodate the come and go of soloists.

The grand finale, *Arabesque Cookie*, based on Tchaikovsky's *Arabian Dance*, is a full display of what a jazz orchestra assuming the role of classical chamber orchestra can do. From the first notes of the bamboo flute in the introduction, the arranger-composer gives notice of his ambitions. Three trombones play Tchaikovsky's first theme (CD 0:20) in imitation, the last with wah-wah, backed by a Latin groove with prominent tambourine. Tchaikovsky's second theme is introduced (0:46) with the unusual scoring of bass clarinet and regular clarinet playing in very low and very high registers, respectively, to create an eerie sense of spaciousness. The effect of all of this sonic invention is less exotic than it is otherworldly.

The exposition of the main themes yields (1:35) to a passage of florid arabesques, effuse and luxurious, clarinet waves that effectively set off the deliberate progress of the primary themes. Extension of the main themes follows, with fresh scoring and melodic development, but this is suddenly interrupted (2:56) by a fresh breakout of a completely new groove. This one is a distinctly jazz groove, and it supports an improvised solo from Hodges. The surprise is quickly joined by another (3:13): when the main thematic group reenters, the solo becomes an obbligato on top of it. Strayhorn has discovered a new and happy way to synthesize the idioms of jazz and classical. Tchaikovsky ended *Arabian Dance* with some nice turns between major and minor versions of the same chord. Strayhorn reduces the device to a simple statement of an isolated major chord (3:44) that sits in the middle of the texture like a cool beam of light. Increasing layers in the background generate great richness. When the Latin groove with tambourine returns for the finish, followed by recapitulation of the main themes and a gradual winnowing, everything feels exactly right.

In September 1963, Ellington, Strayhorn, and the band began a trip through Syria, Jordan, Afghanistan, India, Ceylon, Pakistan, Iran, and Lebanon, sponsored by the U.S. State Department. Their assignment was part of an extended program of "cultural presentations" designed to chip in soft support for the cold war against the Soviet Union. Ellington, always diplomatic, handled the assignment well, and there was tremendous enthusiasm for the music. The assassination of President Kennedy in late November brought the tour to a quick end, but the band was later hired for similar tours, including one to Japan in 1964.

The idea for *The Far East Suite* arose as a set of reflections on the first tour in 1963. Four movements were composed and premiered individually in early 1964. Then five more pieces were added in 1966 to give the suite its final form. Among this second set of pieces was *Isfahan*, which dated from before work with the State Department began (the first title was *Elf*), and also *Ad Lib on Nippon*, a multipart piece Ellington created with clarinetist Jimmy Hamilton during the tour of Japan. The remaining three were composed by Ellington for the 1966 recording dates.

Another majestic ballad from Strayhorn almost steals the show. *Isfahan* had nothing to do with the Middle East at the point of its conception but was simply given a new name and inserted because the music is so good. The tempo is just a whisker faster than *The Star-Crossed Lovers*, though it is hard to imagine that sensual lingering has ever been expressed in music as delightfully as it is here. Phrases extend, caesuras stretch out, ideas repeat with slight yet nimble difference, and Hodges's operatic presence brings every harmonic-melodic dodge to its maximum potential. Contributing to the magic are the inner lines of the sax section, smaller wheels of chromatic sparkle spinning inside the more majestic arc of Hodges's line. When the time comes for him to ascend to an anguished climax the whole band joins in full support.

If *Isfahan* is not quite the show stealer that *The Star-Crossed Lovers* was for *Such Sweet Thunder*, that is because of the great material from the original group of four movements, including two from Ellington. These carry direct references to music the two composers heard on their 1963 tour. *Amad* and *Depk* are two of my favorites among compositions firmly attributed to Ellington during the 1960s. Both are superb ensemble pieces, with rhythmic verve and harmonic intensity. *Amad* has long stretches of static harmony, an allusion to Middle Eastern music. After the introduction the piece clicks into a strong groove based on a two-note riff, with the orchestra adding layers and moving through call-and-response figures. This is Ellington at his earthiest, the band popping with excitement. Lawrence Brown's caravanesque trombone solos represent a Muslim call to prayer. *Depk* is more harmonically traditional in an Ellingtonian sense, with nicely paced modulations and effective spurs of dissonance from the leader. Inspired by a wedding dance from Jordan, it moves with spirited ease between four-bar, six-bar, and three-bar groupings, then kicking into triple meter. This is all pulled off with polish and elegance, none of it sounding contrived. Ellington's piano playing for both of these pieces shows why he was often considered to be the most important member of the rhythm section.

Ellington recalled the origin of Strayhorn's *Bluebird of Delhi*. A mynah liked to come around the window of Strayhorn's hotel room. "He was always talking to it," Ellington remembered, 'How are you today? Good morning! Do you want something to eat?'" There exists an ancient tradition in classical music of imitating birds, but I'm not sure how many of them convey this level of crisp vitality. Part of what gives the call such vivid definition is the harmonic setting, which can be described as "bitonal," another trick from the high modernist workbench (and not at all foreign to Ellington), here presented as exotic mimesis. As the movement unfolds, the bird, played by clarinetist Jimmy Hamilton, relaxes a bit, flies around and checks things out, turns corners of adventure, rips into a peak of exaltation, and restates its exotic call for the finish.

Strayhorn's *Agra* is named after the location of one of the most inspiring architectural monuments in the world, the Taj Mahal. The structure was built by the fifth Mughal emperor as a tomb for his favorite wife, Mumtaz Mahal, who died during childbirth. The connection between Strayhorn's music and the architecture is more mysterious than what arose from Whistler's misty brushstrokes, Tchaikovsky's ballet score, and Shakespeare's mischievous Puck. He decided to feature Harry Carney, who delivers one of his greatest performances, an outpouring of expressive timbral nuance. Carney's baritone sax is appropriately weighty for this topic, but the music is also moody and somewhat enigmatic, with flickering changes of mode. Most of the piece is built around a drone, again a reference to music from the region. In contrast, the stunning introduction intertwines a series of climbing harmonies, full of tension, carried by Carney's effusive saxophone.

These pieces from Strayhorn are among his last. In 1964 he was diagnosed with cancer. Composing and arranging over the next couple of years was sporadic. In June 1965 a concert devoted to his music was presented in Manhattan, with the composer himself at the piano, performing with Clark Terry, Bob Wilber, Willie Ruff, and others. The concert, wrote critic Dan Morgenstern in *DownBeat*, demonstrated "that Strayhorn is much more than Ellington's alter ego . . . Everything he plays is invested with a rare sense of form and development . . ." One of the last numbers he revised, a ballad for Hodges, was grimly named *Blood Count*. The end came on May 31, 1967.

At the funeral Ellington spoke eloquently about his colleague's "freedoms"—"freedom from hate, unconditionally; freedom from self-pity . . . freedom from fear of possibly doing something that might help another more than it might himself; and freedom from the kind of pride that could make a man feel he was better than his brother or neighbor." Strayhorn's family had difficulty gaining ownership of his musical manuscripts, however, with Ellington's sister Ruth claiming them for the Ellington business, Tempo Music. "Billy worked for Edward. Therefore, his work was rightfully Edward's," she explained. That's how things looked to the Ellingtons. She had watched Strayhorn enter Ellington's life and watched him leave it twenty-eight years later, so she had an informed perspective.

In the seven years Ellington lived after Strayhorn's death, his stature just kept growing. Strayhorn's illness inspired him to reflect on his own mortality, yielding a "Concert of Sacred Music" that was performed in September 1965 at Grace Cathedral in San Francisco. A video recording of the whole concert, made for television, can easily be located on the web. The concert mainly features revisions of old material. When Hodges performs *Come Sunday* you can almost see the golden light of the Holy Spirit streaming down on his upturned, concentrated gaze. Gospel singer Queen Esther Marrow is followed by jazz singer Jon Hendricks and the Grace Cathedral Choir. Ellington's modest and humble lyrics move between biblical quotations and more universal messages. Virtually all of the music carries a grandeur that soars in the cathedral setting. For the exciting conclusion Ellington brought out tap dancer Bunny Briggs, put him in counterpoint with a scatting Hendricks, and framed him by the choir and the jazz orchestra for an up-tempo arrangement of *Come Sunday* that he named *David Danced Before the Lord*. The Sacred Concerts stand as a spectacular example of Ellington's conceptual power. Mixing secular and sacred music was hardly new in the African American tradition, but the way he put the whole thing together was tremendously effective. Sacred Concerts became his primary creative outlet during the last years, with extensively new and revised versions for the Cathedral of Saint John the Divine in New York City, Westminster Abbey in London, and many other places.

The Sacred Concerts seemed to put Ellington at the center of all African American culture, and with the mid-1960s victories for civil rights this was a position of tremendous symbolic value. He was no longer just the leader of and composer for the greatest jazz band in history, but someone who embodied the best of African American cultural history. Like a king, he symbolized everything that was good—nobility, dignity, loyalty, equanimity, elegance,

4.5 Sacred Music Concert with Lena Horne, December 1965, Fifth Avenue Presbyterian Church, New York City

aspiration, optimism, perseverance, resilience, confidence, daring, originality, intellect, brilliance, and transcendence.

He was invited several times to the White House, where his father had worked as a servant. Honorary doctorate degrees streamed in. The Ellington canon stood as an unmatched accomplishment. It meant different things to different parts of the population, and it carried special significance for jazz musicians, fans, and advocates. With rock and pop music exploding in popularity and with jazz patronage struggling, Ellington was the best possible person to validate the entire tradition. His accomplishment was clearly equal to any cultural achievement anywhere, without apology.

But among all the possible meanings of the Ellington phenomenon that were embraced during these triumphant years the idea that he occupied the driving center of a creative collective was usually missing. The essential members of the collective were relegated to the shadows, from which they might emerge briefly but not too long or with too much emphasis. The king absorbs everything. The idea that Ellington's best work depended on collaboration was far from anyone's mind.

Two sleights of hand had to be performed over and over again by Ellington's publicists and by hosts of writers. First was the willful ignoring of collaborative realities. Second was a set of lexical acrobatics over the word "composer" and the assertion that this creative activity was distinct from what soloists, improvisers, and arrangers did. Both relate directly to the legacy of the ring shout, where the impulse to explore all openings for creative agency flourished. There is a long history of distinguishing Ellington from mere tunesmiths on the one hand and mere jazz improvisers, who are not composing in "the real sense of the word" (Hodeir) or are not composing at all (C. Lambert). And the biggest distinction those worried about his status had to firm up is between the jazz composer and the jazz arranger. These rigid boundaries have been essential for the Western notion of the great composer, but they were fairly useless in jazz. The groundwork was laid in New Orleans, where Buddy Bolden improvised blues to make his mark, Joe Oliver tinkered with collective improvisation, and Louis Armstrong worked over his solos until he got them the way he wanted them. Early jazz in New Orleans overflowed with performer-centered creativity.

Even though commercial pressures from copyright and marketplace distinction brought greater interest in compositional definition, the blurring of these creative categories remained commonplace. This practical reality has hardly been limited to jazz. You can find it in James Brown's funk ensembles, in Richard Smallwood's gospel ensembles, and throughout traditions that were shaped by the legacy of the ring shout.

What were Ellington's greatest skills? Certainly a knack for instrumentation. He gained mastery of the three-minute form, and he was daring about organizing his material. Like so many jazz musicians, he was fascinated with harmony. Schuller insisted that harmony was, in fact, "his strongest suit."

Or, we could say that his strongest suit was *maximizing the creative potential of his musicians in the service of compositional definition*. At age twenty-seven, the failed composer discovered a new way to generate fresh music by extending material from his soloists through framing and conceptualizing, nipping and tucking, harmonizing, and arranging and enhancing with contrast and form. He spent the rest of his life relentlessly plumbing collaborative practice for every possible scrap of value. He got the best of his musicians' melodies, the best of their arranging ideas, the best of their editing, the best of their creative use of timbre, and the best of their fully formed compositions. To that he added whatever seemed to fit and the whole enterprise soared. The genius collaborator kept the whole thing miraculously going for forty-some years, through a combination of business savvy, interpersonal skills, creative daring, and determination that truly put him, his band, and his music beyond category.

○　○　○

Across the Atlantic, in the late 1950s, another group of musicians stumbled into an equally successful approach to creative collaboration. They had even less contact with the African American musical vernacular than Ellington had when he was growing up. Nevertheless, it was the basis for the music they made together. Their provincial town in the north of England was a port with historic connections to the United States, and the timing was right. Postwar, working-class Liverpudlians found much to admire from the United States, and the communal verve of the ring-shout legacy made its mark. It would have been difficult to script their unlikely story in a novel and make it believable, but such are the quirks of history.

PART II

The Beatles

CHAPTER 5

EARLY BEATLES *and*
ROCK AND ROLL

"Warmed-Over Soup"

IN THIS BOOK I make the case for a series of indirect connections
between the Duke Ellington Orchestra and the Beatles, connections
that emerged from patterns in musical-social history and shaped noteworthy results—creative collaboration to an extraordinary degree,
the merger of compositional vision with vernacular music-making,
and the combination leading to music so compelling and distinctive
that it looms very large in the history of twentieth-century music.
The connections follow historic parallels between jazz and rock and
roll. Both started out close to the vernacular "base." Both drew from
participatory music-making that spread through slavery like the fire
of the Holy Spirit and continued to inspire African Americans for
many generations.

Blues composer W. C. Handy (*St. Louis Blues, Memphis Blues*)
had an epiphany around 1905. In Cleveland, Mississippi, he heard
a small band of guitar, mandolin, and bass playing what he called
"over-and-over strains," with no distinct beginning and no predetermined end, just cycle after cycle of repetitive music that invited
improvisation and got people moving. Handy had been taught as a
child how to sight-read complicated classical music using do-re-mi
solfege. But when he saw the donation hat for the small band in

Cleveland fill up with silver dollars, he learned a lesson about musical markets.

Improvisatory treatment of a well-known tune, based on a single strain played many times, was standard practice for dance music on the plantations, typically little string bands of violin, guitar, and bass viol. If Handy had lived long enough to drop by the Crawdaddy Club in London in 1963, he would have been amused by a string band of British teenagers who called themselves the Rolling Stones whipping fans "into a tribal-like frenzy" as they played a song by the Mississippi guitarist Bo Diddley for forty-five minutes. Somehow, the over-and-over approach had sprouted in staid London, where one writer even trotted out the old "jungle music" put-down.

New Orleans, with its wind instruments, was the center of early jazz, and the string lineage that evolved into rock and roll took off in nearby Mississippi as African American musicians figured out how to use the guitar to their advantage. In the 1940s the crackle of electricity gave blue notes, hard initial attack, and the fixed and variable format a fresh and snappy postwar, migratory identity. John Lee Hooker, from Coahoma County, Mississippi, recorded *Boogie Chillen'* (1948) with his new electric guitar. When Muddy Waters landed in Chicago from Issaquena County his sister teased him that his acoustic guitar was hopelessly out of fashion. Blues presented a big range of possibilities, but there was always the option of making a virtue out of simplicity. Howlin' Wolf, from White Station, Mississippi, recorded *Moanin' at Midnight* (1951) with one chord, repeated riffs, heterophony, and a traditional melodic profile of descending "sawtooth" design: the song reached number ten on the rhythm and blues (the new name for race recordings) charts. Muddy Waters did something similar at a slower tempo with *Hoochie Coochie Man* (1954). Early rock and roll was connected to the blues and also to the Sanctified Church, the training ground for "Little Richard" Penniman as it had been for Louis Armstrong a few decades earlier. Penniman recorded

Tutti Frutti in New Orleans in 1955, aiming to capture some of the excitement of Ray Charles's *I Got a Woman*, with its overt gospel leanings. Penniman gave up rock and roll for the ministry a few years later, brought back into the fold by reformed rocker Joe Lutcher, whose hits included *Rockin' Boogie* (1948).

Like the word "jazz" in its early years, "rock and roll" was associated with sex, which made radio broadcasters hesitant to use it at first. Rock and roll was an impertinent but down-home alternative to the golden age of jazz sophistication, with simple chords, simple riffs, rough voices, and conventional melody types. Novelty records created a crack of an opening into the white market. "If I could find a white man who had the Negro sound and the Negro feel, I could make a million dollars," quipped record producer Sam Phillips.

Rock and roll reset the relationship between white popular music and the black vernacular. The result was a double-wave pattern in the broad sweep of music history in the United States, as if everything started all over again relative to the 1917 explosion of jazz, with a flagrant return to amateur participation, easy to learn and perform, fun to move to, and clearly connected to African Americans. This explains the startling consistency in institutional ridicule of early jazz and rock and roll, the same condemning terms used again and again—"primitive," "jungle," "basement," "Negro threat," and allusions to sexual degeneracy.

Jazz musicians smugly noted the distance their music had traveled—distance upward—since its humble origins. Strayhorn turned out a droll arrangement of *I Want to Hold Your Hand* for the Ellington Orchestra. Dizzy Gillespie made his way to the Beatles' dressing room at their Ed Sullivan debut, asked for autographs, and then announced that he planned to swap them for two Count Basie records. "I haven't come to hear you," he needled, "I just want to get a good look at you."

Jazz and rock have stayed around so long because the basis for each idiom turned out to be so flexible. In the 1950s a fresh style, audibly connected to amateur practice, again emerged from the African American community and conquered the nation. Neither trajectory has yet been exhausted. Early rock and roll was a baseball cap turned backward, a light embrace of African American danger. Black music and dance became youthful white weapons of choice for a fresh round of generational warfare, with victories measured in terms of peer-group bonding, independence of taste, and sexual liberation, all fueled by unprecedented levels of teenage consumerism.

White interest could go deep, just as it did in the 1920s with Mezz Mezzrow and the alligators. "Actually I think we both wanted to be black," said songwriter Jerry Leiber, referring to his composing partner Mike Stoller. "Black people had a better time. As far as we were concerned, the worlds we came from were drab by comparison. I was alienated from my own culture and searching for something else." Leiber and Stoller hung out in black neighborhoods and dated black women. Their reach for black authenticity produced a string of hits, from *Hound Dog* to *Stand by Me*. As a teenage misfit in Port Arthur, Texas, Janis Joplin took refuge in black music and local beatniks. She preferred Willie Mae Thornton's *Hound Dog* to Elvis's. Her sister Laura reported that Janis thought of herself as the "first white-black person." Since she knew very few black people, her imagined identity was formed through listening to records. Johnny Otis, a son of Greek immigrants who got into every possible dimension of the R and B world, grew up in a largely black neighborhood in Berkeley, California, and decided as a teenager that "if our society dictated that one had to be either black or white, I would be black."

Rock and roll instantly diversified, just as jazz had during the 1920s. In *Good Rockin' Tonight* (1948), Wynonie Harris delivered a mellow, seductive voice over an easygoing boogie-woogie, with hand clapping in the background conjuring a participatory atmosphere. Elvis Presley (1954) bumped up the tempo and covered the song with a melodrama of shifting vocal timbres, from high and edgy to low and smooth. Pat Boone, second only to Elvis in rock and roll sales, tamed and softened his covers of black hits with "legitimate" diction, tone, and phrasing. Boone recorded Fats Domino's *Ain't That a Shame*, then Little Richard's raucous *Tutti Frutti*. Richard sometimes dressed on stage as the Queen of England, but Boone's clean persona inspired General Motors to hire him as their spokesman. Elvis, Bill Haley, the Everly Brothers, Buddy Holly, and the Beatles all covered Little Richard. White taming of black music was not uniform. There were many ways to do it. The phenomenon was built into the social structure of the United States with its felt need to keep African Americans subservient, a people with nothing to lose and a great deal of musical splendor to offer.

Elvis turned out to be good not just at singing the black man's music but also dramatic intensity, a combination that brilliantly articulated youthful rebellion. In Hibbing, Minnesota, Bob Dylan heard Elvis and felt like he "wasn't going to work for anybody and nobody was going to be my boss. Hearing him for the first time was like busting out of jail." Lennon said almost the same thing to a friend in Liverpool. Teenage rebellion in the 1950s was largely inarticulate, a feeling more than an ideology. It clustered around a set of images, James Dean, motorcycles, Teddy Boy suits, and the juvenile delinquents in *Blackboard Jungle* who snapped their fingers to rock and roll when they weren't smashing the jazz records from the 1920s that their teacher lovingly collected, music that was, ironically, rebellious when it was originally created but now (in the movie at least) occupied a bourgeois niche of conventionality and respect.

Vaguely articulate also was the inseparability of rock and roll as racial and sexual taboo. Dancing was safer than riding a motorcycle but thrilling nevertheless. This is what Pat Boone was softening almost to the point of surface disappearance, while Elvis flagrantly flashed it. "Rock and roll has its place, among the colored people," acknowledged U.S. Congressman Emanuel Celler, but Elvis's hip shaking violated "all that I know to be in good taste." In a moment of candor Elvis concurred: "The colored folks been singing it and playing it just like I'm doing now, man, for more years than I know . . . I got it from them. Down in Tupelo, Mississippi, I used to hear old Arthur Crudup bang his box the way I do now . . ."

Each Beatle stressed the importance of *Heartbreak Hotel*, the big bang that reached across the ocean in May 1956. Elvis sounded like he was about to jump off the hotel roof. "When I first heard *Heartbreak Hotel*, I could hardly make out what was being said," remembered Lennon. "It was just the experience of hearing it and having my hair stand on end."

"It was the way [Presley] sings it as if he is singing from the depths of hell," added McCartney.

Then came *Hound Dog*, with machine-gun snare drum, vibrant polyrhythmic groove, participatory hand clapping, and formal simplicity, Elvis snarling on the blue third like no white singer had ever done before, at least in Lennon's experience. Nineteen fifty-six became the year of Elvis, and Lennon was floating: "Before Elvis there was nothing," was how he felt.

Relative to early jazz, the rock and roll reset was marked by a different set of instruments, with electric guitars replacing the New Orleans winds, and there was also a difference in function: early jazz was instrumental and dance oriented, while rock and roll was simultaneously a genre of song and dance. Unlike Ellington, the Beatles were focused only on songs. When critics wanted to invoke classical music in their praise of Ellington they dropped names like Ravel and Bartók; with the Beatles it was Schubert and Schumann, two masters of songs.

The song orientation of rock and roll combined with its Everyman aura to create the singer-composer. Rock and roll turned away from the fancy lyrics, chords, forms, and melodies of the professional songwriters and thrived on lack of pretense, with no need for bourgeois legitimation. There is not much that separates a poppish rock song like McCartney's *Can't Buy Me Love* from jazz songs by the Gershwin brothers, as Ella Fitzgerald, the master of *The Great American Songbook*, must have realized when she covered it immediately after its release. The main difference is lack of any trace of pretentiousness. Buddy Holly and Chuck Berry were the primary singer-composer models for Lennon and McCartney, followed by Roy Orbison and Fats Domino. Anybody could write a rock-and-roll song. That was the message, and no one was happier to receive it than two teenagers from Liverpool.

Lennon, McCartney

"We've been playing this music for eight years," Lennon observed in 1964, identifying what musicologists call a "style period." Decades form an easy way to bring history's limitless sprawl under control, but Lennon's periodization cuts right across. It seems natural to track music in the 1950s and '60s, but for him the important boundary was 1956, the year of Elvis.

We could say, from a developmental point of view, that Lennon was born (1940) to rebel. His parents were both fun-loving slackers. The first five years of his life were unstable, with his father Alfred mostly absent and his mother Julia absent often enough, her sisters filling the void. In 1946 sister Mimi asserted custody rights, declaring Julia an unfit mother and demonstrating the sturdiness of her own situation, with a husband whose family owned a business and a comfortable home. John became the ward of his aunt and uncle before his sixth birthday.

Mimi's four-bedroom home, named "Mendips," was solidly middle class, a notch or two (or maybe three in the case of Starr) above the other Beatles in comfort and opportunity. A visit to the Lennon and McCartney homes in Liverpool today, supplemented by a peek at the exteriors of homes lived in by Harrison and Starr, is the most eye-opening Beatles pilgrimage one can make. Lennon was born low but raised considerably higher than the other

5.1 Lennon's childhood home, Mendips, with acoustically resonant vestibule

three, which still surprises many people, especially the comparison with McCartney.

Lennon always spoke well of Mimi, though others criticized her unreasonable expectations, irrational outbursts, and haughty condescension. Uncle George was a softy, alcoholic but easygoing, which must have made Mimi feel even more the need to drive the child toward achievement and decorum. It all went well enough during his preteen years. He and Uncle George read the newspaper together every night. The child put his aunt's full bookshelves to good use, and by age ten he was familiar with Edgar Allan Poe, James Thurber, Robert Louis Stevenson, and (his favorite) Lewis Carroll. Childhood friend Pete Shotton said that "John's ultimate ambition was to one day write an *Alice* himself." Mimi remembered him being fond of Balzac and insisted that she could note that influence in his mature songwriting. The two talked about literature and he embellished for her the stories he had read, using his strong imagination. He loved to draw satirical cartoons and caricatures. He relied heavily on friends for emotional support. "He always had to have a partner," remembered Shotton. "He never could abide the thought of getting stuck out on his limb all by himself."

The inheritance of outsider tendencies from his parents, the tensions of the first five years of his life, Mimi's authoritarian dominance—all of this was more than enough to generate a rebellious adolescence. He was impulsive, creative, easily bored, out of sync with conventional paths of achievement, a risk taker. When he reached his teens Julia reappeared and provided extra fuel. A witty person who loved music and dance, she felt no obligation to monitor her son's progress toward middle-class respectability, leaving good times as the basis for their renewed relationship. She bought him his first guitar and encouraged his interest in rock and roll. He told a story about lying in bed with her, fully clothed, around age fourteen, accidentally touching her breast and wondering to himself if more was possible. She was ambiguous, definitely a friend, vaguely a mother, not really a parent. "At heart," his stepsister wrote, "Julia was still almost a teenager herself who easily identified with John and his friends." One of John's friends remembered her playing guitar and singing for them the bawdy *Maggie May*, a folk song from Liverpool that had become the latest hit by the Vipers Skiffle Group (produced by George Martin for Parlophone). Lennon's first band, the Quarrymen, covered the song and the Beatles did too on the album *Let It Be*.

As a teenager he was trouble at school and in the streets. "I did my best to disrupt every friend's home," he remembered. Some detention sheets from Quarry Bank High School show Lennon written up for "sabotage," "just no interest whatsoever," and "repeated misconduct." "Even I sometimes worried that he seemed destined for Skid Row," admitted Shotton. He wore the stylish "Teddy Boy" clothes that made boys look tough. And he was magnetic. George Harrison remembered him as, in the early days, something like an army sergeant who inspires soldiers through the sheer force of personality to march to their deaths. "He had a lot of power," Harrison explained. His close mates were usually younger, which automatically sorted out the matter of who would be the leader. He specialized in daggers of wit that constantly deflated what others took seriously.

Lennon said that rock and roll saved him, but it was skiffle that turned him and everyone else he knew in that redeeming direction. Lonnie Donegan's *Rock Island Line*, one of the first records he purchased, sold three million copies in 1955 and 1956. Donegan pounded on his guitar and howled, a vigorous antidote to bourgeois conformity. He had stylistic connections to African American music and in this song took Huddie "Lead Belly" Ledbetter as his model. It was easy to form a skiffle band, with a couple of guitars and a washboard, then kazoo, broom-handle bass, comb, and waxed paper added as desired. Lennon insisted that Shotton pick up the washboard, even though he was devoid of musical ability: "Of course you can take part, anyone can," Lennon told him. There was absolutely no pretense. You learned a few simple chords and started playing together, a noisy but happy pastime for a street gang. Some five thousand skiffle bands popped up across the United Kingdom in 1956.

"The guitar's all right, but you'll never earn your living with it," lectured Mimi in words that are now legendary, but that warning was surely repeated by countless parents over the next fifteen years. When he failed O-level exams, she scurried to get him into the Liverpool College of Art as a last resort.

The standards for getting into art schools were loose, "somewhere they put you if they can't put you anywhere else," as Lennon remembered it. In Chapter 1, I suggested that the talents of both Ellington and Lennon as visual artists had something to do with their abilities to freshly conceptualize what a piece of music could be. It has been well established how the institution of British art schools helped turn rock and roll in England away from

American models and toward the 1960s construction of "rock," a white genre with aspirations more complicated than those of its American antecedents. Lennon stands at the head of a long and important list of British rockers who attended art schools—Keith Richards, Jimmy Page, Ray Davies, Pete Townshend, Eric Clapton, Syd Barrett, and many others.

In the 1950s jazz was the bohemian music of choice for art students in England, just as it was for beatniks in the United States. But with his allegiance to rock and roll—and with limited performing skills—Lennon couldn't stand jazz. His most important contact at art school was Stuart Sutcliffe. The two were close friends and shared an apartment. Sutcliffe was the real deal, a talented painter who embraced the visual avant-garde. He introduced Lennon to Impressionism, to the heroic, outsider status of Van Gogh, and to Kerouac, Corso, and Ferlinghetti. Lennon in turn dragged Sutcliffe into his rock-and-roll band, insisting as he had with Shotton that lack of talent was no obstacle. After Sutcliffe left the band in 1962, Lennon confided to a friend, "Me best mate, actually. I miss him not being around, even though he was rubbish on the bass."

Rock and roll in Britain was framed as a youthful opportunity to stick it to middle- and high-brow pretentiousness, and it also represented the United States. "Are We Turning Our Children into Little Americans?" worried a headline. Rock and roll was energetic youth music from the wealthiest, most powerful, most modern country in the world, so what was there for a British teenager not to like? "I was brought up on Americana," Lennon insisted. The genre could not be anything but American, but just to sharpen the point the Beatles sang "She loves you, yeah, yeah, yeah" with American slang, prompting McCartney's father to quip, "Why not yes, yes, yes?"

On their first plane trip across the Atlantic, a nervous McCartney raised the question, "Why should we be over there making money? They've got their own groups. What are we going to give them that they don't already have?" That says a lot about the orientation of the early Beatles.

What it meant for rock and roll to be associated with African Americans in young Liverpool minds is harder to pin down. The Beatles were generous in their praise of black musicians, but they could not have been very clear about what it meant to be black in the United States, culturally or politically, or even who was who. They initially thought Buddy Holly was black, for example. Lennon was no Jerry Leiber or Janis Joplin, imagining himself as a white-black person. When he heard Little Richard's *Long Tall Sally* in 1956, the song hit him as powerfully as Elvis did, but he had bought into Elvis's hero status so completely that he had difficulty accepting any rivals. "How could they both be happening in my life, *both* of them?" he remembered. The conflict dissolved when he found out that Richard was black, which automatically, he later acknowledged with regret, set the hierarchy straight, Elvis still on top.

○   ○   ○

By 1955, Paul McCartney (b. 1942) had moved with his family to a council house a little more than a mile from Mendips. Though the family struggled financially, McCartney grew up in an environment that was warm and secure. He had a good relationship with his father, Jim, who offered an example of how to incorporate music into a stable life. Jim worked for a cotton trading company—one of many connections between Liverpool and the New World—went to bed at 10 p.m. every night, and abstained from alcohol. His wife, Mary, worked part time as a midwife. Jim supplemented his income playing piano in a little dance band and he even wrote a few tunes. The home piano was the center of weekly gatherings for the extended family, everyone standing around and singing along. Mary hoped her son would become a doctor. His father remembered how, as a boy, Paul "seemed to have the sort of mind that could easily grasp things that used to take a lot of concentration from other boys." He was a clever mimic.

Yet during his midteen years he stubbornly turned antischool and had to be held back, taking classes with boys a full year younger. He shared with the other two of the "original three" this trajectory of disenchantment. Harrison was also held back, while Lennon was so far gone that being held back must have seemed hopeless. Harrison once explained how he "loved my association with John and Paul because I had something in me which I recognized in them—which they must have or could have recognized in me, which is why we ended up together." The most direct way to gloss that statement is that they were each intelligent yet determined not to succeed in school. "Now there were three of us who thought the same," remembered Lennon. Family ties were strong enough to keep them from becoming completely alienated. They turned their backs on institutional paths of success and embraced rock and roll. "They were such a gang of rebels," said one friend who turned down an invitation to play bass guitar with the group. "They didn't care about anything."

Paul was introduced to the piano by his father, then ukulele by a cousin, followed by trumpet, and then, in the glow of skiffle and Elvis, to the guitar at age fourteen. His father did not feel threatened by the new music; he even hooked up a speaker extension so that Paul could listen to Radio Luxembourg, the primary source of rock and roll, in his bedroom. But by this time McCartney had already absorbed some of his father's musical tastes for popular music from the 1920s and '30s. "I grew up steeped in that music-hall tradition," he remembered—songs like *I'll Build a Stairway to Paradise, Chicago (That Toddlin' Town)*, and *After You've Gone. When I'm 64*, composed around age sixteen, emerged directly from that connection. He was passionate about rock and roll and it served a social purpose in his peer group, but he never would have said, as Lennon did, that before Elvis there was nothing. By the time he met Lennon he had already put together a notebook of his own songs. His father tried to get him to study formally but he resisted. Like Irving Berlin, he never learned to read music.

Around age fifteen McCartney won a talent contest at a summer camp singing *Tutti Frutti* in imitation of Little Richard. If this had happened in the hills of Virginia we would understand it in terms of blackface minstrelsy, but it is hard to extend that label to a fifteen-year-old whose experience with black people was slight or nonexistent. (Yet England was the birthplace of blackface minstrelsy, and *The Black and White Minstrel Show*, complete with blackface makeup, was a favorite on British television from 1958 all the way to 1978.) When his father heard the imitation he was nonplussed. He didn't realize until much later, when the Beatles were touring with Little Richard himself, how accurate it was; he thought his son had been making it all up.

The main point is that at age fifteen McCartney was performing a parody. He was not finding a place for himself in a tradition but articulating distance from it. Within a few years that had changed and *Long Tall Sally* became a featured number for him, a showstopper at the Cavern, in Liverpool. With African American music there must have often been, in the experience of British musicians and fans during these years, a back and forth between parody and something more normalized—or something vaguely in between. This is important to remember when we think about differently configured meanings for rock and roll in England, relative to the United States.

If McCartney had developed as a composer without Lennon and without the collaboration of the band, he might have turned out to be the Berlin or Gershwin of rock and roll. Like them, he worked in a song idiom built around African American musical markers of light syncopation and light blue notes. Unlike them, however, but like Ellington, he developed as a collaborative composer and as a composer-performer.

On July 6, 1957, Lennon's group the Quarrymen played at a

church festival, and McCartney stopped by to check them out. He watched as Lennon forgot the lyrics for *Come Go with Me*, and he admired his ability to make up new ones. Afterward, he introduced himself. He borrowed Lennon's guitar, showed him how to tune it, and played Eddie Cochran's *Twenty Flight Rock*, all the chords and all the lyrics, followed by a Little Richard medley. The basic terms of their relationship were instantly set in place: verbal facility and leadership meeting strong musical chops and performing confidence. McCartney soon joined the band. The drummer remembered McCartney telling him what to play during his very first rehearsal. He started biking over to Lennon's house, where he was impressed by the bookshelves and by Lennon's ability to put a typewriter in motion. Mimi didn't approve of Paul's inferior class position and Jim didn't approve of John, obviously a troublemaker.

They liked to hang out in the little vestibule at Mendips, exercising its bright acoustics. They figured out chords for songs

5.2 McCartney and Lennon at the Casbah Club in Liverpool, 1958

like *Blue Moon*, and McCartney added vocal harmony, just as his father had taught him and as he liked to do with his brother, Mike. Partnering like this became commonplace as teenagers sunk into the straightforward pedagogy of the music: listen to a recording over and over, figure out the chords on the guitar, and start singing. Their relationship was built into the participatory ethos of rock and roll. Anyone could jump in, which meant that there would be a lot to learn from one another. Lennon showed his younger friend a little book he had put together with his own stories and cartoons, so McCartney brought along his own little book of self-composed songs, with lyrics written out, chords identified by letter name, title at the top. "He was already more of a songwriter than me when we met," remembered Lennon. McCartney soon began a notebook for their joint efforts, and he wrote "Another Lennon-McCartney Original" across the top of each page.

On July 15, 1958, Lennon's mother Julia was struck down and killed by a drunk driver. He remembered being "frozen inside"; it was years before he was able to talk about her death. McCartney had lost his own mother on October 31, 1956. The tragedies brought the two teenagers closer to each other. The fourteen-year-old McCartney had dealt with his pain by composing *I Lost My Little Girl*, which he later described as "a corny little song based on three chords." It must have been obvious to his father that the song was not an innocent tale of romance but a sublimation of grief. Ten years later Lennon explicitly lamented the loss of his mother in *Julia*, a tender and vulnerable exposure, an unprecedented song that wove poetic nuggets from Kahlil Gibran into a delicate proclamation of love. Lennon's breakthrough probably inspired McCartney's *Let It Be*, which alludes to mystical visits from "mother Mary." The differences between *Julia* and *Let It Be* speak to the differences between the two composers in 1968, one looking for personalized expression, the other less confessional and more universal, more formal in both senses of the word (musical form and formal decorum), disguising his autobiographical reference as a hymn to the Blessed Virgin of his mother's Catholic faith. This series of songs captures a lot about their relationship, one leading, then the other, in different ways at different times and with different results.

They brought their phrases and tunes to each other and found ways to create together, as they would continue to do all the way through 1969. A few of them had potential—*One After 909*, *Love Me Do*, *P.S. I Love You*, and *I'll Follow the Sun*. Lennon's acceptance of McCartney's musical superiority formed one basis for their twelve-year partnership. "Paul was always more advanced than I was," he remembered. "He was always a couple of chords ahead and his songs usually had more chords in them. His dad played the piano—he was always playing pop and jazz standards and Paul picked things up from him." Lennon's verbal facility was also obvious. Just as McCartney loved to doodle around with wordless melodies and chords, so did Lennon love to sketch out lyrics.

"John was always writing poetry and lyrics," remembered his aunt. "He never had a pencil out of his hand. He'd write something down, then screw up the bit of paper and throw it away and start again." Their partnership could easily have developed in another way, with McCartney poised to become the George Gershwin of rock and roll, Lennon his Ira. What made the difference was the value system of rock and roll: the musical side was simple enough to include Lennon, the lyric side simple enough to include McCartney. They both worked on music and both on words, sometimes separately, sometimes sequentially, sometimes together, finding their way toward an integrative flexibility.

Their personalities were different, too, as the world would soon realize. Lennon, slightly introverted, volatile, impatient and sarcastic, and "very tough," as Harrison put it, "had that ability to be gentle and soft and lovely but he was *acid* too. He gave that hard edge to the Beatles."

McCartney was (and is) slightly extroverted, steady, willing to revise over and over again. "John brought a biting wit, I brought commerciality and harmony," adds McCartney. A familiar image is that Lennon was inclined toward rock edginess, McCartney toward pop tunefulness. In their post-Beatles years, especially, they seem to have been so different that one has to wonder how they managed to pull off such an intimate partnership. Or to frame the question in a slightly more pointed way: how did they find common musical ground?

The answer is that they didn't have to. The 1950s found it for them.

Hi Fi and Lo Fi, White and Black, Pop and Rock

During the 1920s, jazz energized dance music, popular songs, and even symphonic music as it was adapted by musicians black and white, working for both kinds of audiences, to open up a dynamic field of creativity. Something similar occurred in the 1950s and '60s with rock and roll. Lennon and McCartney didn't have to work very hard to find a creative middle ground between rock edginess and pop prettiness because the American market they were imitating had been vigorously exploring the possibilities all through the late 1950s.

We could think of the process, as it played out in the United States, as shaped by three sets of binary pairs—hi fi and lo fi, black style and white style, pop and rock. Within the pairs, each term defined what the other was not. The three pairs overlapped, though they did not map onto each other precisely. In a loose sense the same concepts were part of the 1920s, with jazz instead of rock in the third pairing. What made commercial music in the late 1950s tick was the sheer delight in promiscuously blending the categories. Ambitious musicians found whatever advantage they could through original combinations. The possibilities were endless, though this did not undermine assumptions of categor-

5.3 Duke Ellington, Mr. Hi-Fi, Florida 1955

ical differences. These mental constructions shaped how people heard and evaluated music. There was a lot of room to find your own way, to discover your own brand of hi fi and lo fi, with certain amounts of musical whiteness and musical blackness, a virtually infinite potential for commingling.

Hi fi, a nickname for phonograph players (short for high fidelity), promised advanced technology. In order to have high fidelity on the receiving end you had to have it on the producing end, too. The larger record companies formed elaborate production models that established their products as elite. Hi fi thus became a way of conceiving music that was popular and also slightly elevated, a fresh manifestation of the American middle brow. If you listened to hi-fi music on your pricey hi fi, you were aligning yourself with wealth. My favorite nod to this comes from the *New York Times* (November 22, 1953, p. 43): "Playing records with a diamond stylus is not merely swank."

Record companies in the 1950s brought unprecedented thoroughness to this business model. When Ellington started making records in the mid-1920s, "race records" were very loosely supervised. The company cared about the style of music he recorded and about contractual details, but little else. By the 1950s they had put in place a hierarchical model with employees lined up in an efficient chain of command.

PRODUCER. The producer was in charge of everything inside the studio. Mitch Miller was probably the most famous producer of the decade. An oboe player trained at Eastman School of Music, Miller brought solid middle-brow tastes to pop recording. "I never compartmentalized it [pop versus classical] in my own mind," he said. "The same rules apply you know—taste, musicianship, balance, get the best sound out of the artists." Beatles' producer George Martin had a similar background. (His oboe teacher at the Guildhall School of Music and Drama, Margaret Eliot Asher, was also the mother of Jane Asher, Paul McCartney's main squeeze from 1963 through 1968. The Asher family introduced the untutored musician to classical music, avant-garde music, contemporary art, and much more. In other words, the high end was working on him both inside and outside the studio.)

COMPOSER. Composers of hi-fi, middle-brow music carried forward the golden age of popular song, with interesting melodic contours enhanced by a complementary flow of chords. Producers like Miller did not hesitate to tinker with the score as they saw fit—as Phil Spector would do one day with *The Long and Winding Road*, to McCartney's astonishment. The preferred musical form for hi-fi songs was AABA. The best material went into the A section; the contrasting B section, or "bridge" (Lennon and McCartney called it the "middle eight"), made the return all the more satisfying. Contrast serves to heighten beautiful design, the hi-fi composer's specialty. The melody brought the lyrics to life with magical synchrony of prosody, syntax, and meaning.

ARRANGER. Record companies in the 1950s hired their own arrangers to give them a distinct sound, just as the leading bands of the Swing Era had done. "A record is in a sense like a play," reflected Goddard Lieberson, president of Columbia Records. "It requires a beginning, a denouement and an end." Mitch Miller liked to combine instruments in unconventional ways, not as daringly as Ellington but to make a fresh statement, what he called the "sweet surprise."

STUDIO MUSICIANS. The Beatles ran smack into the institution of studio musicians at their very first recording session when Martin, dissatisfied with Pete Best's drumming and then with Best's replacement, Ringo Starr, insisted on bringing in studio drummer Andy White for *Love Me Do* (with Starr embarrassingly reassigned to tambourine). When the Beatles' image of authenticity solidified, that kind of replacement was no longer possible. Hi-fi studio musicians included backup singers, professionals with superior control of intonation, covered tone, and blend. A rare Beatles usage is the exception that proves the rule of how important vocal authenticity was for them: in *I Am the Walrus*, the Mike Sammes Singers sound completely out of place, a deliberate quirk that extends the surreal atmosphere of the song.

SINGER. Lead singers were under contract, just like actors at the big movie studios. In the early 1950s they were the biggest names in music—Bing Crosby, the Andrews Sisters, Tony Bennett, Kay Starr, Patti Page, Frank Sinatra, Nat King Cole, Peggy Lee, and so on. They had polished voices, flexible and with range, control of loud and soft, and a judiciously used vibrato. They favored the conventions of a professional singer's diction, and they delivered nicely rounded phrases. With his hit record *Cry* in 1951, Johnnie Ray hammered a crack in the wall of this vocal dominance thanks to, as Miller put it, his "unique way of sobbing through a song." He's "just selling hysteria, he's not singing," complained Patti

Page. Ray paved the way for Elvis, who brought the wall tumbling to the ground.

ENGINEERS. Sound engineers and technicians were an essential part of the hi-fi mix, taking care of overdubbing, tracking, mic selection and placement, reverb, and balance. The Beatles pushed their engineers to break rules, to make every record sound different, and they had many precedents before them. Musicologist Albin Zak identifies the 1950s as a golden age for the pop record as a creative product distinctly different from "live" musical performance. As their success and confidence grew, the Beatles got in the kitchen of the engineers and extended their creative control.

The lo-fi antipode to all of this was the specialty of small, independent recording studios, known as "indies." A lo-fi indie studio did not have to be in New York City or Los Angeles, where well-paid singers, musicians, and composers lived, but could be anywhere (Clovis, New Mexico, for example) in any kind of building (a general store, for example). Owner, producer, and engineer might all be the same person. How could a tiny indie compete with the big companies? By going in the opposite direction with a record that sounded like it was made in a garage, embracing the do-it-yourself American ethos. Everyone had more spending money in the 1950s, even young people eager to separate from their parents. It was no accident that low-budget indies became the launching pad for Everyman rock and roll.

At any point along the way, the unpretentious lo-fi alternative could turn the hi-fi profile on its head. Instead of sounding trained, polished, and with coached diction, singers sounded natural and rough, with black or hillbilly diction. Musical instruments could be identified as lo fi—harmonica and tambourine (*Love Me Do*), hand clapping (*I Want to Hold Your Hand* through *Here Comes the Sun*), a cardboard box filled with cotton instead of drums (Buddy Holly's *Not Fade Away*). There was no hi-fi arranger. Every musician simply made up his or her own part according to vernacular practice, with a sense of how each belonged to the whole, "just playing, you know, by feel," as a musician at Sun Records in Memphis put it. The over-and-over-again approach that Charles Coffin heard in Port Royal, South Carolina, and that W. C. Handy heard in Cleveland, Mississippi—"paralyzing monotony," as Mitch Miller ridiculed it when faced with declining hi-fi sales—took the place of finely tuned beginning, middle, and end. Fade-outs helped with the endings. Blues form was a strong alternative to the pleasant varieties of AABA design, perhaps even blues form straight, just one chorus after another, catchy refrains and pretty bridges nowhere in sight (Elvis's *Heartbreak Hotel* and *Hound Dog*).

Composers of lo-fi melodies did not try to compete with the careful twists and turns of the hi-fi craftsmen. There might be very little contour at all, just hovering around a single pitch or two (Buddy Knox's *Party Doll*, Lennon's *Lucy in the Sky with Diamonds*). In the area of harmony, blues once again provided a model with its three simple chords, which were not even used in the correct conservatory way. Lyrics could be stripped down to emotional outbursts, nonsense even ("tutti frutti ah rootie"), with the implication that words are trivial; what matters is the emotional intensity of the music. McCartney explained the puzzle of how the Beatles could cover a girl-group song like *Boys*, recorded by the Shirelles: "We just never even thought, 'Why is [Ringo] singing about boys?' . . . We loved the record so much that what it said was irrelevant, it was just the spirit, the sound, the feeling. The joy when you did that 'bab shoo-wap bab bab shoo-wop.' That was the great fun of doing *Boys*."

Rough and amateurish engineering could also be an asset. Electric guitar and voice are distorted in Howlin' Wolf's *Moanin' at Midnight*, as if the outpouring of emotions overwhelms the equipment. (We may assume that Lennon was aware of precedents like this when he insisted on a dash of feedback at the beginning of *I Feel Fine*.) The authenticity of amateurish production seemed like a useful strategy to George Martin when he thought to record the Beatles' first album live, in Liverpool at the Cavern. When that turned out to be impractical they recorded the whole thing in a single day back at the Abbey Road studio, saving *Twist and Shout* for the end, so that Lennon's voice would be ragged after the long day of work.

The loose structure and rough-and-ready values of rock and roll created openings for singer-composers like Chuck Berry and Buddy Holly, and the same conditions made it easy to add, subtract, and tinker with tunes. Record producers were already primed to intervene, since that was their job. The easy give-and-take of lo-fi rock and roll made this seem natural.

From the Brill Building era there are plenty of stories about collaboration among composers. Leiber and Stoller were a words-and-music team, but they routinely stepped into each oth-er's territory, something like the Gershwin brothers. Doc Pomus and Mort Shuman enjoyed the same flexibility. Songwriters who were friends across partnerships might help each other when they got into a jam. Pomus began the song *Young Blood*, for example, but it remained, in his words, "a very average hack song until Jerry and Mike helped me and did a serious rewrite." Episodes like this generated long strings of names on disc credits. Leiber and Stoller didn't like the look of that so they invented a single pseudonym ("Elmo Glick") to represent them jointly.

And it was easy to extend co-composing into recording studios. When someone walked in with "their song" it was the producer's job to recognize the good ones and turn them into hits. History overflows with conflicting accounts of who composed what, from Motown's *Money (That's What I Want)* to Percy Sledge's *When a Man Loves a Woman*. When Leiber and Stoller asked Ben E. King at the end of a session if he had any additional material, King sang a version of *Stand by Me*, inspired by some gospel songs he knew. Leiber and King fleshed out the lyrics, Stoller added standard R and B chords, a Latin bass line, and percussion, and Stoller and

Stanley Applebaum framed the results with a string arrangement. The collaborative blending of lo fi with hi fi produced gold.

Culturally speaking, no binary opposition in the history of the United States is more basic than black and white. Racialized terms of musical expression saturated the marketplace in the late 1950s, pushing and pulling products in various marketing directions. For many this must have been subliminal: few dancers at the local hop thought of themselves as the first white-black people in their towns. But that does not mean it was irrelevant. They were not just shaking their hips. "If I hadn't seen [the Beatles] I'd never have dreamed they were white," gushed Little Richard in 1962. "They have a real authentic Negro sound." Even if Richard was chuckling to himself a little when he made that observation, he was pointing to something important about the creation and reception of their music.

One way to approach the topic is through the distribution of stylistic features. If a performance has clear markers of black vocal style, with lots of blue notes, "worrying" pitch, conversational phrasing, strained timbre, sawtooth melodic prototype, or gospel-style melismas; if the fixed and variable model is strongly cast as a way to organize rhythm; if the performance follows a musical form of successive choruses with no hook and no bridge; if it uses few chords or standard blues chords, or standard gospel chords; if it includes heterophony, call and response, or riffs; if it features vocal effects on an instrument; if it conjures a participatory atmosphere with hand clapping, tambourine, spoken commentary, and call and response, all mimicking church services—if a record from the 1950s leans in these directions, you can bet on this: it was crafted by black musicians who were targeting a black audience. Every one of these features had a perceived "opposite" on the white end of the racial-musical spectrum. It was easy for musicians to blend it all together for expressive purposes or sales or both, thus generating what more than one writer from the 1950s called "mongrels."

Because the voice is so personal, singing was heavily loaded. Muddy Waters sang what he called "deep blues," his aim being to score hits on the R and B charts; crossover did not factor. His prominent blue notes and extended displays of conversational rhythm and phrasing were points of black musical virtuosity. Whites could "play so much, run a ring around you playing guitar," he noted, "but they cannot vocal like the black man." It is true: no white singer has ever sounded like Muddy Waters. Even Chuck Berry's bending of pitch sounds modified in comparison. Lennon imitated Berry and modified further still (the connection is clear in *Carol*).

Light blue notes, judiciously sprinkled around, traveled best across the racial divide. They became a firm stylistic signature for McCartney. They are still there, ever so slight, in his elegant ballades (*Yesterday*, *Eleanor Rigby*), where they stand as the only connection to rock and roll. Gospel-style melismas, so common in R and B in the late 1950s (listen, for example, to the early Tamla/Motown singles), tended not to cross into white bands. The Beatles reserved strained vocal timbre for special cases, especially "shout" numbers in finale position. McCartney brought the house down (he was already in the basement) at the Cavern with *Long Tall Sally*. *Twist and Shout* was their preferred finale number in 1963 and 1964—it was replaced by *I'm Down*, a Little Richard imitation. Later examples include *Helter Skelter*, designed to keep up with a turn in 1968 toward rock authenticity, and *Hey Jude*, a statement of communal values enhanced by McCartney's gospel flares in the extended second half.

Jazz was where the fixed and variable model for organizing rhythm found full and virtuosic treatment in the United States. R and B tended to be much simpler, often based on the unpretentious but effective "back beat," accents on beats two and four, with cross rhythms and syncopations bouncing off that foundation. That was the model for rock and roll. During their early years the Beatles routinely add cross rhythms on bass, drums, rhythm guitar, and hand clapping, with light syncopation a standard feature of the vocals.

Chords associated with blues could also allude to black authenticity, for example, the "one chord" juiced up with a "flat seven." Rather than explain from the ground up what all of that means, I'll simply cite an example—the crackling opening of *I Saw Her Standing There*. This chord instantly locates the song on the black side of the racialized spectrum. It flies in the face of formally schooled Western harmony, with the flat seven destabilizing the home chord, normally a place of resolution. From the point of view of textbook harmony it is an aggressive move that undermines the tonal system as it was worked out in Europe over many centuries. The chord comes from a tradition that values loading a single musical gesture with as much intensity as it can handle. (Strained timbre serves the same purpose.) For blues musicians it expressed a traditional African approach to music-making. Gershwin occasionally slipped a chord like this into his elegant harmonic-melodic designs. McCartney puts it front and center in *I Saw Her Standing There*.

Just as typical for the Beatles was a gesture that was marked in the other direction, a little pop flourish at the end. *She Loves You* explodes with the energy of lo-fi American optimism, edgy syncopation, little snaps of counterrhythm, and splashing, aggressive cymbals, but the song finishes with a poppish major sixth that sits on the final chord like a maraschino cherry. The flat seventh that opens *I Saw Her Standing There* points unequivocally to black music, and this decorative sixth is a 1950s convention that points in the direction of pop. The chord confused George Martin, who told Harrison to drop it. He thought it sounded corny, like an old vaudeville flourish, but the Beatles insisted. A few years later Harrison crafted *Something* around equally poppish harmony, his melody gently dropping down to a major seventh in the first phrase to signal the sweetness of the smiling girl, the kind of detail that made *Something* a favorite of Frank Sinatra. Like the rest of their

5.4 Chuck Berry, 1950s

contemporaries, the Beatles could have things both ways. Even though *I Saw Her Standing There* begins with gritty black intensity, it ends with a mellow ninth on top of the final chord.

I Saw Her Standing There was directly inspired by Chuck Berry, the lyrics from *Little Queenie* and the opening chord, the guitar riff, and the boogie-woogie bass from *I'm Talking about You*. In Liverpool the Beatles came to be known as Chuck Berry specialists. Relative to Berry, *I Saw Her Standing There* is faster and more aggressive. McCartney's opening phrase also has more musical definition than the counterpart. Lennon added the sly suggestion that the listener knows what the singer means about the girl being just seventeen, an early example from a long list of lyric upgrades for his partner's works in progress. This is not just a better line: it is an invitation to the listener to take the song as an intimate moment of storytelling.

Musical form may seem like a dry, abstract matter that shouldn't have anything to do with racially marked culture, but it did. The bridge, the contrasting section in AABA form that makes the return to A sound fresh, pointed in the hi-fi direction, while a simple succession of blues choruses indexed vernacular practice, where the emphasis was not on elegant design but easy participation and performer-based intensity. It is not that musicians always did things one way or another, rather that these marked tendencies could be manipulated and used purposefully.

Lennon's *I Feel Fine* is a classic demonstration of the Beatles landing on the side of white pop in the area of musical form. He was inspired by a riff from *Watch Your Step* (1961), by Bobby Parker, who was in turn inspired by Ray Charles's *What'd I Say* (1959). (Lennon knew both records thoroughly and referred to *Watch Your Step* as "son of *What'd I Say*.") Listening to the recordings in chronological sequence provides a lot of insight into how the blending Beatles positioned themselves.

The first thing to do is track the riffs, where each composition began. They are obviously connected. Following Lennon's lead, Starr adapted drum patterns from the Charles and Parker recordings to combine with the riff and form a vigorous groove. In vocal qualities, the Beatles differ strikingly from their models. Charles and Parker sing with vocal ornaments that would have been at home in the black church, while Lennon delivers his melody fairly straight, with only slight blues inflections. Charles and Parker interact with their backup singers in call and response, again connecting to communal practices, while Lennon's lead is simple enough for his companions to add direct harmonies in the fashion of the Everly Brothers (just like the McCartney brothers had done at home).

But the most startling moment comes when Lennon breaks out of the verse and into the bridge ("I'm so glad . . ."). If you first listen to the Charles and Parker recordings, which have no bridge, this comes as a shock. This formal difference creates, all by itself, a huge gap between *I Feel Fine* and music more firmly aligned with the African American vernacular. It reveals the Beatles' enthusiasm for the craftsmanlike, *fait parfait* designs of the hi-fi songwriters. By 1964, Lennon and McCartney had become good at creating bridges that are not simply filler but have their own appeal.

A bridge places the melody and chords of each section in a relationship of contrast and complementary design. The bluesy vocals in *What'd I Say* and *Watch Your Step* do not emphasize variety of melodic design but instead serve as a basis for expressive blues notes, detachment from the beat, conversational delivery, and strained timbre, the kinds of things African American performers had been specializing in for centuries. AABA form, on the other hand, requires the composer to chisel out two sections, each with its own melodic-harmonic image. Putting these two formal packages alongside each other—as they frequently were on radio and on turntables—makes one sound pretty and the other raw, one decorative and the other genuine, one crafted and reserved and the other spontaneous and demonstrative. These qualities are not absolute but relational, and, as I have argued, this set of relationships was highly active during the Beatles' formative years. The Beatles liked the exciting groove of the black recordings, and they blended that with a sense of design fitting to white pop to create *I Feel Fine*.

The kind of pop, that is, that dominated the late 1950s, when the everyday magic of the indies was charming record-buying youth in the United States to the tune of two-thirds of the market for singles by 1957, causing the bloated hi-fi sector to writhe in pain. When Sinatra's record sales and television show started to tank, he let rip an infamous tirade, the hiss and snarl of a cornered rat: rock and roll, "the most brutal, ugly, desperate, vicious form of expression," was "written for the most part by cretinous goons." Those in more flexible positions found ways to adapt. Even Patti Page and Pat Boone could be marketed as rock and rollers. The sense of opposition between rock and roll and pop did not disappear, but it was also obvious that there were infinite ways to combine the two. Of our three binary oppositions, the one between pop and rock and roll was the most unstable during Lennon's style period of 1956–1964.

There was no way to control the sprawling energy of creative blending. Leiber and Stoller came to the chaotic middle from a different direction when they added strings to R and B records, their attempts initially dismissed by producer Jerry Wexler as a "radio dial picking up two stations at once." Mongrelized mixing across the triple spectrums offered a feast of creative synthesis. A creative *team* had structural advantages, an automatically larger range. A team assembled on an ad hoc basis could produce stunning results like *Stand by Me*, but a team built around tight friendships with long experience together could multiply that by one hundred.

Such was the fluid environment that Lennon and McCartney jumped into, ready to make their mark. Their success inspired them to become professional songwriters. "We were really looking at being a Rodgers and Hammerstein," remembered McCartney. His partner seems to have agreed. Asked in an early 1963 interview about his ambitions, he answered, "to write a musical," which brings one up as short as the bridge in *I Feel Fine*. What is important is not so much that he literally wanted to write a musical but to become the most famous composers of popular music in the world. The image of Lennon as a devotee of "pure" rock and roll became deeply important to him in later years, but it should not be projected too heavily onto his formative years as a composer. To the contrary, a career as the next Rodgers and Hammerstein (or alternatively, as Lennon once said, the "British Goffin and King") seemed like a glorious thing.

And for Lennon, being a professional composer meant being a collaborative composer. The group did not become "John Lennon and the Beatles" (or Johnny and the Moondogs, as they briefly were in 1959) because it was crystal clear how much the leader needed his younger friend. McCartney was to Lennon as Stuart Sutcliffe had been to him in art school, the supertalented mate who was smart enough to keep up and could bring him along professionally. Had Lennon been able to see a collaborative opening for himself in visual art in 1958, he might have gone in that direction, with Sutcliffe at his side. The art school-rock connection is not simply a biographical detail but a central part of the story of the 1960s. Musicologists Simon Frith and Howard Horne conclude that "those who were in art school brought into music making attitudes that could never have been fostered under the pressures of professional entertainment." The Beatles confirm that observation, in both a positive sense and a negative one.

For during their formative years—and really all the way through the end of 1965—Lennon and McCartney accepted the pressures of professional entertainment as a fact of life. This made them who they were. It was only after they had reaped financial rewards exceeding those of any other musician, after they had indeed become the next Rodgers and Hammerstein, that they felt secure enough to bring bohemian attitudes into their music. By then they had internalized the craft of composing popular songs so deeply that the outsider attitude came through that filter.

This internalization put them out of sync with younger, more committed art schoolers like Townshend, Clapton, and Barrett, who did not rise on the same track of pop-song mastery. By 1968, Lennon was feeling the tension acutely, and it became a primary cause of the Beatles' breakup. But in 1964 there was no such tension. It is sometimes claimed that the Beatles were Lennon's group in the beginning, then McCartney's group by *Pepper* or even *Revolver*. But McCartney won the most important victory early on when he joined Lennon to the Rodgers and Hammerstein vision. "I become whoever I'm with," Lennon said in 1975. The only way he could ever have even considered going in that direction was by hitching his wagon to McCartney. The way into this collaborative model was paved by the interactive history of African American music, a model the visual arts did not have. High on creativity and intelligence but low on discipline and training, collaboration offered Lennon his best and probably only chance.

CHAPTER 6

FOUR-HEADED
MONSTER

JAZZ AND ROCK EMERGED roughly four decades apart, two cultural explosions that altered a huge range of music. Like Ellington, the Beatles stepped into a well-formed scene and found fresh ways to collaborate. But the two groups publicly defined themselves very differently. Ellington was known as a great composer who had a canny knack for using his soloists, while the joint songwriting of Lennon and McCartney became the centerpiece of a group profile that was nonhierarchical. Mick Jagger said the Beatles were like a "four-headed monster" when he first met them, never doing anything outside of the group.

Eric Clapton agreed: "It was an odd phenomenon. They seemed to move together, and think together, it was almost like a little family unit."

"The bigger the Beatles got the closer we became," affirmed Starr.

To paraphrase Lennon, the creative collective was born in Liverpool and grew up in Hamburg, Germany. When they first arrived, in August 1960, they stepped into a highly sexualized environment of strip clubs, porn cinemas, and bordellos. Harrison described Hamburg as "the naughtiest city in the world," and Stuart Sutcliffe called it a "vast amoral jungle."

The city shaped their music through five extended stays over three years. They did whatever it took to grab the attention of drunken sailors, gangsters, strippers, and especially prostitutes, who signaled gratis interest and jostled for their attention. (Prostitutes were required to carry a clean-bill-of-health card, dubbed by the Beatles a "ticket to ride.") Their music was thus designed to generate sexual adventure. This was not a new development in music history, though the phenomenon has rarely been as streamlined as it was here. The result was a bright and energetic sound, the drive of macho male sexuality, vigorous, youthful, and instantly engaging.

They also learned to be outrageous. They acted out pretend fights, threw Nazi salutes, dressed like a cleaning woman, imitated a crippled walk, mooned the audience, played prostrate from the floor, and jumped unpredictably into the crowd. A lot of this came from Lennon, who might sing a song in his underwear or with a toilet seat around his neck. They pushed their voices to extremes. A rendition of Ray Charles's risqué *What'd I Say* might last an hour. Everything was fueled by amphetamines and alcohol, setting in place lifestyles brimming with substance use and abuse.

A small group of artsy outsider types, including Astrid Kirchherr and Klaus Voormann, befriended them. For these Germans the musicians from Liverpool seemed to resolve tensions left over from the war by bringing American music to Germany via Britain. Kirchherr invited them to her family home for meals. They were impressed by her bedroom, painted black with black carpet and black bedspread, a tree branch wrapped in aluminum foil dangling from the ceiling. The "Exis," as Lennon nicknamed Kirchherr and her friends, turned their backs on German culture and took inspiration from France, including existentialist philosophy. Kirchherr moved in with Sutcliffe and the two were engaged to be married before his untimely death from a cerebral hemorrhage in 1962. The two artists enjoyed a passionate relationship of equals, wearing each other's clothes in public and inspiring each other to create. Their relationship predicted the synergy of John and Yoko, six years later.

Kirchherr took some stunning black and white photographs of the Beatles. Their budding magnetism and tough image splendidly combined with her moody sensibility to produce an unprecedented set of documents, far removed from the typical celebrity shots of professional musicians. They are unmatched artifacts of the Hamburg years.

The Exis opened up the Beatles to a fresh set of cultural forms, mainly black leather jackets and the famous haircuts, modeled on the French and called "Caesar" haircuts. There is a story about McCartney putting on a spoof of reading poetry by Yevtushenko, as if the group were beatniks, demonstrating both an awareness of and a sense of distance from bohemian taste. How bohemian detachment played out musically is less obvious. It certainly encouraged them to wear a badge of difference, which turned out to be useful back in Liverpool between the Hamburg trips. "There was always an underlying ambition to go in a slightly artistic direction, whereas a lot of our fellow groups didn't have that," reflected McCartney. This meant willingness to explore obscure repertory and eventually offer their own compositions.

There was plenty of fun with prostitutes, and the warm friendship of the Exis was valued highly, but the main social orientation of the Beatles in Hamburg was to spend time with one another. They were young, untethered from family, friends, language, and customs, with inverted hours, threats of violence, and living conditions that were cramped, cold, and unsanitary. It was a challenge to survive, and they survived together, especially Lennon, Sutcliffe, McCartney, and Harrison, with drummer Pete Best usually off to himself. All experiences were shared, even the women. They watched as Harrison lost his virginity, cheering after he finished.

Verbal patterns of wit, irony, and social critique defined their tight social group, a coded, intense, dynamic, and insular style of interaction to form what biographer Barry Miles has called a

6.1 The five-piece Hamburg band, 1960

"hermetic Liverpool bubble around them." Keeping up with the witty banter, as much as anything musical, was what made it hard for Best to fit in. Born out of a developmental, late-teenage need and cultivated through Lennon's leadership, the bubble became the basis for their success. You can glimpse it in descriptions of Lennon and McCartney generating song lyrics together. The finished lyrics often communicate a feeling of a direct connection, and also an edge of competition, sharp and fresh. It is not surprising that they feel conversational since they were generated through actual conversations.

Later, after the move to London, they were joined by a group of Liverpool friends who enlarged the bubble and also contributed to lyrics, including Neil Aspinall ("John often asks Neil for ideas for the last lines of songs," observed biographer Hunter Davies), Mal Evans (the pretend Pepper band was his idea), Terry Doran (who suggested filling the holes in Albert Hall), and Pete Shotton (*Eleanor Rigby*). It seems likely that contributions like these extended beyond what has been documented, a hidden layer of the collective.

The bubble helped define their public image. Their closeness could be seen in their dress and haircuts, heard in the stage patter, the rock ensemble, and the vocal harmonies, imitating the Everly Brothers. Sometimes the three main singers sang at once, "a very charming image," as a Hamburg fan put it. The Beatles sang and sang and sang. Lennon and McCartney learned how to hold an audience in Germany. Regular rotation of the lead vocal became part of their egalitarian ethos, with featured numbers even for Sutcliffe (*Love Me Tender*) and Best (*Matchbox*), and a regular slot for Harrison.

Eight months younger than McCartney and a full twenty-eight months younger than Lennon—and an inch shorter than both of them—Harrison, part of the "original three," calmly assumed a subordinate position, like a row of children in a family birth order. He pretty much stayed there for the rest of the band's existence, with a circumscribed upgrade in late 1967 through the strength of his immersion in India. Lennon "seemed incapable of taking [Harrison] very seriously," remembered Shotton. "In John's eyes, George was still the little kid who tagged along, who happened to play the guitar and thereby gained his entrée into the band, but essentially remained (like Ringo) little more than an assistant, a second class Beatle." George Martin remarked how the same was true of McCartney, who could not be bothered to help Harrison with his compositions. Yet Harrison was intelligent enough to keep up and fully committed to the music. He learned when and how to mediate. "John and Paul would butt into a conversation, George would stand there and wait patiently until you brought him in," reported a Hamburg friend. He waited patiently for his brief guitar solos, for his turn in the vocal rotation, to get his compositions placed on LPs, and finally, at the very end, to be given the A side of a single.

Hamburg rewarded them for playing and singing more aggressively than the average Liverpool band, faster, louder, with passionate vocals and hard attack. They were drawn to rock and roll on the African American end of the spectrum—Ray Charles, Chuck Berry, Little Richard, Gene Vincent, Jerry Lee Lewis, and Elvis. As they bounced back and forth between Hamburg and Liverpool they firmed up a style that was out of step with the British mainstream, dominated by Cliff Richard and the Shadows, who were selling a softer, more middle-of-the-road version of American pop rock. "They liked us because we were kind of rough, and we'd had a lot of practice in Germany," remembered Harrison. "There were all these acts going 'dum de dum' and suddenly we'd come on, jumping and stomping, wild men in leather suits." Lennon stood with legs slightly parted, aggressive and sexual, mesmerizing girls in the front rows. They smoked and ate on stage, turned their backs to the audience and bantered inside jokes. *Long Tall Sally* induced hysteria. Cynthia Lennon described the Cavern scene: the Beatles "would grab their audience musically, emotionally and sexually, take them with them for the ride and when the trip was over would leave them totally exhausted yet screaming for more. I had never seen anything like it. It was fantastic."

Their embrace of African American numbers—dozens of them, like Arthur Alexander's *Shot of Rhythm and Blues* and Richie Barrett's *Some Other Guy* (both released in Britain in 1962), for example—distinguished them from the Liverpool competition. They did not have the musicianship to compete with bands like the Blue Angels, who produced pristine versions of Roy Orbison songs, or the Remo Four, who mastered Chet Atkins–style guitar picking, so they went in a different direction. They even sang some call and response (*Stay, New Orleans, Twist and Shout*). The Beatles were "no. 1 [in Liverpool] because they resurrected original style rock 'n' roll music, the origins of which are to be found in American Negro singers," explained Bob Wooler to the readers of *Mersey Beat* in August 1961. They became known as Chuck Berry specialists and covered a dozen of his songs. One observer insisted that "to play Chuck Berry covers in a dance hall in Liverpool in 1962 was an open act of defiance."

On an intuitive level there must have been a sense that African American stylistic markers naturally reinforced their egalitarian profile. Through the miracle of the phonograph, the energy of the ring shout had skipped across the Atlantic, hopped the North Sea, and returned to England with a difference. They became "part of the crowd," as one musician described the Cavern. "Or the crowd was a part of them . . . all the jokes and all the shouting. They were very, very funny, and spontaneous, and the nearer the front you were the more evident it was."

Lennon and McCartney were brimming with confidence in the autumn of 1961. "They reminded me of those well-to-do Chicago lads Leopold and Loeb, who killed someone because they felt superior to him," insisted Wooler. "Lennon and McCartney were 'superior human beings.'" At the end of the year, Brian Epstein offered to manage the band with the promise that he would pump a lot of his own money into the project. He persuaded them to drop some of the more severe affronts to bourgeois convention. His secretary typed up a list of guidelines—no smoking on stage, no swearing, no joking with girls, trim your guitar strings. They could smoke off stage, but only filtered cigarettes, not the low-class unfiltered "rollies." Epstein taught them how to bow: bend from the waist and count "1-2-3." Lennon believed that Epstein's primary talent was fashion. Though he grumbled about the new uniforms, which made them look like the hated Shadows, he came around since their income was improving, loosening his tie and undoing the top button of his shirt as modest gestures of rebellion.

Music always has the potential to communicate more than one thing at a time, and Epstein was steering the Beatles toward a straightforward package: the music was rough, sexy, and slightly dangerous, while the visual presentation was tamed, safe, and professional. The strategy was completely compatible with 1950s blending in the United States, as their trans-Atlantic success soon confirmed.

Epstein convinced them to work out a thirty-minute set and repeat it, instead of spinning out in unpredictable lengths and sequences. He probably had some influence on repertory (though this has been denied). When he started peddling them to record companies he offered an eclectic mix. As the owner of a record store he knew where the money was flowing, and the sensible thing was to push them toward the middle. They were fond of a range of American styles, from country to Broadway, especially when they had in front of them the precedent of a cover by an American rock-and-roll group. At an audition for Decca Records on New Year's Day 1962, they performed fifteen songs. Motown's *Money (That's What I Want)*, Berry's *Memphis, Tennessee*, the Coasters's *Searchin'*, and Holly's *Crying, Waiting, Hoping* were all pieces they loved to play. More strategic was *September in the Rain*, a standard from 1937 that Dinah Washington had recently revived. *Take Good Care of My Baby*, by Carole King and Gerry Goffin, was a current and very poppy number one for Bobby Vee, while *'Till There Was You* and *Besame Mucho* profiled McCartney's romantic side.

The New Year's Day audition included three originals—*Hello Little Girl*, *Like Dreamers Do*, and *Love of the Loved*. These were early efforts. Lennon and McCartney had been composing together since the beginning of their friendship, but Hamburg put their songwriting on hold. Mark Lewisohn, who has chronicled and studied this period with precision and insight, concludes that they did not compose a single song in 1961. It is as if the ferocious drive to become professional performers overwhelmed them, with no energy or ambition left for composing. Composing and performing during these early years were pretty much separate activities. People wanted to hear hits they recognized, not mediocre songs they didn't. Lennon's close friendship with Stuart Sutcliffe may have been another factor for the composing hiatus, since it slightly distanced McCartney from the leader. But the bottom line is that they understood their future in 1960 and 1961 in terms of performance. Toward the end of 1961 they started to slip an original song or two in at the Cavern.

Epstein's goal in offering three original numbers to Decca was to give the band a distinct identity, but he also understood a key part of the music business: big payoffs could be collected when an original got recorded by other people. This was precisely the direction Duke Ellington had tried at age twenty-five. A career as a songwriter was not dependent on a career as a performer, but the two could mutually benefit. At these moments in their respective biographies, Ellington, hoping to be the next Irving Berlin or George Gershwin, was in sync with Lennon and McCartney, aiming to be the next Rodgers and Hammerstein. They diverged with collaborative models during the next phases, with Ellington merging composition with performance through arrangements for featured soloists, while Lennon and McCartney got better and better at songwriting and extended creative control to details of arranging and record production.

The spur they needed was a contract with Parlophone, a division of EMI. Epstein met with George Martin in London on May 9 and signed up for a session on June 6. It was a tremendous breakthrough. Martin requested new material (new relative to the Decca material he had already heard), and the excitement revived the songwriting partnership. The immediate results were *P.S. I Love You*, *Ask Me Why*, and *Please Please Me*.

When Lennon, McCartney, Harrison, and Best stepped out of their beat-up white van and into the EMI studios on Abbey Road in June they entered an industry much more thoroughly organized than anything they had experienced. In due course they met Martin, the studio producer, who would shape their music and extend the creative collective.

In Chapter 5 we looked at how much control a recording studio could assert. A record producer acts something like an editor in a publishing house. All novelists expect to deal with an editor.

They may not like it, but they accept it as part of business. In Victorian England publishers went further than most by imposing specifications about stories and characters on authors like Charles Dickens, much as record producers put forward new songs for groups to record based on the most recent hits. Artists inevitably have to negotiate, at some point, the tension between their own ideals and the expectations of a target audience, but in this arena the important calculations were made by the publisher. As Dickens grew successful he took creative control, which is pretty much what happened to the Beatles.

It is easy to miss how the record producer as editor represented a new force in music history. Classical composers do not have editors, at least not in the same way that novelists have them, and they never have. Even composers of popular music like Gershwin or Joplin would have been surprised to bump up against an editor of sheet music messing with the details of their songs. No one told Stephen Foster to use more subdominant chords for expressive effect, or W. C. Handy to have less syncopation in a second strain for contrast. In the classical tradition, musical notation, theory, and complexity of design all combine to minimize editing, while the status of the great composer makes it taboo. The combination of vernacular practice, with normal conditions of regularly changing content, and the relatively modest status of the composer of popular music created an opening for the studios. The LP upped the ante of financial investment and led to centralized control. Any musician who entered a studio with a strong creative agenda faced a real chance for direct conflict.

Ellington achieved legendary status before the studios fully flexed their muscles, which must have helped him in negotiations like this. Plus, the entire idiom of jazz had donned an artistic halo by the 1950s, which shielded it from the heavy interventions of pop. The businessmen controlled the pop system as thoroughly as their Victorian counterparts had controlled serialized novels—or more. Record companies notoriously paid very little, but they offered massive, unmatched publicity. There were good reasons to bow to the company way. "You'd sell your soul to get on a little record," remembered Starr.

Lennon and McCartney were stubborn and independent, but it did not take them long to recognize Epstein's business savvy; now they saw how much Martin had to offer. For *Love Me Do*, their first Parlophone record (recorded September 1962), Martin had McCartney sing the hook instead of Lennon so that Lennon could enter on harmonica. McCartney was nervous, but the overlap worked. *Please Please Me* (recorded November 1962) was a slow number in its original conception, but Martin told them to jack up the tempo. For *She Loves You* (recorded July 1963) his advice was to open the song with the high-energy chorus. These turned out to be excellent edits that earned for Martin the Beatles' trust.

The dynamics between record producers and performers fell across a big range, from the dictatorial (Phil Spector) to the savvy businessman as arbiter of taste (Berry Gordy) to unquantifiable relationships of give-and-take. Roy Orbison and producer Fred Foster worked together to shape and reshape *Only the Lonely*, *Pretty Woman*, and *It's Over*, three of Orbison's biggest hits. Martin was canny enough and flexible enough to succeed in a creative relationship that turned out to be relentlessly quirky and unpredictable. He had the right combination of humility and confidence, which helped him see, in a given moment, how much his young employees needed and wanted. "I could recognize that an idea coming from them was better than an idea from me," he admitted. Since the Beatles were already used to collaborating, and since Martin's suggestions were lifting them to the top of the charts, he became part of the creative collective. "George Martin always has something to do with it, but sometimes more than others," McCartney explained. "Sometimes he works with us, sometimes against us . . . Sometimes he does all the arrangements and we just change them." Engineer Geoff Emerick noted a less tangible contribution: "Martin's legacy will not just be the scoring and arranging he did but his willingness to accommodate the Beatles as they stretched their artistic wings and learned to fly."

Martin organized the first session on June 6, 1962, to test the three vocalists. He wanted to see who was the best singer, which would lead to a marketing strategy. The norm was to have a front man backed by a group. "I desperately wanted my own Cliff," he remembered. "I was so hidebound by Cliff Richard and the Shadows that I was looking for the one voice that would carry them." Since the Shadows were selling massive quantities of records that was not such a bad plan. He quickly narrowed to two. It would be either "Paul McCartney and the Beatles" or "John Lennon and the Beatles."

In the end, he did not push for a front-man format, though he did insist that drummer Pete Best was not good enough to record. Nominations for the "fifth Beatle" regularly rotate through six candidates—Sutcliffe, Best, Epstein, Martin, Yoko Ono, and Billy Preston—and in June 1962 one fifth Beatle was aiming to raise standards by getting rid of one of the others. The original three were more than ready, so Epstein passed on the bad news to Best and promptly went to fetch Starr, whom Harrison had already been promoting within the group. Like Harrison, Starr was sharp enough to keep up and savvy enough to know how to fit in, musically and socially. He was witty, with a knack for clever phrases, and solid enough musically.

Starr's entry completed what assistant Neil Aspinall called "the chain," a key for scanning the group hierarchy: Lennon brought in McCartney, who brought in Harrison, who brought in Starr. The sequence also worked on the levels of social class and physical height, subliminal mechanisms for defining how they all lined up. Five to six inches shorter than the others (Lennon for a while called him "the dwarf"), less educated, and from a background of considerable poverty, Starr did whatever was asked of him. A journalist described him astutely in 1966 as "less complicated and more mature than the others, which makes him restful company and a

6.2 Ringo's childhood home

charming host." Harrison looked out for him and made sure that he rotated hotel room assignments, now with Lennon, next with McCartney, back and forth, quickly integrating him into the group. The unassuming drummer never presented himself as a rival in any way. With creative sparks flying more and more intensely as the decade unfolded, these personal qualities proved valuable.

Epstein had given Martin a list of the band's repertory, but Martin wanted them to record a song called *How Do You Do It?* The Beatles hated it. Behind the scenes, Martin was being urged by his boss to develop their original numbers, so against his better judgment he agreed to record *Love Me Do*, an early song they had recently reworked with harmonica and a new bridge. Compared with *Hello Little Girl, Love of the Loved*, and *Like Dreamers Do, Love Me Do* stood way over on the lo-fi end of the spectrum. It begins with the I-7 chord that opens *I Saw Her Standing There*, instantly communicating blues. Lennon thought it might have been the first-ever recording of a British band with harmonica. Martin intuitively recognized the implicit logic that tied everything together: this was an egalitarian group, not a soloist with accompaniment, and that image was compatible with unpretentious, lo-fi, African American-derived music. An added dose of genuineness came from the fact that they wrote the song themselves.

The record was released in October 1962. It has been reported that when Epstein heard it he sank into a funky depression. It's easy to see why. *Love Me Do* is so threadbare and raw, a simple melody with just three chords, not at all the middle of the road and sharing nothing with the number one hits tumbling out of Cliff Richard and the Shadows. When singer-guitarist Tony Sheridan, who had worked with the Beatles in Hamburg, heard it he croaked with scornful laughter. "What a load of crap," he scoffed, astonished by the low-level simplicity. Indeed, it would be a long time before the Beatles again recorded a song that was quite so basic. "We actually had a sense of being different," said Harrison, and *Love Me Do* made that crystal clear.

Love Me Do was credited to "Lennon and McCartney," just like the entries in the little notebook McCartney began keeping in early 1958. Epstein hired a lawyer to make their partnership contractual and explicit: everything composed by one of them would be credited to both, regardless of the level of joint authorship, even if one of them was working with someone else. They talked about ordering their names to reflect the primary composer in each individual case, and there were some experiments in this direction during 1963. But it did not take long before they settled on the formula of always listing Lennon's name first. They sensed the mischief that would inevitably follow from ordering the names according to primary composer and the boost that would arise from a consistent formula, the ordering of which could be blamed on the alphabet and which implicitly confirmed the hierarchical chain.

The decision to cosign everything was the business piece that promoted all future collaboration. It was much cleaner than Ellington's ecosystem of giving raises and privileges to musicians who supplied their melodies, riffs, and pieces. Cosigning meant that each could freely contribute to the other's songs, and it meant a powerful addition to their emerging public image. Not only did the Beatles write their own songs, they wrote them together. Collaboration was not only visible and audible, it was *inscribed*.

Ellington preferred to keep the fluid dynamics of interactive creativity in the shadowy background, and his decision was completely normal for the times—and most times. When Dickens, for example, acquired enough capital to start his own business, he hired writer Wilkie Collins (among others). The two of them wrote together, "side by side at two desks in [Dickens's] bedroom at Gad's Hill," as Collins described it, for many years. But Collins's participation has been routinely erased, minimized, and misconstrued, the usual issues of copyright and the status of solitary genius close at hand.

The Beatles embraced a collaborative image partly because of the egalitarian nature of the vernacular tradition, partly because of their closeness, and partly through an intuitive sense for how commercially appealing this model could be. People went nuts over the idea of a democratized rock-and-roll band saturated with creative camaraderie. Collaboration became part of what their music *meant*. This held all the way to the breakup. The informed listener hears *Hey Jude*, for example, as a song generated by a tight group of friends. Together they articulate a communal vision of healing that saturates the piece from beginning to end. This had a lot to do with the song being recognized as number one of the entire decade in many polls.

Ellington skewed a communal image and promoted the idea of his own genius; he was known as "The Duke." In Britain, the Beatles were known as "The Boys."

Composers of the Year

Thanks to relentless boosting from Epstein and an organized purchase campaign from the Liverpool fan clubs, *Love Me Do* reached number seventeen on one of the UK charts, high enough to open up England for them. The *London Evening Standard* ended 1963 by calling it the "year of the Beatles." The *New Musical Express* agreed: "In the distant future, when our descendants study the history books, they will see one word printed against the year 1963—Beatles! Just as convincingly as 1066 marked the Battle of Hastings, or 1215 the Magna Carta, so this year will be remembered by posterity for the achievement of four lads from Liverpool." A well-placed churchman publicly requested the band to update a Christmas carol, *O Come All Ye Faithful, Yeah! Yeah! Yeah!*, and Dora Bryan crooned *All I Want for Christmas Is a Beatle*. Topping it all off was the classical music critic for the London *Times*, William Mann, who called Lennon and McCartney the "outstanding English composers of 1963."

Cynthia Lennon remembered how "John and Paul were writing their songs with incredible ease" during the winter of 1962–1963. They had spent 1960 and 1961 memorizing dozens and dozens of pop-rock songs and internalizing stylistic norms while composing very little. In early 1963 their creativity started to burst out, and with a big step up in quality. No one was counting *Hello Little Girl, Like Dreamers Do, Love of the Loved,* or *Love Me Do* among their epoch-making accomplishments. What made them composers of the year were *Please Please Me, I Saw Her Standing There, From Me to You, She Loves You, All My Loving, It Won't Be Long, Hold Me Tight,* and *I Want to Hold Your Hand.* With these songs they cracked the blending code and came out on top.

Please Please Me was the first big success, and it was thoroughly collaborative. The original inspiration came from Roy Orbison. Lennon started composing the song in May 1962, around the time they were covering Orbison's *Dream Baby* (composed by Cindy Walker). Judged by lyrics alone, the singing persona of *Please Please Me* stands in a pleading, helpless position, an Orbison specialty. Lennon's original tempo was slow, atmospherically vulnerable, the kind of thing that was carrying Orbison to the top of the charts. In spite of their headstrong cultivation of hypermasculine sexuality, they were exploring vulnerability as an option. When the tempo was sped up at Martin's suggestion the energy became more of a demand than an Orbison-style plea, which has confused some observers to take the song as a plea for oral sex, so powerful is Lennon's macho presence.

Lennon's fingerprints are there in the neat synchronization between words and music in the bridge ("I don't wanna sound . . ."). He carried the emerging song to his partner, literally to his house on Forthlin Road, where the two of them sat down one afternoon in the front parlor and set to work at Jim McCartney's piano. Two fifteen-year-old girls happened to be hanging around (this kind of connection with Liverpool fans was not unusual in 1962), and one of them later described the two composers sitting side by side on the piano bench, "mostly working on the chord changes, with a lot of joking and messing about."

It is easy to make a few inferences. Lennon did not grow up with access to a piano, while McCartney had been learning about chords from his father on this very instrument for years. (You could say that this piano was the only material advantage McCartney had over Lennon while growing up.) Greater mastery of chords was McCartney's calling card. McCartney's likely contribution to *Please Please Me* as they joked around on the piano bench would be the chords for the repeated words "come on," which nicely built up tension into the release. Lennon took *Dream Baby's* triple repetition and made it more concise, and his partner's chords lifted the song to a higher level.

The collaborative mix also included McCartney's single-note vocal harmonization of Lennon's melody, a technique he had learned in school. The vocal duet is bright, energetic, fresh, and collective: with the harmonizing part ringing out on top the listener has no way of separating the two lines hierarchically. An egalitarian vocal ensemble becomes part of the compositional product, and we are an ocean away from Orbison's lonely pleading. As McCartney later said about *There's a Place*, another number from around this time, "I took the high harmony, John took the lower harmony or melody. This was a nice thing because we didn't actually have to decide where the melody was till later when they boringly had to write it down for sheet music." Martin sped up the tempo and asked for harmonica (following *Love Me Do*). Harrison took the harmonica riff and played it continuously throughout the song on his guitar, like a blues riff. Assistant Producer Ron Richards told him it was too much: simply play the riff "in the gaps," he advised, which made it less bluesy and more poppy. Starr added strong drumming, Lennon a strong vocal lead, and McCartney some nice details on bass. Such was the fluid give-and-take behind their first number one hit.

Ask Me Why, on the flip side of *Please Please Me*, also started with Lennon. The chords of the A section imply composition on a guitar. The nicely contrasting bridge ("I can't believe . . ."), however, moves through an augmented chord, and it is easy to again imagine McCartney, always a couple of chords ahead of his partner, at work on the Forthlin Road piano. This same pattern of chords opens the bridge of *Don't Ever Change* (composed by King and Goffin), released by the Crickets in the spring of 1962 and quickly covered by the Beatles. There is also a melodic difference between the two sections of *Ask Me Why*: in the A section, the melody follows the chord tones in a very straightforward way, while the bridge features more nonharmonic tones, again suggesting different composers.

They recorded their first album in a single day, February 11, 1963, and after it was released in March it went on to hold the number one position for thirty weeks, generating national tours, television appearances, and a regular radio show on the BBC. The BBC show gave listeners a chance to hear the musicians in conversation. Their interactive verbal style had gone through several phases with still more to come: in Hamburg it took high form as the hermetic bubble, on stage it incorporated raucous insults and outrageousness, and at the Cavern it was tweaked with neighborly charisma and faux-private shows for the swooning girls. Now it was properly tamed for the BBC.

They did not tame their Liverpudlian identity, however. Each Beatle plus Epstein experienced blatant prejudice in London before their explosive success. "London is so very strange about the north of England," confessed Dick Rowe, the Decca producer who famously turned the group down. "There's sort of an expression that if you live in London you really don't know anywhere north of Watford. Liverpool could have been Greenland to us then." Starr remembered trying to dance with girls in London and being rejected repeatedly because of his accent.

But against all odds Liverpool had suddenly become an asset. In a press release from the fall of 1962, Epstein mentioned the city twelve times in three pages. Publicity photographs had the band standing in bombed-out ruins from the war. The musicians asked why there always had to be mention of their home city. After Epstein explained it to them they started to exaggerate their accents in interviews, reviving the speech patterns that Mimi Smith and Mary McCartney had worked so hard to snuff out. When they finally reached the national stage their jangling guitars, splashing cymbals, and bright voices were attached to images of Liverpool and a sense of hardwired difference.

LIVERPOOL WAS WORKING CLASS. Liverpool had long been known as a rough city of immigrants, slums, smog, and working docks, and those associations were hardly diminishing in 1963. It continued to hold some of the highest rates in England for poverty, unemployment, crime, and alcoholism. Some fifty thousand families still relied on outhouses. "It's *Liverpool*, where Z-Cars comes from" explained a fan, referencing a gritty crime drama from BBC television.

LIVERPOOL WAS WITTY AND IRREVERENT. "Being born in Liverpool you have to be a comedian," insisted Harrison. Lennon was an expert in the local tradition of undermining virtually any stated value with daggers of sharp wit. All displays of self-satisfaction were read as attempts to separate from the common crowd and dealt with accordingly. "If one [Beatle] seemed in danger of taking himself too seriously, the others knocked it out of him," observed Harrison's first wife, Pattie. Class resentment found outlets through witty attacks on the upper crust, "blunt northern humor," as McCartney put it. *The Goon Show*, with Spike Milligan and Peter Sellers, which all of the Beatles listened to faithfully during their teenage years, demonstrated how to professionalize class-slaying bluntness by gobbling up British pomposity and rendering it toothless. "It's a highly prized commodity, a laff," explained Beatles publicist Derek Taylor, "especially in Liverpool where there's hardly anything to laff at unless you laff at all the sadness and poverty."

LIVERPOOL WAS MIXTURE. Three of the four Beatles (Starr was the exception) had mixed ancestry, Irish and English, a fairly typical feature of the working class. Liverpool had the first "Chinatown" in the world, a huge American presence during the war, Jewish refugees from the pogroms, and a steady history of permanent disembarkation. A climate of cultural mixing must have made it easier for the Beatles to open up to alternative cultural values, first from the United States, then from India. They had nothing to protect.

LIVERPOOL WAS COMMUNAL. When success made it possible for Starr to buy his mother Elsie a nice house, properly detached and far from the Dingle slums, she had a mixed reaction. The neighbors were so far away, and where was the corner store? Impoverishment had a deeply communal side. Houses shared walls, streets were narrow, and courtyards gave architectural form to neighborliness. This could be deadly, with easy transmission of disease through unsanitary conditions, but it also brought a culture of shared intimacy that people liked, fertile ground for the ancient communal practices of African American music-making to land upon.

As their fame grew during 1963, Liverpool infused their image with a nice little mixture of foreign yet still one of us. Their musical connections to the United States were obvious, but they were also clearly distinctive, which was read as British, something genuine that had popped up in a remote corner of the homeland. "But they're not black, Grandma . . . They're white . . . and they're British!" was how a press release from late 1962 framed them. Beatlemania was a symbolic ascent of the underprivileged classes, and that was something the entire nation was ready to endorse in 1963. "This working-class explosion was all happening and we were very much a part of it," explained McCartney, "making it okay to be common." More than a matter of screaming teenage girls, Beatlemania included a communal, working-class identity, youthful and modern but also willing to play by the rules.

In the United States rock and roll was firmly connected to a caste system based on race. England organized social hierarchies no less thoroughly through class, and this structural difference helps explain the differing receptions of rock and roll. Basically, it made it easier to cover the phenomenon in a blanket of white Britishness than it was, across the Atlantic, to cover it in a blanket of white Americanness. By symbolically lifting class boundaries in a spirit of national solidarity the Beatles could stand as British icons up and down. (It could even be argued that when they came to the United States in January 1964 their British translation of music that had been so strongly inflected with race in the United States helped de-racialize the phenomenon.)

Some have argued that Beatlemania was fueled by the Profumo affair, the spy-sex scandal of mid-1963, though it is perhaps more accurate to say that the scandal got legs because of deeper frictions within British society, which in turn promoted the Beatles' success. The friction involved a synthesis of class structure and cultural values with traditional Britain, cast as decadent, elitist, and stifling, pitted against an inclusive reach for modernity. Tradition gathered around images of the aristocracy and the Conservative party, modernity around youth and the United States. "We want the youth of Britain to storm the new frontiers of knowledge, to bring back to Britain that surging adventurous self-confidence and sturdy self-respect which the Tories have almost submerged with their apathy and cynicism," puffed Harold Wilson at the end of 1963. As devotees of American music the Beatles were in a good position.

They also radiated authenticity. McCartney noted in 1964 how "quite a few people mention the word 'genuine'" when explaining why they liked the Beatles. Interpretations of the group as having a campy vibe in the early years miss this central ingredient. As teenagers they disdained phoniness and were drawn to music they considered pure and uncompromising. The integrated parts of their public identity (no leader but a group of equals, tight camaraderie, singer-songwriters who composed together, Liverpudlian working class, Everyman authenticity, democratized rock and roll) so powerfully fueled an aura of genuineness that the leaks were easy to overlook (the exaggerated accents, the hierarchical chain, Lennon's middle-class background, the contradiction between safe appearance and dangerous sound). That they wrote their own songs and wrote them together trumped everything.

Their performance at the Royal Variety Show on November 4, 1963, solidified their standing as institutionally sanctioned rebels. With the Queen Mother and Princess Margaret in attendance, McCartney started their short set by singing *'Till There Was You*, and Lennon ended it with the raucous *Twist and Shout*. In Chapter 5 we watched music travel through different social-musical configurations, and here is another classic example. *Twist and Shout* began life as *Shake It Up Baby*, composed by Phil Medley and Bert Russell and recorded by the Top Notes (1961). This first version stood on the far end of the lo-fi spectrum, a simple riff tune over and over again, call and response, no chorus, no bridge, no hook, with minimal variety in harmony and texture. When Medley and Russell reworked it for the Isley Brothers and gave it the title *Twist and Shout*, they added a six-bar middle section that moved through an exciting buildup on a single chord of tension, with strong additive rhythm and rising "ahhhs" from the vocalists, growing louder and swelling to a climax.

Louis Armstrong could have been thinking of the Beatles' *Twist and Shout* when he said that rock and roll was nothing but warmed-over soup from the Sanctified Church. They took the Isley Brothers' performance and simplified the instrumentation while adding more repetition and harder attack. Lennon sang with feral intensity, making it hard not to come along with him. They made the middle section even more exhilarating with seemingly random and polyrhythmic vocals, a scripted gospel eruption—or, if you like, a scripted sexual eruption. The *Sunday Times* asked a medical professional to comment on the sexual side of Beatlemania and he had this to say in late 1963: "You don't have to be a genius to see the parallels between sexual excitement and the mounting crescendo of delighted screams through a stimulating number like *Twist and Shout*." The added focus on the middle section with its harmonic tension and explosive release articulated masculine sexuality in a big way. The obvious sexual tension in songs like this has led to the category "cock rock," one of musicology's more memorable terms. Additional Beatles' entries could include *I Saw Her Standing There*, *I Want to Hold Your Hand*, and *A Hard Day's Night*.

When he introduced *Twist and Shout* at the Royal Variety Show, Lennon famously extended an invitation: "On this next number I want you all to join in. Would those in the cheap seats clap their hands. The rest of you can rattle your jewelry." He delivered those lines with a polite nod to the royal box and a sheepish grin. It was a rapier thrust that hit the mark. The entire nation loved the quip as they read about it in newspapers and watched

6.3 Princess Margaret greets the Beatles, 1965

it on television. Lennon cheekily imagined England as a giant ring shout, a cheerful gesture of national unity. The context was very different from the American emphasis on African American mimicry and affirmation of the caste system. Even royalty could playfully form the "base" as the shouters at Port Royal, South Carolina, would have said in 1863, while the community's most talented members on center stage contributed syncopation and vocal intensity. It was already apparent before the Royal Variety Show that Beatlemania was open to everyone. Lennon adorned this crowning moment with just the right dash of slightly irreverent Liverpudlian wit. "If we could put in something [in composing songs] that was a little bit subversive then we would," remembered McCartney. Measuring that little bit became a fine point of Beatles' intelligence.

Being the Rodgers and Hammerstein of British rock and roll helped the Beatles lighten up social-political tensions in early

1960s Britain, and the movie *A Hard Day's Night* put it all in artistic shades of black and white. Liverpudlian Alun Owen scripted the movie with the hometown dialect, known as "Scouse." One could see on screen the close male camaraderie, the unpretentious exuberance, the Liverpool accents, the witty irreverence, the long hair and nice suits, the working-class cheekiness and charm. The laughter of *A Hard Day's Night* was a binding laughter, a glue joining the four Beatles, one to all and all to one, the audience to them, England as a nation. As the director Richard Lester put it, "The Beatles sent the class thing sky-high; they laughed it out of existence." In their bright, energetic music you could hear the collaboration of the band and the two composers who, for the first time, wrote every single song on the album, the collaborating commoners trumping top-down genius. "We're rather crummy musicians," quipped Harrison, to which McCartney added, "We can't sing, we can't do anything, but we're having a great laugh."

From there the Beatles made genuineness a defining feature of the countercultural 1960s, a dividing line that automatically separated them from an enterprise like Motown, which had an impressive array of talent and its own collective style. Berry Gordy perfected his version of the old-school studios, with emphasis on a streamlined sequence of production. It worked for him. Gordy regulated everything: "artists performed, writers wrote, and producers produced," lamented Otis Williams, one of the singing Temptations. "In his paternal, sometimes condescending way, he let it be known that he wasn't interested in having an artist who wrote and produced." Smokey Robinson, who has written over four thousand songs and was the lead singer in the Miracles, was the exception who proved that rule when he was promoted as vice president of the business. Otherwise, Gordy resisted the singer-songwriter model until 1971, when Marvin Gaye demonstrated its value with *What's Going On?* In some ways Gordy was like Ellington, the father figure of a family-like business. Gordy zeroed in on the expertise of session men, backup singers, solo singers, and songwriters, lined them up under contract and put the sprawling "family" into semicollaborative competition with one another. The process was more fluid than the typical studio and perhaps a bit more ruthless.

The *Times*' William Mann assured the nation that Beatlemania was more than carnivalesque ritual, that Lennon and McCartney's distinctive blend was full of quality. For this, McCartney's skill with chords was essential. When he first heard the Beatles, singer-songwriter Taj Mahal was impressed by the density of chords, "almost a chord for every word," it seemed, and he mentioned *From Me to You*. Composition of that song started on a bus, the two composers tossing phrases back and forth. Harmonic variety includes a G-minor chord to open the bridge ("I got arms . . ."), an unusual direction given the C-major focus of the verse. McCartney said this was a daring step that opened up possibilities for him (indeed, the same unusual relationship, transposed, marks the beginning of the bridge in *I Want to Hold Your Hand* from a few months later). The minor "five" chord turns the bridge in a softer, more tender direction, a foil to the drive of the verses. McCartney realized how catchy *From Me to You* was when he heard a mailman humming it on the street.

I Want to Hold Your Hand was also created "eyeball to eyeball," as Lennon put it, the two of them sitting side by side on a piano bench in the basement of the Ashers' house. Again McCartney led the way in chords. While they were composing the verse he landed on a chord that inspired Lennon, who, sensing the right touch of design, shouted out, "That's it! Do that again!" Epstein had asked for something that would sell in the United States. *I Want to Hold Your Hand* is strong with harmonic and melodic tension building to release, first into the catchy hook that defines the song (more precisely: the hook includes a buildup of tension *and* the release), and then at the end of the bridge, returning back to the verse.

Already familiar with double messaging, they built a song around that principle, with macho musical drive overwhelming the innocent, handholding lyrics. The urgency of the music makes it clear that the singer wants to do more than hold the girl's hand. The swells and upward leaps and explosive release topple the coyness of the lyrics almost to the point of irony. Dylan heard the song on the car radio and admired its craft. "Their chords were outrageous," he said, "just outrageous, and their harmonies made it all valid."

Critic Alec Wilder wrote about the "hard sell" of Gershwin's most popular melodies, aggressive textures of driving, catchy gestures with lots of repetition. When Epstein asked Lennon and McCartney to tailor a song for the United States they responded with something similar. *I Want to Hold Your Hand*'s introduction hits the ground running (*She Loves You* is a precedent), both harmonically and metrically, with a syncopation thrown in for added kick. Crafted design is balanced with lo-fi hand clapping. The emphatic drum set reinforces details of design. Contrast is used effectively, with the relative tenderness of the bridge ("And when I touch you . . .") leading back to the intensity of the verses by way of repeated references to visibly manifesting love. The song brims with dynamic energy, youthful optimism, and confidence. Writer and political activist Václav Havel described its impact in Czechoslovakia: "Suddenly you could breathe freely. People could associate freely, fear vanished, taboos were swept away, social conflicts could be named and described."

For the breathtaking climb of Beatlemania Lennon's cleverness with words was as important as McCartney's knack for chords and melody. This could mean a felicitous phrase or image (for example, *I Saw Her Standing There*) and it meant the marriage of pithy verbal gestures to memorable musical gestures. Most songs by Lennon have this kind of union, for example, *Revolution*, where the first line sails up to the stressed syllable of the most important word. He once alluded to this in an interview:

> See I remember in the early meetings with Dylan: Dylan was always saying to me, "Listen to the words, man!" and

I said "I can't be bothered. I listen to the sound of it, the sound of the overall thing."

The story is one way to calculate the differences between folk and pop. "The sound of the overall thing" may be understood to mean the *synergy* between words and music, which is more important than the words or music by themselves. It is challenging to achieve this when the music comes first, as it often did with Lennon's partner.

For the Beatles, vocal melody stood above everything. One of McCartney's great gifts has been melodic design, the bread and butter of the hi-fi composers. The verse of *I Saw Her Standing There* does not sound much like the Chuck Berry models McCartney was listening to because of its strong melodic arc, supplemented with slightly unusual progressions that decorate and push at strategic points along the way, all of it building tension that resolves into the hook. The boogie-woogie groove serves actual dancers but it also supports the melodic-verbal narrative of the imaginary dance described by the singer. The bridge ("Well my heart . . .") moves to a conventional blues chord, but it is, again, more than that. As handled here the chord creates a state of suspended animation, the reverie of a booming heart fixated on the seventeen-year-old object. The melodies of Beatlemania in 1963 unfold in crisp and simple bits to make extended shapes, which are in turn governed by a formal purpose that enhances everything. That was the craft that made them composers of the year.

It was Lennon's blessing and his curse to have a collaborator who could write great melodies that he would always fall short of. At certain moments in his tragically abbreviated life the comparison chewed him up. As the Beatles matured in 1965 and 1966, he discovered how to deal with the problem of living in his partner's shadow by contributing in ways that would never have occurred to McCartney.

The final analysis of how Lennon and McCartney became

the Rodgers and Hammerstein of rock and roll must reassert the importance of unquantifiable collaboration, with more back and forth, more mutual editing and brainstorming than anyone will ever know. In late 1962 a fan flew back with the band to Liverpool on their final return from Hamburg and watched the two principals sitting next to each other on the plane. "They definitely needed each other," she remembered. "They always seemed to be laughing together, scribbling on bits of paper and laughing some more." They boosted each other's confidence. McCartney described how they put their demo tapes together:

> To learn a guitar part we would both play exactly the same thing, so it was really like double-tracking a guitar. If we played it to anyone there'd be two guitars pumping out this same thing, two voices often singing the same melody line, so you just got double-strength everything, double-strength Daz. It was a loud demo rather than just one guy wondering enigmatically whether the song was okay or not. The two of us knew it was okay and played it forcefully, we convinced each other.

And they wrote for each other as primary audience, each striving to match the other's expertise, internalizing shared gains and eagerly looking forward to what was next.

The Departure

When Lennon said, in 1964, that he and his bandmates had been "playing this music for eight years," he was offering a view of the past and perhaps sounding out a prediction. The Beatles were hardly alone in looking for ways to expand the boundaries of rock and roll. Among their musical contemporaries the most important departure was, unquestionably, Bob Dylan (b. 1941), who heavily shaped their artistic maturity.

6.4 Dylan in London, 1965

Around the same time that Lennon and McCartney were harmonizing in the Mendips vestibule, the teenage Dylan was leading a band that covered Elvis, Little Richard, and Gene Vincent in Hibbing, Minnesota. At age eighteen he moved to Minneapolis to attend the University of Minnesota and settled into a coffee shop scene that had some things in common with the art school scene in Liverpool. But Dylan immediately went in a very different direction. "The thing about rock and roll is that for me anyway it wasn't enough," he remembered. "*Tutti Frutti* and *Blue Suede Shoes* were great catch phrases and driving pulse rhythms and you could get high on the energy, but they weren't serious or didn't reflect life in a realistic way."

Lennon and McCartney perfected their songwriting by studying pop-rock blends, while Dylan was shaped by folk music. His primary model was Woody Guthrie, and he admired plenty of African American singer-songwriters as well. He moved to New York City, worked his way up the ladder of venues, and in the summer of 1963 became the darling of the Newport Folk Festival. *Blowin' in the Wind*, released in May on the album *The Freewheelin' Bob Dylan*, established him nationally after it was recorded by Peter, Paul and Mary. Dylan performed *Blowin' in the Wind*, with its pleasant, sing-along refrain and drifty charm, at the March on Washington for Jobs and Freedom in August. Also on *The Freewheelin' Bob Dylan* is *Masters of War*, a severe sermon and uncompromising indictment of the war machine that Eisenhower had warned against in his farewell speech to the nation in

January 1961. These songs extended the folk tradition while they were solidly part of it, serious and reflecting life, as Dylan put it.

In 1963 he also composed love songs that didn't much resemble either traditional folk songs or pop songs. *Don't Think Twice, It's All Right* touches on the ambiguity of a relationship, a sense of wanting more fused with resignation over not being able to get it. Now that the love has past, the singer is moving on, and he recommends that the woman do likewise. Bits of the message are stated categorically, but nothing is resolved. The listener senses that the singer is trying to bring himself to some definite position through the act of singing, that the title is ironic. *Don't Think Twice* stands near the beginning of a great series of songs about the complexities of romance. *She Belongs to Me* (1965), for example, had considerable impact on Lennon. The title said one thing but the lyrics implied that the power structure of the relationship was exactly the opposite.

Yet Dylan's most daring work was composed under the influence of Beat hero Arthur Rimbaud (1854–1891). This "God of Adolescence" (André Breton) had devoted followers among the Beat poets, to whom Dylan was paying close attention. Allen Ginsberg pinned a Rimbaud quotation on his dormitory room wall at Columbia University, and Jack Kerouac wrote a poem entitled simply "Rimbaud." The most startling song on *The Freewheelin' Bob Dylan*, *A Hard Rain's a-Gonna Fall*, could be heard as a response to the Cuban missile crisis of October 1962, but there is no folk-song precedent for the dense, hallucinatory imagery, which followed Rimbaud's style of vivid, free association, a "derangement of the senses," as the French poet put it, a disordering of rational constructions. "The poet makes himself a seer," insisted Rimbaud. "I have seen the low sun spotted with mystic horrors . . . I have dreamed of the green night with dazzled snows"—those lines and others from Rimbaud's most famous poem, *The Drunken Boat*, caught Dylan's attention. Absinthe and hashish helped fuel the Frenchman's dreamy landscapes, while in New York City marijuana and amphetamines usually did the trick.

"Je est un autre" (I is someone else) wrote Rimbaud, a detached and fluid point of view. "When I read that the bells went off," said Dylan, "it made perfect sense." In early 1964 those bells took lyrical shape in *Chimes of Freedom* with its extraordinary array of images. Rimbaud's drunken boat coasted through fantastic lands filled with hysterical cows, blue wine, rotting whales, clouds with purple clots, avalanches of water, and small electric moons, while in *Mr. Tambourine Man* a musical instrument becomes the means of magical conveyance. *Subterranean Homesick Blues* from the album *Bringing It All Back Home* (early 1965) dipped down below street level to give fresh definition to the bohemian experience. The Beat poets had safely harnessed their musical tastes to progressive jazz, which relieved them from having to worry about any verbal content, but Dylan was set on changing their minds. *Subterranean Homesick Blues* combined a stream of vivid non sequiturs, "chain saw lyrics" as George Martin described them, with music flavored by Chuck Berry. Dylan's Rimbaud-inspired songs also had a huge impact on Lennon, though it took longer for him to figure out how to make the style his own. He eventually solved the problem with *I Am the Walrus*. The album cover of *Bringing It All Back Home* was an easier idea for the Beatles to pick up: it is safe to assume, I think, that the distorted lens used in the photograph influenced the cover of *Rubber Soul*.

The Beatles stumbled on *The Freewheelin' Bob Dylan* in Paris in early 1964, and they played it together at their hotel, over and over again during an eighteen-day stay. Now they had a new singer-songwriter-hero. All but two of the songs on *Freewheelin'* were composed by Dylan himself, and it is perhaps no coincidence that their next album, *A Hard Day's Night*, was the first to include their own originals and nothing else. When the Beatles and Dylan met in August 1964, with Dylan discreetly ushered up to the band's suite in the Delmonico Hotel, there was mutual respect while Dylan turned them on to marijuana, a first toke for several of them.

It took Lennon and McCartney much longer to step out of their pop-rock comfort zone than it took the folk singer from Minnesota, partly because of backgrounds that were more provincial (Dylan came from a family of business owners) and partly because it was not easy to reconcile an exploratory impulse with the fantastic rewards of Beatlemania. When they expanded their ranges Lennon and McCartney went in different directions, following different inspirations. Eventually their independent trajectories created problems, but for the duration of the band's existence respective gains were folded into the collaborative relationship, lifting the group higher and higher. Starr called *Rubber Soul* the "departure album," and it is easy to see it as a milestone, but the process was more varied and gradual than a single moment like that implies.

McCartney's departure came first. It may be dated to around January 1964, which is when George Martin remembered first hearing *Yesterday*, an innovative and potent song that burst out of the melodic-harmonic conventions of pop rock.

The music came to him in a dream, the composer has reported. He was worried he had heard it somewhere and simply forgotten the source, so he played the tune for friends and asked if they knew it already, singing with place-holding lyrics ("scrambled eggs, oh my baby how I love your legs"). This birth story is believable if we put it in a larger context: he had been studying, critiquing, imitating, and mastering the craft of songwriting intensively for a year and a half. His prep work included hi-fi numbers like *'Till There Was You*, an attractive model for him with its nicely shifting chords and chiseled leaps, a beautiful design that must have inspired *And I Love Her*, which Lennon referred to as McCartney's "first *Yesterday*."

McCartney is often called a great melodist. That is a nice thing to say about a composer, yet it is easy to misunderstand. It means that the melodies have grace and elegance and fit the human voice with ease. Great melodists rely on natural talent, but they also work hard. Gershwin, another great melodist, insisted that the melodies for his songs caused him just as much effort as his semi-classical pieces. There can be no doubt that McCartney worked over melodies in this way, too, but since he never learned how to read notation he never wrote anything down. When there is no material trace of the stages of improvement it can seem like the music just popped out, the product of natural gift rather than hard work. *Yesterday* must have been related to many sessions of noodling around at the piano and guitar and months of careful study.

'*Till There Was You, And I Love Her,* and *Yesterday* all have great melodies, but that does not mean those melodies were designed to stand alone. The melody works with harmony to create a beautifully designed musical *structure,* and this is what accounts for *Yesterday*'s astonishing success—the song has apparently been played on the radio and covered more than any other from the twentieth century. Its richness of design is something like a sonnet by Shakespeare, with patterns of rhyme, phrase, metaphor, allusion, assonance, syntax, and so forth, everything carefully integrated, a small artistic gem.

McCartney's control of harmony was a key part of Beatlemania, and this song represents a further blossoming. He cited a connection between *Yesterday* and jazz chords he remembered his father playing on the family piano. This would probably be a series of harmonic turns, the kind of thing jazz pianists frequently insert (for example, ii-V7-I in jazz parlance). In *Yesterday* these little progressions nimbly animate the melody. The tightly constructed melody of the "A" section would feel too confined and deliberate without this added layer of dynamic energy from the chords.

The reason musical structure is so important here is that it lies at the heart of expression. The structure effectively conveys shades of emotions. The A section begins starkly, with the simple word "yesterday," a sigh on two pitches. As the phrase expands it brings a touch of minor-mode sadness, confirmed by the gesture at the phrase end, which musically and verbally rhymes with the stark opening. The next phrase brings a feeling of resignation, a sense of so-be-it acceptance achieved through what musicians call a "plagal" progression of chords; the progression is familiar as the "amen cadence" due to its standard position at the end of church hymns. McCartney later used the gesture to develop the same mood even more extensively in *Hey Jude* and *Let It Be*. The final phrase of the A section repeats the plagal progression but ends with a ray of hope, communicated through the melodic rise to the third of the chord.

These emotional shadings are discreet and reserved. They are brought into focus by the musical rhymes that refer back to the initial, stark statement, with verbal rhymes to match ("far away," "here to stay," "yesterday"). With less richness in the chords, the melodic-verbal rhymes would feel too deliberate, too heavy. As it is, the balance is just right, and the four rhymes play both a formal and an expressive role.

After such a lovely A section, the bridge ("Why she had to go . . .") could have been a throwaway, but instead it is an inspired complement. No moment is wasted in this song. The bridge opens with starkness, but it immediately explores a new mood when bass line and melody move in opposite directions. The energy feels expansive, and it offsets the constraint of the A section. Taj Mahal appreciated the harmonic density of early Beatles songs, and here, in the first phrase of the bridge, we do indeed get a change of chords on every single syllable. In contrast to the shifting turns of the A section the bass now keeps going in a single direction. We could say that there are three neatly coordinated layers of independent musical activity—melody, chords, and bass. McCartney is never as daring as Ellington in his use of chords, but daring is not what he is after. What is skillful is the integration of all compositional elements in the service of emotional enrichment.

6.5 Brian Epstein and George Martin, 1964

The Beatles did not know what to do with *Yesterday*. The dilemma sat there for well over a year, until they finally recorded it in June 1965, with McCartney the only Beatle performing. There was talk of giving composer credit solely to him, since it was so obviously a one-man show; doing that might have hastened the end of the Beatles. Martin suggested adding strings. He was probably led in this direction by a quirky recording from the previous May called *Eine Kleine Beatlemusic*, released by a group called Barock and Roll, formed for the purpose of arranging a batch of Beatles hits for string quartet. Framing their music as classical had come to seem natural, and this title put the Beatles in comparison with Mozart; the album reached the British charts. Martin's string arrangement for *Yesterday* sticks closely to McCartney's guitar work. He asked the composer if there was anything he wanted changed, and McCartney suggested a small blue note in the cello (the song's only connection to rock and roll) and a single held note in the violin for the final section (a prominent dash of restraint).

Analysis could go into a lot more detail, but one feature that should not be missed is the irregular phase lengths. Contrary to most popular songs, the first section is seven bars long, not eight or some other multiple of two. On this level, beginning the second verse on the word "suddenly" is a pun, an abrupt return that is skillfully handled and not immediately obvious. This formal freshness works well with the song's tone of understated reserve. Asymmetrical phrasing was a technique Lennon and McCartney (like Ellington) regularly came back to, all the way through the very end (*Don't Let Me Down* has groupings of five beats, for example), the asymmetry keeping things fresh when handled with rightness of design.

Martin once said that a key to the Beatles' success was a sense of British restraint, and it is easy to think of *Yesterday* in those terms. McCartney asked that the strings not sound syrupy, that the players use only slight vibrato. The melodic discourse does not feel much like an opulently emotive ballad. As William Mann phrased it in a related critique, the emotions do not spill into "artificial sentimentality." This musical-emotional atmosphere, crisp and understated yet emotionally potent, became one of McCartney's trademarks. Martin understood the principle well in his arrangements. Counterexamples like Phil Spector's arrangement of *Long and Winding Road*, with over-the-top wordless chorus and orchestra that tip the delicate balance, demonstrate how in tune Martin was with McCartney.

Suddenly the Beatles' range of expression opened very wide. On the day he recorded the vocal lead for *Yesterday*, McCartney did the same thing for *I'm Down* (in Little Richard style) and *I've Just Seen a Face* (blue-grassy folk rock).

Lennon said that he admired *Yesterday* but did not envy it. His own inclination toward simpler music meant that his compositions begged for enhancement, and his partner was always eager to oblige. McCartney contributed introductions (*Lucy in the Sky with Diamonds*), enriched melody and chords (*In My Life*), countermelodies (*Help!*—McCartney called this addition a "descant," a term that goes back to the Middle Ages; it must have been another technique he learned in school, like his single-note harmonization for *Please Please Me*), intricate and dominating details of an arrangement (*Tomorrow Never Knows*), solo details and riff accompaniment (*Come Together*), and completion and restructuring (*Don't Let Me Down*).

It is easy to see how *Yesterday* could have left Lennon feeling a little uneasy, since the song asserted McCartney's independence at the same time that it made glaringly obvious his high value to the team. It would be several years before Lennon grew confident enough to make a musical statement that would be left untouched by his partner. By my calculation that statement is *Julia*, one of the most personal songs Lennon ever wrote. There is Lennon in the fall of 1968, bravely alone with guitar and voice, urged to independence by his new romantic and creative partner, Yoko Ono.

Lennon's own departure from the boundaries of pop rock was based on a direct response to Dylan. This happened gradually through 1965–1966. The results turned the group in an avant-garde direction, and they were no less important for the band's mature phase than McCartney's musical excellence.

Through study of folk songs, Beat poetry, and Rimbaud, Dylan had opened up fresh possibilities, but it was not a simple matter for the Rodgers and Hammerstein of rock and roll to start filling their number one hits with this kind of volatility. Lennon had read Kerouac while working on his bohemian slouch in art school, and he enjoyed hanging out with the sexy Exis in Hamburg, but all of that was kept at arm's length while he advanced his musical career, first in performance then in composition. This changed in 1965. Lennon said that Dylan's example helped him become more personal about his songs, and there are many successful demonstrations of that from this wonderful year.

He bought himself a cap like the one Dylan wore on the cover of his first album, then an acoustic guitar and a neck strap for his harmonica, while the others made fun of his devotional mimicry. His challenge was to channel some of the attitude and style of Dylan's sprawling narratives into pop-rock songs, with requisite hook, chorus, and bridge, dropping all pretentiousness and keeping things simple. *I'm a Loser* was followed by *You've Got to Hide Your Love Away*, the first Beatles song lacking electrical instruments. A Dylanesque vocal snarl came easy to Lennon, but, unlike Dylan, the hook dominates in this song. Poppish, turtlenecked flutes replace the folk singer's harmonica. Lennon's song *Help!* became one of his personal favorites. He later claimed that the desperation in the lyrics was autobiographical, and that the song was a product of self-reflection and subjective writing inspired by Dylan.

In the fall of 1965 the Rolling Stones landed their first number one American hit with *(I Can't Get No) Satisfaction*. Jagger and Richards had Lennon and McCartney in their sights from the start. The connection between the two pairs deepened after the latter demonstrated how to co-write a song right before the former's eyes, literally finishing off *I Wanna Be Your Man* and handing it to their younger friends as a gift to record in 1963. Lennon and McCartney's *Day Tripper* may be heard as a direct response to *Satisfaction*, with *Day Tripper*'s riff topping the Stones, though Lennon and McCartney smartly did not try to compete with Jagger's charmingly rambling lyrics.

Day Tripper and *We Can Work It Out* (on the flip side) were both thoroughly collaborative. Lennon once said that his conception of songwriting was a matter of "doing little bits which you then join up." Just as Ellington combined melodies from different composers as an automatic way to generate contrast, so did Lennon and McCartney. *We Can Work It Out* is a classic example, with McCartney starting the tune and Lennon helping with the minor-mode bridge ("Life is very short . . ."). Harrison suggested triple-meter effects for the bridge, a further point of contrast with the verse.

In My Life was another of Lennon's personal favorites, and he again credited the inspiration to Dylan. Like many of Lennon's songs, this one started with words. The first stage of the lyrics described a bus trip from Mendips to Penny Lane, seeing places where he had lived and making an inventory of what they evoked. Extensive revision produced a landmark in Beatles lyrics, reflective and compelling. The lyric sophistication of *In My Life* matched the musical sophistication of McCartney's *Yesterday*.

As with Ellington, there are many occasions when the who-wrote-what investigation cannot be resolved. Lennon acknowledged his partner's help with the "middle eight" (though there isn't one, exactly) and some chords while claiming the melody for the verse as his own—and feeling that it was one of his finest melodic achievements, at that. Yet, to the contrary, arguments that see the fingerprints of McCartney all over this lovely melodic arc are persuasive. Beatle experiments with fresh instruments in 1965 are usually successful, for example, the flutes of *You've Got to Hide Your Love Away*, the strings of *Yesterday*, the simple sitar of *Norwegian Wood*. For me, the pseudo-harpsichord of *In My Life* is one of Martin's missteps. He must have been aiming for a classical touch analogous to the strings of *Yesterday*, but the Baroque fussiness detracts from the sincerity and directness of the song. Nevertheless, this song did a lot to help define the maturity of *Rubber Soul* in late 1965.

Norwegian Wood has Lennon pursuing Dylan more directly, with a cryptic, ballad-style narrative that draws musical inspiration from (in McCartney's view) Irish folk music. As in *She Belongs to Me*, the singer-persona finds himself at a disadvantage in a relationship. The mystery of Dylan's Egyptian ring is matched by the Norwegian wood, which is never explained, just part of the ambiguous atmosphere. (Commentators who tiresomely try to explicate the Norwegian wood miss the point and the Dylan connection.) Harrison bravely sprinkled in some exotic spice with his new sitar, and McCartney helped with the bridge. Lennon's "nowhere man" could be considered a cousin to Dylan's Mr. Jones, the clueless establishment figure in *Ballad of a Thin Man*. But of course there is again difference. Lennon makes the figure more sympathetic by including the audience: each of us, he says, is a little bit like the nowhere man. In the summer of 1965 the Byrds brought Beatles' vocal harmonies and rock accompaniment to Dylan's *Mr. Tambourine Man*, and their recording soared to number one. The Beatles returned the compliment by matching the Byrds' dope-soaked tempo and dreamy atmosphere precisely in *Nowhere Man*. They also topped the Byrds' jingly jangly guitars by cranking up the brightness on Harrison's guitar solo as far as it could go, ignoring the warnings of the nervous studio engineers.

With *Yesterday* and *Rubber Soul*, the Beatles were moving toward art, with McCartney's classy ballades at the center. *Michelle*, another product of McCartney sitting at a piano fooling around with chords, became the only Beatles song ever to win a Grammy. As with *Yesterday*, McCartney sings in a way that holds the song back from sentimental excess, now defined as French cool. Elements of the song date back to the Liverpool days, when the composer liked to command a piano at parties for the art students, who smoked Gitanes cigarettes and wore French berets. Harrison contributed a pleasantly wistful guitar solo, Lennon had the idea of the ecstatic outburst "I love you" for the bridge (inspired by Nina Simone's *I Put a Spell on You*), and a friend who taught French helped with the lyrics.

McCartney was expanding the Beatles' musical range while Lennon was doing the same thing with lyrics. Elvis had long ago demonstrated the advantages of stylistic flexibility, and in 1965 the Beatles were keen to discover how far they could go. They mixed in humor with songs like *Drive My Car* and *Dr. Robert*, darkness with *Girl* and *Run for Your Life*, and sour sarcasm in Harrison's *If I Needed Someone*. Everything was Beatlized through

strategically placed vocal harmonies, tight musical form, compelling word-music synthesis, memorable tunes complemented
by effective chords, judicious arrangements, seductive grooves,
humor, and emotional restraint. The mellow and acoustic emphasis of *Rubber Soul* (especially the North American version) made it
sound to Brian Wilson of the Beach Boys like a coherent whole, a
"collection of folk songs." Bette Midler heard the album as a "tidal
wave of enthusiasm, ideas and alternatives." McCartney called it
"the beginning of my adult life."

Ellington was a major part of jazz becoming art, and in 1965
the Beatles were doing the same thing with rock and roll. The
key for Ellington was a new relationship between arrangement
and instrumental solo; for Lennon and McCartney it was an
exploration of new song types, a spinning out of lyrical-musical
possibilities. Ellington took advantage of the jazz niche of the
performer-composer, and in the mid-1960s singer-songwriters
were in a strong position. Singer-songwriters good at both words
and music were in the strongest position of all, which made the
skill set of Lennon and McCartney tough to beat.

Ellington achieved artistic diversity by building pieces around
the various styles of his soloists, the Beatles by absorbing diverse
influences and taking them further. The sitar on *Norwegian
Wood*, tentatively performed by the band's junior member, turned
out to be a seed for an even bigger range. An even more radical
step would soon follow, but there was a twist involved: their most
dramatic innovations could only be accomplished in the recording studio, not on the stage. Since the biggest money was now in
record albums this turned out not to be a problem. The Beatles
were filling their music with so much variety, originality, and
excellence that it was hard to put a finger on what category they
belonged to. The simplest thing to do was let the sense of categor-
ical differences simply collapse, and there were plenty of precedents for that.

CHAPTER 7

RETREAT

Phase Two: Into the Mind and Into the Studio

WE HAVE ARRIVED at a natural line of division in the Beatles' career. Phase one was a period of professionalization, mastery of craft, and rise to spectacular success. It put in place the egalitarian rock-and-roll band, and it included the decision by Lennon and McCartney to cosign all compositions. Working-class toughness, youthful energy, stage charisma, tight rock and roll, fresh and original compositions, and a vigorously modern (in a very specific, localized British sense) image of authenticity lifted the Beatles to megacelebrity. "This isn't show business," said Lennon in late 1963, "it's something else. This is different from anything that anybody imagines. You don't go on from this. You do this and then you finish." Had they not continued, the Beatles would have been noteworthy collaborators, but they would not have been grouped together with someone like Duke Ellington.

Phase two, from 1966 through 1969, was shorter, as if the energy was so intense that it simply could not be sustained. Cynthia Lennon described 1966 and 1967 as something "like a Walt Disney nature film where the process of blossoming and growing was shown at high camera speeds." These years are sometimes portrayed in terms of fragmentation and individualization, yet many of the greatest successes were thoroughly shaped by collaboration. Phase two involved a double retreat—into the mind and into the recording studio. Frustrated on multiple levels with public performance, they simply decided to stop. The album *Revolver* was worked out in the Abbey Road studios with high attention to detail and no intention of live performance. The studio became their compositional laboratory. Few other rock bands could demand resources like this. The main precedents were avant-garde, state-funded composers like Karlheinz Stockhausen, whose work was of great importance for the Beatles.

At the same time that they retreated into the studio their songs became more introspective. Inspired by his experiments with LSD, Lennon set about to express his inner explorations musically, his mates following like foot soldiers behind a charismatic field commander. With the songwriting skills of the Rodgers and Hammerstein of rock and roll and with the web of interactive creativity as starting points, the innovations of 1966–1969 lifted the Beatles higher and higher in prestige. The Beatles "are the wisest, holiest, most effective avatars the human race has ever produced," gushed Timothy Leary in 1967, and to more than a few admirers that sounded like it might actually be true.

The last four years of the group's existence divide fairly neatly according to the calendar. Early 1966 began with *Revolver* and closed with the single *Strawberry Fields Forever/Penny Lane*. The first half of 1967 was dedicated to *Sgt. Pepper's Lonely Hearts Club Band*, the second to *Magical Mystery Tour*. There was a lot going on during the period from *Tomorrow Never Knows*, the first song recorded for *Revolver*, through *I Am the Walrus*, the first song recorded for *Mystery Tour*, but the outstanding feature was the development of a psychedelic worldview. This phenomenon overlaps with the growing influence of Indian music and religion, addressed in the final chapter.

Revolver

"The people gave their money and they gave their screams," noted Harrison, "but the Beatles gave their nervous systems, which is a much more difficult thing to give." Of the four, Lennon paid the steepest price.

In the spring of 1965, Lennon, his wife Cynthia, Harrison, and Harrison's girlfriend Pattie attended a dinner party hosted by their dentist, who secretly spiked their coffee with LSD. Lennon eventually found a reliable source for the drug and took what seemed to him like a thousand trips. "I used to eat it all the time," he remembered. He was heavily influenced by the book *The Psychedelic Experience: A Manual Based on the Tibetan Book of the Dead* (1964), by Timothy Leary, Ralph Metzner, and Richard Alpert. Psychologist Leary and his Harvard colleagues dove head first into the stunning possibilities of LSD, using the legal drug themselves and monitoring streams of volunteers. *The Psychedelic Experience* is one of the most audacious artifacts from a decade bursting with outrageousness.

Leary and his coauthors presented LSD as a shortcut to Buddhist enlightenment. They dedicated the book to Aldous Huxley, who had studied the religious use of peyote by Native Americans in the Southwest and Mexico. Leary turned to High Asia instead. It seemed like a matter of cosmic poetry that the Tibetan diaspora, caused by the horrific Chinese takeover of a peaceful country, roughly coincided with public access to chemically synthesized hallucinogens. Leary seized on an ancient book that had been translated in the 1920s and given, by Walter Evans-Wentz, the name *The Tibetan Book of the Dead*. When the actor Peter Fonda told Lennon, in the summer of 1965 in Los Angeles, during Lennon's second trip, that he knew what it was like to be dead (a phrase that turns up in *Revolver*'s *She Said She Said*), we may suspect an unacknowledged reference to Leary and Evans-Wentz. This trip and this comment seem to have helped Lennon click into the momentum and write songs about it.

When qualified Tibetans started to translate and teach in Western languages, they published several superb editions, with commentary, of the text Evans-Wentz had struggled to interpret.

7.1 Allen Ginsberg, Timothy Leary, and Ralph Metzner, 1965

It is easy to see how bold and, to be blunt, how stupid Leary was, as he extracted what he thought were pithy instructions from a richly textured religion that recommends long, patient, and multidimensional cultivation of wisdom and compassion. Nevertheless, it cannot be denied that LSD was something of a game changer for Western society, with Leary and the Beatles among the prime movers.

The Psychedelic Experience gathered legitimacy by association with Evans-Wentz, Huxley, Carl Jung (who wrote the preface to the 1960 edition of *The Tibetan Book of the Dead*), and Tibetan

Buddhism, and it framed LSD as a matter of spiritual quest rather than party-down hedonism. "I suppose now what I'm interested in is a Nirvana, the Buddhist heaven," said Lennon in late 1967. "LSD was the self-knowledge which pointed the way in the first place." Tibetans regard the author of the original book, the great teacher Padmasambhava, as the second Buddha because he successfully planted the vajrayana tradition at Samye monastery in the ninth century. From him it was a clean line back through centuries of Buddhist lineages, all the way to Shakyamuni Buddha himself, ca. 500 BC. Like Lennon, many readers of Leary's manual had at least a dim awareness of this radiant aura of authority.

The Psychedelic Experience advised its users to read the book out loud to each other while tripping. If you were by yourself, you could prepare a tape recorder ahead of time and play it back while you took the drug; this was Lennon's solution. Lennon loved to share drugs (first alcohol, then amphetamines, then marijuana) with his buddies, but for now he was a solitary seeker, tucked away in his suburban mansion and destroying his ego as instructed by the Harvard psychologists.

His song *Tomorrow Never Knows* was the first number recorded for the album *Revolver*. He began the song by cribbing one of the best lines from Leary's introduction: "Whenever in doubt, turn off your mind, relax, float downstream." He had learned from Dylan how to make a love song more personal and how to inject elements of mystery, then figured out how to match catchy hooks to a concise critique of bourgeois conventional values. In the spring of 1966 he was prepared to go further. Beatles fans could buy the latest album and let Lennon be their guide.

McCartney remembered his partner singing his new song while "rather earnestly strumming in C major" on his acoustic guitar. He wondered to himself what Martin was going to think. The Beatles held a lot of power in the recording studio, but even they had to deal with commercial realities. This new song had no bridge, no refrain, a very dull melody, and only one chord. It made no concession whatsoever to pop prettiness. With its austere, preachy message it resembled a song like Dylan's *Masters of War*. In the future Lennon would figure out how to soften this rhetorical mode, his lyrics becoming less like a sermon and more evocative while the title and refrain sum up the exhortation succinctly (*All You Need Is Love, Come Together, Give Peace a Chance*).

McCartney was good at taking songs from Lennon and making them musically better, but this challenge had no precedent. Good composers are often stimulated by limitations, and that turned out to be the case here. *Tomorrow Never Knows* is the first great example of a breakthrough song conceived by Lennon that was then hugely transformed through collaboration. The simplicity of the music and the audacity of the lyrics were an invitation to his partner to think boldly.

One could connect the single chord of *Tomorrow Never Knows* to folk music or to blues, but the more explicit reference for the Beatles was northern India, the region of the Buddha's birth. The Byrds had just demonstrated (March 1966) "raga rock" in *Eight Miles High* (backed by *Why*), with drone, static harmony, and sitar-like guitar solos, and Harrison had been immersing himself in the real thing for several months, hanging out with Ravi Shankar while putting his guitar aside. Around the same time (April 1966) that the Beatles started to work on *Tomorrow Never Knows*, Harrison brought some musicians from London's Indian Music Association into the EMI studio to play sitar, tamboura, and tabla on his song *Love You To*. For *Tomorrow Never Knows* tamboura and sitar in the background were enough to authentically connect to India.

McCartney had an idea for a drum pattern. In his very first rehearsal with the Quarrymen, back in 1957, he had intervened with the drummer, and that continued with the Beatles. Engineer Norman Smith, who worked with them from 1962 through

Rubber Soul, said that "Paul had a great hand in practically all the songs we did, and Ringo would generally ask him what he should do." For *Tomorrow Never Knows* he recommended a syncopated pattern (which he had already taught Starr for *Ticket to Ride*) to replace the simpler pattern Starr had chosen (which can be heard on *Anthology*). Lennon once praised McCartney and Starr as first-class rock musicians who could go head-to-head with anyone. Some of their best work drives Lennon's lyrically rich but musically modest songs: *Tomorrow Never Knows* is one example, *Rain* another, *Come Together* the last. It made a difference that the sound quality for bass and drums was improving in 1966, thanks to EMI experiments with microphone placement, direct bass feed into the console, and stuffing sweaters into the bass drum.

Lennon told Martin that he wanted his voice to sound like the Dalai Lama chanting from a remote mountain in the Himalayas. Perhaps they could suspend him in a harness, he wondered, dangling from the ceiling, with microphones in a large circle around him, rigged in such a way that he could rotate around the room, his voice drifting in and out. This being impractical, the engineers ran his microphone through Leslie speakers, a rapidly rotating configuration designed for the organ, yielding an unprecedented transformation of the human voice.

But the most important musical touch came with a set of tape loops conceived by McCartney. Lennon was dismissive of the avant-garde, which for him meant "French for bullshit"; he later explained this position as "intellectual-reverse-snobbery." "I don't go in for much of those culture things," he said in 1964. "Just drop a name and Paul will go. I'd rather stay at home when I'm not working." LSD intensified Lennon's inward-looking leanings, while megacelebrity gave McCartney unlimited access to new art, movies, music, and ideas, whatever caught his fancy. Many are still surprised to learn that it was McCartney rather than Lennon, the abrasive radical, who brought in the innovative techniques used so effectively in *Tomorrow Never Knows*, *Strawberry Fields Forever*, and *A Day in the Life*. It was McCartney who selected a photograph of Karlheinz Stockhausen for the cover of *Sgt. Pepper*.

McCartney's turn toward European modernists resembles Strayhorn's interest in the harmonies of Ravel and Bartók twenty years before. Jane Asher's family had been putting a nice variety of high-end stimulation in front of him, and in 1965 and 1966 this included abstract modernism. Her brother Peter joined with friends John Dunbar and Barry Miles to form the Indica Gallery and Bookstore, where McCartney liked to hang out (and where Lennon stumbled upon *The Psychedelic Experience* and, later, Yoko Ono). McCartney met, at some point during these years, Luciano Berio, William Burroughs, Andy Warhol, Michelangelo Antonioni, and many other thinkers and artists. "I am trying to cram everything in, all the things I've missed," he said in the spring of 1966. "People are saying things and painting things and writing things and composing things that are great, and I must know what people are doing."

The London Days of Contemporary Music Festival dedicated two sold-out evenings to Stockhausen's music in December 1965. The composer himself spoke and answered questions. He brought along tapes of his electronic compositions, prepared at his famous Studio for Electronic Music in Cologne. A tape of *Mikrophonie II* included excerpts from his 1956 electronic composition *Gesang der Jünglinge*, which was created with unmatched hi-fi equipment. McCartney may have heard about the December events; we know for certain that he attended concerts and lectures given by Cornelius Cardew, a close disciple of Stockhausen, in January 1966. He told Cardew that he appreciated the importance of challenging the status quo, but that the music "went on too long."

Gesang der Jünglinge, available on LP, became his favorite Stockhausen, as it is for many others. The piece uses musique concrète, tape recordings of everyday sounds placed in an unfamiliar context and distorted in inventive, disorienting ways, for example, by playing them backward. The real-life sounds of *Gesang der Jünglinge* were sung by a boy soprano. The innocence and purity of the voice, along with the lyrics—a biblical story of miraculous salvation from fire—contribute to the drama and supernatural atmosphere. In the fantastically imaginative context of the composer's electronic sound world, the boy is thrust into a fiery cosmos, breathing air from a different planet, singing for his life.

With oscillographs and filters, Stockhausen analyzed the physical characteristics of the singing and figured out how to create similar sounds electronically. Then he merged the two, back and forth. Sometimes the voice is multiplied, sometimes fragmented, and often enough it is coherent and comprehensible. Percussive consonants blend with electronic clicks, vowel timbres blend with adjusted sine waves, and the pitches of the song blend with a microscopically controlled spectrum of electronic pitch. Different levels of musical reality blur together. As Stockhausen once explained in a different context, "what is like becomes only approximately like; correspondences only correspond approximately."

The Beatles took musique concrète and ran with it. They used it for humor and charm in a good number of McCartney's songs (*Yellow Submarine, Penny Lane, Back in the USSR, Maxwell's Silver Hammer*), then for modernist dislocation in songs written primarily by Lennon (*Tomorrow Never Knows, Benefit of Mr. Kite, Strawberry Fields For-*

7.2 Karlheinz Stockhausen, ca. 1960

ever, *I Am the Walrus*). *Gesang der Jünglinge* (and probably other pieces, too) showed them how to introduce electronic sound with a dramatic flair.

McCartney constructed a rudimentary recording studio at his home. In 1965, Stockhausen had experimented with tape loops in pieces like *Solo*, which was designed to be performed by a single instrumentalist supported by four technical assistants. The assistants create, on the spot, tape loops of what is being played, they manipulate the sound according to various methods, and then they play back the loops as part of the unfolding performance. In April 1966, McCartney planned something similar for the emerging *Tomorrow Never Knows*.

The rock quartet had already recorded the foundation on track one of the studio master, and now the loops, guided by McCartney, were worked by a collection of white-coated studio technicians and engineers, some manning the tape recorders and some mixing at the sound board. Just like Stockhausen, McCartney and his colleagues painstakingly cut, pasted, threaded, and finagled the tapes, which were variously saturated, sped up, played backward, and sprinkled across the master tape. It was all put together in real time in the studio, not very different from a performance of *Solo*. One of the loops, a B-flat major chord played by a symphony orchestra, helped compensate for the lack of harmonic variety in Lennon's tune. This lowered-seventh degree (relative to C) is a sonic spot where African American music meets music from India—it may be heard as a reference to soul pieces like Stevie Wonder's *Uptight (Everything's Alright)* and/or as a reference to ragas. Another loop sounded vaguely like an Indian instrument. The famous seagull cackles are similar to sounds from Stockhausen's *Solo*. There is a backward guitar solo: the listener recognizes an electric guitar and can sense a shape to the line, but the attack, decay, and melodic details are off-kilter, difficult to conceptualize—correspondences that correspond only approximately.

"The idols now, the people that I can appreciate now are all much more hidden away in little back corners," said McCartney in early 1967 as he explained how Stockhausen and John Cage had replaced Elvis as his primary heroes. A little bit of avant-garde went a long way for the Beatles in 1966. Stockhausen shunned surface patterning and especially repetitive rhythms, while the rock-band foundation of *Tomorrow Never Knows* is that and little else, a single chord, unvarying riff, a simple melody, over and over. The added tape loops are treated as erratic riffs that randomly enter, fade away, and return.

Early titles for this song were "The Void" (a reference to Buddhist teachings on emptiness) and "Mark I." *Tomorrow Never Knows*, a throwaway quip from Starr, was intended to "take the edge off the heavy, philosophical lyrics," as Lennon explained in retrospect. Harrison later insisted that Lennon didn't fully understand the lyrics and their implications. No doubt that was true, but musicians do not necessarily have to master the philosophies that shape their times. They simply have to have enough connection that they are able to bring that energy to life through music. Even with partial and intuitive understanding they can still come up with powerful results.

One often reads that the Beatles were starting to dissolve with *Revolver*, spinning out in centripetal directions and losing the collectivity of their early years. This is completely misleading. In fact, the two most important songs on *Revolver* were thoroughly collaborative. McCartney's *Eleanor Rigby* is no less a creative breakthrough than Lennon's *Tomorrow Never Knows*, though more subtly. Songwriter Jerry Leiber described it as "evocative and complete. Everything is intact, lyrically and musically, and the arrangement, production and vocals are all integrated. I don't think there has ever been a better song written than *Eleanor Rigby*." Everything was integrated in spite of the fact that at least six people helped create the words, music, and arrangement. McCartney crafted a strong musical structure and verse one of the lyrics. Others then contributed more lyrics, the idea for the chorus, and the string arrangement to fill out his original conception.

McCartney and Lennon first met at St. Peter's Church in Liverpool, and they occasionally hung out in the church cemetery (also the location where Lennon lost his virginity), which includes the grave of one Eleanor Rigby, though McCartney claims not to have been aware of this when he named the main character. He sang verse one in the spring of 1966 to a gathering of friends from Liverpool. Ideas flew back and forth. Starr came up with the poignant images of the preacher writing a sermon not to be heard by anyone and darning his socks in isolation. Pete Shotton, Lennon's friend since childhood, solved the problem of how to end the song: have the two lonely principals come together through Eleanor Rigby's death and burial by Father McKenzie. Harrison contributed the hook, the cry for the lonely people. It is sung by the backup singers, who universalize the narrative like a Greek chorus, pithily condensed. There were several Beatles' precedents for using a refrain as a throat-gripping opening, but this song's seriousness gives the device special force. Martin had the idea of combining the refrain and the chorus at the end.

Eleanor Rigby is a ruthless indictment of the Western church and society, which is not capable of saving anyone. It is a stark postwar representation of despair. As Harrison explained in the spring of 1966, "All of this love thy neighbor and none of them are doing it. If Christianity's as good as they say it is, it should stand up to a bit of discussion." Exposing the church's failure cleared the way for the atheist Beatles' spiritual turn to the East. The rhetorical strategy is narrative rather than exhortative (in contrast to Lennon's *Tomorrow Never Knows*), a more effective approach for a pop song. Still, this song was a shock. The predominating E-minor chord is relieved with blunt, temporary dips to C-major that only make the minor all the more dreary.

At the same time that he was developing a taste for the high-modern avant-garde, McCartney was getting to know classical music from the Baroque period. He asked Martin to write something in the style of Italian composer Antonio Vivaldi for the background to *Eleanor Rigby*. Martin had recently seen the movie *Fahrenheit 451* and had the music for that film in mind when he scored the string octet. It is one of Martin's most effective arrangements, enhancing and not claiming too much attention, just like a good film score. McCartney wanted to place the microphones close to the strings to get a raw sound, and he asked for reduced vibrato, like *Yesterday*. Again we see him locating an emotional sweet spot, with proper British restraint. The crispness of his melody balances the harmonic dreariness. Against all odds, this powerful synthesis of music and words drove the song all the way to the top of the pop charts.

McCartney's interest in Baroque music generated two more excellent results in 1966. I sense an undocumented case in the instrumental introduction to *And Your Bird Can Sing*. This driving line is full of vigor and originality, and it recalls a Bach ritornello—for example, the *Fifth Brandenburg Concerto* (BWV 1050, movement 1), or the *Concerto for Violin* (BWV 1042, movement 3). Like these Bach examples, the "ritornello" for *And Your Bird Can Sing* just keeps going in even rhythmic values, winding unpredictably without any syncopation and with plenty of memorability. The line is very fresh and hardly the kind of thing Lennon could have come up with. Bach and McCartney are very different composers, but these passages offer a way to put them in comparison, with McCartney emerging in fine standing.

The other Bach connection for McCartney in 1966 was *Penny Lane*, one of the most sparkling songs in the Beatles canon. The composer tuned in one evening to a BBC television broadcast of Bach's *Second Brandenburg Concerto*. The next day he asked Martin to hire the piccolo trumpet player, David Mason, who would add a track to *Penny Lane*, his melody dictated to Martin by McCartney. The song is built on a pleasant, allegro bass line, a jaunty stroll through suburban Liverpool. Building on a technique used for

Good Day Sunshine, *Penny Lane* cleverly modulates (movement from one key area to another) at each chorus, a musical skip into the bright blue sky that perfectly expresses the cheerful optimism of the lyrics. As each verse reverts to the jaunty stroll, the music settles back to the home key; the words "meanwhile back" become a pun analogous to "suddenly" in *Yesterday*. The master stroke arrives when the final chorus surprisingly modulates a step higher still. Everything is dynamic, uplifted, and fresh.

When Brian Wilson heard *Rubber Soul* it seemed to him all of a piece; he set out to match and beat it with the unified *Pet Sounds*. *Revolver* went in a different direction and became the first Beatles step toward the LP as collage. Collage (from the French *coller*, to glue) was another innovation from Georges Braque and Pablo Picasso, every bit as important as cubism for their climb to the high peak of early-century modernism. The artists glued playing cards, musical scores, nails, wallpaper, newspapers, and advertisements into painted scenes. Since the found objects carry implied meaning and since they do not usually belong together, the technique automatically brings humor and irony. From Braque and Picasso the practice spread and became a foundational principle of high modernism (and postmodernism). In the Beatles' LPs, the varied objects that form collages are types of songs carrying different styles, different types of lyrics, and different sound worlds, the latter intensified by studio innovations. The LP as a collage, full of discontinuity, humor, and irony, is quite different from the LP as a suite: one stresses continuity, the other rupture. The LP suite came naturally to Ellington and Strayhorn as they cultivated associations with classical composers, while the Beatles stumbled into the LP collage in the heady mix of hip London, in 1966.

We have already seen a huge range of expression marked by *Tomorrow Never Knows* and *Eleanor Rigby*. *Revolver*'s collage also includes Harrison's *Love You To*, which, though marred by poor lyrics, makes good use of musicians from India playing uncompromisingly Indian music on sitar, tabla, and tamboura. From there *Revolver* just keeps going. In the early stages there was talk of making the entire album in the United States, at Stax Records or Motown. Though the plan was abandoned, the thought gave birth to McCartney's *Got to Get You Into My Life*, with its R and B horn section and equal-stress four-beat groove. Satire in the riff-based and effective *Taxman*—Harrison's best song to date, with help on the lyric from Lennon and solo guitar from McCartney—adds yet another dimension.

The range of geographic influence on the Beatles included a swath of cutting-edge Los Angeles. Peter Fonda's remark about knowing what it is like to be dead was the starting point for Lennon's *She Said She Said*, which Harrison helped "weld" together by combining three previously independent starts. Joining up little bits, as Lennon described his process of composition, in this case produced jolts of expressive discontinuity similar to the beautiful non sequiturs of Ellington. Clever shifts of meter and phrasing conjure the unpredictable swings of a mysterious conversation and a sudden lift into childhood reverie, all of it carried with superb musicianship from the band. The splendid single *Rain* was made around the same time. With heavy use of varispeed tape manipulation and backward guitar and voice, *Rain* does the Byrds, with their draggy tempos and sitar-style guitars, one better. Also coming from Los Angeles were the latest ballades by Brian Wilson, directly inspiring two from McCartney. A huge spread of charmingly capricious chords, anchored by a delightfully expansive melody, portrays the singer's ubiquitous love in *Here, There and Everywhere*, while *For No One*, the negative counterpart, achieves a lyrical but chilling melancholy.

Capping off this unprecedented breadth was the sing-along *Yellow Submarine*, perfectly crafted for Starr. Here is another song by McCartney that got filled out with lyric help from others (including singer-composer Donovan Leitch). The downward-dwelling submarine shares a dropout sensibility with Dylan's *Subterranean Homesick Blues*, but emotionally those two songs occupy opposite worlds. Everything in *Yellow Submarine* is simple and happy. As a singer, Starr's common-man persona had been crisply defined with *Act Naturally* in 1965. The clever leap of *Yellow Submarine* was to put him at the center of a song that is all about camaraderie. With each fancy breakthrough the Beatles were drifting away from the Everyman ethos, but songs like this, which from now on could only be sung by the unassuming drummer, continued to reassert the image of a communal core.

The step toward the album as a collage was the accidental by-product of independent explorations, but this approach dominated all subsequent Beatles albums. It proclaimed their obvious superiority for the simple reason that no one else could come close to such a huge panorama of music, accomplished at such high-level skill. *Revolver*'s impressive range emerged from McCartney's musical flexibility and ability to transform various models, from Lennon's commitment to bringing his experience of LSD into his songs, and from Harrison's growing connections to India. One can identify the centripetal energy that tracks forward all the way to the band's disintegration, but the beauty of *Revolver*, *Sgt. Pepper's Lonely Hearts Club Band*, *The White Album*, and *Abbey Road* is the balance between this outward thrust and the strong sense of Beatles identity, internalized so thoroughly that it shines through everywhere.

While the Beatles were deep into *Revolver* the Beach Boys released *Pet Sounds*, which made a huge impression on McCartney. "Without *Pet Sounds*, *Sgt. Pepper* wouldn't have happened," insisted Martin. *Pet Sounds* changed the way McCartney thought about his creative role, or at least confirmed a direction he was already inclined to take.

Wilson's ballads *God Only Knows* and *You Still Believe in Me* bowled him over, and McCartney also made a close study of Wilson's bass lines. He had already blossomed as a composer who could coordinate melody, chords, bass line, and form, but any pop composer could find inspiration in Wilson's craftsmanship.

The broader impact from Wilson came through a sense of how to micromanage studio production and arrangements. Wilson was getting into the kitchen of the producer and the engineer and flaunting their luxurious eight-track tape recorders, double the size available at EMI. Wilson had in front of him models like producers Phil Spector and Jerry Leiber, who combined composition, arranging, editing, engineering, and producing. Wilson, the composer-performer, was ready to claim an even bigger range. "He alone in the industry—at the pinnacle of the pop pyramid—is full creator of a record from the first tentative constructions of a theme to the final master disc," wrote Liverpudlian Derek Taylor, who was generating publicity for both the Beatles and the Beach Boys in 1966. Taylor's high praise must have hit McCartney like a taunt.

In *Pet Sounds* you can hear Wilson romping through the studio with evident joy. Unexpected combinations of instruments (the "sweet surprise," as Mitch Miller used to call it) pop out all over the place—accordion on a soft bed of strings, flutes backed by ukulele, English horns mixing with Hammond organ, a dramatic tympani stroke with heavy reverb coming out of nowhere like a bolt of lightning, altered piano, bass clarinet followed by bicycle horn or sleigh bells, smart drumming, funky bass, liberal doses of synthesizer, and the Beach Boys' interweaving voices on top of everything. The loving attention to detail matches and extends the beautifully crafted songs. Composer, performer, arranger, and producer are united in the mind of one extremely musical person.

Wilson was good at what we might call the "dynamic arrangement." Instead of having the same accompaniment for each statement of verse or bridge or refrain, the arrangement keeps changing over the three-minute recording. This kind of thing was standard practice in the Swing Era, but rock musicians had to discover it for themselves. *Sloop John B*, Wilson's stunning transformation of a simple folk song, is a terrific example. The song opens with some kind of percussion, hard to identify but sounding like a tick-ing clock and accompanied by a swirling motive on synthesizer. In verse one the bass enters gradually, then becomes more active, while glockenspiel and percussion add light touches in the background. Verse two brings more active percussion and light vocal harmony, the swirling synthesizer staying steady. Genuine rock accompaniment arrives in verse three, along with extended vocal harmonies. Verse four is suddenly much more active, with a sudden disappearance of the instruments dramatically highlighting the brilliant and complex vocals. A drop in activity marks verse five, out of which pops much more aggressive percussion. The last chorus begins with a marchlike cadence that carries the song into fade-out as the ship sails away, leaving the listener wanting more.

In southern California, Wilson was also experimenting with LSD and reading *The Psychedelic Experience*, a step or two ahead of Lennon. He tried to articulate a turned-on point of view in *Hang on to Your Ego*, but his bandmates convinced him to recompose the lyrics and rename it *I Know There's an Answer*. They could not follow him. (Al Jardine: "To be honest, I don't think I even knew what an ego was"; Mike Love: "I wasn't interested in taking acid or getting my ego shattered.") In fact most of what Wilson was doing for *Pet Sounds* was too far out for his bandmates. He was on his own, exploring new territory without the support Lennon enjoyed from the four-headed monster.

Wilson's move was not a collaborative one but just the opposite: he took control of activities that were usually done by others in sequence. McCartney observed the example and did something different with it. Just as Ellington merged composition, performing, and arranging, and enhanced his position at the center of a creative process that remained highly collaborative, so did McCartney. The others could join him or not, anywhere along the process. As long as the Beatles were able to move flexibly through various combinations of creative procedures—and they did this through *Abbey Road*—they stayed strong.

Perhaps the most marvelous Beatles demonstration of a

dynamic arrangement is *Strawberry Fields Forever*. The 45 single that distributed this song with *Penny Lane* is the greatest Lennon-McCartney pairing, not only because of the excellence but also because the compositions reflect the group dynamics so well. These songs were intended to be the first step toward an album about Liverpool and the magic of childhood. As McCartney explained in January 1967, "I'd like a lot more things to happen like they did when you were kids, when you didn't know how the conjuror did it, and were happy to just sit there and say, 'Well it's magic.'" *Strawberry Fields Forever* is about a place experienced in isolation, *Penny Lane* is about a community hub. One turns to introverted reverie with mysterious depth, the other to extroverted motion and surface brilliance. Yet the musical riches of *Strawberry Fields Forever* were the product of creative collaboration, while those from *Penny Lane* came largely from a superb musical design created by one person.

From *Pet Sounds*, *Strawberry Fields Forever* takes the "fade-in" at the end, fondness for musique concrète, and the vast array of instruments, including synthesizer, to which it adds swarmandal from India and backward cymbals while subtracting Beach Boys vocals. "I played [*Pet Sounds*] so much to John that it would be difficult for him to escape the influence," remembered McCartney. In the meantime, Wilson had upped the ante of studio hyperfocus with *Good Vibrations*, which, in late 1966, was soaring through the charts to become the greatest Beach Boys hit ever. But the Beach Boys did not have George Harrison, looking to India; they did not have John Lennon, studying Dylan and boldly thinking about how to reconceive song lyrics; and they did not have Paul McCartney, checking out the high-modern avant-garde. There were no barriers to McCartney's study of Wilson's dynamic arrangements, just a huge opening to pour the gains into the Beatles' studio retreat.

Dylan showed Lennon how to make rock-and-roll lyrics deeper and broader, and Wilson showed McCartney how to turn a recording studio into a compositional laboratory. As Dylan was to Lennon, so Wilson was to McCartney, midcareer models for new directions.

All of this helps explain a central fact about collaboration in phase two: *musically*, McCartney's direct impact on Lennon's songs tends to be far greater than Lennon's on McCartney's. Partly this has to do with the nature of each creative mind. Lennon's fresh, outside-the-box lyrics tend to emerge with relatively simple music, while McCartney's refined musical structures leave little room for his partner to contribute. In a limited way, the situation is analogous to Ellington and Strayhorn: Ellington liked to combine themes, chords, instruments, and moods in a freewheeling process of mixing, adding, subtracting, and rearranging (Lennon: "doing little bits which you then join up"), while Strayhorn designed intricate musical structures that he regarded as complete and perfect. Ellington sometimes chopped up Strayhorn's musical structures, upsetting his assistant, but no one messed with McCartney's. The difference has to do with the different hierarchical textures. Ellington's leadership was never in doubt. By 1966, McCartney was assuming a position as chief Beatle in charge of musical production without actually taking the title.

With his ego-destroying project advancing grimly, Lennon acceded to his partner's new role. On one level he could relax, knowing that his songs were in good hands. He was pushing the group beyond "safe" music, and McCartney helped him do it successfully. McCartney appreciated Lennon's "battering ram" mentality, which he himself lacked. On another level, Lennon was inclined to withdraw. "I was really going through a 'What's it all about?' phase," he remembered. "This song writing is nothing, it's pointless and I'm no good, not talented and I'm a shit and I couldn't do anything but be a Beatle . . . And it lasted nearly two years! I was still in it in *Pepper*! I know Paul wasn't at that time: he was feeling full of confidence but I wasn't." Lennon's crisis put McCartney in the central position.

In the early 1970s, when he looked back with some bitterness and a lot of faulty memory, Lennon complained about what McCartney and Martin had done to some of his greatest songs. "I should have tried to get near my original idea, the monks singing," he insisted for *Tomorrow Never Knows*—"I realize now that was what it wanted." He wished *Strawberry Fields Forever* had been simpler, without the fancy studio treatment. We are lucky it wasn't. We should not see this as a dysfunctional period for the collective. According to Shotton, who remained involved through 1968:

> There never was, and probably never will be, a group more self-contained or tightly knit than the Beatles were in those days; the way their talents and personalities harmonized was little short of miraculous. Until about 1968, I never witnessed, or even heard about, a single serious disagreement between any of them . . . Paul was the only Beatle who posed any challenge to John's authority and preeminence with the group. Much as John might have found it easier to handle those who—like George and Ringo—seemed to take it for granted that *he* was the king of the castle, Paul was the only one he considered more or less his equal. John particularly admired and respected—yet at the same time slightly resented—Paul's independence, his self-discipline, and his all-around musical facility; all qualities in which John felt relatively lacking.

It is not that everything was always rosy. The point is that they found a new equilibrium in 1966 and 1967, one suited to the group's evolution.

Sgt. Pepper's Lonely Hearts Club Band

Lennon had intended *Strawberry Fields Forever* to be the first song for the next album, but it quickly got redirected to a single with *Penny Lane*. It must have become clear that the theme of childhood memories of Liverpool was too limiting, that the album could reach further without that particular anchor. Ideas were bounced around and a new theme gradually emerged. Personal assistant Mal Evans suggested that they introduce a pretend band, the Beatles' alter ego. They had heard a funny story about Elvis sending his Cadillac on tour as a substitute for himself. The pretend band, existing only on the phonograph record, could represent the Beatles since they were no longer going to perform in public. McCartney noted the eccentric band names of West Coast psychedelia, and Sgt. Pepper's Lonely Hearts Club Band was born. A pretend audience appeared on the cover and roared its approval several times over the course of the record, presented in such a way that it was obviously fake.

But the power of *Pepper* goes well beyond pretending. Lennon later complained that the songs are not topically unified, but that apparent lack is actually part of the magic. The concept is loose enough to allow an array of music so diverse that it mimics the glorious chaos of life itself. The implicit theme is the psychedelic worldview, which could be summed up most simply as *nothing is real*. "It's a fantastically abstract way of living that people have got into without realizing it," said McCartney in an interview with Barry Miles from January 1967. "None of it's real." The most important thing to say to people is "It isn't necessarily so, what you believe. You must see that whatever you believe in isn't necessarily the truth . . . because the fact that it could be right or wrong is also infinite, that's the point of it. The whole being fluid and changing all the time and evolving." Conventional views of reality fall apart when you see things from a higher point of view, which opens up a world of brilliance, playfulness, wonder, and love.

The most serious songs on the album—A *Day in the Life, Within You Without You, Lucy in the Sky with Diamonds*—articulate this view clearly enough, while the others fill out the album with brilliance, playfulness, wonder, and love. All of it is done with compelling and unprecedented music, tuneful and accessible. The diversity and studio imagination of *Revolver* are ratcheted up, and those qualities become part of how the album defines itself. This is the recipe for the greatest album in rock history.

When you bought the album you saw the spectacular photo on the cover before you heard the music. It is no coincidence that the most famous rock album has the most famous rock album cover. The cover helps define the theme, and in this way it represents the greatest collaboration between rock musicians and a visual artist. The Beatles enjoyed access to the very best—the best piccolo trumpeter, the best Indian musicians living in London, the best photographers, and so forth. McCartney's friend Robert Fraser, who happened to be the London dealer for Andy Warhol, knew that Warhol was designing an LP for the Velvet Underground (released March 1967). He thought that the Beatles should follow suit and suggested Peter Blake, who produced his most famous work of art for the benefit of something beyond the status of his own portfolio.

The cover first of all defines the pretend band as a psychedelic one, with dayglo uniforms and the suggestion of a fissure between past and future. The imaginary audience gathers for what might be a funeral, with a solemn statue kneeling at a flower-strewn grave inscribed "Beatles." The psychedelic incarnation has taken over. The power of the cover depends on the technique of visual collage. The pretend band, the only thing "real" in the photo, stands in front of an imaginary audience of Warholian celebrities in irregularly clunky, vaguely life-size, cardboard cutouts.

The touch of Warhol, picking up on the faux reality of celebrity representation and turning that into a softened and extended theme, reminds us how the most famous visual artist of this decade so closely parallels the Beatles. The Beatles were formed by the view that their primary purpose was popular success, with more artistic goals coming later and always tempered by commercial instincts, deeply ingrained. They shared this pattern with

Warhol, who developed his talents in graphic design and window displays before he became an artist. Furthermore, Warhol's work was highly collaborative, following the norms of commercial art.

As with Warhol, *Pepper* emphasizes artifice. Some of the celebrities are colorized, many are black and white, and there is no attempt to bring them into a uniform scale. The variety of visual representation continues with the wax Beatles, the ceramic dolls, the cloth doll, the Hindu goddess, artificial palm trees, a collage of untamed semiotics. This is conceptually compatible with the musical collage inside, so each strengthens the other. Visually and musically, brilliant detail, pointing in many different directions and working on different levels of "reality," overwhelms logic. This was the trick that made it possible for the Beatles to work on a bigger canvas.

The double retreat led them directly to this point. The imaginary world of the album cover has no existence apart from the photograph of it, just as the musical world inside cannot exist apart from the phonograph record. (Three phase-two album titles point toward the phonograph: *Revolver* is the revolving LP, *Pepper* is the band that exists only on the LP and nowhere else, and *Abbey Road* is the address of the recording studio. *Pet Sounds* was the likely antecedent for this way of thinking.) The disadvantages of phonograph recordings are clear: the sound quality is artificial, there are no performers to relate to, and the record is often heard in social isolation. An advantage is how the phonograph encourages imaginative engagement from the listener, allowing the range of musical meaning to spread beyond what it might in live performance. No record has ever embraced these possibilities better than *Pepper*.

With *Strawberry Fields Forever* moved to a single, Lennon turned his attention to a new start for the album. This song became *A Day in the Life*. He understood how an innovative number could set the tone and shape direction, as *Tomorrow Never Knows* did for *Revolver*. The sequence of these three songs defies

anyone who wishes to paint
the Beatles as more concerned
with mass success than artistic
innovation, for each is utterly
noncommercial. Each builds on
the previous effort and beats it.
Each began as a simple song by
Lennon and through collaboration reached an endpoint that
he never could have imagined by
himself. *A Day in the Life* was a
collaborative tour de force.

7.3 Lennon, May 1967

We have seen Dylan precedents for a number of Lennon's
songs. *A Day in the Life* leans toward *Ballad of a Thin Man*. The
singing persona of the initial verses laughs gently at the institutional trappings of conventional Britain (the House of Lords,
the English Army, and the Royal Albert Hall). It is usually the
case with most artists that an original point of inspiration does
not help very much with interpreting the final result. In this case
Lennon was responding to a newspaper report of an actual death
by car accident, but the song is not a statement of mourning and
not even tragic. The situation has something to do with blowing
one's mind, we are told, a phrase that meant something positive
in 1967, and the storyteller is laughing. This sets the tone for the
entire song, which is about the futility of a shallow and pretentious mind-set and an invitation to join a more expansive view.

Lennon brought verse one to his songwriting partner, not the
finished script of *Tomorrow Never Knows* or *Strawberry Fields* but
a rushed work in progress. "The way we wrote a lot of the time,
you'd write the good bit, the part that was easy, like 'I read the
news today' or whatever it was . . . ," recalled Lennon, "then when
you got stuck or whenever it got hard, instead of carrying on, you
just drop it; then we would meet each other, and I would sing
half, and he would be inspired to write the next bit and vice versa."

McCartney contributed the slight but powerful refrain, the invitation to turn the listener on, which was taken by the BBC as a drug reference and caused a radio ban.

That Lennon did not carry to his partner a finished script opened up a simple procedure from the old days, now dramatically extended: one songwriter creates a verse and the other complements it with a bridge. In this case, the bridge ("Woke up . . .") is close to being a complete song in itself, composed and sung by McCartney. It defines a persona that is clearly distinguished from the one in the verses, sung by Lennon. It is the finished musical articulation of this structure that makes the song so spectacularly successful. The results were so unprecedented and powerful that *A Day in the Life* was immediately compared (by *Newsweek*) with T. S. Eliot's poem *The Waste Land*.

The great conductor-composer-critic Leonard Bernstein described how "three bars of *A Day in the Life* still sustain me, rejuvenate me, inflame my senses and sensibilities." Lennon sings as if from a distance, with understated delivery. He is recorded with an exceptionally long delay, and his lines are punctuated by piano chording never heard before, a huge sound coming from afar and portending storms ahead. The texture is vast yet empty. McCartney asked a reluctant Starr to invent drum fills instead of simply keeping time. The results—likewise muffled and big at the same time—are superb.

The famous orchestral cacophony first appears as a transition into the bridge, a ferocious swirl of energy that gradually overtakes the initial haze. McCartney had been hanging out at the electronic studio of Peter Zinovieff, an independently wealthy PhD from Oxford who loved to experiment with sequencing, randomness, and musique concrète. Martin remembered that McCartney wanted a "spiraling ascent of sound, suggesting we start the passage with all instruments on their lowest note and climbing to the highest in their own time." McCartney's concern was to balance audacity with accessibility. "The worst thing about doing something like this is people get a bit suspicious," he can be heard saying on a rolling tape picking up studio chatter. "Like, 'come on, what are you up to?'" In a January interview he spoke about the risk of moving too far ahead too fast. He saw himself as a link to avant-garde electronics. His caution was born from full acceptance of his role as a musician whose primary task is to connect with the audience.

After the chaotic transition swells and bursts, the song lands on a thumping piano quite different from the ominous piano of the verses. McCartney, now the singer, is recorded full, close, and dry, very different from Lennon's surreal detachment. From this aural trickery we understand the purpose of the transitional chaos: it transports the song from one persona to another, not a typical strategy in popular songs. It takes us from the knowing outsider to the hopeless insider. The new persona is straight, hurried, conventional. It could be Mr. Jones himself rushing through his quotidian hassles, getting his tea, catching the bus, though he is more sympathetic than Dylan would have him, a bit like you and me.

The scoring at the end of the bridge, during the dream, is skillfully done. After the song crisply returns to the verses and their initial atmosphere, the absurdity of the conventional world is pushed to the limit with the counting riddle of four thousand holes at Albert Hall. The farcical tone and quickened pace prepare for the bigger chaos to come. With the final release into oblivion, the supernaturally long piano chord resolves all dramatic tension and punctuates the kaleidoscopic brilliance of the entire album. (An earlier idea was to chant "om" here, a sacred syllable that represents the universal essence and advises caution against nihilistic interpretations of this moment.) Still, the Beatles, in 1967, were not inclined to leave seriousness dangling, so British record buyers were treated to one last joke, the goofy, inner-groove tape loop that popped out surprisingly just before the phonograph arm was about to lift and return to its place, analogous to the laughter at the end of *Within You Without You*.

In song lyrics, Bob Dylan could spin circles around anyone. Brian Wilson could match anyone in musical craft. Neither could combine the two at the deep level of symbiosis achieved by Lennon and McCartney. And nobody else could, either.

If Lennon was good at launching a breakthrough song that provided intellectual gravity, McCartney was the one who got the album started with the title track and the second track, *With a Little Help from My Friends*. It was smart to open with high-energy rock—and rock that was very up to date, it should be noted. McCartney's chords for the theme song do not connect to Chuck Berry but to Jimi Hendrix's *Purple Haze*, just released in March. (Hendrix returned the compliment by covering the *Pepper* theme at the Saville Theatre three days after the album was released. Then McCartney bowed in Hendrix's direction once again by repeating these chords in the theme song for *Magical Mystery Tour*.)

It was even smarter to move directly into *With a Little Help from My Friends*, a jaunty tune with *Penny Lane*'s tempo and ambience. The song was conceived for Starr, acting naturally as the fictional Billy Shears, the lyrics filled out with extensive back and forth between McCartney and Lennon. *With a Little Help from My Friends* has the humble drummer close to the mic and close to the audience. "Of course you can take part, anyone can," Lennon said to his teenage friend Pete Shotton when he tried to get him to join his skiffle band, even though Shotton was completely devoid of talent. In 1967 the sophisticated Beatles were in danger of losing their connection to the unassuming side of rock and roll, but Starr's unpretentious voice and persona helped keep it going. The accommodating drummer held things together musically and socially, and he freshly defined their communal image in *Yellow Submarine* and *With a Little Help from My Friends*.

The two opening tracks, both based on pretend names, already mark a range of playful expression. Beatles humor, with origins in Scouse sarcasm and *The Goon Show* mimicry, two traditions of undermining the hegemony of British aristocracy, was a major part of *Pepper*'s nothing-is-real, psychedelic vision. Humor is often about shifting meaning, a sudden glimpse of an unfixed point of view. The *Pepper* band is not just funny in its military uniforms, it is surreal. Humor is infused into so many of the *Pepper* songs that it becomes thematic, a way of puncturing all limiting concepts and opening into a bigger view of life that is "fluid and changing all the time and evolving," as McCartney put it.

Lucy in the Sky with Diamonds follows to form a deftly effective psychological sequence for the first three tracks: the pretend, theatrical fun of the opening track is public and extroverted; then comes the inner-circle warmth and tight camaraderie of track two; track three retreats further into a private, visionary world. When Lennon later complained that the concept of the album "doesn't go anywhere," he was ignoring this subtle progression.

Lucy in the Sky complements *A Day in the Life* in that the latter critiques the conventional world while the former celebrates the higher view. Like so much of *Pepper* it features hard-to-identify sounds crafted in the studio, correspondences corresponding approximately. Backward tape loops, now old hat, give way to more subtle engineering to define unique qualities for each song, the result of some four hundred hours of studio time spread over four and one-half months. *Lucy* has been criticized for the bald separation between its drifty verses and vigorous chorus. More sympathetically we could hear the chorus as a burst into ecstasy and an experience of childlike wonderment. Lennon was adamant about the origin of the title in a watercolor painting made by his four-year-old son, Julian, rather than the initials "LSD." The importance of this detail to him indicates his devotion to *Through the Looking Glass*, which he read passionately as a child, and the sense that the vivid and imaginative qualities described in both song and book are accessible to everyone, even without the drug.

The concept for an album of songs about Liverpool may have been inspired by *In My Life* and *Eleanor Rigby*, two songs full of empathy. In the meantime, Lennon's experiments with LSD turned him in the direction of edgy and boundary-breaking originality. "We're fed up with making soft music for soft people," he told Martin in November 1966. That left it to McCartney to pick up the warmer side and achieve emotional balance, an assignment for which he was fully primed.

Getting Better embodies the balance all by itself. McCartney brought the emerging song to his partner, and in a single line—the call and response that it isn't possible for things to get worse—Lennon complicated his partner's optimistic tilt; more darkly, he added the bridge about beating his woman. The two composers routinely added to each other's lyrics like this all the way through the *Ballad of John and Yoko*. With *Getting Better*, Lennon's adjustments took a straightforward song and put it in motion, lifting it into the album's play of humor and shifting meaning. Musically, the song crackles with forward-moving energy, sensitive design, and warm tunefulness. Beatles biographer Hunter Davies watched the production of it and filed a report. "Paul instructed the technician on which levers to press, telling him what he wanted, how it should be done, which bits he liked best," said Davies. "George Martin looked on, giving advice where necessary. John stared into space." With fiancée Jane Asher on a three-month theatrical tour of the United States, January through March, McCartney was ratcheting up his micromanagement of the studio.

McCartney's *Fixing a Hole* builds on the point of view of *Strawberry Fields Forever*. William Mann, the classical music critic for the *Times*, heard this song as "cool, anti-romantic, harmonically a little like the earlier *Yesterday* and *Michelle*." It is easy to miss the excellence of an unpretentious song like this. As composer Ned Rorem put it, with McCartney as his example, "genius doesn't lie in not being derivative, but in making right choices instead of wrong ones." One difference between *Pepper* and an innovative album like Pink Floyd's *The Piper at the Gates of Dawn* is that a

7.4 McCartney rehearsing "A Day in the Life," Abbey Road studio, February 1967

second tier (for *Pepper*) track like *Fixing a Hole* is musically stronger, by far, than anything on *The Piper at the Gates of Dawn*.

At the very warm end of McCartney's *Pepper* spectrum stands *When I'm 64*, perhaps the most maligned song on the album, even though it works well as a unique part of the collage of social and entertainment registers. The song dates from when McCartney's father, Jim, was still a primary musical influence on his teenage son. Beatles scholar Walter Everett has suggested that the spur for its revival was the chart-making success of *Winchester Cathedral* by the New Vaudeville Band in October 1966. While *64* evokes the music hall with its bouncy rhythms and conventional melody—it remains a work of juvenilia at this level—it is not simply a dip into nostalgia. McCartney's insight was to see how, with the right arrangement and dose of winky humor (Lennon contributing the chuckling names of the grandchildren), the "schmaltz," as he put it, could be lightened up and occupy a satisfying slot in *Pepper's* heady mix.

The clarinets of *64* are effective, and so are the harp and strings of *She's Leaving Home*, though for different reasons. The clarinets rescue 64 from camp, while the harp and strings of *She's Leaving Home* bring into relief the delusionary world of the hopeless parents; along with the falsetto singing they help define this domestic perfection as a transparent illusion. The implicit theme of the album—"It isn't necessarily so, what you believe"—strengthens this song and vice versa. Musical tenderness solicits empathy for the clueless parents, and the departing daughter quietly emerges as an unnamed heroine who has turned on, dropped out, and freed herself from bourgeois conformity.

Lovely Rita offers another dose of McCartney's captivating blend of warmth, humor, and tunefulness. It was funny to imagine the world's most eligible bachelor losing his hair and mending a fuse, and funny to think of him bedding the meter maid, as he does at the song's end with comic reenactment of the panting sex from Ray Charles's *What'd I Say*. Once again musical warmth lifts the song above simple comedy: it tells us that the meter maid is rather fetching.

What is so artistically persuasive about *Pepper* is how the kaleidoscopic dance of imagery, the tapestry of emotions, the play of humor, is all so beautifully energized by the music. Edgy songs from Lennon are an important part of the texture. *Good Morning Good Morning*, with its shifting patterns of beats and sneering transitions, is a mate to *A Day in the Life*; the protagonist has a harder time scuffling through the world in the former than he does in McCartney's bridge for the latter. *Being for the Benefit of Mr. Kite* is childlike, colorful, and wondrous, a psychedelic calliope, brilliantly realized, the musical equivalent to the dayglo uniforms on the cover. Other musicians in 1967 were exploring psychedelic styles, but none could match either the Beatles' range or their musical magnetism. That is why *Pepper* was one of a kind: the safest thing was to go in another direction.

One song remains, and it is the most challenging on the whole album—Harrison's *Within You Without You*. Like *Tomorrow*

Never Knows, it is something of a sermon, a starting point for lay-
ing out a philosophy that would yield to less preachy efforts in
the future. Except for the pun in the title and brief refrain it is
completely serious, so serious that Harrison felt he had to lighten
the atmosphere by throwing in canned, nervous laughter from the
imaginary audience at the end of the track. The point of view is
based on religious teachings from India dating back thousands
of years. The music also takes inspiration from North India,
introductory *alap* in free, unmeasured rhythm, followed by a *tala*
rhythmic cycle and melodic material that is close to modes of *raga*.
Martin worked with the violinists and cellists to get raga-style
bending of pitch and rhythm, amplifying the seriousness of the
song with Western classical instruments and suggesting rap-
prochement between East and West (following the lead of the
Ravi Shankar-Yehudi Menuhin collaboration *West Meets East*,
released January 1967).

Pepper would have been terrific without *Within You Without
You*, but its presence clarifies and deepens everything else. *A Day
in the Life* is a potent critique of materialistic values, and *Lucy in
the Sky* offers psychedelic rapture; *Within You Without You* firmly
grounds the psychedelic view in Vedic spirituality. If one is sympathetic, it can subtly define the entire album. The pretend band
and fake audience, surreal circus tricks and empty suburban rush
hour, failing families and superficial happiness, the fetching meter
maid and handsome Paul losing his hair—the entire fantasy may
be understood as the "wall of illusion" (*maya* in Sanskrit). The
album's sprawl suggests a universal reach. *Within You Without
You* states plainly that each of us can dissolve the wall of illusion
and experience limitless love and ultimate truth.

Harrison needed five full minutes to ground *Pepper*'s dazzling
psychedelic fantasy in the nurturing embrace of Mother India.
There was talk of trimming but he stood firm. It was risky to take
the psychedelic inquiry in this direction. The song pointedly asks
where you, the listener, stand. *Nowhere Man* observed how each

of us can be a little blind, just seeing what we like to see. Now the full antidote is placed at the beginning of side two of the Beatles' greatest album. Lennon gave *Tomorrow Never Knows* a throwaway title to deflect the song's seriousness, but the title *Within You Without You* leaves no possibility of escape. Stephen Stills had Harrison's lyric engraved on a stone monument in his backyard, and Lennon eventually praised it as Harrison's best composition.

Within You Without You and *A Day in the Life* bookend *Pepper's* second side, two five-minute-plus, mind-blowing songs, each aiming to define not just the album but an entire epoch. *A Day in the Life* was instantly recognized as a masterpiece, though *Within You Without You* did not fare that well, partly because of the Indian music, partly because of the didacticism. Not everyone has understood it in the way I have described, as gathering *Pepper's* psychedelic world under a Vedic tent. "Harrison now seems to take seriously . . . the kind of homilies that used to make the Beatles giggle . . . 'self-discovery' and 'universal love,'" snorted Robert Christgau in *Esquire*, with condescension that has been rampant in literature on the Beatles. Nevertheless, that was certainly where the Beatles were headed in 1967—that is, they were headed to India.

The recording studio turned out to offer the best way to musically articulate a psychedelic vision, and the combination landed the Beatles in the realm of art like no other rock group. Reviewing *Pepper* in the *New Yorker*, Lillian Ross felt that there was only one possible comparison: "The Beatles, like Duke Ellington, are unclassifiable musicians." As with Ellington, diversity of expression arose from the plurality of voices, setting them apart from all competition. Their closest rivals at the top of art rock, Dylan and Wilson, sounded monochromatic in comparison. The composer of *The Times They Are a-Changin'* was open enough to appreciate *I Want to Hold Your Hand*, but he is said not to have liked *Pepper*. Wilson was struck by the folk-rock homogeneity of *Rubber Soul* and he aimed to better it; compared with *Pepper*, *Pet Sounds* does indeed sound homogeneous. There was no way that Dylan or Wilson or anyone else could compete with *Pepper*'s brilliant display. Nobody else had the four-headed monster's magical mix of talent, collaboration, and mastery of craft.

Like other musical monuments that define their times, *Pepper*'s status was less one of trendsetter and more a matter of unapproachable awe. It set a standard that was a burden even for the Beatles.

Love, Death, and Mystery

While the foursome increasingly oriented to India, the second half of 1967 brought several surprises and a crippling tragedy. On June 25 they sort of performed (part prerecorded and part live) Lennon's *All You Need Is Love* for a television broadcast that reached around the globe. The show included segments from many countries, a gesture of international harmony. The Beatles were selected for the grand finale. The love in this song is the same love that will save the world in *Within You Without You*. The opening with *La Marseillaise* seems to say that the Beatles are offering an international anthem for the revolutionary Summer of Love.

When Harrison actually visited Haight-Ashbury he was shocked by the squalor and sloppiness of come-one-come-all hippiedom. The Beatles had just released their fanciest artistic statement of all. They were at one with high-end technology. How could they align themselves with the casual strumming and free jam sessions of Golden Gate Park? A sing-along was the clever solution. It didn't matter that the rest of the lyrics for *All You Need Is Love* were vague and mediocre. Beatles wit and tunefulness (and skillful use of irregular phrasing) carried the day.

Then Brian Epstein died from a drug overdose, leaving the group with a tremendous loss, professionally and personally. There had been growing dissatisfaction with Epstein's contractual arrangements, still in place from the early days, and it has even been suggested that *Baby You're a Rich Man* (another combi-

7.5 San Francisco, summer of 1967

native song, part from Lennon and part from McCartney) was a
dig at his sustained harvest of Beatles profits. Nevertheless, they
still depended on him. "Just as Paul had assumed some of the
production duties from George Martin," observed Emerick, "he
now filled Brian's shoes as well." McCartney's first initiative was
to move forward on the *Magical Mystery Tour* movie, which combined the British institution of the mystery bus tour, where you
buy a ticket without knowing where the bus is destined, with Ken
Kesey's psychedelic bus adventure. The movie flopped, though it is
not as bad as its reputation. With a little tinkering and reworking
it could have been excellent. A halfhearted album with the same
title was patched together.

We could define the psychedelic phase of the Beatles' career as beginning with *Tomorrow Never Knows* (April 1966), reaching its apex with *Sgt. Pepper*, and ending with *I Am the Walrus* (September 1967). *I Am the Walrus* takes that aesthetic seriously. Like *Tomorrow Never Knows*, *Strawberry Fields Forever*, *A Day in the Life*, *Come Together*, and *I Want You*, *I Am the Walrus* was a conceptual breakthrough that received royal treatment from the collaborative team. Lennon once said that it took him a while to figure out how to follow Dylan's example, and the Rimbaudian Dylan of *A Hard Rain's a-Gonna Fall*, *Mr. Tambourine Man*, and *Chimes of Freedom* was the most difficult challenge of all. *I Am the Walrus* is his great, crowning victory.

Behind the direct influence of Dylan and the indirect influence of Rimbaud lay, once again, Lewis Carroll, who wrote a poem called "The Walrus and the Carpenter" and created the character Humpty Dumpty (the eggman) for *Through the Looking Glass*. The messianic opening phrase of *I Am the Walrus* was derived from the very first page of Maharishi Mahesh Yogi's commentary on the Bhagavad Gita: "I am That, thou are That, and thou are That and all this is That." But the rest of the song chases Rimbaud as channeled through Dylan, the poet as visionary who disorders the rational world of the senses. Non sequiturs spill out in all directions in a chain of micronarratives about dead dogs, English gardens, and flying policemen. In both *Strawberry Fields* and *A Day in the Life* the singer looks on with amused detachment (in his own tree, reading the newspaper, watching a film) at the folly and shallowness of conventional Britain. In *Walrus* he has grown ten feet tall. He is an eggman and a walrus, and he cries while the rational world darts around in sharp, brittle fragments.

The lyrical imagery is vivid, but what makes *I Am the Walrus* so powerful—and what distinguishes it from anything Dylan ever wrote—is the musical-lyrical synthesis, the combination once again yielding a song with no precedent. *I Am the Walrus* is the ultimate (for the 1960s) realization of Rimbaudian aesthetics.

They began recording barely a few days after Epstein's death. A distracted Starr was having trouble concentrating, so McCartney picked up a tambourine, stood in front of him, and kept time, "like a human click track," as Emerick put it. The studio engineer found yet another fresh way to defamiliarize Lennon's voice with a cheap mic and an overloaded preamp. The siren-like, oscillating melody is effectively embedded in high-profile and inventive harmonies that swirl around in a way nicely described by critic Ian MacDonald as a "perpetually ascending/descending M. C. Escher staircase." Martin's superb arrangement turns ordinary cellos into savage instruments of revenge against those who would kick around an outsider genius like Edgar Allan Poe.

McCartney and Lennon had been experimenting at home with random combinations of sound and video by turning the sound off from the television and joining the visual with records and radio. Lennon brought the twirling radio dial into *Walrus*. The Mike Sammes Singers were hired to deliver the joker's laugh. The great novelist Milan Kundera wrote in *The Book of Laughter and Forgetting* about the laughter of the devil, which denies the world's rational coherence, and the laughter of the angels, affirming harmony and beauty. If Richard Lester's movie *A Hard Day's Night* was all about the fun-loving laughter of harmonious angels, *I Am the Walrus* conveys the logic-slaying laughter of the devil. The song was paired with *Hello Goodbye*, another terrific piece of music that shows McCartney's knack for making things complicated where they need to be complicated, with independent melody, bass, chords, guitar riff, and vocal call and response, then simple where they need to be simple. *Hello Goodbye* overshadowed *Walrus* in the marketplace, to Lennon's great irritation.

CHAPTER 8

GROW A
LITTLE TALLER

"WE'D ALL LEARNED to grow together and some days one of us would grow a little taller"—that was how Starr described Beatles symbiosis. During the last few years of the group's existence, Harrison unexpectedly led the way. The Quiet Beatle took seriously what others merely dabbled in, and his full immersion in India lifted the entire group. His effort infused their music with reflection, depth, and compassion. It distanced them from the art-school rockers—as Keith Richards snickered, "I'm quite proud that I never did go and kiss the Maharishi's goddamn feet." It's true, Richards never came close to writing songs like *Across the Universe, Hey Jude*, and *Here Comes the Sun*. Harrison's embrace of India was central to the crowning phase of the Beatles' career, which confirmed their status as the musicians who defined the 1960s.

While they were filming *Help!* in early 1965, Harrison discovered a sitar on the set. The weakest of the five Beatles films, *Help!* is a postcolonial farce that ridicules the primitive, ignorant, and barbaric (from a British point of view) sides of India. The Beatles hated the film. Harrison remembered his mother listening to music from India on the radio when he was a child. Emboldened by precedents like the Kinks' *See My Friends*, he flipped British condescension and felt an attraction. By October he was able to add a touch of exoticism to *Norwegian Wood* with a simple sitar solo. Also during filming for *Help!* came a chance introduction, on location in the Bahamas, to Swami Vishnudevananda, who gave each Beatle a copy of his book *The Complete Illustrated Book of Yoga*. The Swami signed and dated Harrison's copy, February 23, 1965, which happened to be Harrison's birthday. He took that as an auspicious sign.

In the spring of 1965, Lennon and Harrison were also introduced to LSD. Lennon was intrigued by how Leary connected the drug to Eastern mysticism, but Harrison took that linkage more seriously: "For me it was like a flash, the first time I had acid, it just opened up something in my head that was inside of me, and I realized a lot of things . . . [LSD] happened to be the key that opened the door to reveal them. From the moment I had that, I wanted to have it all the time—these thoughts about the yogis and the Himalayas, and Ravi's music."

The first musical fruit of his new passion was *Love You To* (from *Revolver*), which relies heavily on musicians from London's Indian Music Association. The song provided Harrison with a new niche. He put his guitar aside and made the sitar his primary instrument all the way until the end of 1968. In the summer of 1966 he met Ravi Shankar in London and took some lessons. This fortuitous connection could not have been bettered. Shankar was a sitar virtuoso who made it his life's goal to promote the North Indian raga tradition in the West. For him, the primary purpose of music was devotional, to reach God, which made him the perfect person to bring Harrison into not only music but also religion. Lennon and McCartney took Dylan and Brian Wilson as remote models for new phases in their compositional careers, but Harrison found a mentor who was willing to personally bring him along. Shankar was "the only person who ever impressed me," Harrison once said (having forgotten the impressiveness of the teenage Lennon). Shankar in turn appreciated Harrison's humility.

It was as if a hidden intelligence in the Beatles' hierarchy was now emerging, with Harrison's modest position relative to the two principals allowing him to take bigger risks, a classic "last born" situation: Harrison, the youngest of four children and the youngest in the band of four, had less reason to defend the status quo. He was open to a rebellion more radical than those ahead of him cared to pursue.

Anyone who wishes to scan his turn to India in terms of "orientalism"—a vigorous European tradition of manipulating stereotypes from the exotic "East" for trivializing purposes, a form of control only slightly more subtle than blackfaced minstrelsy—misses two central points. First, his goals were to learn musical and spiritual *practices*; second, his engagement was driven through direct contact with powerful mentors. His teachers regarded these traditions as universal treasures of humanity that should be available to everyone. They wanted the best of India's heritage to travel across cultural boundaries. Access to top talent was an important part of many Beatles' successes, and in this case, especially, fast-track, high-level tutoring gave potency to the group's connections to India, accounting for the impressive results.

In one of his first lessons, Harrison got up to answer the telephone, and as he stepped across his sitar Shankar whacked him on the heel, scolding not to disrespect his instrument. Around the same time that art-schooler Pete Townshend was introducing nihilistic gestures like smashing his guitar on stage, Harrison was being taught by the only person who ever impressed him about the fundamental concept of respect and how to manifest it in his life. ("I started my own rebellion against these rebellious youths," Shankar once said.) It is a simple moment that symbolically represents the spiritual orientation that shaped the last phase of the Beatles' career. The Beatles would not be putting anarchy and nihilism in a primary position. Nor would they reduce their stunning variety of expression to straight-ahead rock, an increasingly popular construction of authenticity. Lennon was tempted by all of those trends. But what gave the Beatles so much heart, what made them the ultimate representatives of the 1960s counterculture, was the firm infusion of a genuine spiritual tradition into their music.

In the autumn of 1966, Harrison traveled with his wife Pattie to India for seven weeks. He was impressed by the role religion played in the lives of ordinary people, not something reserved for Sunday morning but a way of life. Pattie learned to play the *dilruba* while George studied intensively with Shankar. They met Shankar's guru, who instructed them on the law of karma. They saw sadhus living in poverty, and they visited the sacred cremation grounds of Benares, along the banks of the Ganges. Shankar gave concerts that lasted until four in the morning. They spent several weeks with the virtuoso and his entourage on a houseboat in Kashmir, practicing and talking endlessly about music and religion. "I got the privileged tour," Harrison observed. When they returned to London, he embraced his sitar with fanatical devotion, taking breaks to practice yoga and meditation, mixed with LSD.

From Shankar, Harrison received a copy of *Autobiography of a Yogi* by Paramahansa Yogananda, and from Shankar's brother a copy of *Raja Yoga* by Swami Vivekananda. Yogananda (1893–1952) took it as his mission to bring Hindu spirituality to the West, while Vivekananda (1863–1902) had pursued the same goal earlier. "Each soul is potentially divine," wrote Vivekananda. "The goal is to manifest that divinity." Those words moved Harrison deeply. He closely studied *The Bhagavad Gita* with Yogananda's commentary volume. *Autobiography of a Yogi* includes photos of the author and his guru Swami Sri Yukteswar Giri, *his* guru Lahiri Mahasaya, and *his* guru Babaji. Harrison put all four of them on the cover of *Sgt. Pepper's Lonely Hearts Club Band*, and he put his new composition *Within You Without You* on the LP itself. The year separating this song from *Love You To* was a period of full immersion in the music and spirituality of India. He absorbed Ravi Shankar's point of view and did not perceive any boundary between the two.

With informal ease, *Within You Without You* conveys the Vedic teachings he had been contemplating, just as if he and his friend Klaus Voorman were hanging out and chatting (as he described the origin of the lyrics). The three books that we know he was reading—*Autobiography of a Yogi, Raja Yoga,* and *The Complete Illustrated Book of Yoga*—are all first-rate expositions in English of the Vedic tradition. This song bound his interest in India to his emergence as a songwriter, the two growing more sophisticated in tandem. The integrity of the song gained the goodwill of his bandmates. In a striking way, mid-1967 found the four of them (or at least the three creative principals) on the same page with regard to the Eastern foundations of the psychedelic inquiry. "God is in the space between us," said McCartney. "God is in the table in front of you . . . It just happens I've realized all this through acid."

In August, Pattie persuaded her husband, who persuaded Lennon and McCartney, to attend a lecture in London given by Maharishi Mahesh Yogi. The Maharishi presented meditation as something that anyone could benefit from, without religious trappings. "If we'd met Maharishi before we had taken LSD, we wouldn't have needed to take it," insisted Lennon. The Maharishi invited them to join him for a group retreat in Wales, but on the second day Brian Epstein, back in London, suddenly died. They abandoned the retreat, but not the Maharishi, who encouraged them to join him in Rishikesh, India, an area favored by renunciants in the sacred foothills of the Himalayas, where he had a residential center funded by cigarette heiress Doris Duke.

Plans were made to visit in February. Meanwhile, they meditated and kept in touch, McCartney and Harrison visiting the Maharishi in Sweden and Lennon and Harrison in Paris. "You know I feel I can handle anything at the moment and I never felt like that before," said Lennon. "[This is] the greatest period for us in an inner sense." His close friend from childhood, Pete Shotton, saw how good it all was for Lennon. One evening Shotton was watching television with the four musicians when Lennon suggested they turn the sound off and meditate. Shotton sneaked a peak during the twenty-minute session and noted Harrison and Lennon in deep concentration while Starr watched a silent soap opera on the TV set; Starr shot Shotton a wink. "We were looking for something more natural," explained McCartney in August. "This is it. It's not weirdy or anything, it is dead natural. Meditation will be good for everyone."

"I hope the fans will take up meditation instead of drugs," advised Starr.

McCartney composed *The Fool on the Hill*, which he defined as a song about the Maharishi, and Lennon answered with *Across the Universe*. *The Fool on the Hill* is a strong song, but *Across the Universe* is one of Lennon's best. It was never developed on record to a finished state worthy of its quality. *Across the Universe* deals with the imagery of mystics. In his book *On the Bhagavad-Gita: A New Translation and Commentary with Sanskrit Text* (1967), the Maharishi describes a mind no longer imprisoned by a "field of

8.1 McCartney, Jane Asher, Mike McGear, Lennon, Cynthia Lennon, and Pattie Harrison at the Maharishi's lecture in London, August 24, 1967

sorrow" or "waves of joy." The accomplished meditator becomes "an unbounded ocean of love and happiness. His love and his happiness flow and overflow for everyone in like manner." Lennon's song is indebted to these lines and it quotes the mantra *"Jai guru deva"* (Victory to the guru-god), which was chanted in homage to the Maharishi by his followers.

There was an idea to put *Across the Universe* on the B side of McCartney's *Lady Madonna*, but Harrison's *The Inner Light* was chosen instead. A McCartney favorite, *The Inner Light* was recorded with a superb ensemble of five Indian musicians, with Harrison's vocal added back in London. Harrison was nervous about singing the lead, but McCartney encouraged him and got him through. It is a simple song about the power of meditation, the lyrics based on the classic Taoist text *Tao Te Ching* by Lao-tzu. In *The Inner Light*, the weight of *Within You Without You* gives way to enchantment and whimsy, with Pink Floyd's *Chapter 24* as a possible inspiration.

The four musicians arrived in India in mid-February. Starr, nervous about the food and his weak stomach (a condition that began in childhood), brought a suitcase filled with canned beans. Cynthia Lennon felt her husband drifting away. In fact, he was indeed strolling down to the post office every day to both drop off a letter to and pick up one from Yoko Ono. But for the most part, Rishikesh was a happy time. It put them all on the same page, renewed the Beatles as a communal enterprise, launched dozens of new songs, defined *The White Album*, and put the Maharishi's teachings on "transcendental meditation" on the map like nothing else could have.

The retreatants woke up every day to the screams of peacocks and monkeys. They dressed in white, ate vegetarian food, practiced meditation, listened to the Maharishi's lectures, met with him in private audiences, and hung out together in the cool mountain air. The Maharishi presented meditation as a simple but flexible practice that could help with anything in life, lead to

8.2 Donovan, Harrison, and the Maharishi in Rishikesh, along the Ganges, 1968

cosmic consciousness, and bring harmony to the world. Lennon quizzed him about the "big brass band" that was in his head when he meditated. McCartney remembered how he "got to a really good place" through meditation. "I felt like I was a feather, floating over a hot air pipe." Mia Farrow was there with her sister Prudence, who was unsettled and stuck to her room. Prudence was determined to fast-track her meditative path. Maharishi asked Lennon to coax her out for a little bit of social time, which led to the four Beatles lining up outside her door and singing the emerging *Dear Prudence*. Farrow saw the Beatles as belonging to a "land of light, and of youth, strength, and certainty; they seemed beautiful and fearless."

The Maharishi banned drugs, and they respected that request with the tiny (for them) exception of some joints. There were no easy ways for them to experience communal living, and Rishikesh turned out to be the solution. It was a holiday of healing and socialized creativity. "For creating it was great," remembered Lennon. "It was just pouring out." They brought along acoustic guitars

and spent a lot of time strumming and fooling around, composing dozens of songs that filled the next three albums and beyond.
(Lennon's 1971 *Jealous Guy*, for example, began life at Rishikesh with the title *Child of Nature*, a companion to McCartney's
Mother Nature's Son.) McCartney estimated that twenty of the
thirty songs on *The White Album* started in Rishikesh. "John and
George were in their element," explained Cynthia. "They threw
themselves totally into the Maharishi's teachings, were happy,
relaxed and above all had found a peace of mind that had been
denied them for so long . . . To John nothing else mattered. He
spent literally days in deep meditation . . ." In a postcard from
Rishikesh, McCartney wrote to Starr (who had already left) that
"John and George have each done 7 hours, but we've [he and Jane
Asher] only managed 2½ so far."

Starr departed after two weeks and McCartney stayed for five.
"I'm a new man," he told a friend. Lennon and Harrison stuck
with it for eight weeks, though their departure unfolded badly.
Urged on by Lennon's friend, the jealous and scheming Magic
Alex (John Alexis Mardas), they falsely accused the Maharishi of
sexual impropriety and deception. The guru had no idea what was
going on and asked why they were leaving so suddenly. Lennon
snarled, "Well, if you're so cosmic, you'll know why." He silently
interpreted a flash in the Maharishi's eyes to say, "I'll kill you, you
bastard." With that, the novice reduced his teacher to the level of
the Liverpool streets. "I felt that what we were doing was wrong,
very wrong," remembered Cynthia. The Maharishi found out the
hard way how celebrity sparks could backfire. From parts of the
Western world there was an almost audible sigh of relief, an echo
of the response to Elvis joining the Army in 1958, a collective
satisfaction that this disavowal of meditation, the Maharishi and
Indian spirituality would bring a return to normalcy—whatever
that could possibly mean in the spring of 1968. McCartney and
Harrison later apologized to the Maharishi. Many more people
today remember Lennon's accusations than the apologies.

The bottom line, as each of his bandmates have noted, was that Lennon had better things to do. It is easy to imagine how difficult it must have been for him to break with the Maharishi, who had helped him considerably, but this was just one part of a huge transition in his life. He composed a tacky little song to commemorate the moment. *Sexy Sadie* is an indictment of the guru he had been so beholden to (the deflecting title came at Harrison's request, replacing the original title, *Maharishi*). The triumphant quality in this song should not be missed. It is as if Lennon's fragile ego has realized that it cannot possibly defend itself against the potency of these teachings and practices. *Sexy Sadie* confirmed that this was now past. He was free to turn his back on meditation and embrace his new lover, avant-garde conceptual art, and heroin.

The White Album

The retreat was so creatively fertile that it required a double LP. In place of the elaborate fantasy of *Pepper*'s album cover there is just a white cover, designed by the artist Richard Hamilton, with the name of the group faintly embossed.

The album has been described as a postmodern statement. This is the kind of grandiose analysis that made the Beatles chuckle, a fancy way to grapple with the lack of a unifying concept and the sprawling diversity. For the first time they include fragments, a postmodern specialty. The range of *Pepper*'s collage is matched and doubled. Lennon's taste for satire is echoed by Harrison. McCartney offers warm ballads, fun-loving narratives, and hard rock. Lennon embraces full-frontal avant-gardism and raw blues. Vaudeville, lullaby, doo-wop, swing, blues, a nature anthem, old-fashioned rock and roll, cutting-edge heavy metal, and country all mix it up. Humor is everywhere, in the music and in the lyrics, ironic, punning, childlike, coy, raucous, silly, slapstick, sly, playful, and over the top. "Both John and I had a great love for music hall, what the Americans call vaudeville," explained

McCartney. Musical parodies (Beach Boys, Dylan, Donovan, Tiny Tim, The Who, etc.) go in more directions than one can count. All of the past is available for play in the present, and nothing gains dominant traction.

The postmodern array (if one wishes to call it that) is stunning, but for me what stands out are the reflective songs that represent Rishikesh most directly, with its communal synergy of acoustic guitars, meditation, and relaxed sociability—*Dear Prudence, While My Guitar Gently Weeps, Blackbird, I Will, Julia, Mother Nature's Son, Long, Long, Long, Revolution 1, Cry Baby Cry*, and *Good Night*. No more soft music for soft people, declared Lennon as *Pepper* was incubating, but Rishikesh and the Maharishi changed his mind. These songs are tender, contemplative, and full of heart. They have nothing to do with postmodern cynicism and everything to do with the very best of the countercultural 1960s. They define the soulful center of the album.

Blackbird is another example (*Eleanor Rigby, And Your Bird Can Sing, Penny Lane*) of McCartney discovering inspiration in classical music from the Baroque period. He cited a bourrée by Johann Sebastian Bach as an influence on this song. The connection has to do with the richness of independent lines (though the impact from an étude by Fernando Sor seems more direct). *Blackbird* ranks among McCartney's best work. It is heartfelt but impersonal when compared with *Julia*, Lennon's startling step into publicly exposed vulnerability. Lennon builds his lyric around a couple of Kahlil Gibran's aphorisms and presents it with soul-bearing tenderness. Lennon instructed Martin to arrange his lullaby *Good Night*, composed for his son Julian, with over-the-top camp, but Martin wisely ignored him. Here is a wonderful exception to the Beatles' allergy to straightforward sentimentality. Starr's unpretentious persona makes it work. Engineer Geoff Emerick remembered the other three standing behind him as he worked to get the vocal right, urging him on in four-headed-monster fashion. No other Beatles album ends like this.

While My Guitar Gently Weeps helps focus the album's contemplative side. Modest images gently drift in and out of the lyrics—unlimited love latent in every human being, a little Zen sweeping of the floor to clear away self-centered clutter, the sad heart of the compassionate, knowing observer. These sentiments work well with the minor/major contrast between verses and bridge, and they are enriched by the introduction and descending bass lines, with effective layers of percussion in the background. Without a trace of self-consciousness, the song synthesizes African American blues with an Eastern perspective. As provincial outsiders with no culture to protect, the Beatles had reached a global perspective.

The title promises strong guitar work. Harrison's initial idea to have an edgy, backward guitar solo may be taken as a confession that he was simply not up to the task. It was a good decision to abandon that plan and ask his friend Eric Clapton to add the weeping guitar. Usually in Beatles songs, instrumental solos do not command too much attention but lend support to the total effect. *While My Guitar Gently Weeps* is the exception, justified by the title. The guitar is an equal partner from the moment it enters in lovely call and response with the singer. Clapton's solo, one of the greatest he has ever recorded, magnificently gives life to the aspiration of the lyrics. It is paced skillfully from the first note to the last as a coherent statement, deep blues that powerfully extend Harrison's compositional script. Clapton took a good song and made it great.

Along with the Indian musicians who played on *Within You Without You*, this is an example of creative collaboration brought in from outside the circle of four plus one. The absence of credit recalls Ellington's dissemblance, which is somewhat ironic given how central collaboration was to the Beatles' image. The lads from Liverpool did it all together, and they did it all by themselves. It was easy to stretch that configuration to include George Martin, with his technical know-how and classical training, graciously bringing "the boys" into the professional realm, but it was a different matter to bring in someone like Clapton. Just as Ellington and his publicists worked hard to sustain the image of a great artist who didn't need anyone else, so did the self-sufficient collaborative circle of the Beatles become a fixed boundary that required maintenance and secrecy.

The White Album is often read as a marker of the band's fragmentation and the end of collaboration. The main rebuttal to this is that most of it was generated during the communal retreat in Rishikesh. The three creative principals were moving independently, but Rishikesh and the long buildup to it put them all on the same page. There were still stunning moments of collective effort back in London, above all *Dear Prudence*. Here is another great example of a strong script from Lennon brilliantly developed by the creative team, including swirling, sitar-like guitars, superb drumming and piano touches from McCartney, and a deliberate ascent on Harrison's guitar for the finale that, when it reaches its peak, forms an absolutely perfect moment.

There was one collaboration with an outsider that was not hidden but instead occupied the painful center of a whirlwind controversy. Lennon and Ono, the most famous intervenor in Beatles history, worked together on *Revolution 9* for *The White Album*. In 1968 the Beatles recorded three pieces with "Revolution" in the title, two on *The White Album* and one on a single, one slow and acoustic, one raucous and electric, the third bizarre and avant-garde. How the three fit together—which has often been misunderstood—documents Lennon's personal turbulence in 1968 in a vivid way.

The up-tempo single, entitled simply *Revolution*, was released first. It was issued as the B side of *Hey Jude* in late August, five days before the Rolling Stones' *Street Fighting Man*, and on the first day of the Democratic National Convention in Chicago. The gentlemen's agreement between Beatles and Stones to stagger releases and avoid head-to-head competition collapsed in this case. *Street Fighting Man* was immediately banned on radio stations in Chicago, a city overwhelmed with rioting and arrests. The main musical impression one has from this *Revolution*, with its raucous guitar distortion and screaming lead vocal, is an explosion of rage. Yet the lyrics suggest something else.

This *Revolution* is a classic case of mixed messaging, a technique the Beatles had mastered in the early days, when Epstein tidied them up while they played tough rock and roll. Their songs were sexually charged and daring on the musical side, while the lyrics were safe and polite. For *Revolution*, Lennon badgered the studio engineer to distort the guitars harder and harder to match the intensity of his voice. The lyrics, on the other hand, say that the singer is repelled by political radicalism and all calls for violence. Instead he advocates a "revolution in the head," as the great Beatles commentator Ian MacDonald put it. Violence and hatred simply lead to more of the same. Count me out when it comes to Mao or any other destructive ideology, sings Lennon. This position earned the Beatles a warm endorsement from *Time* magazine while the radical Left lashed out bitterly.

The first key to understanding the triple *Revolution* conundrum is that Lennon conceived the foundational song in Rishikesh. For the Maharishi, spirituality trumped politics, which is a common position for religious leaders everywhere. It would not be surprising if the basic ideas of Lennon's song came straight out of his teacher's evening lectures. Having returned to London, in May he made a demo tape and put the song forward as the first to be recorded for the new album. This would be the major statement, the new album's equivalent of *Tomorrow Never Knows* and *A Day in the Life*. But by then he had reconceived the song. During the month or so after his return he spent a lot of time holing up with Ono, whose ideas about modern art were well informed, well practiced, and well articulated. The revolution of the song became an *artistic* one, replacing the spiritual one he had turned his back on.

At his suburban London home, he and Ono offered to a tape recorder what one critic has described as "whistling, caterwauling, groaning, wailing, moaning, shrieking, samplings of old records, the sounds of guitars being tuned and strummed, background noise, scraps of conversations." This material eventually filled the album *Two Virgins*, and it was a warm-up for the sound collage that ultimately became *Revolution 9*. The collage of *Revolution 9* had little

8.3 Ono and Lennon, July 1, 1968

in common with the album-track collage of *Pepper*, which was based on a variety of tunes, chords, engineering, imagery, and verbal narratives. It was instead a wild ride through fragments of barely identifiable tunes, orchestral warm-ups and doodlings, backward tape loops, electronic distortions, radio shows, and loads of random speech.

McCartney had dabbled in a one-off experiment of freak-out electronica called *Carnival of Light*, which was never intended for commercial release but made for fun and restricted playback at a happening in London in February 1967. Ono was no dabbler. She was born into immense privilege and wealth in prewar Tokyo. Like her conceptual-art predecessor Marcel Duchamp, she used her position of security to launch a career of full-throttle adventurism. With bohemian leanings in place she auspiciously landed at Sarah Lawrence College in 1953. In 1956 she moved to the Lower West Side, married to a young Japanese composer who was fascinated with the music of John Cage. This put her on a fast track into the downtown world of happenings filled with randomness, absurdity, and high concept. This group of artists took Duchamp's principle of regarding ordinary objects in special ways and added dynamic performance and audience interaction, though with far less humor.

In 1964, Ono published a book with the title *Grapefruit*, a collection of small poems that instructed the reader in quirky exercises of the imagination. In 1965 she premiered her legendary *Cut Piece* at Carnegie Hall, inviting audience members to mount the stage where she sat, pick up the scissors she provided, and cut away parts of her dress. Her 1966 *Film No. 4* was dedicated to a series of closely cropped human buttocks in motion.

Ono was smart enough to keep up with Lennon—he declared that this was rare in his experience with women—and in an excellent position to tutor him in a set of bold artistic principles. He had gotten a whiff of avant-garde art at the Liverpool College of Art and then in Hamburg with the Exis, but he kept all of that "bullshit" at a distance while climbing the ladder of Beatle fame. In May 1968 he was feeling differently. His close friends Stuart Sutcliff and Astrid Kirchherr had worn each other's clothes as an expression of how intellectually, artistically, and romantically close they were. Since Lennon was nine inches taller than Ono, that was not an option, though they could both wear similar white outfits. "She's me in drag," Lennon informed the world. He told a close friend that she was to him as Don Juan was to Carlos Castaneda.

The collage *Revolution 9* began life as an extension of the original song from Rishikesh. With help from Harrison and Ono, Lennon strategically set to work while McCartney was out of the country, knowing that his songwriting partner was not going to endorse this new direction. "Not bad," was McCartney's dismissive response to a first hearing. "You have no idea what you're talking about," sputtered Lennon. "This should be our next bloody single!"

"I agree with John, I think it's great," chimed in Ono, supportively. The collage grew and got cut from the slow tempo, acoustically based song from Rishikesh, which was now given the title *Revolution 1*. At Lennon's insistence, his experiment found a place on the double album as a separate track called *Revolution 9*.

Lennon wanted *Revolution 1* to be the flip side of the single with *Hey Jude*, but the others were wary that the slow tempo would not sell. His solution was to transform the song once more, now into an up-tempo rocker. Certainly he was aware of the soon-to-be-released *Street Fighting Man*. The opposite receptions of the two songs must have burned. In terms of hip credentials, nothing could top getting banned from the radio, and nothing could be worse than praise from *Time* magazine combined with scathing criticism from the Left.

What happened next was an effort to ameliorate his position with a single word. When *The White Album* came out in November, it included *Revolution 1*, with acoustic guitar and slow tempo, not too different from a demo tape made in May and presumably not too different from the song Lennon composed on the ashram's rooftop. But the word "in" was added after the singer advises those advocating destruction that they must count him out. It was a little flash of provocative ambivalence. It certainly seemed like a response to the scathing criticism, a slight nod of agreement that yes, there will be situations that demand violent revolution, a meek assertion that Lennon was not hopelessly bourgeois. The added "in" does not appear on the lyric sheet attached to the album, and it does not appear on the early demo. It very much looks like a late, strategic addition, post *Time* magazine and *Street Fighting Man*.

Often it is a mistake to lean too heavily on biography for interpreting art. Songs like *Dear Prudence* or *Let It Be*, for example, have precise biographical origins, but the narratives of those origins limit understanding of the end product more than they enlighten. In this case, however, biography explains a lot. Lennon's interior confusion produced three mutually contradictory *Revolutions*. It's worth imagining how a single *Revolution* might have stood as the dominant song on the album. Had Lennon yielded to Martin and his bandmates rather than to Ono as he developed the song, this hypothetical *Revolution* might have given the entire album more depth and definition, much as *A Day in the Life* did for *Pepper*. Instead, the triple *Revolutions* work against one another.

Emerick described the four Beatles, during work on *The White Album*, leaving the studio very late one night, headed to a club for some fun, and then returning for an impromptu session of work at four in the morning, which doesn't sound like a break-down of camaraderie. Yet there certainly were strains during the five months of production. Starr actually quit the band for two weeks, frustrated with McCartney's mix of cajoling him to do better and then surreptitiously redubbing his drumming. Were there limits to McCartney's micromanagement? "It got a bit like, 'I wrote the song and I want it this way,'" Starr remembered, "whereas before it was 'I wrote the song—give me what you can.'" Even more damaging was Lennon's insistence on bring-ing Ono into the studio, a move that astonished the others; he even brought in Magic Alex, whom he considered an electronic genius but has been portrayed by others as a complete charlatan. Best-friend-as-needed Starr was nominated to make a friendly visit to Weybridge. "Listen, John, does Yoko have to be there *all the time?*" he gently asked.

McCartney's *Ob-La-Di, Ob-La-Da* became a pressure point. The song came to define for Lennon everything that was wrong about his partner. One of Paul's "granny songs," he called it. After long stretches of intense rehearsal, with McCartney having diffi-culty finding the right tempo, Lennon stormed out of the studio in anger. When he returned a few hours later he walked in and threw his new fondness for heroin in his partner's face, shouting, "I am more stoned than you have ever been! In fact I am more stoned than you will ever *be!*" Then he sat down and pounded out the granny song with a new tempo that turned out to be the one ultimately used.

"You" in Lennon's proclamation was primarily McCartney,

secondarily the other two, ultimately anyone who was not in the tree he and Ono now occupied. Emerick reports that the next day, when they set upon recording the backup vocals, "the bad feelings of the past weeks seemed to evaporate. That's all it took for them to suspend their petty disagreements." But the die was cast. Heroin had become part of Lennon's all-encompassing entrancement with Ono. Their deep connection through the drug locked in his sense of separateness from the others and fueled his fascination with her ideas. His songwriting partner had kept up with him through alcohol, amphetamines (cautiously), pot, and LSD (even more cautiously). It was obvious that he was not going to go for heroin. And in the summer of 1968, Lennon was starting to gain confidence that it might be okay if McCartney was not in his tree, anyway.

Out of this grand mess arose two of McCartney's best-known songs, *Hey Jude* and *Let It Be*, both composed in the summer of 1968. *Hey Jude* was initially conceived as consolation for Lennon's young son, Julian, and *Let It Be* was based on a dream where his mother appeared to comfort him in the midst of the band's squabbling. The sense of gentle reassurance and resignation in each song builds musically on the "amen cadence," discussed in Chapter 6 with reference to *Yesterday*.

Hey Jude and *Let It Be* are both easy to like and hard to analyze. Their surface simplicities are traps for any critic. The long, mantra-like second part of *Hey Jude*, based on a *doubled* version of the amen cadence and judged over-the-top by some, gives it communal empathy and universal weight. The gesture of nonverbal comfort is dutifully backed by the interpersonal strength of the world's most famous group of friends. Lennon told his partner to keep the outlier line about moving the shoulder, put there as a placeholder, thus adding a small dose of mystery. Harrison wanted to add call and response with his guitar, something like Clapton did for *While My Guitar Gently Weeps*—he wanted to enter this special song more fully—but McCartney vetoed that in favor of simplicity, irritating Harrison. The swell through the lyrical first part and the long, gradual fade through the mantra-like second are masterfully controlled.

The atmosphere of *Let It Be* includes church references to Mother Mary, the amen effect, simple, hymnlike chords, Starr's bell-like cymbals (directed by McCartney), and a Hammond organ. Two different guitar solos from Harrison were issued, one on the single and the other on the album, both strong and documenting his renewed dedication to the instrument. *Hey Jude* and *Let It Be* are songs of elegance and warmth, and they both sit in the sweet spot of the singer's range. Spiritual qualities of acceptance and compassion are central to their appeal. This is usually missed, even though it should be obvious: these two songs were the finest fruits of McCartney's sustained attention to the Maharishi's teachings, capped by the Rishikesh retreat.

Get Back

The month of January 1969 was set aside for what came to be internally called the "*Get Back* Project" and ultimately got the title *Let It Be*. The original conception of the monthlong project included a television show, a live performance, and an LP. The TV show would document how the Beatles worked together to create their songs over the course of the month, how they went, in McCartney's metaphor, from a blank canvas to a fully finished painting. A live performance would premiere the songs and the LP would crown the whole thing.

The idea of filming the band's working method was a competitive response to Jean-Luc Godard's *Sympathy for the Devil (One Plus One)* (released November 30, 1968), which showed the Rolling Stones creating and improving the title song over many sessions. There is enough good footage in the film *Let It Be* to give it a taste of success. When it is supplemented by the excellent study *Get Back: The Unauthorized Chronicle of the Beatles' Let It*

Be Disaster, by Doug Sulpy and Ray Schweighardt, we have very thorough documentation of the entire month.

The stage performance was the key to the project and also its biggest obstacle. Back in the summer of 1966 the Beatles had given up touring and embraced the creative possibilities of the recording studio. Three years later it was not easy to leap back, pre-*Revolver*, to a simpler kind of music that did not depend on studio tracking. The rewards of strong musicianship and playing well together had carried them through the Hamburg years, and the hope was that these could pull them together again, as a counterforce to the centripetal momentum of independent interests. A month in the studio would get them in shape to play on stage, a bootstrapping embrace of nine to five discipline, as McCartney explained. A return to rock and roll became a rallying cry for unity.

Each of them bought into the concept. Harrison and Starr must have viewed it as a way to reestablish themselves as integral partners. Yet they were also concerned about venues. Starr flatly refused to travel abroad and Harrison refused to perform on a ship, two ideas that were tossed around. The rooftop performance on January 30 solved the venue problem since it was local, yet kept fans and hysteria at a safe distance.

McCartney's feelings about live performance must have also been divided, though for different reasons. On the plus side, he was a confident performer and missed playing in public. The creative drawback would be that the songs would have to be crafted in such a way that they did not depend on studio tracking. The final recording could be doctored, but the conception of the songs had to reflect what the quartet could produce on stage, which could not be significantly altered. In the early years, when their music was less ambitious, the quartet carried a song all by itself. But McCartney was now an expert in bringing songs to completion through brilliant studio detail. The quartet was used to recording a "backing track," but that was rarely conceived to stand alone; rather, it was the foundation for a bigger compositional vision. In

January 1969, as they ran through a song like *Across the Universe* and pondered how to develop it without tracking, Lennon threw up his hands in frustration and asked for an up-tempo number.

Harrison had been hanging out in the fall of 1968 with The Band, in upstate New York, and he mentioned that group as a model for their new direction. In The Band's 1968 album *Music from Big Pink*, the five-piece group plays lean and tough, with tightly constructed songs. Harrison envied their egalitarian spirit, which reminded him of the early Beatles. In 1966, Brian Wilson became McCartney's model for extending creative control into the studio, and now The Band was Harrison's model for a return to songs that could be performed on stage. The Band's down-home singing nicely matched their songs about old-timey country life, moonshine, crazy dogs, and pre-pickup-truck southern narratives, all delivered with sincerity. That theme would not be something the Beatles could easily explore, since they reserved their country slots for light satire on the one hand and Starr's winning simplicity on the other. But no one was better than the Beatles at absorbing a model and transforming it, so it is easy to understand Harrison's enthusiasm.

Ironically, McCartney's songs tend to be the ones that can flourish with the least amount of arrangement. He embraced the decision to drop tracking and fancy studio production, to get "more natural, less newspaper taxis" as Lennon put it (alluding to *Lucy in the Sky with Diamonds*), and move toward a fresh sense of authenticity. January 1969 could be a communal retreat something like Rishikesh, without the Maharishi but with electricity and all of the conveniences of home.

Lennon loved the idea of live performance and no tracking, but he was really the most conflicted of all. The documents from January 1969 make clear that the main problem, indeed the main factor in the breakup of the Beatles, was Lennon. He brought to the daily sessions the debilitation of heroin addiction and the distraction of his relationship with Ono. Without heroin it might have been possible to overcome all the other issues and reach the promise of the project. "I was stoned all the time and I just didn't give a shit," he later admitted. Day after day, Lennon shows up late, forgets what they had just rehearsed, can't carry a part, doesn't finish writing songs, can't write new songs, and can't contribute to shaping the songs he has introduced. The others realize that if they push too much he will quit. Harrison's intelligent stroke was to match The Band and go to a quintet by adding keyboardist Billy Preston, who filled out the sound, covered up inadequacies, and added solo interest.

At the Royal Albert Hall in December 1968, Lennon and Ono appeared at an event called the "Alchemical Wedding." They sat in a large black bag for forty-five minutes, barely moving. Covered up by the bag, the audience was supposed to tune into a level of communication deeper than visual or aural. The two felt that they could communicate without words. During the January sessions, Lennon sometimes sat in silence, insisting that Ono speak for him.

In addition to bagism and aleatoric music, he was excited by the current turn toward hard rock, with Cream, The Who, and Jimi Hendrix leading the way. He performed *Yer Blues* with Clapton, Keith Richards, and Mitch Mitchell for the film *Rock and Roll Circus*, also in December. As soon as the song was finished he quickly ushered in Ono, who then screamed into a microphone while the surprised rock stars jammed. Rock purity was in the air. Jon Landau wrote in *Rolling Stone* magazine that *The Fool on the Hill* and other examples of "rock 'art'" were "pious, subtly self-righteous, humorless and totally unphysical." He lamented how "the joyfulness and uninhibited straight-forwardness which is such an essential side to all rock and roll was often lost in the shuffle. Rock became cerebral." Language like that multiplied during the 1970s, after the Beatles dissolved. For example: *Pepper* was "the moment when the music went off the rails almost for good."

It all recalls John Hammond's 1943 complaint that Duke Ellington had "alienated a good part of his dancing public . . . By becoming more complex he has robbed jazz of most of its basic virtues and lost contact with his audience." Such were the perils of turning the African American musical vernacular in the direction of art. This antiart position was the flip side to mid-1950s and early 1920s chatter about rock/jazz dragging Western civilization into the barbaric Negro jungle. A rigid set of conceptual frames on each end of the spectrum was readily available to pump up like a balloon. The only thing needed was some hot air.

The authentic side of rock and roll was especially meaning-ful to the art-school rockers who had begun their careers in the Beatles' wake. By 1968 they were strong enough to advance a set of values that excluded the Beatles' artistic turn. Lennon would struggle with this problem for the rest of his tragically abbreviated life: how to use his talents as a composer of pop hits while holding on to anticommercial purity?

For all of these reasons, it is not surprising that the first week in January was heavily dedicated to oldies, from Carl Perkins's *Tennessee* to Cliff Richard's *Move It* to Elvis's *Good Rockin' Tonight*. The band seemed happiest with a number they had covered back in Hamburg or Liverpool. This was an easy way to get them pointed in the direction of no tracking. For Lennon, especially, the oldies were bubbling up to surface consciousness, as we can see from several of his new songs for 1969: *Don't Let Me Down* was partly derived from Little Richard's 1957 *Send Me Some Lovin'*; *I Want You* from Mel Tormé's 1957 *Coming Home Baby*; and *Come Together* from a Chuck Berry mix.

Lennon and Harrison both suggested that the band might recast some of their own oldies for the concert, but McCartney brushed that idea aside. The closest they got was *One After 909*, a Lennon tune from way back in 1960, perhaps the first Lennon-McCartney original performed for the Liverpool public. One gets the feeling that this inclusion was a gesture of sympathy from the others, a recognition that in his present condition Lennon was having trouble coming up with new material.

The infamous rancor of early January can be blamed on a lot of things. There was the cold environment of the Twickenham studio, chosen for its movie-making advantages. Though they were relatively close in point of view about musical direction, there were still substantial differences. Harrison brought out his new song *All Things Must Pass*, and while McCartney was encouraging, Lennon pushed for something more up-tempo. Again and again they tried it, Harrison talking about how The Band would have performed it and mentioning his inspiration from Timothy Leary's poetry, trying to hook Lennon in. An acoustic version was considered, also a set of backup singers in the style of the Raylets. Harrison predicted that the Beatles would regain harmony when they could each approach songs composed by the others as if they were their own. In frustration, he decided to withdraw *All Things Must Pass*, explaining that he would save it for proper treatment in the studio.

Sulpy and Schweighardt observe the different working methods of the three creative principals coming through during the January sessions. McCartney tends to have a vision of the final product in his mind. His approach is to work over all the little parts—riffs, solos, drumming, everything—again and again until everyone gets them the way he wants them. Harrison prefers to play through a new song multiple times, allowing each player to gradually develop his own details. Lennon is so disengaged that he cannot lead his own songs forward.

On January 7 they bluntly confronted their collective problems, with a lot of venting audible through the studio microphones, some of which sat in full sight while others were hidden and unknown to the musicians. They have never fully recovered from Brian Epstein's death, Harrison says. McCartney admits that they haven't been having very much fun, and he cites lack of discipline, bad attitude, and lack of commitment to a quality product. Harrison bristles and tells McCartney to go find musicians he'd be happier with. Lennon yawns. McCartney reminds Harrison of how to let go of negative thoughts through transcendental meditation. Harrison again brings up the example of The Band, but it must have been pretty evident by now that the Beatles were not up to the standards of musicianship of The Band, not in January 1969. There is talk of ending the group's existence. Lennon wants to play some up-tempo rock and roll. According to Martin (who was not regularly present), Harrison and Lennon actually came to blows.

On January 10, Harrison announced that he was quitting and left the studio in a huff, throwing off years of frustration from second-class citizenry. Lennon told the other two that he thought it would be easy to persuade Eric Clapton to take Harrison's place and finish the project. But Harrison came back, with the stipulation that they expand to a quintet by adding Billy Preston. Harrison intuitively understood where to turn to jump-start communal music-making: to the gospel tradition, the strongest modern manifestation of the ring-shout heritage. No musician knows how to fit in better than a gospel pianist. The Beatles first met Preston in 1962, when he was sixteen years old and touring through Hamburg backing Little Richard. On January 22 they moved back to Apple studios and started fresh with Preston. Like a squabbling family, they all behaved better in front of the guest. George Martin called Preston an "emollient." Preston filled out the sound and added bright solos. Lennon was so impressed that he wanted to keep him in the band permanently.

Many writers have read the January project as a failure. If *Abbey Road* is your measure of success, then it is very easy to come up short. But there are reasons to value this undertaking.

First there is the stunning introduction of fifty-two new songs over the course of the month. Michael Lindsay-Hogg, the director hired to make the film, asked McCartney at one point about the decline of his songwriting partnership with Lennon. McCartney responded that this was mainly due to physical separation and simply not spending as much time together as they had in the

8.4 The rooftop concert, January 30, 1969

early days. Rishikesh in the spring of 1968 and the January 1969 sessions were the successful corrections to that problem.

The rooftop concert on January 30, at 3 Saville Row, was also a success. All four of them were delighted with the performance. After it was over they can be heard bubbling with enthusiasm, eager to take a break and get back to the studio, Harrison ranting about how the police had no right to stop the concert. They performed five songs, four of them created and developed through January sessions with an eye toward no tracking.

I've Got a Feeling is the last example (except for the medley of *Abbey Road*, which did not involve much interaction with Lennon) of a Lennon-McCartney hybrid, with songs from each composer combined to make something stronger than either individual effort. McCartney worked patiently to help Lennon get the descending guitar slide at the transition just right. At one point in January Lennon insisted that he and McCartney had experienced simultaneous dreams the night before. Lennon had lost interest in his partner's granny songs, and he was passionately searching for an artistic vision that would include his soon-to-be wife, but the songwriting partners were still exceptionally close. It is a complete mistake to project the anger of *How Do You Sleep?* back to January 1969.

As intended, the January documents reveal a lot about how the Beatles took a blank canvas and turned it into a finished product. "It's complicated now," says McCartney at one point. "If we can get it simpler, and then complicate it where it needs to be complicated." That is a sophisticated approach to composition. Ellington said something similar: "Simplicity is a complex form, and the more involved you get you're going to find out how complex simplicity is." This kind of focus on detail, which is difficult to track and isolate in analysis, undoubtedly accounts for much of the high-level appeal of what the Ellington Orchestra and the Beatles achieved. The ability to focus in this way was part of the skill sets for both Ellington and McCartney.

Don't Let Me Down started as a song by Lennon. Over the course of the month the whole band worked it over, again and again. McCartney took the fragments Lennon had composed and arranged them to produce the finished order. He recommended dropping a line for the chorus and a repeat of the title phrase to open the song. Harrison changed the rhythm, they experimented with the bridge, Harrison tried the wah-wah, McCartney dictated rhythms to Starr, and all four of them bantered critiques back and forth as the song got better and better. When Preston entered the ensemble Lennon cued him for a solo. The commercial single, the B side to *Get Back*, is as much a product of collaboration as *Please Please Me* had been in early 1963. McCartney fretted that he was being too dominant, and he suggested that each of them take the lead in developing his own songs. Lennon was not sure that this would work, and it is clear how dependent he was on his partner.

Get Back, which gave a working title to the whole project, is the closest of the rooftop songs to the January jam sessions. In spite of the discord, the month was filled with countless hours of good-time yucking it up, dancing, clowning, joking, riffing, and the pure enjoyment of playing music together. "No matter how bad it was in the studio, and some days it was quite bad," remembered Starr, "when the counting came in we were all there. If someone counted it in we all gave everything." Through dozens of sessions, Harrison came up with the three quick chords that help define *Get Back*, much as his riff for *And I Love Her* helps define that song. McCartney alternately improvised the melody and lyrics while the group played along, then went home and revised independently on his own, back and forth, a working method that must have been followed many times, just as it was by Ellington. His melodic gift carried the song to the top of the charts. Starr's drumming is energizing, and Preston adds a crisp, bluesy solo. His contribution to the Beatles in 1969, like Clapton's to *While My Guitar Gently Weeps* and like the Indian musicians to *Within You Without You*, suggests one way the Beatles might have developed had they stayed together: keeping the core intact and extending the creative dynamics to include performers of this quality. That kind of trajectory would have resembled the long-term dynamics of the Ellington band, a collaborative mandala with a fixed center that drew on the strengths of others who came and went.

The four songs performed on the rooftop could have easily been supplemented by *Oh! Darling, I Want You, Come Together, I Me Mine, Old Brown Shoe*, and *Octopus's Garden* (worked on by Harrison and Starr on January 26) to make a terrific album. All it would have taken was willingness to see it through. Instead, the music was shoved into the wrong-sized shoe without end-stage participation from McCartney and Martin. If Billy Preston demonstrated the potential of an extended mandala, Phil Spector showed, in his production of the album *Let It Be*, how difficult it could be for an outsider to enter the Beatles' creative world. McCartney was appalled by Spector's treatment of *The Long and Winding Road*. He had been developing the song at the piano during January. He had in his ear Samuel Barber's *Adagio for Strings*, and you can hear the impact of that lovely piece (for example, in the rising lines in the bridge, "Many times I've been alone . . ."). Spector pushed the song over the fine line of Beatles restraint, with syrupy strings and a wordless chorus of professional singers. We can only pity him for having been assigned a hopeless task—to bring the song to fruition with quality that the creative quintet reached so often through untraceable alchemy developed over many years, and to do it all by himself, as an outsider.

The End

Lennon's break was slow and painful, but there was musical success along the way. There was still tension in the making of *Abbey Road*, with Ono attending regularly and offering suggestions. (Emerick, the engineer, remembered Harrison snorting, "That bitch! She's just taken one of my biscuits!") But the atmosphere was more productive and professional, with, in Emerick's view, Lennon less acerbic, McCartney less officious, and Harrison more confident than ever. Their fresh commitment to good behavior was prompted, no doubt, by bracing awareness of genuine financial difficulties. In any event, positive energy hops off the vinyl. The song scripts range from good to excellent, vocal harmonies sparkle, musicianship is solid, the production is superb, and the medley is a classic summary of the Beatles' aesthetic of collage. Starr suggested naming the album after the address of the recording studio, another confirmation that, while the Beatles engaged with many different types of meaning during their career, what they were ultimately about was music.

Lennon's songs are still the most interesting to talk about. Side one of *Abbey Road* is bookended by two that stake out very different territories. *Come Together* is a high-verbal, Rimbaudian scramble, while *I Want You (She's So Heavy)* could be described as an anti-Dylan and antipop demonstration of the aesthetics of obsession.

Lennon demoed *Come Together* for the others on acoustic guitar, and McCartney's first suggestion was to slow down the tempo and aim for a "swampy" kind of sound. As usual, his response to his partner's bare-bones music was spot on. McCartney came up with the electric piano part, and his bass riff inspired a splendid little mosaic groove of drums, bass, and vocalization that musically defines the song. When the Beatles first heard Dylan's *Subterranean Homesick Blues*, back in 1965, they were stunned. The impression it made was still resonating in 1969. Like *Subterranean Homesick Blues*, *Come Together* leans on Chuck Berry.

I Want You was conceived as another major statement that would dominate the album. The title matches one by Dylan, certainly no coincidence. "Listen to the *words*," Dylan once told Lennon, and Dylan's own *I Want You* is a terrific example of words worth listening to. Lennon's titular match has only twelve words for seven minutes and forty-seven seconds of music—which would be, by the way, thirty-six seconds longer than *Hey Jude*. *Hey Jude's* heartfelt communal swell is replaced with manically obsessive love. *I Want You* is a denial of pop prettiness as well as Dylanesque wordplay, a denial, you could say, of the two primary influences on Lennon as a composer (McCartney and Dylan). What saves the song is another perfect match between words and music.

I Want You and, from side two of *Abbey Road*, *Because* are Lennon's final efforts to create Beatles songs that reflect Ono's artistic sensibility. For *I Want You* that meant minimal words and maximum intensity. The band sounds terrific in part one of the song, with Billy Preston fully engaged on organ, McCartney dazzling on bass, and tight ensemble playing from everyone, the result of a lot of practice, including thirty-five takes on the first studio day. Part two is based on an ostinato. This is not a riff related to black music, like *Day Tripper* or *Come Together*. Instead it is humorless, sexless, and obsessional, which is what Lennon wanted.

The main problem with *I Want You* is the lapse in part two, where Lennon takes command of a synthesizer and yields an incoherent spillage of nonsense. "Louder!" he shouted, "I want the white noise to completely take over." When he said that, Emerick noticed a smile cross Ono's face while McCartney sat in grim silence, his head between his knees. Lennon did have an inspired idea of how to end the song, though—simply cut the tape with a scissors, a gesture of symbolic violence and an abrupt, unexplained end to the obsession, a cut inspired, perhaps, by his wife's most famous work of art, *Cut Piece*. If Preston had been given more room in part two, with the synthesizer taken out of Lennon's hands, and if McCartney and Martin had been given free rein to imaginatively develop it, *I Want You* might have turned into something on the order of *Tomorrow Never Knows*. When Lennon invited his partner to take the lead in executing his strong concepts the results were spectacular, but those days were rapidly coming to a close.

Because is a lovely, haunting number, lit up with vocal harmony arranged by Martin. "John and Paul were a unique blend," reported a listener in 1960, in Liverpool. "They sounded like the same person and they sounded like a *record*." Here is the rainbow ending to that unique blend, an unconscious salute to the resonant vestibule at Mendips with Harrison dutifully finding his place. McCartney conducted the original three with hand gestures for five hours to get the phrasing precise, while Starr sat silently at the side, eyes closed in sympathetic concentration. Lennon liked the addition of Martin on electric spinet since it provided a classical touch, a nod to the initial inspiration of the piece in Beethoven's *Moonlight Sonata*, which Ono had played for him at home.

Abbey Road is usually talked about as McCartney's album, but his stand-alone pieces actually lag behind those of his fellow composers. *Oh! Darling* is a handsome Fats Domino/Little Richard tribute. One can almost imagine it making the charts in the late 1950s, nestled between *Ooh! My Soul* and *Little Darlin'*, but of course it is more than an imitation. Harrison's guitar accompaniment works splendidly with the emotional buildup, and

McCartney's vocal is superb. *Maxwell's Silver Hammer* was, in Harrison's words, "imposed" on the band. On the plus side, this song exhibits the same levels of great musicianship and great production as every other number on *Abbey Road*. It might have been more at home as a snippet on side two, Maxwell entering alongside Polythene Pam and Mr. Mustard and exiting just as quickly.

Lennon disliked the side two medley, maybe because it trumped *I Want You*, but this is where McCartney shines. Lennon legitimately pointed out that there is no coherent theme that ties the songs together, though a few gestures do lend light coherence. Three songs on side two feature the sun. *You Never Give Me Your Money* is reprised toward the end of the medley. If Lennon could have gotten it together to sit down for an afternoon with McCartney, he easily could have strengthened the whole thing. The medley solved the problem of what to do with so many fragments left over from January and even Rishikesh. Lennon called it "Paul's opera." It is opera that blends the semitragic with the comic, the semitragedy being the Beatles' farewell, the comedy a postmodern play of styles and moods.

McCartney had been sneaking little insider messages into a couple of the January songs, especially *Get Back*, where Ono is thinly disguised as Loretta (Lennon complained that the singer looked straight at her when he sang the refrain), and Jojo (John/Yoko) is also advised to get back to where he belongs. Plus there was *Two of Us*, which is partly about having fun with Linda Eastman, partly about his songwriting partner. The medley-opera on side two of *Abbey Road* sprinkles vague references to the imminent collapse of the band throughout. *You Never Give Me Your Money* alludes to perhaps the most insurmountable of all Beatles squabbles—the fierce disagreement over management and the last of the disasters following from Brian Epstein's untimely death (*Magical Mystery Tour*, Apple, Magic Alex, manager Allen Klein). The song introduces the "sweet dream" that came true and now has nowhere to go, which can be none other than the ascent of four Liverpool scruffs to the top of the world. In January, Lennon had suggested to McCartney that they cover a song called *I Had a Dream* as their final single. The Beatles were well positioned to talk about dreams. Through their fans, they confronted, in glaring spotlights, the dreamlike quality of individually constructed reality every single day of their famous lives.

Golden Slumbers is based on a poem by Thomas Dekker from 1603. McCartney uses the lullaby to acknowledge how the *Get Back* wish of return to a golden age of Beatles camaraderie is now impossible. *Carry That Weight* has Starr closely mic-ed on the sing-along, his humble aura representing the collective identity of the group. No single Beatle will be able to achieve on his own what the four of them had achieved together, and they will each have to carry the weight of their unmatchable collaborative accomplishment. McCartney was the superior musical talent, but he understood the implications of the breakup. Mr. Mustard and his sister Pam add comic relief, with Lennon slathering on a Scouse accent.

What is so thrilling about the medley, and what makes it feel like an opera, are the brilliant changes of mood, all of it carefully calibrated with elegant fade-outs, mysterious fade-ins, effective modulations and changes in tempo, dynamic peaks and swoons, and terrific vocals. *You Never Give Me Your Money* itself moves through three moods, each in a different tempo, from wistful to hustling to dreamy. The song uses twenty-one different chords. *Sun King*, building on Fleetwood Mac's *Albatross*, extends the relaxed expansion of *Because*, punctured by the jokey fake Spanish-Italian. Starr's inventive drumming stirs the variety of tempos throughout. He hung towels on his tom-toms and beat them with tympani sticks for *Mean Mr. Mustard*. Harrison's guitar licks count among his finest as a Beatle, especially the crackling explosions of *She Came in through the Bathroom Window*. McCartney's full vocal range is on glorious display everywhere. The medley is a bath of sonic luxury. The Beatles had started their recording career by claiming the extreme lo-fi end of the spectrum with *Love Me Do*, and they ended it with hi-fi production that must have made even Mitch Miller pause in admiration.

The blending principle of rock and roll absorbed during the late 1950s and early 1960s was extended, by the end of 1965, to a musical range no one else could touch. After that they went further with studio imagination and fresh concepts. The album as a kaleidoscopic collage was presented in *Revolver*, thematicized in *Pepper*, and doubled in *The White Album*. Now the principle was condensed into sixteen minutes of continuous music, a rotating crown of jewels that reflects dazzling light in all directions.

For *The End* McCartney convinced a reluctant Starr to take a drum solo. He patiently coached him through many takes out of which a final conflation was patched together. Then the other three sat around jamming solos on their guitars, McCartney answered by Harrison, who is answered by Lennon, and so on. Acknowledging the special moment, Lennon tactfully suggested to his wife that she retreat to the control room. Emerick saw the three of them looking "like they had gone back in time, like they were kids again, playing together for the sheer enjoyment of it . . . They reminded me of gunslingers, with their guitars strapped on, looks of steely eyed resolve, determined to outdo one another . . . No animosity no tension at all—you could tell that they were simply having fun." Emerick engineered each guitar slightly differently to emphasize the distinct voices.

The End finishes with McCartney's closing couplet about the love anyone generates in life being equal to the love that is, in turn, received. ("It proves he can think," snapped his partner.) McCartney said he was inspired by the epigrams that conclude Shakespeare's sonnets. It was the end not only of the Beatles but of the 1960s, perfectly phrased. *Her Majesty* got tacked on like the laughter of *Within You Without You* and the silly, sped-up voices after *A Day in the Life*—Scouse insistence that nobody take themselves too seriously.

8.5 Harrison with Ravi Shankar, August 1967

Starr offered a reflection in *Anthology* that is one way to frame the epigram of *The End*: "There were some really loving, caring moments between four people . . . a really amazing closeness. Just four guys who loved each other." Their offering of music was also an offering of love, a music-love synthesis at the core of the band's experience and their cultural meaning.

The End is a perfect finale to *Abbey Road* and the Beatles' story, but let us give the last word in this collaborative study to Harrison, the youngest Beatle, who reached musical maturity in 1969, at age twenty-six. His contributions to the last Beatles' years brought heart and vision, an antidote to the occasional slippage of McCartney into pop glibness and Lennon into edgy cynicism. Harrison grew taller, and the others came along. *Here Comes the Sun* and *Something*, his two best songs, go a long way toward making *Abbey Road* the charmer that it is.

Here Comes the Sun is weightless, infused with magnetizing light. Like *Let It Be* and *Julia*, it is a song of simple richness. Musically it is relaxed yet assertive, an attractive blend. The extended syncopations of the verses and chorus, delivered with a light touch, burst into raga-inspired licks of threes and twos. The musical freshness does indeed resemble sunshine bursting out on a rainy April day in London. Starr called the sun mantra, which is set to a slightly longer raga pattern, an "Indian trick" that was hard for him to pick up, though once he did he enhanced it splendidly with his imaginative fills. The message of solar rebirth is completely realized through the music and the slender lyrics, which gently point in a spiritual direction with no need for sermons. The arrangement, with understated strings, winds, and Moog synthesizer, is exquisite.

Something is a simple song of elegance and loving awe. Sinatra famously called it the greatest love song in fifty years, a big shift from his paranoid assault on rock and roll from 1957, but it was the Beatles who had changed more than he had. A gentle riff defines the song. When, to introduce the bridge, the riff deftly carries the tune into an unexpected modulation, lifting it into a larger space, it is still possible, after so many hearings, to get goose bumps. This leads to a surprising expansion beyond the comfort of the verses that feels exactly right. The drums pick up and so do bass, strings, organ, and voice. The arrangement for the bridge ("You're asking me . . ."), collectively generated, is a musical masterpiece. Harrison learned about the power of modulation from McCartney, and he also internalized his partner's sense of balance between emotional richness and restraint. The combination made *Something* the second most covered Beatles song ever—after *Yesterday*.

Emerick was impressed at how well Harrison delivered the central guitar solo on the same take that the orchestra was also playing. The solo may be his finest. There is an enchanting take of McCartney playing his bass while scatting Harrison's solo and lifting everything through his feeling for counterpoint. Harrison resented McCartney's active bass line, which he took as a symbol of his domineering attitude. But here, as in so many other Beatles songs from 1966 forward, it enriches the piece immensely.

Harrison wanted to have a long section of doodling freak-out music in the middle of *Something*, but Martin wisely deleted it. In its place Martin composed a warm string arrangement, a soft bed of loving touch. *Something* is modesty lifted into the territory of the sublime.

A third Harrison composition, *All Things Must Pass*, was available for *Abbey Road* as well. Either Harrison held it back for his solo album or the Beatles hierarchy (the chain) could not accommodate three strong songs from the youngest member on a single album. Had it been included, it would have been hard to resist naming this farewell album after the song. *All Things Must Pass* has a touch of majesty (thanks partly to lyrics copied directly from a poem by Timothy Leary) that would have brought into focus the spiritual tint that shines through *Here Comes the Sun*, *Because*, and *The End*. It might have made this the greatest Beatles album of all.

Yet McCartney's micromanagement was central to the success of *Abbey Road*, just as it had been for *Pepper* and *The White Album*. The others complained that he was overbearing, during (Starr and Harrison, but not Lennon) and after (Harrison and Lennon) the group's existence. No doubt he was.

With the Beatles, there were two tacit understandings that facilitated decision making: first, the relationship between Lennon and McCartney, which gave Lennon leadership status while always leaving an opening for McCartney's improvements; and second, the hierarchy of the "chain." As both started to weaken, McCartney took over, seeing things through much as Ellington did by vetting, revising, improving, and forging ahead. The complaints against Ellington were along the lines of "You're not a composer, you're a compiler," while those against McCartney were symbolized by Harrison's sarcastic barb, "Whatever it is that will please you, I'll do it." McCartney's musical superiority was respected by the others at the same time that they resented it. *Abbey Road* represents the respect, *Let It Be* (the album) the resentment.

Imagine

A tape from January 1969 caught Lennon singing a phrase of *Imagine*, the song that is identified with him like no other. The song still held its power almost fifty years later when Madonna sang it for an impromptu postconcert (and postterrorist attack) gathering at Place de la République in Paris (December 2015). *Imagine* may be heard as Lennon's most successful resolution of the contradictory influences coming from the two primary collaborators in his life.

He got the structure and concept for the lyrics from Ono's poetry anthology *Grapefruit*, where several poems begin with the word "imagine." He acknowledged that the lyrics owed so much to her that he could have plausibly listed her as co-composer, though of course he didn't. *Imagine* is thus a witness to the most commonly unacknowledged creative collaborator of all, regardless of art form, genre, or period—the dutiful wife.

Imagine may also be heard as a response to McCartney's *Let It Be*, a song that bothered Lennon. (On the *Let It Be* album, Phil Spector wickedly introduced the title track with Lennon cutting it down to size, singing in falsetto voice, "now we sing 'Hark the herald angels come.'") McCartney's song is about resignation and resolve. Lennon's is about resolve but not resignation, and it explicitly argues in favor of ditching religion (since it includes the idea of hell), possessions (since they lead to greed), and countries (since they breed war). These concepts separate people from one another, and their absence, in the author's view, leads to liberation and peace.

If *Imagine* had appeared on his first solo album, *Plastic Ono Band*, I doubt that anyone would be talking about it today or singing it in the Place de la République. On that album Lennon experimented with a kind of musical primitivism, raw and bare and therapeutic. Instead, *Imagine* relies on bourgeois musical conventions as much as any of McCartney's granny songs. This works with the lyrics to strike just the right note of invitation, sincerity, optimism, and inclusiveness. Lyrically, the song is a full-frontal attack on bourgeois convention, while bourgeois musical gestures—"chocolate coating," as the composer begrudgingly acknowledged—pull the listener in. He turned to the musical language he had spent years soaking up with McCartney as his guide. The entire verbal-musical construction is sleek and tight, without a wasted word or note, yielding a classic statement.

Imagine was started before the breakup and it solves in a unique way the riddle of how to blend the two greatest artistic influences in his life. Like each of his former bandmates, he then struggled to meet expectations established during his career as a Beatle. The question will always arise: why weren't any of them as good after the breakup as they were when they were Beatles? There are at least three answers.

First is that the 1960s were over, literally and figuratively. To be more precise, the idealism of the 1960s was no longer pushing ahead. Idealism did not disappear but it did not remain the cultural force it had been. Different cultures arrange their artistic values differently, with varying points of emphasis between the arts, and youth engagement in the 1960s put a remarkably high emphasis on music. Like many great artists, the Beatles were directly plugged into the liveliest currents animating their exciting times.

The second answer is that the three creative principals, once they stopped being Beatles, tried very hard *not* to be Beatles. They tried to stake out individual identities that did not involve their past. As Beatles they wrote to impress one another, but as post-Beatles they wrote to distance themselves from one another. It is hard to create great art with a negative agenda, to be unlike someone, something. The artist is limited, cramped, before he even starts.

And the third reason, of course, is that they had learned to rely on one another in countless ways. They were used to collaborating, and each of them continued to do that. But they did not do it with musicians who shared their deep history. A solo artist will find it very difficult to give up the method he or she has developed and start collaborating with someone else. Vice versa, any collaborative artist who gets used to exchange and stimulation will feel like something is missing when it is taken away. Personal closeness brings trust, which makes room for constructive conflict, which lifts the achievement higher. As Starr put it, "disagreements contributed to really great products."

What was extraordinary about Ellington and the Beatles was their skill in synthesizing group dynamics of the African American vernacular with commercial expectations of compositional definition. The combination came with built-in structural conflict that had little to do with any particular set of individuals. Collaboration like this depends on leadership, which directly introduces a paradox, since to be a good leader means to be exceptional in some way. As McCartney confessed, in a candid assessment of January 1969, "it was getting too democratic for its own good, you know?"

Some still hold a grudge against him for being overbearing, but given who he was and what the group turned out to be, the most musically gifted Beatle really had no choice. Part of what made them special was insistence on the finest compositional result, the one that beat not just everybody else but all previous efforts. It's lonely at the top, even when—or *especially* when—you are surrounded by your best friends in the world.

NOTES

Epigraph

v "There is such" "Paul McCartney: A Giant among Rock Immortals." 2007.

Prelude

xi "Coffin described": Epstein 1977, 301–2.

xii "In the postwar years": Payne 1968, 254; Stuckey 1987; Floyd 1995.

xii "Ethnomusicologist John Chernoff": Chernoff 1979, 154.

xiii "base": Handy 1957, 76–77.

xiii "The predictability": Epstein 1977, 295.

xiii "marvelous complication": Ibid.

xiii "Robert Anderson": Ibid., 296.

xiii "They'd all take": Raboteau 1978, 245.

xiii "One observer quipped": Jackson 1967, 62.

xiv "Louis Armstrong learned": Brothers 2006, 43 and 40.

xiv "Armstrong 1966": Armstrong 1966, 57. Ellington agreed: "Rock 'n' roll is the most raucous form of jazz, beyond a doubt; it maintains a link with the folk origins, and I believe that no other form of jazz has ever been accepted so enthusiastically by so many." Hamm 1995, 163.

xiv "All that music": Jones and Chilton 1971, 45–46.

Introduction

xvii "his revisionist account": Sheff 1981, 117. For a review of Lennon's revisionist history, see Weber 2016, 67–113.

xviii "Some of the finest": For example, Wilfred Mellers (1973, 32): "Though only during the first year or two did Lennon and McCartney actually compose *together* . . ." (emphasis in original). Ian Macdonald was similarly fooled.

xix "Becker argues": Becker 1982, 91.

xx   "Editorial intervention in literature": Stillinger, *Multiple Authorship and the Myth of Solitary Genius.*

xx   "The differences are structurally determined": Andrew Durkin (2014) makes the opposite case, that Ellington's collaborative ways were not qualitatively different from those employed by someone like Beethoven. He observes, for example (p. 58), instances of Beethoven heeding the advice of other musicians, as well as borrowing melodies created by someone else. To me, the differences are so dramatic, with Ellington cultivating a central focus on what can be achieved through direct collaboration and Beethoven not (while still part of the kinds of interconnections Becker associates with an "art world"), that we need a vocabulary to identify them. "Collaboration" seems like the right word.

xx   "sad farewell": MacDonald 2005, 356.

xxii   "as Lennon put it": Sheff 1981, 132.

xxiii   "a backing track": Journalist Maureen Cleve (Turner 2009, 74) described the process for filling out the song *A Hard Day's Night*: "The song seemed to materialize as if by magic. It consisted of John humming to the others, then they would all put their heads together and hum and three hours later they had this record."

xxiii   "Starr summed up"; Martin and Pearson 1994, 72.

xxiv   "McCartney said": Miles 1967.

xxv   "like a script in a movie": The analogy is suggested by Albin Zak 2010, 191.

xxvii   "Richard Taruskin": Taruskin, "Introduction: The History of What?," *Oxford History of Music.*

Chapter 1: Ellington and Early Jazz

3   "I had never heard anything like it": Ellington 1973, 47–49. Ellington gave the date as 1921, but this has been clarified by John Chilton; see Tucker 1991, 75, for discussion.

5   "remembered clarinetist Garvin Bushell": Bushell 1988, 25.

6   "Bechet took Hodges": Ellington 1973, 48.

6   "One observer explained": The relationship between church and early jazz in New Orleans is discussed in Brothers 2006, 31–54.

7   "impulse for wildness": Leonard 1962, 38.

7   "gushed saxophonist Bud Freeman": Freeman 1974, 8.

7   "became a Negro": Mezzrow 1946, 111 and 210.

8   "I don't know how many castes": Nicholson 1999, 7–8.

8   "Chesterfield gentleman": Ibid., 4, 1–2.

8   "The way the table was set": Ibid., 23.

8   "Ellington acknowledged": Tucker 1993b, 7–8.

9 "My strongest influences": Hasse 1993, 135.

10 "tone parallel": Tucker 1991, 12.

10 "In our house": Cohen 2010, 9.

10 "old standard operatic things": Tucker 1993b, 11.

10 "jungle music": Nicholson 1999, 79.

10 "All through grade school": Ellington 1973, 17.

10 Ellington's (and Strayhorn's) *A Drum Is a Woman* (1956) coincidentally shares imagery with Lennon's *Lucy in the Sky with Diamonds* (1967). The narrator speaks about a song he once heard sung by Madam Zajj, the leading figure in the suite. The madam beckons all comers into her "emerald rock garden just off the moon" where "cellophane trees grow a mile high," and where the fruit "tastes like the sky." There is also a diamond-encrusted hot-house. The connections to Lennon's *Lucy in the Sky with Diamonds* (1967) are striking. I doubt that Lennon knew this obscure narrative; the similarities come from the mutual love of both composers for the work of Lewis Carroll. The point is that the two visually oriented musicians found their way to a similar set of vivid images. On Ellington's love of Carroll, see George 1981, 136.

10 "Harvey Oliver Brooks": Nicholson 1999, 8.

11 "stray tips": Tucker 1991, 44–45 and 59–62.

11 *Heliotrope Bouquet*: Berlin 2016, 156.

12 "Sometimes he had two or three": Nicholson 1999, 19.

13 "Duke drew people": Teachout 2014, 2.

13 "There was an awareness": Peter Jenner in Green 1988, 61.

13 "If anybody taught Ellington": Nicholson 1999, 32.

14 "He didn't want it": Ibid., 40.

15 "This colored band": Teachout 2014, 49.

15 "forget all about the sweet music": Nicholson 1999, 47.

15 "for all-colored Broadway productions": Woll 1989.

16 "Ellington's most recent biographer": Teachout 2014, 112 and 254.

17 "It simply hasn't the verve": Wilder 1990, 415.

17 "Once you put your horn": Nicholson 1999, 50.

19 "My biggest ambition": Ellington 1973, 87 and 109.

20 "Fletcher Sr. refused": Allen 1973, 3.

20 "But before he knew it": On Henderson, see Magee 2005.

21 "fistful of nickels": Nicholson 1999, 81.

22 *Sugar Foot Stomp*: Magee 2005, 88; Brothers 2014, 149–150.

23 *Carolina Stomp*: Magee 2005, 90–96.

23 "changed our whole idea": Ibid., 94.

23 "Modernism will always": Peyton, *Chicago Defender*, November 14, 1925: 7.

24 "The musicians got paid to rehearse": Hodes and Hansen 1977;
Schuller (1968, 134–174) remains the essential introduction to
Morton.

25 "You clap your hands": Brothers 2014, 234–237; Brothers 2006, 143.

26 "Gunther Schuller": Schuller 1968, 157.

26 "According to Barney Bigard": Bigard WRC 1969.

27 "Johnson described": Brown 1986, 185.

29 "He [Cook] lacked the interpersonal skills": Riis 1989, 42.

29 "I can see him": Ellington 1973, 95.

29 "First you find": Ibid., 97; Nicholson 1999, 45.

29 "I'd sing a melody": Collier 1978, 245; Tucker 1993b, 241.

30 "Bechet described": Nicholson 1999, 57.

Chapter 2: The Miley Method and the Ellington Problem

31 "Picasso and Braque": This paragraph derived from Antliff and
Leighten 2001.

31 "We were prepared to efface": Rubin 1989, 19.

32 "two mountaineers": Ibid., 47.

32 "his wife": Braque and Picasso were not alone among early modernists
in sharing their progress so closely. An equally celebrated example is
T. S. Eliot asking Ezra Pound to review his emerging draft for *The
Waste Land*. In 1921–1922, Pound sharpened his blue pencil and
boldly reduced the text by half, while revising in the margins a lot of
what remained. Pound described himself as the "midwife" of Eliot's
poem. More than one scholar regards his intervention as so strong that
he should be credited as coauthor. Eliot's wife Vivienne also worked
over the drafts. Stillinger 1991, 121–38.

32 "Miley's life": Tucker 1993b, 454–58.

33 "growling at each": Nicholson 1999, 56.

33 "Lewandos": Baumgartner (2012) organizes and reviews much of the
literature on this piece.

33 "The strength comes from the inseparability": As dancer and critic
Roger Pryor Dodge argued, with Miley as his primary example,
freak music with manipulated timbre "can inspire the player to subtle
melodic invention"; Tucker 1993b, 456. See also Schuller 1968, 322
and 326.

34 "Mary Austin": Austin 1926, 476; see Brothers (2014, 222–75) for
discussion.

35 "The band became": Nicholson 1999, 48.

35 "backbone of the band": Ibid., 53.

35 "The recording begins": Tucker 1988, 88.

36 "People heard it": Tucker 1991, 243.

36 "the hair on your head rise": Brothers 2014, 63.

37 "Saxophonist Otto Hardwick": Lasker 1994, 35.

38 "Bub is responsible": Tucker 1993b, 27.

38 "The title *East St. Louis Toodle-O*": Baumgartner 2012, 35.

38 "entering the realm of art": Becker (1982, 149) quotes philosopher Arthur Danto: "The moment something is considered an artwork it becomes subject to an *interpretation*. It owes its existence as an artwork to this, and when its claim to art is defeated, it loses its interpretation and becomes a mere thing. . . . art exists in an atmosphere of interpretation and an artwork is thus a vehicle of interpretation." Ellington's explanation for the title was "The Black and Tan was a speakeasy of the period where people of all races and colors mixed together for the purpose of fulfilling their social aspirations"; Stanley Dance, liner notes to *The Ellington Era, 1927–1940, Volume One* (Columbia C3L 27).

39 "she had been performing with him": Williams 2002, 111–112.

39 "*Creole Love Call* was filled out": On Rudy Jackson's role in *Creole Love Call*, see Tucker 1991, 236–42.

40 "Miley was an idea man": Nicholson 1999, 53.

40 "He was responsible for many licks": Ellington 1978, 24.

41 "he needed Ellington": Roger Pryor Dodge in Tucker 1993b, 457.

41 "It is possible to theorize": Schuller 1992, 41 and 39. Also Schuller 1968, 326–27: "Although the extent of Miley's contribution has not yet been accurately assessed, there seems little doubt that those compositions that bear Bubber's name along with Ellington's were primarily created by Miley. These include the three most important works of the period . . . *East St. Louis Toodle-Oo, Black and Tan Fantasy*, and *Creole Love Call*."

42 "what Langston Hughes called": Hughes 1926, 693; Tucker 1993b, 135.

43 "If music is a language": Maus 1989, 1–80.

43 "There are reports": Tucker 1993b, 467, 463–465, and 458; Nicholson 1999, 53.

43 "One writer even referred": Tucker 1991, 242.

44 "This played out in South Side Chicago": Brothers 1997, 185–86.

44 "You've got to learn to stop hollering": Jackson 1966, 59.

45 "Whenever his theme song": Ellison 2003, 681 and 682.

46 "Darrell claimed": Tucker 1993b, 127–28 and 57–65.

47 "primitivist thinking": On primitivism, see Brothers 2014, 222–275.

47 "emotional holiday": Tichenor 1930, 485.

47 "Rudolph Fisher": Fisher 1927, 398.

49   "decoration of the interior": Haskins 1977, 33; Singer 1992, 100.

49   "The big attraction are the gals": Vail 2002, 9.

49   "Spike Hughes": Nicholson 1999, 74.

50   "Benny Goodman and Charlie Parker": Goodman 1939, 231; Morton 2008, 31.

50   "so beautiful it sometimes brought": Ellington 1973, 119.

50   "full of ideas": Ellington 1978, 109.

50   "an absolute song factory": Teachout 2014, 163.

50   "Ellington's frequent failure": Ibid., 271.

51   "Cootie Williams was hired": Nicholson 1999, 89.

51   "open faucet": Serrano 2008, 108. Chapter 11 of Serrano is an excellent introduction to the obstacles in assessing Tizol's compositional achievement.

52   "Yeah he did some bad things": Serrano 2008, 118.

52   "Juan was disgusted": Ibid., 117.

52   "a very big man": Ibid., citing Ellington 1973, 55–56.

53   "The opening strain": See the analysis, with transcription, by Jeffrey Magee, in Magee 2015, 91–93.

53   "Radio was a surprise benefit": Wall 2012, 197–222.

53   "The band was first heard": Cohen 2010, 32.

53   "started to reference": Peyton *Defender*, August 10, 1929: 7.

53   "Louis Armstrong remembered": Singleton IJS 1975.

53   "they all rushed back": Teachout 2014, 92.

54   "Black Paul Whiteman": Barnes 1929, 7.

54   "talent on his grandmother's side": Ellington 1978, 10–12.

56   "mostly my own": Bigard 1986, 64.

56   "We had a little six-piece": Nicholson 1999, 340; Tucker 1993, 43.

56   "I had to laugh": Bigard IJS 1976.

56   "first tune I wrote": Tucker 1993, 89.

56   "Each member of his band": Ibid., 270.

57   "Gary Giddins has described": Miley's role was noted by Schuller (1968, 336), citing Ulanov (1946, 94); Giddins 1986, 110.

57   "Lyricist Don George described": George 1981, 29.

57   "experimenting with chords": Schuller (1986, 47–50) offers a pithy discussion of Ellington's effective and innovative use of harmony.

58   "I understand that he got a lot": Bigard 1986, 64.

58   "Trumpeter Freddie Jenkins described": Nicholson 1999, 111.

58   "Vodery's chromatic tendencies": Howland 2009, 40–43; Teachout 2014, 93; Tucker 1996.

58   "Doctor of music": Braud 1957.

59   "Ellington was the right person": Schuller 1968, 340.

61 "He put Harry's name": Nicholson 1999, 194; Stewart 1972, 119.

61 "Ellington's pretty smart": Bigard 1976.

61 "we used to call ourselves": Nicholson 1999, 126.

61 "origin story": Teachout 2014, 113.

61 "I don't consider you a composer": Collier 1987, 130.

61 "compiler of deeds": Teachout 2014, 115.

62 "It wouldn't cost him": Ibid., 116.

62 "My loot": Hasse 1993, 327.

62 "might get credit": Williams 2002, 117.

62 "You'll be talking": Tamarkin 2008.

62 "helped subsidize": Hajdu 1996, 141.

62 "he inspired a togetherness": George 1981, 148.

63 "The musicians understood": On the contracts, see Nicholson 1999, 80.

63 "Writers aiming to glorify Ellington": For a useful review of literature on Ellington from this point of view, see Whyton 2010, 127–152; see also Durkin 2014.

64 "Mills to promote Ellington as a great composer": This theme is developed by Cohen, 2010, especially Chapter 2.

64 "I made his importance": Cohen 2010, 63.

64 "increasing veneers": Ellington 1978, 38.

64 "Mills wanted Duke to be the star": Nicholson 1999, 159.

64 "Critic Abbe Niles wrote": Tucker 1993b, 40–41.

65 "bore the indelible stamp": Ibid., 59–61.

65 "composed, scored and played": Ibid., 61. Darrell's readers included composer Percy Grainger, who would, in October, invite Ellington to a composition seminar at New York University; Rexroth 2007, 77.

65 "Sell Ellington": Teachout 2014, 4.

65 "the involved nature of my numbers": Tucker 1993b, 49.

68 "Managers and promoters": Ibid., 55.

68 "The chief number": Ibid., 51.

68 "Ellington's pay reached the highest": Cohen 2010, 99–100.

68 "We worked clean": Bigard 1986, 52.

Chapter 3: The 1930s: An "Accumulation of Personalities"

69 "The Wizard of Oz": The process is exceptionally well documented in Harmetz 1977.

70 "I don't remember": Harmetz 1977, 163.

70 "generous parade": Schuller 1989, 59.

71 "We would have an arrangement": Nicholson 1999, 18.

71 "Everyone made suggestions": Magee 2015, 88; see also Hardwicke in Nicholson 1999, 71.

71 "Everybody pitches": Tucker 1993b, 475; see also Rex Stewart 1972, 96.

71 "filling the holes": Braud 1957.

71 "All bands at that time": Nicholson 1999, 121.

71 "Bechet taught": Serrano 2012, 182. Bechet was in New York City in 1932, playing in a band led by Tommy Ladnier.

72 "1933 article": Tucker 1993b, 101.

72 "1944 *New Yorker*": Ibid., 227. Serrano (2012, 203) considers the likelihood that the quoted dialogue between Tizol and Ellington in this article was invented by the author of the article.

72 "Tizol the extractor": Stewart 1991, 154; Nicholson 1999, 127; Bigard 1986, 63.

72 "How much Tizol edited": A 1933 article in *Time* magazine described how "Ellington lets all his players have their say but listens particularly to the shrewd advice of pale Cuban [sic] Juan Tizol." Teachout 2014, 140.

73 "what he called extended compositions": Howland 2009, 179.

73 "The idea came from Mills": Nicholson 1999, 118–19; Ellington 1978, 34; Ellington 1973, 82; Howland 2009, 159.

73 "New York University": Rexroth 2007, 79.

74 "connections to Gershwin's": A. J. Bishop in Tucker 1993b, 349.

75 "It would be a pity": Lambert in Hasse 1993, 154; Wilder in Tucker 1993b, 258–61. Howland (2009) locates the formal models Ellington was using, especially the extended pieces of Paul Whiteman. Zenni (2001) addresses the issue from the point of view of "structural unity."

75 "first jazz composer of distinction": Lambert 1937, 187–88.

75 "in a soliloquizing mood": Tucker 1993b, 244.

75 "The thirteen-minute *Reminiscing*": Howland (2009, 171–76) makes the case that Ellington's preferred conception was limited to the first three parts.

75 "Schuller was impressed": Schuller 1989, 75.

76 "Aren't there marked similarities": Tucker 1993b, 215–16.

76 "silence becomes part of the performance": Katz 2010, 77.

77 "We had a recording date": "Duke Ellington Tells the Secrets of His Success," *Chicago Defender* (national edition), October 2, 1937: 9.

78 "sic-ing that stuff": Murray and Ellison 2000, 61.

78 "platinum-blonde girl": Teachout 2014, 290.

79 "make new, unadulterated": Tucker 1993b, 112.

79 "the first jazz composer": Lambert 1937, 187.

79 "Usually the Negro element": Ibid., 180–187 and 199.

82 "Every aspect of my life": Erenberg 1998, 39.

83 "Ellington explained": Tucker 1993b, 371.

84 "It has been claimed that he sold": Brothers 2014, 434.

87 "Cootie Williams said": Collier 1978, 164.

87 "Otto Hardwick composed": Teachout 2014, 152.

87 "Two women were arguing": Tucker 1993b, 341.

90 "Duke got his name": Teachout 2014, 162.

90 "Corner after corner": Ibid., 164.

91 "Spanish melodies": Serrano 2012, 224–25.

92 "Tizol biographer": Ibid., 208.

93 "every orchestra began to play": Ibid., 331.

93 "Duke took credit": Collier 1978, 187.

94 "Our type of music wasn't really for black people": Teachout 2014, 159.

94 "authentic Negro music": Quote from Tucker 1993b, 135.

94 "weird chords have grown stale": Stratemann 1992, 132; Hasse 1993, 196.

95 "Negro leaders could": Teachout 2014, 161.

95 "Swing is stagnant": The articles are reprinted in Tucker 1993b, 132–40.

95 "Basie's outstanding": Tucker 1993b, 139.

96 "Refining the basics": Murray 2016, 10.

97 "Where the preacher": Quoted in Giddins and DeVeaux 2009, 216.

97 "We always had somebody": Giddins and DeVeaux 2009, 220.

99 "an accumulation": Tucker 1993b, 339.

99 "He studied violin": Büchmann-Møller 2006, 62.

99 "He was featured in front": Teachout 2014, 202.

99 "Those precision notes": Ibid.

100 "He could improvise": Tucker 1993b, 435.

100 "His amazing talent": Stewart 1991, 196.

100 "Webster's entry": Date from Stratemann 1992, 150. Biography for Webster from Büchmann-Møller 2006.

101 "Ben Webster is not only": Nicholson 1999, 217; Büchmann-Møller 2006, 70–71.

101 "A lot of guys": Büchmann-Møller 2006, 70.

102 "Shuckin' and Stiffin'": Ibid., 69–70.

102 "I just wrote": Büchmann-Møller 2006, 69. This insistence that Webster composed the main theme of *Cotton Tail* has usually been missed in discussions of this piece, but Hinton's report is clear: the piece began with a theme composed by Webster that was offered to Ellington. We will never know how much the final theme resembled Webster's original, but the original must have been attractive, or it wouldn't have caught Ellington's attention.

103 "Making a study of Hawkins": *DownBeat* commented how Webster was moving closer to Hawkins; see Büchmann-Møller 2006, 70. On Strayhorn hanging out at Minton's Playhouse and studying early bebop, see Hajdu 1996, 74.

103 "Stanley Crouch": Tucker 1993b, 496.

103 "The lively chorus for saxophone": Stewart 1972, 129.

104 "The flexible Webster": Büchmann-Møller 2006, 68.

104 "ten-bar phrases": Ibid.

105 "miracle year": Teachout 2013, 209; Schuller (1989, 48) refers to "the famous masterpieces of the early 1940s, the creative zenith of Ellington's career."

106 "ten-bar lengths": On the phrase lengths see also Schuller 1991, 118 n. 39.

107 "introduction was composed by Billy Strayhorn": Van de Leur 2002, 34 and 290–91.

Chapter 4: Billy Strayhorn

109 "Our species": Steinbeck 1970, 151.

110 "Mr. Ellington, this is the way": Hajdu 1996, 50.

111 "Billy Strayhorn was my right arm": Ellington 1973, 156.

111 "Strayhorn was born": This biographical sketch is derived from Hajdu 1996.

113 "He would ask me": Hajdu 1996, 13.

113 "I think my brother": Ibid., 18.

113 "learned everything": Ibid., 14.

113 "He kept to himself": Ibid., 16.

114 "What he realized": Ibid., 32.

114 "He began composing *Lush Life*": Van de Leur 2002, 16–17; Hajdu 1996, 34.

114 "Every now and then": Hajdu 1996, 34.

116 "There wasn't a lot of guys": Ibid., 70.

117 "The harmonic language of *Passion Flower*": Van de Leur 2002, 28–30.

117 "At that time people weren't writing": Hajdu 1996, 87.

117 "You'll do whatever": Ibid., 57.

118 "a tendency to emphasize Blanton and Webster": For example, Berish (2014, 113): "Arguably the most significant hiring was bassist Jimmie Blanton, in October 1939."

118 "In the winter of 1940-1941": There was also a recording ban on ASCAP composers that made attribution to Strayhorn a necessity; see below.

119 "flinging a pot of paint": Anderson and Koval 2002, 215.

119 "The main theme of *Chelsea Bridge*": See Hajdu 1996, 50–54. Strayhorn denied having known the Ravel, and it is certainly possible that
the connection was coincidental, the result (as Walter van de Leur has
kindly pointed out to me) of experimenting with similar progressions.

119 "originality at the expense of beauty": Van de Leur 2002, 53.

119 "From the moment I first heard": Ibid.

119 "Webster loved": Gioia 2012, 60.

121 "He already had a passion for collecting": Hajdu 1996, 77.

121 "try things out": For example, see Van de Leur 2002, 103.

121 "It sounded as if Stravinsky": Hajdu, 86. For detailed analysis and
transcription, see Van de Leur 2002, 38–43.

121 "renaissance in elaborate": Ellington 1973, 153.

122 "It didn't work out": Hajdu 1996, 82; Van de Leur (2002, 34) notes the
contradiction between Strayhorn's account and the surviving manuscript evidence.

123 "fragmented": Schuller 1989, 131.

123 "an extended palindrome": A precedent for the palindromic form is
Ellington's 1930 "Jolly Wog" (Givan 2014, 179).

124 "The shaken-up order": Plus, Ellington pulls a neat trick with the
sequence of key areas, with theme C flowing to theme B and theme B
flowing to theme A in a way that seems to resolve the initial tension of
B moving to C in the first part.

124 "The vitality is in step": Greene (2011, 224–32) carefully documents
relationships between *Ko-Ko* and earlier Ellington compositions.

125 "sailed over all": Hasse 1993, 241.

125 "*Ko-Ko* dates": Green 2011, 225, n. 34.

125 "The effect resembles": Transcription by David Berger and Alan Camp-
bell, *Edward Kennedy "Duke" Ellington: Ko-Ko United Artists Study
Score Series*, p. 12. Transcription of the passage from *Take the "A"
Train* in Van de Leur 2002, 48. On characteristic scoring tendencies
and dissonance placement associated with Ellington (closed-position
scoring, lower-register dissonance) and Strayhorn (open-position scoring, upper-register dissonance), see Van de Leur 2002, 75–78.

126 "Schuller admired": Schuller 1989, 118.

126 "Billy got a great full sound": Hajdu 1996, 94.

126 "It was so natural": Gerald Wilson quoted in Hajdu 1996, 94.

126 "I'd see Billy walk": Hajdu 1996, 82; see also George 1981, 78–79.

126 "composing together on the telephone": Van de Leur 2002, 89 and 104.

126 "In music you develop": Ellington 173, 156.

127 "I don't think your strain": Tucker 1993b, 225.

127 "It is unlikely that the surviving evidence": Hence I find this claim from

van de Leur (2002, xxii) to be overstated: "the ultimate proof of author-ship lies in the respective and distinctive styles of the two collaborators, which is not only visible on paper but first and foremost audible."

127   "summit of Ellington's compositional achievement": Teachout (2013, 210), following Schuller's "the creative zenith of Ellington's career" (1989, 48).

127   "It was easy for Ellington to make": There was also a new twist in the business model caused from outside the band. In January 1941 the American Society of Composers and Publishers, representing Elling-ton and many other composers, got tangled up in a dispute with major radio networks over how much money could be collected for airing their members' compositions. The immediate result of this dispute was a boycott of ASCAP-registered tunes, including Ellington's. He was thus forced to emphasize compositions from Strayhorn and also his son, Mercer, during 1941.

128   "Strayhorn reworked the arrangement": Van de Leur 2002, 63.

128   "the 1941 musical": On *Jump for Joy*, see Hajdu 1996, 90–94 and Teachout 2013, 221–34.

129   "take Uncle Tom out": Tucker 1993b, 148.

129   "Negro is the creative voice": Ibid., 147.

129   "That killed me": Cohen 2010, 194.

129   "Ellington and Strayhorn wrote the music together": See Van de Leur 2002, p. 294 n. 27, for a precise list of Strayhorn's contributions to *Jump for Joy*.

129   "We should have listed": Hajdu 1996, 92.

130   "Strayhorn's essential contribution": Van de leur 2002, 62.

130   "Ellington had been talking about": Tucker 1993a, 69–73.

130   "It's time a big": Ibid., 76

131   "greatest pre-performance": DeVeaux 1993, 130.

131   "Mercer Ellington explained": Teachout 2013, 238. Recent readings of *Black, Brown and Beige* include Barg and Van de Leur 2013, Howland 2009 (Chapter 4), and Schuller 1989, 141–50.

132   "Critics complained": Quoted in DeVeaux 1993, 128.

132   "no one in 1943 would have even thought to question": To glimpse how pervasively Ellington's co-composers have been written out of the reception of this music, consider these misrepresentations from Gunther Schuller's liner notes for an LP reissued by the Smithsonian Institution (published 1978, reprinted in Schuller 1986, 51–59): *Lost in Meditation* is called "vintage Ellington," and Tizol is identified as play-ing it "with sovereign suavity" though not identified as the composer; *I*

Let a Song Go Out of My Heart is described as one of Ellington's "superb vehicles" for Hodges though not identified as one of Hodge's compositions; *Don't Get around Much Anymore* is "Duke's own hit of 1940" with no mention of Hodges; *Prelude to a Kiss* is "one of Ellington's most celebrated ballad songs," with no mention of Hardwick; *Cotton Tail* is presented as "Ellington's own," with no mention of Webster; and *Mood Indigo* is Ellington's "all-time classic" with no mention of Bigard.

132   "Paul Bowles": DeVeaux 1993, 137. Howland 2009 (Chapter 4) argues that the formal model for Ellington was Paul Whiteman's "symphonic jazz."

132   "The Negro was put": DeVeaux 1993, 134.

132   "It has been suggested": Barg and Van de Leur 2013, 445.

133   "long meter": Evans 1982, 42–43, quoting Eddie "Son" House.

133   "breathtaking performance": It has always been assumed that *Come Sunday* is one of Ellington's greatest melodic accomplishments. But if we take the Ellington problem seriously—meaning that we cannot simply assume that Ellington composed all of the music credited to him—then we should be particularly alert whenever Hodges is near. It has been ignored until recently that Ellington borrowed one of Ben Webster's tunes for the section called *Emancipation Celebration*. Büchmann-Møller (2006, 71): "The unadulterated theme [from Ben Webster's *Dearie*] pops up as the conclusion to *Emancipation Celebration* in the *Black, Brown and Beige* suite."

133   "Strayhorn wrote about a third": Van de Leur 2002, 88.

133   "without knowing": One recent writer (Berger 2014, 251), believing *Sugar Hill Penthouse* to be Ellington's creation, calls it "the ultimate in sophistication and refinement."

133   "his jazz waltz": Van de Leur 2002, 92.

133   "Hodges was making": Hasse 1993, 273.

134   "George pitched": George 1981, 52–56.

135   "The band's radio audience did not know": Van de Leur 2002, 96.

135   "Critic Alec Wilder wrote": Tucker 1993b, 259.

135   "Ellington gave him stock": Hajdu 1996, 120.

136   "It was a pleasure you know": Teachout 2014, 114.

136   "Billy could have pursued": Hajdu 1996, 79–80.

136   "Ellington wanted the recognition": Ibid., 101.

136   "Mr. Ellington's score": Ibid., 104.

136   "In April 1947": Ibid., 109.

136   "He encouraged me not to compromise": Ibid., 117.

137   "Leonard Feather wrote": Schiff 2012, 167.

137 "Ellington's royalty stream": Hajdu 1996, 141.

138 "His contributions are so substantial": Van de Leur 2002, 117;
Teachout 2014, 268.

138 "Strayhorn's arrangement of *The Tattooed Bride*": Lambert (not knowing that the arrangement is Strayhorn's) 1999, 150.

138 "only Ellington's name listed as composer": Ted Gioia (2012, 358)
notes a "surprising" lawsuit from the Strayhorn estate challenging the
copyright of *Satin Doll*. "One wonders what the two artists themselves
would have thought of this litigation," writes Gioia, "given the smooth
give-and-take that characterized their professional relationship over
a period of three decades." To that one can only say two things: (1) on
the inside, things were not as smooth as they appeared on the outside;
and (2) in terms of credit, it was mostly Strayhorn who did the giving,
Ellington the taking.

138 "It was a situation": Hajdu 1996, 131.

138 "Mercer Ellington said": Ibid., 196.

139 "We had a relationship": Ibid., 192.

139 "He had a very very very": Ibid., 194.

140 "He had a trick of hearing the breath": Ibid., 132.

140 "He could have done a million": Ibid., 136.

140 "The actual source of his frustration": Ibid., 122.

141 "The group worked out the arrangement": "Duke Ellington often wrote
tunes from phrases his soloists played," writes Mingus biographer Gene
Santoro (2000, 116–17), "but Mingus went one better. He created a
whole arrangement out of the way his musicians played what he gave
them." See also Priestly 1984, 66, 77, and 106.

141 "dark church": Mingus's sister Grace quoted in Gabbard 2016, 22–23.
See also Priestly 1984, 4, and 67; Saul 2003, 165.

142 "The charming way he says it": Gabbard 2016, 47.

142 "He routinely embarrassed": "You never knew who was going to be
screamed into submission or humiliated," observed his wife Sue. Saul
2003, 395.

142 "gave me his complete open mind": Gabbard 2016, 320; also Priestly
1984, 99.

142 "Alfred Hitchcock": Hitchcock in the movie *Hitchcock/Truffaut*,
directed by Kent Jones (2015).

143 "Can you do it": Teachout 2014, 286.

144 "doing little bits": Davies 2009, 281.

144 "The final polishing": Tucker 1993b, 321–22. The analysis of Strayhorn
and Ellington as having these different working methods is developed
by van de Leur, especially Chapters 4–6. Van de Leur articulates the

differences between the two composers (2002, p. 78): "Where concepts tended to govern Strayhorn's writing, Ellington seems to have worked case by case, proceeding from chord to chord, from passage to passage, as if designing each sound and phrase separately, without necessarily adhering to a chosen musical technique. As a rule, Ellington kept infusing new and musically unrelated ideas into the musical fabric of a given piece."

145 "The problem was": Van de Leur 2002, 116.

146 "He kept the promise": Ibid., 116.

147 "devoted to Shakespeare": "We were with literally the top Shakespeare scholars in the world, and Strayhorn didn't have a thing to apologize for," remembered the festival's founder, Thomas Patterson. "His knowledge was very deep." Quoted in Hajdu 1996, 163.

147 "comparisons with Debussy": Schiff 2012, 187.

148 "overly scented confections": Lambert 1999, 281.

148 *Up and Down* is a musical illustration of Puck": Schiff (2012, 4–5) suggests that Strayhorn might have identified with Puck, who, in Shakespeare's play, puts things in motion from behind the scenes much as Strayhorn did in the Ellington collective.

149 "the best work that Mr. Ellington": Hajdu 1996, 170.

149 *A Tone Parallel to Harlem*": Howland 2009, 280–88; Berger 2014, 253–56.

149 "the final thirty seconds": Hajdu 1996, 140.

149 "Brian Priestley": Priestley 2014, 61.

150 "Duke was a professional": Hajdu 1996, 210.

150 "The ballet had risen": Barg 2013, 797.

150 "It's always a struggle": Hajdu 1996, 204.

151 "Ellington's aim": Lambert 1999, 219.

151 "The surviving manuscripts establish": Van de Leur 2002, 137–39 and 275–76. Lisa Barg (2013) interprets Strayhorn's *Nutcracker* as "a vehicle for (queer) modernist experimentation" (p. 798).

152 "The scoring is among": Lambert 1999, 218.

152 *Sugar Rum Cherry*": On *Sugar Rum Cherry*, see Barg 2013, 800–802.

153 *Arabesque Cookie*": Barg (2013, 810) argues that "the formal, sonic, and programmatic features in *Arabesque Cookie* can be allied with figurations of gay Harlem Renaissance artists of queer desire and identity."

153 "In September 1963": On Ellington and the State Department tours, see Von Eschen 2004, Chapter 5.

155 "He was always talking to it": Ellington 1973, 199.

156 "that Strayhorn is much more than Ellington's": Hajdu 1996, 240.

156 "freedom from hate": Ibid., 257.

156 "Billy worked for Edward": Ibid., 259.

157 "Like a king": Or, as the actor Richard Burton put it (George 1981, 257), "The concentrated essence of everything that's gifted and courteous."

159 "Hodeir and Lambert": Hodeir in Tucker 1993b, 227; Howland 2009, 177 on tunesmiths. Gabbard (2016, 305) quotes Mingus, writing in *DownBeat*, June 1, 1951: "Charlie Parker is in his own inimitable way creating complete, clearly thought-out compositions of melodic line every time he plays a solo, as surely as one was ever written down by Brahms or Chopin or Tchaikovsky."

159 "distinction between jazz composer and jazz arranger": Schuller (1989, 202): "It is a crucial factor that the Lunceford band—this applies as well to Webb, Calloway, and several other of the major black orchestras of the thirties—was not a *composer's* orchestra, like Duke Ellington's, but an *arranger's*," wrote Gunther Schuller, the most influential writer on Ellington's music (emphasis in the original).

159 "The groundwork was laid": Schuller (1968, 350) approvingly quotes Frances Newton (aka Eric Hobsbawn): Ellington "solved the unbelievably difficult problem of turning a living, shifting and improvised folk music into *composition* without losing its spontaneity." One could instead argue that, on the one hand, the New Orleanians had already done this; on the other, it was the technology of recordings that really made the difference, more than anything.

159 "his strongest suit": Lavezzolo 2001, 112.

Chapter 5: Early Beatles and Rock and Roll

163 "Handy had an epiphany": Brothers 1997, 181.

164 "into a tribal-like frenzy": McMillan 2013, 47.

164 "jungle music": Miller 1999, 198.

165 "radio broadcasters hesitant to use it": Ibid., Chapter 1.

165 "If I could find a white man": Ibid., 72.

165 "I haven't come to hear you": Braun 1964.

166 "Actually I think we both wanted": Miller 1999, 64; see also Emerson 2005, 7.

166 "first white-black person": Joplin 2005, 64, 72, and 76; Adelt 2010, 101.

166 "if our society dictated": Otis 1968, 12.

166 "Presley bumped up the tempo": Miller 1999, 81.

167 "wasn't going to work for": Sounes 2011, 27.

167 "Rock and roll has its place": Miller 1999, 133.

168 "The colored folks been singing": Tick 2008, 585.

168 "When I first heard": Keogh 2004, 39.

168 "It was the way Presley sings": McCartney quoted in BBC News, August 5, 2005.

169 "We've been playing": Giuliano 1994, 5.

169 "born to rebel": On the topic of developmental experience shaping rebellious behavior, see Sulloway 1996.

171 "He always had to have a partner": Shotton and Schaffner 1983, 24.

171 "At heart Julia was": Riley 2011, 59; see also Shotton and Schaffner 1984, 58; Lewisohn 2013, 239 and 320; Davies 2009, 16–17.

171 "*Maggie May*": Lewisohn 2013, 335.

171 "I did my best": Sheff 1981, 136.

171 "sabotage": Kozinn 2013, C3.

172 "He had a lot of power": *George Harrison: Living in the Material World* 2012.

172 "Of course you can take part": Riley 2011, 59; Shotten and Schaffner 1984, 84.

172 "The guitar's all right": Davies 2009, 242.

172 "somewhere they put you": Riley 2001, 87.

172 "It has been well established": Frith and Horne 1987; Green 1988, 32–33.

173 "Me best mate": Flannery 2013, 165.

173 "Are we turning": Lewisohn 2013, 282.

173 "I was brought up": Ibid., 192.

173 "Why should we be over": Braun 1964, 91.

174 "seemed to have the sort of mind": Lewisohn 2013, 338.

175 "held back": Ibid., 375 and 462.

175 "loved my association": Ibid., 518.

175 "Now there were three": Davies 2009, 45.

175 "They were such a gang": Lewisohn 2013, 575.

175 "I grew up steeped": Miles 1997, 23.

178 "He was already": Sheff 1981, 147.

178 "a corny little song": Miles 1978, 71.

179 "Paul was always more advanced": Lewisohn 2013, 515; "I'm not going to waste my life" 2009, 10; Shotten and Schaffner 1984, 91; Miles 1978, 80.

179 "John was always writing poetry": Lewisohn 2013, 579.

179 "very tough": Ibid., 629.

180 "John brought a biting": Inglis 2000, 83.

181 "These mental constructions": The foundation for my discussion is Zak 2010.

182 "I never compartmentalized": Zak 2010, 48.

183 "A record is in a sense": Ibid., 49.

183 "sweet surprise": Ibid., 54.

183 "unique way of sobbing": Ibid., 58–9.

185 "just playing you know by feel": Ibid., 102.

185 "paralyzing monotony": Ibid., 73.

185 "We just never even thought": Miles 1997, 82.

186 "Brill Building": Emerson 2005.

186 "Leiber and Stoller": Myers 2012a.

186 "Doc Pomus and Mort Shuman": Emerson 2005, 42 and 163.

186 "a very average hack song": Ibid., 31.

186 "Leiber and King fleshed": Emerson 2005, 128; Myers 2012a.

187 "If I hadn't seen the Beatles": Lewisohn 2013, 1412 and 1437.

188 "play so much run a ring": Palmer 1982, 260.

188 "Chuck Berry specialists": Flannery 2013, 215.

191 "son of *What'd I Say*": Lewisohn 2013, 1244.

192 "two-thirds of the market": Zak 2010, 81.

192 "the most brutal ugly": Emerson 2005, 17 and 169.

193 "There was no way to control": Zak 2010, 201.

193 "radio dial picking up": Myers 2012b.

193 "We were really looking at": Lewisohn 2013, 13.

193 "to write a musical": Braun 1964, 13.

193 "most famous composers": Rupprecht 2015, 26; Harker 1992, 238–43.

193 "British Goffin and King": Lewisohn 2013, 1344.

194 "those who were in art school": Frith and Horne 1987, 86.

194 "I become whoever I'm with": Giuliano 1994, 142.

Chapter 6: Four-Headed Monster

195 "four headed monster": George-Warren 2009, 30.

195 "It was an odd phenomenon": Clapton in *George Harrison: Living in the Material World* 2012.

195 "The bigger the Beatles": Starr in *George Harrison: Living in the Material World* 2012.

195 "the naughtiest city": Lewisohn 2013, 700.

196 "ticket to ride": Turner 2009, 122.

196 "fueled by amphetamines": That Germany was where the Beatles were introduced to stimulants was no accident. With a long tradition of excellent chemists and engineers, Germany had been in the forefront of drug development for more than a century. In the late 1930s a new method of synthesizing methamphetamine was marketed under the name Pervitin, which was used widely (Ohler 2016, 41). Pervitin has been recognized as the key ingredient in the German invasion of

France; it kept soldiers in a euphoric state continuously for three days and three nights. "*Blitzkreig* was founded on methamphetamine," one medical historian has insisted (Ohler, 89). Preludin, the latest 1950s amphetamine invention, put the Beatles into overdrive not just in Hamburg but for years to come as an aid to performance and creativity. "Once you had a few beers and the odd pill, you could stay awake for days and didn't give a shit," explained one Hamburg musician (Spitz 2005, 218). This connection between the century's most horrific political movement and its most exciting musical movement stands as one of history's little ironies.

197   "reading poetry by Yevtushenko": Miles 1997, 83.
197   "There was always an underlying ambition": Ibid., 84.
198   "generated through actual conversations": See, for example, Davies 2009, 263–69.
198   "Liverpool friends contributed to the lyrics" : Davies 2009, 260; Shotton and Schaffner, 1984, 214–17.
199   "A very charming image": Spitz 2005, 226.
199   "Seemed incapable of taking Harrison": Shotton and Schaffner 1984, 186; Sheridan in Lewisohn 2013, 888; Brown and Gaines 1983, 221.
199   "John and Paul would butt": Lewisohn 2013, 703.
200   "They liked us because we were kind of rough": McMillian 2013, 18.
200   "Lennon stood": Ibid., 18–19.
200   "Cynthia Lennon described": Lennon 1978, 72.
200   "They did not have the musicianship": Miles 1997, 82.
200   "no. 1 because they resurrected": Lewisohn 2013, 950.
200   "Chuck Berry specialists": Flannery 2013, 215.
201   "to play Chuck Berry covers": Ibid., 219.
201   "On an intuitive level": Lewisohn 2013, 834.
201   "Or the crowd was part of them": Ibid., 866.
201   "They reminded me": Ibid., 966.
201   "His secretary typed": McMillian 2013, 29.
202   "At an audition for Decca": Miller 1999, 192.
202   "Mark Lewisohn": Lewisohn 2013, 843.
202   "Lennon's close friendship with Stuart Sutcliffe": Ibid., 722.
203   "slip in an original song": Ibid., 1151, 1096, 1071, 649, 651, 1056, and 1057.
203   "revived the songwriting partnership": Ibid., 1193.
203   "All novelists expect": Stillinger 1991.
204   "In Victorian England": Sutherland 1976.
205   "You'd sell your soul": Lewisohn 2013, 1323.

205   "Roy Orbison and producer Fred Foster": Lehman 2003, 14–15; 48, 50, 51, 94, and 36.

205   "I could recognize": McMillian 2013, 135.

205   "George Martin always has something": Miles 1978, 93; see also Lennon in Wenner 2000, 8.

205   "Martin's legacy will not just be": Emerick and Massey 2007, 370.

206   "I desperately wanted my own Cliff": Lewisohn 2013, 1222.

206   "Neil Aspinall called 'the chain'": Ibid., 1313.

206   "less complicated and more mature": Gould 2007, 309.

208   "when Epstein heard it": Flannery 2013, 180–81.

208   "Tony Sheridan heard it": *George Harrison: Living in the Material World* 2012.

208   "We actually had a sense of being different": Belmo 2002, 63.

209   "Epstein hired a lawyer": Lewisohn 2013, 1341–43.

210   "side by side at two desks": Nayder 2002, quotation on p. 202.

210   "In the distant future": Sandbrook 2005, 673.

210   "A well-placed churchman": Ibid., 195.

210   "William Mann": "What Songs the Beatles Sang," 1963, *Times* December 27: 4, cited in Sandbrook 2005, 677–78.

210   "John and Paul were writing": Lennon 1978, 90.

211   "mostly working on chord": Lewisohn 2013, 1235.

212   "I took the high harmony": Miles 1997, 95.

212   "play the riff in the gaps": Lewisohn 2013, 1337.

212   "*Don't Ever Change* covered by the Beatles": Ibid., 1241; Miles 1997, 92.

212   "Their interactive verbal style": Lewisohn 2013, 1363–66, 157, 1025, 1328, and 600.

213   "London is so very strange": McMillian 2013, 12; Braun 1964, 31.

213   "Press release from the fall": Lewisohn 2013, 1351.

213   "exaggerate their accents": Ibid., 1396 and 1428.

213   "It's Liverpool, where Z-Cars": Braun 1964, 9; Lewisohn 2013, 1115 and 1418.

213   "Being born in Liverpool": Lewisohn 2013, 1228; Gould 2007, 42; Davies 2009, 1–2.

214   "If one seemed in danger": Boyd 2007, 89.

214   "blunt northern humor": Miles 1997, 159.

214   "It's a highly prized commodity": Lewisohn 2013, 405.

215   "but they're not black": Ibid., 1350.

215   "This working-class explosion": Miles 1997, 98.

215   "Profumo affair": Sandbrook 2005, 629–37.

216   "We want the youth": Ibid., 690.

216   "quite a few people mention": Braun 1964, 32.

217   "You don't have to be a genius": Ibid., 12.

217 "cock rock": Frith and McRobbie 1991.

217 "On this next number": Miles 1978, 54.

218 "If we could put": Miles 1997, 276.

219 "The Beatles sent the class thing": Miller 1999, 217.

219 "We're rather crummy": Gendron 2002, 165.

219 "In his paternal": Early 2004, 53.

220 "almost a chord for every word": Exhibit *The British Invasion* at the Museum of Liverpool, June 2015.

220 "That's it!": Sheff 1981, 117.

221 "Their chords were outrageous": Scaduto 1971, 175.

221 "Critic Alec Wilder wrote about": Wilder 1990, 122.

221 "Suddenly you could breathe": Miller 1987, 5.

221 "See I remember in the early meetings": Miles 1978, 75; Goldman 2013. Lennon's "sound of the overall thing" also included the right consonants and the right vowels; see, for example, his comments on *I Dig a Pony* in Turner 2009, 287.

223 "They definitely needed each other": Lewisohn 2013, 1456.

223 "To learn a guitar part": Miles 1997, 170.

224 "The thing about rock and roll": Sounes 2011, 37.

225 "Allen Ginsberg pinned a Rimbaud": Fowlie 1994, 9.

225 "The poet makes himself a seer": Rimbaud 2000, 403.

226 "When I read that the bells went off": Dylan 2004, 288.

227 "It may be dated to around January 1964": Lewisohn 1988, 59. A different chronology is presented in Miles 1997, 201.

227 "McCartney's first *Yesterday*":Miles 1997, 80 and 81.

228 "Gershwin insisted that the melodies": Pollack 2006, 176.

228 "The melody works with harmony": McCartney alluded to the mutual benefit of working with melody and harmony together: "People think of *Long Tall Sally* and say it sounds so easy to write. But it's [*I'm Down*] the most difficult thing we've attempted. Writing a three-chord song that's clever is not easy." Turner 2009, 113.

228 "He cited a connection": *The Beatles Anthology* 2000, 175.

230 *Eine Kleine Beatlemusic*: Gendron 2002, 172.

230 "McCartney suggested a small blue note": McCartney learned to use single blue notes for effective moments of intensification. In *I'm Looking Through You* the flat seven of the IV chord is saved for the high peak of emotional-musical climax ("You're not the same"). In *Eleanor Rigby*, a flat fifth adds a fleeting moment of deeper poignancy ("Where do they all come from?").

231 "William Mann": William Mann (1963) on the Beatles's version of *'Till There Was You*: "a cool, easy, tasteful version of this ballad, quite without artificial sentimentality."

233   "He bought himself a cap": Bell 2013, 361.

233   "He later claimed": Sheff 1981, 149–50.

233   "doing little bits": Davies 2009, 281.

223   "Harrison suggested triple-meter": Miles 1997, 210.

234   "arguments that see the fingerprints of McCartney": MacDonald 2005, 170; Miles 1997, 277; Davies 2009, 371.

234   "He must have been aiming for a classical touch": This hunch is confirmed by Lennon (Wenner 2000, 8): "I would say, 'Play it like Bach or something, could you put twelve bars in there?'"

234   "Irish folk music": Miles 1997, 221.

235   "Elements of the song date back": Turner 2009, 142.

236   "Brian Wilson ... Bette Midler": Giuliano 1984, 370.

236   "beginning of my adult life": McMillian 2013, 136; Lydon 2003, 12.

Chapter 7: Retreat

237   "'This isn't show business': Braun 1964, 52.

237   "like a Walt Disney": Lennon 1978, 155.

238   "the wisest, holiest": Inglis 2000, 4.

238   "The people gave their money": McMillian 2013, 132.

239   "Lennon paid the steepest price": As Lennon explained (Wenner 2000, 57), he began taking amphetamines in Hamburg and "was a pill addict until *Help!*, just before *Help!* Where we were turned onto pot and we dropped drink . . . I've always needed a drug to *survive*."

239   "thousand trips": Miles 1978, 115.

239   "When the actor Peter Fonda": The documented explanation of Fonda's comment is that he was recalling an experience from childhood.

241   "I suppose now what I'm interested in": Davies 2009, 288–89.

241   "Whenever in doubt": Leary 1964, 6.

241   "rather earnestly strumming": *The Beatles Anthology* 2003.

242   "The Byrds had just demonstrated": Bellman 1997; Heylin 2007, 23–24; Green 1988, 160.

243   "Paul had a great hand": Emerick and Massey 2008, 405.

243   "French for bullshit": Miles 1978, 120; MacDonald 2005, 224.

243   "I don't go in for much of those": Braun 1964, 51.

243   "innovative techniques": Giuliano 1994, 222 and 228; Weber 2016, p. 235 n. 163; Green 1988, 79.

244   "McCartney met": Miles 1997, 180; Inglis 2000, 11; Braun 1964, 53; Green 1988, 77–78.

244   "I am trying to cram": Gould 2007, 313.

244   "The London Days": Cardew 2006, 73–75.

244   "went on too long": Miles 1997, 237. McCartney was also inspired by John Cage. "Cage, he felt, is too random," wrote an interviewer from

March 1966. "I like to get ideas randomly but then develop them within a frame," McCartney explained in what could be taken as an accurate description of the use of tape loops in *Tomorrow Never Knows*, recorded on April 7. Quotation from an unpublished interview by Michael Lydon, March 1966, accessed (March 2017) on the website teachrock.org.

245 "what is like becomes": Harvey 1975, 28; Stockhausen 1958, 74; MacDonald 2005, 224.

246 "rudimentary recording studio": Miles 1997, 239–41, 258, and 291; Spitz 2005, 601; MacDonald 2005, 190; Heylin 2007, 9 and 10.

247 "The idols now": Miles 1967, 9.

247 "take the edge off": Sheff 1981, 153.

247 "Harrison later insisted": *The Beatles Anthology* 2000, 210.

247 "evocative and complete": Swainson 2000, 555.

248 "gathering of friends": Shotton and Schaffner, 1984, 214–17; Davies 2014, 146–47. Lennon's contributions to *Eleanor Rigby* (contrary to his claims) appear to have been negligible; see, for example, Davies 2009, 371.

248 "All of this love thy": Gould 2007, 310.

250 "From Braque and Picasso the practice spread": Oxford Art Online, article "Collage," by Francis Frascina, Marjorie Perloff, and Christine Poggi.

251 "weld together": *The Beatles Anthology* 2000, 97.

253 "He alone in the industry": Heylin 2007, 47.

255 "Well it's magic": Miles 1967, 8–11.

256 "battering ram": Miles 1997, 595.

256 "I was really going through": Miles and Marchbank 1978, 115. Lennon in Wenner 2000, 17: "I was very paranoid in those days [the making of *Sgt. Pepper*], I could hardly move."

257 "I should have tried to get": Miles and Marchbank 1978, 88.

257 "There never was": Shotton and Schaffner 1984, 186.

258 "It is a fantastically abstract": Miles 1967, 10.

258 "It isn't necessarily so": Bromell 2000, 99.

261 "The way we wrote": Miles and Marchbank 1978, 88; Sheff 1981, 183–84.

262 "immediately compared": *Newsweek* cited in Gendron 2002, 195.

262 "three bars": Inglis 2000, 16.

262 "McCartney asked": Emerick and Massey 2007, 149.

262 "Peter Zinovieff": Pinch and Trocco 2002, 278–82.

262 "spiraling ascent": Martin 1994, 56; Noyer 2015, 70.

262 "The worst thing about": Bromell 2000, 98; Miles 1967.

264 "extensive back and forth": Described in Davies 2009, 263–67.

265   "Humor is often about shifting meaning": Psychologist Dacher Keltner
      (2009, 137) describes laughter as "an invitation to enter into the world
      of pretense, it is a suspension of the demands of literal meaning and
      more formal social exchange . . . a ticket to travel to the landscape of the
      human imagination."

265   "doesn't go anywhere": Sheff 1981, 197.

265   "*Through the Looking Glass*": Miles 1997, 312.

266   "We're fed up": Emerick and Massey 2007, 132.

266   "Paul instructed": Davies 2009, 270.

266   "cool anti-romantic": Mann 1967, 96.

266   "genius doesn't lie": Eisen 1969, 155.

266   "One difference": As William Mann (1967, 96) insisted, "any of these
      songs is more genuinely creative than anything currently to be heard on
      pop radio stations."

267   "Walter Everett": Everett 1999, 112; Mann 1967, 94–95.

267   "schmaltz": Martin 1994, 34.

269   "from North India": Everett 1999, 112 and 342; Bellman 1998, 297;
      Moore 1997, 45.

269   "talk of trimming": Emerick and Massey 2007, 186.

270   "Harrison now seems to take": Christgau 1967, 117.

270   "Lillian Ross": Lillian Ross, "Sgt. Pepper," *The New Yorker* June 24,
      1967: 22.

272   "dig at his sustained harvest": Shotton and Schaffner 1984, 256–61.

272   "Just as Paul had assumed": Emerick and Massey 2007, 212.

273   "I am That": Mahesh Yogi 1967, 9; Mendelson 2014, 31; Sheff 1981,
      156.

274   "like a human click": Emerick and Massey 2007, 212; Becker 1982, 91.

274   "perpetually ascending": MacDonald 2005, 266.

274   "Milan Kundera": Keltner 2009, 130.

Chapter 8: Grow a Little Taller

275   "We'd all learned": *George Harrison: Living in the Material World* 2012.

275   "I'm quite proud": McMillian 2013, 176.

275   "Harrison remembered": Riley 2011, 77; Davies 2009, xxxv.

275   "Emboldened by precedents": Bellman 1997, 120–21.

276   "auspicious sign": Davies 2009, 318.

276   "For me it was like": Glazer 1977, 37.

276   "In the summer of 1966": Shankar 1999, 189; Reck 1985, 105; Harri-
      son 1980, 55.

276   "the only person who ever impressed": Tillery 2011, 55.

277   "Last born": Sulloway 1996.

277 "answer the telephone": Boyd 2007, 87.

277 "I started my own": Farrell 1997, 176.

278 "Harrison received": O'Mahony 2008, 23.

278 "Each soul is potentially": Shankar 1999, 195.

278 "all four of them on the cover": Miles and Marchbank 1978, 92; Tillery 2011, 156; Mason 1994, 106.

279 "God is in the space": Miles 1997, 393.

279 "If we'd met": Miles and Marchbank 1978, 32.

279 "You know I feel": Ibid. 37.

279 "One evening Shotton": Shotton 1984, 252.

280 "I hope the fans will": Giuliano 1994, 107.

280 "Across the Universe": Fiona Apple's 1998 recording is a rare example of a cover that actually improves upon the Beatles original. Of course there are many covers of Beatles songs that that successfully reconceptualize original arrangements. My point here is that this arrangement doesn't do that; it simply improves on the original.

280 "field of sorrow": Mahesh Yogi 1967, 155–57 and 366–68.

281 "The Inner Light was recorded": Miles and Marchbank 1978, 97.

281 "based on the classic Taoist text": Belmo 2002; Reck 1985, 113.

282 "big brass band": Farrow 1997, 137.

282 "got to a real good place": Transcendental Meditation 2010.

282 "land of light": Farrow 1997, 138.

282 "For creating it was great": Sheff 1981, 169; Lennon in Wenner 2000, 12: "I wrote the last batch of my best songs [in India]."

283 "John and George were in": Lennon 1978, 170.

283 "John and George have each done": Starr, 2004, 17.

283 "Well if you're so cosmic": Mason 1994, 138–39; Boyd 2007, 116 and 119.

283 "I felt what we were doing": Lennon 1978, 176.

284 "Lennon's fragile ego": Starr (2004, 49) reports, with no date given but probably from around this time: "I can say this now (if he was here John could tell you) but suddenly we'd be in the middle of a track and John would just start crying or screaming—which freaked us out at the beginning. But we were always open to whatever anyone was going through so we just got on with it."

284 "postmodern statement": Ed Whitely, "The Postmodern White Album" in Inglis 2000.

284 "Both John and I had": Miles 1997, 497.

285 "Fernando Sor": The connection to Sor's Study, No. 19, opus 60 in G major (the same key as Blackbird) was brought to my attention by Randy Reed, my colleague at Duke University. Chet Atkins did in fact

record Bach's *Bourrée* in E minor for an album called *Hi Fi in Focus*,
released October, 1957.

285 "Kahlil Gibran": Lennon 1978, 172; Sheff 1871, 160.

286 "Harrison's initial idea": MacDonald 2005, 301.

288 "warm endorsement from *Time*": Platoff 2005; McMillian 2013, 180.

288 "For the Maharishi spirituality trumped": Kent 2001, 84.

288 "evening lectures": Lennon (*The Beatles Anthology* 2000, 298): "I had
been thinking about it [the song *Revolution*] up in the hills in India."
On the Maharishi's politics, Mason 1994, 126–27.

289 "whistling caterwauling": Prose 2002, 337.

290 "Carlos Castaneda": Shotton and Schaffner 1984, 378.

290 "Not bad": Emerick and Massey 2007, 241; O'Toole 2007; Davies
2009, 372.

291 "hip credentials": Adding to the problem for Lennon was his jealousy of
Jagger and the Stones' more rebellious image; see Davies 2009, lvi.

292 "Emerick described": Emerick and Massey 2007, 251.

292 "Starr actually quit": Brown and Gaines 1983, 315–16.

292 "It got a bit like": *Beatles Anthology* 2000, 316.

292 "Listen, John": Brown and Gaines 1983, 296.

292 "I am more stoned": Emerick and Massey 2007, 246.

295 "McCartney explained": Sulpy and Schweighardt 1997, 183.

297 "I was stoned all the time": Miles and Marchbank 1978, 103; Sulpy and
Schweighardt 1997, 198–99; Brown and Gaines 1983, 302.

297 "Alchemical wedding": Connolly 1981, 121.

297 "pious subtly self-righteous": Brennan 2007, 158, 155; Doggett 1998,
115.

297 "went off the rails for good": Heylin 2007, 278.

297 "alienated a good part of his dancing public": Teachout 2014, 10; see
also Heylin 2007, especially Chapter 13.

299 "different working methods": Sulpy and Schweighardt 1997, 76.

300 "According to Martin": Martin and Pearson 1994, 122.

300 "emollient": *The Beatles Anthology* 2003, Episode 7.

301 "simultaneous dreams": Sulpy and Schweighardt 1997, 272.

302 "It's complicated now": *The Beatles: Let It Be* 2002 [1970].

302 "Simplicity is a complex form": Quoted by Clark Terry in *Keep on
Keepin' On* 2014.

303 "No matter how bad": *George Harrison: Living in the Material World*
2012.

304 "That bitch": Emerick and Massey 2007, 286.

306 "Louder!": Ibid., 300.

306 "John and Paul were a unique": Lewisohn 2013, 654.

308 "In January Lennon had suggested": Sulpy and Schweighardt 1997, 209.

309 "like they had gone back in time": Emerick and Massey 2007, 294.

310 "There were some really loving caring moments": *The Beatles Anthology* 2000, 356.

312 "thanks partly to lyrics copied directly": Leary 1997, 51.

312 "Whatever it is that will please you": *The Beatles Anthology* 2000, 316.

313 "A tape from January 1969 caught Lennon": *The Beatles Anthology* 2000.

314 "chocolate coating": Sheff 1981, 179.

315 "disagreements contributed": Miles 1997, 579.

315 "It was getting too democratic": Noyer 2015, 80.

BIBLIOGRAPHY

Adelt, Ulrich. 2010. *Blues Music in the Sixties: A Story in Black and White*. New Brunswick, NJ: Rutgers University Press.

Aldridge, Alan. 1969. *The Beatles Illustrated Lyrics*. London: Macdonald Futura.

Allen, Walter C. 1973. *Hendersonia: The Music of Fletcher Henderson and His Musicians*. Highland Park, NJ: Jazz Monographs.

Anderson, Ronald, and Ann Koval. 2002. *James McNeill Whistler: Beyond the Myth*. New York: Carroll and Graf.

Antliff, Mark, and Patricia Leighten. 2001. *Cubism and Culture*. London: Thames & Hudson.

Aravamudan, Srinivas. 2006. *Guru English: South Asian Religion as a Cosmopolitan Language*. Princeton, NJ: Princeton University Press.

Armstrong, Louis. 1966. *Louis Armstrong—A Self-Portrait: The Interview by Richard Merryman*. New York: Eakins.

Austin, Mary. 1926. "Buck and Wing and Bill Robinson." *Nation* 122 (April 28): 476.

Barg, Lisa. 2013. "Queer Encounters in the Music of Billy Strayhorn." *Journal of the American Musicological Society* 66 no. 3 (Fall): 771–824.

Barg, Lisa, and Walter van de Leur. 2013. "'Your Music Has Flung the Story of "Hot Harlem" to the Four Corners of the Earth!': Race and Narrative in *Black, Brown and Beige*." *Musical Quarterly* 96, 3–4: 426–58.

Barnes, Walter, Jr. 1929. "The Musical Bunch." *Chicago Defender* (November 9): 7.

Baumgartner, Michael. 2012. "Duke Ellington's 'East St. Louis *Toodle-O*' Revisited." *Jazz Perspectives* 6, nos. 1–2: 29–56.

The Beatles Anthology. 2000. San Francisco: Chronicle Books.

The Beatles Anthology. 2003. Directed by Geoff Wonfor and Bob Smeaton. EMI. DVD.

The Beatles: Let It Be. 2002 [1970]. Directed by Michael Lindsay-Hogg. United Artists Entertainment. DVD.

Becker, Howard S. 1982. *Art Worlds*. Berkley: University of California Press.

Bell, Ian. 2013. *Once upon a Time: The Lives of Bob Dylan*. New York: Pegasus Books.

Bellman, Jonathan. 1997. "Indian Resonances in the British Invasion, 1965–1968." *Journal of Musicology* 15, no. 1: 116–36.

————, ed. 1998. *The Exotic in Western Music*. Boston: Northeastern University Press.

Belmo. 2002. *George Harrison: His Words, Wit & Wisdom*. Fort Mitchell, KY: Belmo Publishing.

Berger, David. 2014. "The Land of Suites: Ellington and Extended Form." In *Cambridge Companion to Duke Ellington*, edited by Edward Green, 245–61. Cambridge: Cambridge University Press.

Berish, Andrew. 2014. "Survival, Adaptation, Experimentation: Duke Ellington and His Orchestra in the 1930s." In *Cambridge Companion to Duke Ellington*, edited by Edward Green, 106–20. Cambridge: Cambridge University Press.

Berlin, Edward A. 2016. *King of Ragtime: Scott Joplin and His Era*. New York: Oxford University Press.

Bigard, Barney. 1969. Interview at Williams Research Center, New Orleans, July 25.

————. 1976. Interview at Institute for Jazz Studies, Rutgers University, Newark, New Jersey.

————. 1986. *With Louis and the Duke: The Autobiography of a Jazz Clarinetist*. New York: Oxford University Press.

Bogle, Donald. 2005. *Bright Boulevards, Bold Dreams: The Story of Black Hollywood*. New York: Ballantine Books.

Boyd, Pattie, with Penny Junor. 2007. *Wonderful Tonight: George Harrison, Eric Clapton, and Me*. New York: Harmony Books.

Brackett, David. 2013. *The Pop, Rock, and Soul Reader: Histories and Debates*. New York: Oxford University Press.

Braud, Wellman. 1957. Interview at Williams Research Center, New Orleans, May 30.

Braun, Michael. 1964. *Love Me Do: The Beatles' Progress*. Harmondsworth, UK: Penguin.

Brennan, Matt. 2007. "Down Beats and Rolling Stones: An Historical Comparison of American Jazz and Rock Journalism." PhD diss., University of Stirling.

Bromell, Nick. 2000. *Tomorrow Never Knows: Rock and Psychedelics in the 1960s*. Chicago: University of Chicago Press.

Brothers, Thomas. 1997. "Ideology and Aurality in the Vernacular Traditions of African-American Music." *Black Music Research Journal* (Fall): 169–209.

————. 2006. *Louis Armstrong's New Orleans*. New York: W. W. Norton.

————. 2014. *Louis Armstrong, Master of Modernism*. New York: W. W. Norton.

Brown, Peter, and Steven Gaines. 1983. *The Love You Make: An Insider's Story of the Beatles*. New York: McGraw-Hill.

Brown, Scott. 1986. *James P. Johnson: A Case of Mistaken Identity*. Metuchen, NJ: Scarecrow Press.

Büchmann-Møller, Frank. 2006. *Someone to Watch over Me: The Life and Music of Ben Webster*. Ann Arbor: University of Michigan Press.

Bushell, Garvin. 1988. *Jazz from the Beginning.* As told to Mark Tucker. Ann Arbor: University of Michigan Press.

Cardew, Cornelius. 2006. *Cornelius Cardew: A Reader.* Edited by Edwin Prévost. Harlow, UK: Copula.

Chernoff, John Miller. 1979. *African Rhythm and African Sensibility: Aesthetics and Social Action in African Musical Idioms.* Chicago: University of Chicago Press.

Christgau, Robert. 1967. "Secular Music." Reprinted in Sawyers 2006, 115–19.

Clark, Andrew. 2001. *Riffs and Choruses: A New Jazz Anthology.* London: Continuum.

Clifford, James. 1988. *The Predicament of Culture:* Twentieth-Century *Ethnography, Literature and Art.* Cambridge, MA: Harvard University Press.

Cohen, Harvey G. 2010. *Duke Ellington's America.* Chicago: University of Chicago Press.

Collier, James Lincoln. 1978. *The Making of Jazz: A Comprehensive History.* London: Papermac.

———. 1987. *Duke Ellington.* New York: Oxford University Press.

Compton, Todd. 1988. "McCartney or Lennon?: Beatle Myths and the Composing of the Lennon-McCartney Songs." *Journal of Popular Culture* 22, no. 2: 99–131.

Connolly, Ray. 1981. *John Lennon, 1940–1980.* London: Fontana.

Dance, Stanley. 1977. *The World of Earl Hines.* New York: Da Capo.

Davies, Hunter. 2009. *The Beatles.* New York: W. W. Norton.

———. 2014. *The Beatles Lyrics: The Stories behind the Music, Including the Handwritten Drafts of More Than 100 Classic Beatles Songs.* New York: Little, Brown.

DeVeaux, Scott. 1993. "*Black, Brown and Beige* and the Critics." *Black Music Research Journal* 13, no. 2: 125–46.

Doggett, Peter. 1998. *Let It Be/Abbey Road: The Beatles.* New York: Schirmer.

———. 2009. *You Never Give Me Your Money: The Beatles after the Breakup.* New York: Harper Collins.

Durkin, Andrew. 2014. *Decomposition: A Musical Manifesto.* New York: Pantheon.

Dylan, Bob. 2004. *Chronicles: Volume One.* New York: Simon & Schuster.

Early, Gerald. 2004. *One Nation under a Groove: Motown and American Culture.* Ann Arbor: University of Michigan Press.

Eisen, Jonathan. 1969. *The Age of Rock: Sounds of the American Cultural Revolution; A Reader.* New York: Random House.

Ellington, Duke. 1973. *Music Is My Mistress.* Garden City, NY: Doubleday.

Ellington, Mercer, with Stanley Dance. 1978. *Duke Ellington in Person: An Intimate Memoir.* Boston: Houghton Mifflin.

Ellison, Ralph. 2003. *The Collected Essays of Ralph Ellison.* Edited by John F. Callahan. New York: Modern Library.

Emerick, Geoff, and Howard Massey. 2007. *Here, There and Everywhere: My Life Recording the Music of the Beatles.* New York: Gotham Books.

Emerson, Ken. 2005. *Always Magic in the Air: The Bomp and Brilliance of the Brill Building Era.* New York: Viking.

Epstein, Dena. 1977. *Sinful Tunes and Spirituals: Black Folk Music to the Civil War.* Urbana: University of Illinois Press.

Erenberg, Lewis. 1981. *Steppin' Out.* Westport, CT: Greenwood.

———. 1998. *Swingin' the Dream: Big Band Jazz and the Rebirth of American Culture.* Chicago: University of Chicago Press.

Evans, David. 1982. *Big Road Blues: Tradition and Creativity in Folk Blues.* Berkeley: University of California Press.

Everett, Walter. 1999. *The Beatles as Musicians: Revolver through the Anthology.* New York: Oxford University Press.

Farrell, Gerry. 1997. *Indian Music and the West.* New York: Oxford University Press.

Farrow, Mia. 1997. *What Falls Away: A Memoir.* New York: Nan A. Talese.

Fisher, Rudolph. 1927. "The Caucasian Storms Harlem." *American Mercury* 11: 393–98.

Flannery, Joe, with Michael Brocken. 2013. *Standing in the Wings: The Beatles, Brian Epstein and Me.* Stroud, UK: History Press.

Floyd, Samuel A., Jr. 1995. *The Power of Black Music: Interpreting Its History from Africa to the United States.* New York: Oxford University Press.

Fowlie, Wallace. 1994. *Rimbaud and Jim Morrison: The Rebel as Poet.* Durham, NC: Duke University Press.

Freeman, Bud. 1974. *You Don't Look Like a Musician.* Detroit, MI: Balamp.

Frith, Simon, and Howard Horne. 1987. *Art into Pop.* London: Methuen.

Frith, Simon, and Angela McRobbie. 1991. "Rock and Sexuality." In *On Record: Rock, Pop, and the Written Word*, edited by Simon Frith and Andrew Goodman, 371–89. New York: Routledge.

Furia, Philip. 1996. *Ira Gershwin: The Art of the Lyricist.* New York: Oxford University Press.

Gabbard, Krin. 1990. "Krin Gabbard Replies." *American Music* 8, no. 3: 360–62.

———. 2016. *Better Git It in Your Soul: An Interpretive Biography of Charles Mingus.* Oakland: University of California Press.

Gendron, Benard. 2002. *Between Montmartre and the Mudd Club: Popular Music and the* Avant-Garde. Chicago: University of Chicago Press.

George, Don. 1981. *Sweet Man: The Real Duke Ellington.* New York: Putnam.

George Harrison: Living in the Material World. 2012. Directed by Martin Scorsese. Universal. DVD.

George-Warren, Holly, ed. 2009. *The Rock and Roll Hall of Fame: The First 25 Years: The Definitive Chronicle of Rock & Roll as Told by Its Legends.* New York: Collins Design.

Gershwin, Ira. 1973. *Lyrics on Several Occasions.* New York: Viking.

Giddins, Gary. 1998. *Visions of Jazz: The First Century.* New York: Oxford University Press.

Giddins, Gary, and Scott DeVeaux. 2009. *Jazz*. New York: W. W. Norton.

Gioia, Ted. 2012. *Jazz Standards: A Guide to the Repertory*. New York: Oxford University Press.

Giuliano, Geoffrey. 1994. *The Lost Beatles Interviews*. New York: Dutton.

Givan, Benjamin. 2014. "Ellington and the Blues." In *The Cambridge Companion to Duke Ellington*, edited by Edward Green, 173–85. Cambridge: Cambridge University Press.

Glazer, Michael. 1977. "Growing Up at 33⅓: The George Harrison Interview." *Crawdaddy*, February.

Goldman, Andrew. 2013. "Billy Joel on Not Working, Not Giving Up Drinking and Not Caring What Elton John Says about Any of It." *New York Times Magazine* (May 26): 34–38, 46.

Goodman, Benny, and Irving Kolodin. 1939. *The Kingdom of Swing*. New York: Stackpole Sons.

Gould, Jonathan. 2007. *Can't Buy Me Love: The Beatles, Britain and America*. London: Portrait.

Green, Edward. 2007. "Ellington and the Art of Motivic Composition." *Ongakagaku* 53: 1–18.

———. 2011. "'It Don't Mean a Thing if It Ain't Got That Grundgestalt!'— Ellington from a Motivic Perspective." *Jazz Perspectives* 2, no. 2: 215–49.

Green, Jonathon. 1988. *Days in the Life: Voices from the English Underground 1961–1971*. London: Heinemann.

Hajdu, David. 1996. *Lush Life: A Biography of Billy Strayhorn*. New York: Farrar, Straus, Giroux.

———. 1999. "A Jazz of Their Own." *Vanity Fair* (May): 188–96.

Hamm, Charles. 1995. *Putting Popular Music in Its Place*. Cambridge: Cambridge University Press.

Handy, W. C. 1957 [1941]. *Father of the Blues: An Autobiography*. Edited by Arna Bontemps. London: Sidgwick and Jackson.

Harker, Brian. 2005. *Jazz: An American Journey*. Upper Saddle River, NJ: Pearson Prentice Hall.

———. 2008. "Louis Armstrong, Eccentric Dance, and the Evolution of Jazz on the Eve of Swing." *Journal of the American Musicological Society* 61, no. 1: 67–121.

Harker, Dave. 1992. "Still Crazy after All These Years: What Was Popular Music in the 1960s?'" In *Cultural Revolution?: The Challenge of the Arts in the 1960s*, edited by Bart Moore-Gilbert and John Seed, 236–54. New York: Routledge.

Harmetz, Aljean. 1977. *The Making of the Wizard of Oz: Movie Magic and Studio Power in the Prime of MGM and the Miracle of Production #1060*. New York: Knopf.

Harrison, George. 1980 [2007]. *I, Me, Mine*. San Francisco: Chronicle Books.

Harvey, Jonathan. 1975. *The Music of Stockhausen: An Introduction*. Berkeley: University of California Press.

Haskins, James. 1977. *The Cotton Club*. New York: Random House.

Hasse, John Edward. 1993. *Beyond Category: The Life and Genius of Duke Ellington*. New York: Simon & Schuster.

Hentoff, Nat. 1965. "This Cat Needs No Pulitzer Prize." *New York Times* (September 12): SM64–74.

Heylin, Clinton. 2007. *The Act You've Known for All These Years: A Year in the Life of Sgt. Pepper & Friends*. New York: Canongate.

Hobsbawm, E. J. 1987. "Slyest of the Foxes." *New York Review of Books* (November 19).

Hodes, Art, and Chadwick Hansen, eds. 1977. *Selections from the Gutter: Jazz Portraits from "The Jazz Record."* Berkeley: University of California Press.

Howland, John. 2009. *"Ellington Uptown": Duke Ellington, James P. Johnson, & the Birth of Concert Jazz*. Ann Arbor: University of Michigan Press.

Hughes, Langston. 1926. "The Negro Artist and the Racial Mountain." *The Nation* 122, no. 3181 (June 23): 692–94.

"'I'm Not Going to Waste My Life . . . I Don't Want to Die at 40': Exclusive." (2009). "For 40 years Ray Connolly's taped interviews with John Lennon have gathered dust. Published here for the first time, they give an insight into the unnervingly prescient mind of the Beatle whose premature death stunned the world. Illustration by Erika Simmons; The lost interviews." *London Sunday Times* (September 6): 10.

Inglis, Ian, ed. 2000. *The Beatles, Popular Music and Society: A Thousand Voices*. New York: St. Martin's Press.

Inglis, Ian. 2010. *The Words and Music of George Harrison*. Santa Barbara, CA: Praeger.

Jackson, Bruce, ed. 1967. *The Negro and His Folklore in Nineteenth-Century Periodicals*. Austin: University of Texas Press.

Jackson, Mahalia, with Evan McLeod Wylie. 1966. *Movin' On Up*. New York: Hawthorn Books.

Jones, Max, and John Chilton. 1971. *Louis: The Louis Armstrong Story, 1900–1971*. Boston: Little, Brown.

Joplin, Laura. 2005. *Love, Janis*. New York: Harper.

Katz, Mark. 2010. *Capturing Sound: How Technology Has Changed Music*. Berkeley: University of California Press.

Keep on Keepin' On. 2014. Directed by Alan Hicks. Absolute Clay Productions. DVD.

Keltner, Dacher. 2009. *Born to Be Good: The Science of a Meaningful Life*. New York: W. W. Norton.

Kent, Stephen. 2001. *From Slogans to Mantras: Social Protest and Religious Conversion in the Late Vietnam Era*. Syracuse, NY: Syracuse University Press.

Keogh, Pamela Clarke. 2004. *Elvis Presley: The Man, the Life, the Legend*. New York: Atria Books.

Kozinn, Allan. 2013. "Lennon's School Records: He Was a Bad Boy." *New York Times* (November 11): C3(L).

Lambert, Constant. 1937. *Music Ho! A Study of Music in Decline*. London: Faber.

Lambert, Eddie. 1999. *Duke Ellington: A Listener's Guide*. Edited by Dan Morgenstern and Edward Berger, Studies in Jazz Series, No. 26. Lanham, MD: Scarecrow Press.

Lasker, Steven. 1994. Liner notes. Duke Ellington. *Early Ellington*. Audio CD. New York: GRP.

Lavezzoli, Peter. 2001. *The King of All, Sir Duke: Ellington and the Artistic Revolution*. New York: Continuum.

Leary, Timothy, Ralph Metzner, and Richard Alpert. 1964. *The Psychedelic Experience: A Manual Based on the Tibetan Book of the Dead*. New York: University Books.

———. 1997. *Psychedelic Prayers and Other Meditations*. Berkeley, CA: Ronin.

Lehman, Peter. 2003. *Roy Orbison: The Invention of an Alternative Rock Masculinity*. Philadelphia: Temple University Press.

Lennon, Cynthia. 1978. *A Twist of Lennon*. New York: Avon.

Leonard, Neil. 1962. *Jazz and the White Americans: The Acceptance of a New Art Form*. Chicago: University of Chicago Press.

Lewisohn, Mark. 1988. *The Complete Beatles Recording Sessions: The Official Story of the Abbey Road Years*. London: EMI.

———. 2013. *Tune In. The Beatles: All These Years*. Special extended edition in two parts. London: Little, Brown.

Lydon, Michael. 2003. *Flashbacks: Eyewitness Accounts of the Rock Revolution, 1964–1974*. New York: Routledge.

MacDonald, Ian. 2005. *Revolution in the Head: The Beatles' Records and the Sixties*. London: Pimlico.

Magee, Jeffrey. 2005. *The Uncrowned King of Swing: Fletcher Henderson and Big Band Jazz*. New York: Oxford University Press.

———. 2006. "'Everybody Step': Irving Berlin, Jazz, and Broadway in the 1920s." *Journal of the American Musicological Society* 59: 698–715.

———. 2015. "Ellington's Afro-Modernist Vision in the 1920s." In *The Cambridge Companion to Duke Ellington*, edited by Edward Green, 85–105. Cambridge: Cambridge University Press.

Mahesh Yogi, Maharishi. 1967. *Maharishi Mahesh Yogi on the* Bhagavad-Gita: *A New Translation and Commentary with Sanskrit Text Chapters 1–6*. Harmondsworth, UK: Penguin.

[Mann, William. Printed without attribution]. 1963. "What Songs the Beatles Sang . . ." *London Times* (December 27): 4.

Mann, William. 1967. "The Beatles Revive Hopes of Progress in Pop Music." Reprinted in Sawyers 2006, 92–101.

Martin, George, with William Pearson. 1994. *Summer of Love: The Making of Sgt. Pepper*. London: Pan Books.

Mason, Paul. 1994. *The Maharishi: The Biography of the Man Who Gave Transcendental Meditation to the World*. Rockport, UK: Element.

Maus, Fred Everett, Marion A. Guck, Charles Fisk, James Webster, Alicyn

Warren, and Edward T. Cone. 1989. "Edward T. Cone's *The Composer's Voice*: Elaborations and Departures." *College Music Symposium* 29: 1–80.

McMillian, John. 2013. *Beatles vs. Stones*. New York: Simon & Schuster.

Mellers, Wilfrid. 1973. *Twilight of the Gods: The Music of the Beatles*. New York: Viking.

Mendelson, Edward. 2014. "Who Was Ernest Hemingway?" *New York Review of Books* (August 14).

Mezzrow, Milton "Mezz," and Bernard Wolfe. 1946. *Really the Blues*. New York: Random House.

Miles, Barry. 1967. "Miles Interviews Paul McCartney." *International Times* (January 16–29)" 8–11.

———. 1997. *Paul McCartney: Many Years from Now*. New York: H. Holt.

Miles, Barry, and Pearce Marchbank, eds. 1978. *Beatles in Their Own Words*. New York: Delilah.

Miller, Jim. 1987. *Democracy in the Streets: From Port Huron to the Siege of Chicago*. New York: Simon & Schuster.

———. 1999. *Flowers in the Dustbin: The Rise of Rock and Roll, 1947–1977*. New York: Simon & Schuster.

Moore, Allan F. 1997. *The Beatles: Sgt. Pepper's Lonely Hearts Club Band*. Cambridge: Cambridge University Press.

Morgan, David. 1999. *Monty Python Speaks!* New York: Spike.

Morton, John Fass. 2008. *Backstory in Blue: Ellington at Newport '56*. New Brunswick, NJ: Rutgers University Press.

Murray, Albert. 2016. *Murray Talks Music: Albert Murray on Jazz and Blues*. Minneapolis: University of Minnesota Press.

Murray, Albert, and Ralph Ellison. 2000. *Trading Twelves: The Selected Letters of Ralph Ellison and Albert Murray*. Edited by Albert Murray and John F. Callahan. New York: Random House.

Myers, Marc. 2012a. "Interview: Mike Stoller (Part 3)." *JazzWax* (May 31). Accessed May 2015.

———. 2012b. "Interview: Mike Stoller (Part 4)." *JazzWax*. (June 1). Accessed May 2015.

Nayder, Lillian. 2002. *Unequal Partners: Charles Dickens, Wilkie Collins, and Victorian Authorship*. Ithaca, NY: Cornell University Press.

Nicholson, Stuart. 1999. *Reminiscing in Tempo: A Portrait of Duke Ellington*. Boston: Northern University Press.

Noyer, Paul Du. 2015. *Conversations with McCartney*. London: Hodder.

Ohler, Norman. 2016. *Blitzed*. Translated by Shaun Whiteside. London: Allen Lane.

O'Mahony, John. 2008. "G2: Arts: 'A Hodgepodge of Hash, Yoga and LSD': On the eve of his last ever gig in Europe, sitar giant Ravi Shankar tells John O'Mahony why the 60s got India wrong, how his daughters give him hope—and why Hendrix annoyed him." *London Guardian* (June 4): 23.

Ono, Yoko, ed. 2005. *Memories of John Lennon*. New York: Harper Entertainment.

Otis, Johnny. 1968. *Listen to the Lambs*. New York: W. W. Norton.

O'Toole, Fintan. 1997. "How Stockhausen Made Pop Weird." *Irish Times* (December 15): Weekend, Arts, 6.

Palmer, Robert. 1982. *Deep Blues*. Harmondsworth, UK: Penguin.

"Paul McCartney: A Giant among Rock Immortals." 2007. Interview for *Rolling Stone Magazine*, April 23.

Payne, Daniel Alexander. 1968 [1888]. *Recollections of Seventy Years*. New York: Arno Press.

Perone, James E. 2009. *Mods, Rockers, and the Music of the British Invasion*. Westport, CT: Praeger.

Peyton, Dave. 1925. "The Musical Bunch." *Chicago Defender* (November 14): 7.

———. 1927. "The Washingtonians 'Set New England Dance Crazy.'" *Chicago Defender* (August 27): 6.

———. 1929. "The Musical Bunch." *Chicago Defender* (August 29): 7.

Pinch, Trevor, and Frank Trocco. 2002. *Analog Days: The Invention and Impact of the Moog Synthesizer*. Cambridge, MA: Harvard University Press.

Platoff, John. 2005. "John Lennon, 'Revolution,' and the Politics of Musical Reception." *Journal of Musicology* 22, no. 2: 241–67.

Pollack, Howard. 2006. *George Gershwin: His Life and Work*. Berkeley: University of California Press.

Posner, Gerald. 2002. *Motown: Music, Money, Sex, and Power*. New York: Random House.

Priestly, Brian. 1984. *Mingus: A Critical Biography*. New York: Da Capo.

———. 2014. "Ellington Abroad." In *The Cambridge Companion to Duke Ellington*, edited by Edward Green, 55–66. Cambridge: Cambridge University Press.

Prose, Francine. 2002. *The Lives of the Muses: Nine Women and the Artists They Inspired*. New York: Harper Collins.

Raboteau, Albert J. 1978. *Slave Religion: The "Invisible Institution" in the Antebellum South*. New York: Oxford University Press.

Rattenbury, Ken. 1990. *Duke Ellington Jazz Composer*. New Haven, CT: Yale University Press.

Reck, David R. 1985. "Beatles Orientalis: Influences from Asia in Popular Song Tradition." *Asian Music* 16, no. 1: 83–149.

Reed, Randy. 1997. *Randy Reed's Repertoire*. Durham, NC: R. Reed.

Rexroth, Laura. 2007. "Duke Ellington and Percy Grainger: Black, Brown, and 'Blue-Eyed English.'" In *The Wind Band in and around New York ca. 1830–1950: Essays Presented at the 26th Biennial Conference of the College Band Directors Association, New York, NY, February 2005*, edited by Frank Cipolla and Donald Hunsberger, 76–94. Van Nuys, CA: Alfred.

Riis, Thomas L. 1989. *Just before Jazz: Black Musical Theater in New York, 1890–1915*. Washington: Smithsonian Institution Press.

Riley, Tim. 2011. *Lennon: The Man, the Myth, the Music—the Definitive Life*. New York: Hyperion.

Rimbaud, Arthur. 1966. *Complete Works, Selected Letters*. Translated,

introduction, and notes by Wallace Fowlie. Chicago: University of Chicago
　　Press.

———. 2000. *Rimbaud: The Works: A Season in Hell, Poems and Prose,
　　Illuminations.* Translated by Dennis Carlile. Philadelphia: Xlibris.

Rosenberg, Deena. 1997. *Fascinating Rhythm: The Collaboration of George and Ira
　　Gershwin.* Ann Arbor: University of Michigan Press.

Rubin, William. 1989. "Picasso and Braque: An Introduction." In *Picasso
　　and Braque: Pioneering Cubism,* compiled by William Rubin. New York:
　　Museum of Modern Art.

Rupprecht, Philip. 2015. *British Musical Modernism: The Manchester Group and
　　Their Contemporaries.* Cambridge: Cambridge University Press.

Said, Edward. 1978. *Orientalism.* New York: Pantheon Books.

Sandbrook, Dominic. 2005. *Never Had It So Good: A History of Britain from
　　Suez to the Beatles.* London: Little, Brown.

Santoro, Gene. 2000. *Myself When I Am Real: The Life and Music of Charles
　　Mingus.* New York: Oxford University Press.

Saul, Scott. 2003. *Freedom Is, Freedom Ain't: Jazz and the Making of the Sixties.*
　　Cambridge, MA: Harvard University Press.

Sawyers, June, ed. 2006. *Read the Beatles: Classic and New Writings on the
　　Beatles, Their Legacy, and Why They Still Matter.* New York: Penguin.

Scaduto, Anthony. 1971. *Bob Dylan.* New York: Grosset & Dunlap.

Schiff, David. 2012. *The Ellington Century.* Berkeley: University of California
　　Press.

Schuller, Gunther. 1968. *Early Jazz: Its Roots and Musical Development.* New
　　York: Oxford University Press.

———. 1986. *Musings: The Musical Worlds of Gunther Schuller.* New York:
　　Oxford University Press.

———. 1989. *The Swing Era: the Development of Jazz, 1930–1945.* New York:
　　Oxford University Press.

———. 1992. "Jazz and Composition: The Many Sides of Duke Ellington,
　　Music's Greatest Composer." *Bulletin of the American Academy of Arts and
　　Sciences* 46, no. 1: 36–51.

Serrano, Basilio. 2012. *Juan Tizol: His Caravan through American Life and
　　Culture.* Bloomington, IN: Xlibris.

Shankar, Ravi. 1999. *Raga Mala: The Autobiography of Ravi Shankar.* New York:
　　Welcome Rain Publication.

Sheff, David. 1981. *The Playboy Interviews with John Lennon and Yoko Ono.*
　　Edited by G. Barry Golson. New York: Playboy Press.

Shelton, Robert. 1986. *No Direction Home: The Life and Music of Bob Dylan.*
　　London: New English Library.

Shotton, Peter, and Nicholas Schaffner. 1984. *The Beatles, Lennon, and Me.*
　　New York: Stein and Day.

Singer, Barry. 1992. *Black and Blue: The Life and Lyrics of Andy Razaf.* New
　　York: Schirmer Books.

Singleton, Zutty. 1975. Interview at Institute for Jazz Studies, Rutgers University, Newark, New Jersey.

Sounes, Howard. 2011. *Down the Highway: The Life of Bob Dylan*. New York: Grove Press.

Spitz, Bob. 2005. *The Beatles: The Biography*. New York: Little, Brown.

Starr, Ringo. 2004. *Postcards from the Boys*. San Francisco, CA: Chronicle Books.

Steinbeck, John. 1970. *East of Eden*. New York: Bantam.

Stewart, Rex. 1972. *Jazz Masters of the Thirties*. New York: Macmillan.

———. 1991. *Boy Meets Horn*. Ann Arbor: University of Michigan Press.

Stillinger, Jack. 1991. *Multiple Authorship and the Myth of Solitary Genius*. New York: Oxford University Press.

Stockhausen, Karlheinz. 1958. "Structure and Experiential Time." In *Die Reihe* 2, translated by Leo Black, 64–74. Bryn Mawr, PA: Theodore Presser.

Stratemann, Klaus. 1992. *Duke Ellington: Day by Day and Film by Film*. Copenhagen, Denmark: JazzMedia ApS.

Stuckey, Sterling. 1987. *Slave Culture: Nationalist Theory and the Foundations of Black America*. New York: Oxford University Press.

Sulloway, Frank. 1996. *Born to Rebel: Birth Order, Family Dynamics, and Creative Lives*. New York: Pantheon.

Sulpy, Doug, and Ray Schweighardt. 1997. *Get Back: The Unauthorized Chronicle of the Beatles' Let It Be Disaster*. New York: St. Martin's Press.

Sutherland, J. A. 1976. *Victorian Novelists and Publishers*. Chicago: University of Chicago Press.

Swainson, Bill, ed. 2000. *Encarta Book of Quotations*. New York: St. Martin's Press.

Tamarkin, Jeff. 2008. "Chico Hamilton." *Jazz Times* (November 2008): 16–17.

Teachout, Terry. 2014. *Duke: A Life of Duke Ellington*. New York: Gotham Books.

Thomson, Elizabeth, and David Gutman, eds. 2004. *The Lennon Companion: Twenty-Five Years of Comment*. Cambridge: Da Capo Press.

Tichenor, George. 1930. "Colored Lines." *Theatre Arts Monthly* (June 14): 485–90.

Tick, Judith. 2008. *Music in the USA: A Documentary Companion*. New York: Oxford University Press.

Tillery, Gary. 2011. *Working Class Mystic: A Spiritual Biography of George Harrison*. Wheaton, IL: Quest Books/Theosophical Publishing House.

Transcendental Meditation. 2010. "David Lynch Interviews Paul McCartney about Meditation and Maharishi." Online Video Clip. YouTube. Uploaded April 7.

Tucker, Mark. 1988. "On *Toodle-oo*, Todalo, and Jenny's Toe." *American Music* 6, no. 1: 88–91.

———. 1991. *Duke Ellington: The Early Years*. Urbana: University of Illinois Press.

————. 1993a. "The Genesis of *Black, Brown and Beige*." *Black Music Research Journal* 13, no. 2: 67–86

————, ed. 1993b. *The Duke Ellington Reader*. New York: Oxford University Press.

————. 1996. "In Search of Will Vodery." *Black Music Research Journal* 16, no. 1: 123–82.

Turner, Steve. 2009. *The Beatles, A Hard Day's Write: The Stories behind Every Song*. New York: MJF Books.

Ulanov, Barry. 1946. *Duke Ellington*. New York: Creative Age Press.

Vail, Ken. 2002. *Duke's Diary*. Lanham, MD: Scarecrow Press.

Van de Leur, Walter. 2002. *Something to Live For: The Music of Billy Strayhorn*. New York: Oxford University Press.

Von Eschen, Penny. 2004. *Satchmo Blows Up the World: Jazz Ambassadors Play the Cold War*. Cambridge, MA: Harvard University Press.

Wall, Tim. 2012. "Duke Ellington, Radio Remotes, and the Mediation of Big City Nightlife, 1927 to 1933." *Jazz Perspectives* 6, nos. 1–2: 197–222.

Weber, Erin. 2016. *The Beatles and the Historians: An Analysis of Writings about the Fab Four*. Jefferson, NC: McFarland and Company.

Wells, Simon. 2005. *The Beatles: 365 Days*. New York: Harry N. Abrams.

Wenner, Jann. 2000. *Lennon Remembers*. London: Verso.

Whyton, Tony. 2010. *Jazz Icons: Heroes, Myths and the Jazz Tradition*. New York: Cambridge University Press.

Wilder, Alec. 1990. *American Popular Song: The Great Innovators, 1900–1950*. New York: Oxford University Press.

Williams, Iain Cameron. 2002. *Underneath a Harlem Moon: The Harlem to Paris Years of Adelaide Hall*. New York: Continuum.

Williams, Martin. 1963. *Jelly Roll Morton*. New York: A. S. Barnes and Company.

Woll, Allen. 1989. *Black Musical Theatre: From Coontown to Dreamgirls*. Baton Rouge: Louisiana State University Press.

Wright, Laurie, with Walter C. Allen and Brian A.L. Rust. 1987. *King Oliver*. Chigwell, UK: Storyville.

Zak, Albin. 2010. *I Don't Sound Like Nobody: Remaking Music in 1950s America*. Ann Arbor: University of Michigan Press.

Zenni, Stefano. 2001. "The Aesthetics of Duke Ellington's Suites: The Case of 'Togo Brava.'" *Black Music Research Journal* 2, no. 2: 1–28.

ILLUSTRATION CREDITS

1.1. Photo by Charles Peterson
1.2 Duke Ellington Collection, Archives Center, National Museum of American History, Smithsonian Institution
1.3 Courtesy of Steven Lasker
1.4 The Stanley Dance and Helen Oakley Dance Papers, Special Collection, Yale University
1.5 Courtesy of Steven Lasker
2.1 Courtesy of Steven Lasker
2.2 John D. Kisch / Separate Cinema Archive / Archive Photos / Getty
2.3 Courtesy of Steven Lasker
2.4 The Stanley Dance and Helen Oakley Dance Papers, Special Collection, Yale University
3.1 Courtesy of Steven Lasker
3.2 Duncan P. Schiedt Photograph Collection, Archives Center, National Museum of American History, Smithsonian Institution
3.3 Photo by Charles Peterson
3.4 John W. Mosley Photograph Collection, Charles L. Blockson Afro-American Collection, Temple University Libraries, Philadelphia, PA
3.5 From the collection of Fred Reif
4.1 Courtesy of Steven Lasker
4.2 Courtesy of Steven Lasker
4.3 Courtesy of Steven Lasker
4.4 Paul Hoeffler / Redferns / Getty
4.5 Bettman / Getty
5.1 Claudio Divizia / Shutterstock.com
5.2 Album / Newscom
5.3 Charlotte Brooks / Library of Congress
5.4 Everett Collection / Newscom
6.1 Courtesy of Pauline Sutcliffe / Su / Newscom
6.2 Ben Dome, CelebrityHomePhotos / Newscom

6.3 NI Syndication / Newscom
6.4 Kent Gavin Mirrorpix / Newscom
6.5 Zola Mirrorpix / Newscom
7.1 Everett Collection / Newscom
7.2 akg-images / Newscom
7.3 Pop / Photoshot / Newscom
7.4 Tracksimages.com / Alamy stock photo
7.5 bil paul sixtiespix.com
8.1 Douglas Eatwell Mirrorpix / Newscom
8.2 Pictorial Press Ltd / Alamy stock photo
8.3 STARSTOCK / Photoshot / Newscom
8.4 Freddie Reed Mirrorpix / Newscom
8.5 Bettman / Getty

INDEX

Page numbers in *italics* indicate photographs.